Ruling Europe

The Stability and Growth Pact (SGP) is central to Economic and Monetary Union (EMU) in Europe. Initiated by Germany in 1995 and adopted in 1997, it regulates the fiscal policies of European Union Member States. Following numerous violations of its deficit reference value, the Pact's Excessive Deficit Procedure was suspended in 2003. The decision to suspend was brought before the European Court of Justice in 2004 and the SGP then underwent painstaking reform in 2005. After a period of economic prosperity and falling budgetary deficits, the global economic crisis is putting the system under renewed stress. *Ruling Europe* presents the first comprehensive analysis of the political history of the SGP as the cornerstone of EMU. It examines the SGP through different theoretical lenses, offering a fascinating study of European integration and institutional design. One cannot understand the euro without first understanding the SGP.

MARTIN HEIPERTZ is Senior Officer to the Board of Directors of the European Investment Bank, Luxembourg. He has previously worked in the fiscal policy divisions of the European Central Bank and the German Ministry of Finance and has served as Economic Adviser to the EU Special Representative in Kosovo.

AMY VERDUN is Professor of Political Science, Jean Monnet Chair Ad Personam and Director of the Jean Monnet Centre of Excellence at the University of Victoria, Canada. She is the author, editor or coeditor of fourteen books including *European Responses to Globalization and Financial Market Integration: Perceptions of Economic and Monetary Union in Britain, France and Germany* (2000) and *EMU and Political Science: What Have We Learned?* (2010).

Ruling Europe

The Politics of the Stability and Growth Pact

Martin Heipertz

and

Amy Verdun

CAMBRIDGE
UNIVERSITY PRESS

CAMBRIDGE UNIVERSITY PRESS
Cambridge, New York, Melbourne, Madrid, Cape Town, Singapore,
São Paulo, Delhi, Dubai, Tokyo

Cambridge University Press
The Edinburgh Building, Cambridge CB2 8RU, UK

Published in the United States of America by Cambridge University Press,
New York

www.cambridge.org
Information on this title: www.cambridge.org/9780521197502

First published 2010

Printed in the United Kingdom at the University Press, Cambridge

A catalogue record for this publication is available from the British Library

ISBN 978-0-521-19750-2 Hardback

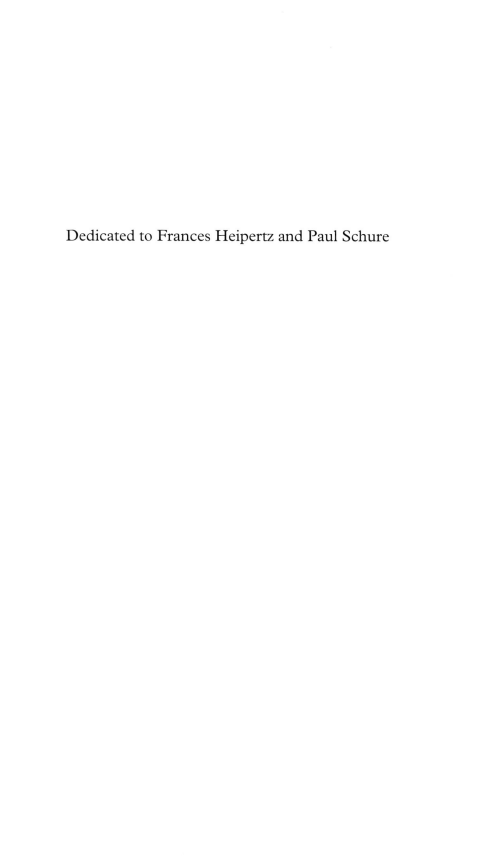

Dedicated to Frances Heipertz and Paul Schure

Contents

List of tables   *page* viii
Foreword by Jean-Claude Juncker, Prime Minister
of Luxembourg and President of the Eurogroup   ix
Preface   xi
Acknowledgements   xiii
List of abbreviations   xvi

1 The politics of the Stability and Growth Pact   1

Part I

2 States, intergovernmentalism and negotiating the SGP   19

3 Opening the box: A domestic politics approach to the SGP   42

4 The functional logic behind the SGP   64

5 The role of experts and ideas   85

Part II

6 Implementation of the SGP in good and in bad times   113

7 From bad times to crisis   128

8 The SGP before the European Court of Justice   154

9 The SGP in times of financial turbulence and economic crisis   174

10 Conclusion: The past, present and future of the SGP and
    implications for European integration theory   196

Appendix   205
Bibliography   296
Index   311

List of tables

Table 1.1 Taxonomy of theoretical approaches to European
integration *page* 12
Table 9.1 General government net lending (+) or borrowing
(-) (as a % of GDP) (1) 182
Table 9.2 General government gross debt (as a % of GDP) 184

Foreword

Since its inception in 1997, the Stability and Growth Pact (SGP) has lived through times both good and bad. It has been berated by politicians, academics, trade unionists and many other participants in the public debate. It has been called simultaneously too rigid and too lax, harmful to economic growth and outright 'stupid'. At the same time, the constituency has grown in number of those who strongly believe in the merits of a rules-based framework to rein in the fiscal appetite of the executive branches and to bring the issue of the sustainability of public finances to the fore of the political debate. Today, the SGP is the cornerstone of European economic policy coordination and surveillance framework for nationally determined fiscal policies in the single currency area. It is as intimately linked with Economic and Monetary Union as is the European Central Bank or the euro itself. Yet every crisis, be it political or economic, puts to the test the effectiveness, the credibility and the political sustainability of the Pact.

In order to withstand the test of time, it has been important to recall repeatedly and to emphasise the economic and political 'doctrine' underlying the SGP, while avoiding dogmatically enforcing its rules without due regard for the specific economic and political circumstances.

In 2004, a combination of economic, political and legal constraints implied that a revision of the fiscal surveillance framework had become unavoidable in order to stop the *de facto* demise of the Pact. Its comprehensive reform that was undertaken in 2005 under the Luxembourg Presidency of the European Union responded to the criticism of insufficient flexibility, introduced greater symmetry in the application of the rules throughout the economic cycle and made the Pact more enforceable. It emphasised the importance of greater *ex-ante* coordination of fiscal policies, leading to the inception of a 'mid-term review of budgetary policies' to be carried out at the level of the euro area and the importance of 'peer pressure' as an effective deterrent.

Although the 2005 reform of the Pact drew a lot of criticism and even triggered 'serious concerns' in some quarters, it was always clear to me that only time could tell whether it had been a success or a failure. In fact, in order to assess the effectiveness of the reformed Pact, it would be necessary to observe its functioning through an entire economic cycle.

Prior to the 2005 reform, the main problem of the Pact had been the asymmetry between 'good' and 'bad' times. In fact, the Pact was not very prescriptive regarding the adequacy of fiscal policy in 'good times'. This has changed with the 2005 reform and the results of the period 2006–8 were indeed very encouraging as structural deficits across Europe shrank quickly, public debt levels dropped and all euro-area Member States gradually exited the Excessive Deficit Procedure.

However, the true test of the Pact started with the world financial crisis in 2008 and the ensuing unprecedented economic downturn. Deficit and public debt levels shot up to levels unheard of since the 1970s. The added flexibility introduced in 2005 allowed us to carry out enhanced surveillance of public finances while remaining within the confines of our fiscal framework. As governments prepare to exit from the unparalleled support measures for the financial sector and the economy at large, it is crucially important that the flexibility provided by the Pact is used with economic intelligence and political guile in order to ensure that it is still around when we need to address the next crisis. In this way, we shall contribute collectively to restoring both much-needed growth and stability in Europe.

To most members of the general public, the SGP is dry material. Yet it is one of the few instruments of EU policy-making that has a tangible and direct impact on the living conditions of all our people. As such, it has often been at the centre of heated discussions and it has been subject to many criticisms. However, an informed debate about the usefulness and sensibility of a policy instrument like the Pact needs to be framed by objective analysis. I therefore congratulate the authors of this book for casting an objective yet critical eye on the issues at stake. The readers will certainly become better informed about the purpose of the Pact and the constraints that have shaped its current existence, thus enhancing their ability to participate fully in the public debate.

JEAN-CLAUDE JUNCKER
Prime Minister of Luxembourg and President of the Eurogroup

Preface

The year 2009 marked the tenth birthday of Economic and Monetary Union (EMU) in Europe. The Stability and Growth Pact (SGP) is one of the cornerstones of that enterprise. EMU itself is perhaps the most ambitious project of regional integration in the world: the merging of national monetary policies first by eleven, later sixteen, nation states into one is unprecedented in modern history. This phenomenal enterprise is characterised by transferring monetary policy to the supranational level on the one hand while retaining national sovereignty over all other fields of economic policy on the other. However, monetary policy is interdependent with the other areas of economic policy, notably the conduct of public finances. The viability and success of EMU therefore depends on the ability of the participating, but independent, nation states to conduct their fiscal policies in a manner that is compatible with the pursuit of a single, common monetary policy.

In theory, EMU functioning well along these lines is a collective good. We know that, short of subjecting themselves hierarchically to some Leviathan (the state), people as well as nations rely on *norms* to ensure the reliable provision of collective goods. One could compare it to a club. If members of a club are found not to contribute – i.e. to free-ride – or even to damage the club goods, the group enforces its norms through *sanctions*. Depending on the club, such sanctions take on various forms, from verbal bullying to brutal fighting. Among sovereign nations, norms are enshrined in treaties and other types of international law, but 'hard' sanctioning is difficult to the extent that the realm of international politics still remains one of a Hobbesian *bellum omnium contra omnes*. Ultimately, a sovereign nation must consent to being sanctioned if an international regime is to persist.

Being an integral part of the institutional architecture of the European Union (EU), the SGP is as of yet the most complex and far-reaching version of such a norm-setting arrangement among sovereign nation states. In fact, it submits important aspects of the very core of parliamentary democracies – i.e. the setting of taxes and the formulation of the public budget – to common principles by regulating the residual between the expenditures and revenues of governments: the budgetary deficit. Issues of public finance go to the heart of a polity. In consequence, the very nature of the SGP is a political compromise among competing national interests. Its purpose is to align national fiscal policies along one common doctrine. As such these rules are complex, intricate and technical.

Despite its highly technical and complex features, the SGP has a tendency to hit the headlines. Repeatedly, it has been the subject of major international controversies in the EU as well as among commentators and academics. Opposing and changing interests and convictions, even cultures, resurface over time and clash in the name of fiscal policy, as framework conditions, above all the macroeconomic environment, oscillate and public finance priorities react to political swings. In this sense, the creation, implementation and adaptation of the SGP over fifteen years provide a prime example of institutional design within the process of European integration and have great potential to highlight the mechanics of the more general, underlying processes at work in the EU among experts and politicians alike.

We had two particular reasons for writing this book. First, the SGP itself is sufficiently important to be understood properly not only from an economics perspective but also from a political science one. Having been exhaustively treated in the economics discipline, we see the need for a book-length, comprehensive coverage of its politics – in order to tell and understand its history since 1995 and to inform readers of its evolution as EMU moves into uncharted territory following the 2008 financial meltdown and the subsequent economic recession. Second, more fundamentally, we believe that the case of the SGP provides important theoretical insights for explaining and analysing the process of European integration more generally. In studying the origins of the SGP, we develop a methodological apparatus that we apply subsequently to the analysis of its implementation and reform as well as in the hard times of autumn 2008 and after. We think that the approach developed in this book could be applied usefully to more instances of integration – economic and other – in Europe and beyond.

Acknowledgements

This book would have been impossible without support. We had both been working on the SGP when we first met at the Max Planck Institute for the Study of Societies in Cologne in July 2002, thanks to its former Director, Fritz W. Scharpf. We collaborated at the Institute on an early version of the book manuscript, focusing our research at the time on the origins of the SGP. Subsequently, work was continued at a joint research visit at 'Sciences Po', Paris, in 2004, before Amy Verdun returned to the University of Victoria in Canada, where she held the Jean Monnet Chair in European Integration, while Martin Heipertz joined the European Central Bank (ECB) in Frankfurt as a fiscal economist, closely following the reform of the SGP as well as its further evolution, in part also during a secondment to the fiscal policy division of the German Ministry of Finance. It was at the premises of the ECB that we produced the penultimate version of the manuscript, in the summer of 2007 during the beginning of the financial crisis – at a turning point in the macroeconomic environment that could some day cause the SGP to return to the fore of European politics, ten years after entering Stage III of EMU. Final revisions to the manuscript were made in early 2009, which enabled us to incorporate some of the effects of the financial crisis on European budgetary policies of autumn 2008 and speculate on its implications for the SGP.

We are grateful for institutional and financial support from a variety of institutions, including notably the Max Planck Institute for the Study of Societies under its Director Wolfgang Streeck, the Social Sciences and Humanities Research Council of Canada (Grant 410–2002–0522 held by Amy Verdun), the Centre d'Études et de Recherches Internationales at Sciences Po and the ECB, which facilitated several extended visits by Amy Verdun to Frankfurt, and the European Commission, who paid for Martin Heipertz' visit to Victoria in January 2009, before he joined the European Investment Bank in Luxembourg. Despite this repeated and generous institutional support, any views and opinions expressed in this book are personal and do not reflect the views and opinions of any institutions with which the authors are affiliated.

Furthermore, we received important feedback along the way for which we are very grateful. Some results of the research were presented over a longer period of time at various conferences and different universities throughout the world at: the NYU Conference in London, 'Building EU Economic Government: Revising the Rules?' 25–6 April 2003; a seminar of the Max Planck Institute for the Study of Societies (MPIfG), Cologne, 29 April 2003; the Oberseminar of the Jean Monnet Chair, of Wolfgang Wessels, University of Cologne, 27 May 2003; the 19th IPSA World Congress, Durban, South Africa, 29 June – 4 July 2003; the European University Institute in Florence on 3 October 2003; the University of Leiden on 6 October 2003; at Simon Fraser University in Vancouver on 24 November 2003; 'Ruling Europe: Theory and Politics of the Stability and Growth Pact', at the UBC Institute for European Studies on 11 February 2004; at the Centre for European Studies, Fudan University, Shanghai, China, 27 February 2004; at the 14th International Conference of Europeanists, Chicago, 11–13 March 2004; at the CERI Faculty Seminar, Sciences Po, Paris, France, on 26 April 2004; at Dalhousie University, Halifax NS, 25 May 2004; at the Second Pan-European Conference on EU Politics: Implication of a Wider Europe, ECPR Standing Group on the European Union, Bologna, 24–6 June 2004; at the European Central Bank, Frankfurt, 21 December 2004; at the 46th International Studies Association Annual Convention, Hawaii, 1–5 March 2005; at the Ninth Biennial International European Union Studies Association Conference, Austin, Texas, 31 March – 2 April 2005; at the London School of Economics and Political Science, 9–10 September 2005; at the Conference at the Viessmann Centre, Wilfrid Laurier University, Waterloo, 28 April 2006; at the Jean Monnet Centre of Excellence Seminar Series, University of Victoria, 7 November 2006; at the 10th International Biennial European Union Studies Association, Montreal, 17–19 May 2007; and at a seminar of the Department of Politics at the University of Virginia in Charlottesville, on 13 February 2009. We wish to thank participants of the above-mentioned conferences and seminars for sharing their insights with us and providing useful and constructive criticism, comments and suggestions.

This book is based in part on fifty-five interviews with key informants, all of whom were close to the actual creation and/or the current politics of the SGP. Their contribution was invaluable for our insights into the matter. Most of our interview partners took around one and a half hours or more to discuss with us their views on the SGP and, where applicable, they filled out a project questionnaire. We found many of them readily available for follow-up questions in the wake of the November 2003 SGP crisis and the 2008 financial crisis. We wish to express a special word of thanks to these officials, many of whom are included in the list below, for their contribution to our understanding of the policy process and their personal views. In addition numerous colleagues and friends at different points were willing to provide us with feedback and suggestions (and we apologise for those whose names we might have left out). We wish to thank: Bill Allen, Michael J. Artis, Jean Artuis, Henk Brouwer, Marco Buti, Albert Caspers, Anne Lore de Coincy, Declan Costello, Wouter Coussens, Patrick M. Crowley, Renaud Dehousse, Bruno Délétre, Dimitrios Doukas, Bernhard Ebbinghaus, Henrik Enderlein, Erik Fasten, Graham Floater, Kyle Galler, Wolfgang Glomb, Daniel Gros, Günther Grosche, Mark Hallerberg, Detlev Hammann, Sebastian Hauptmeier, Helmut Herres, Dermot Hodson, Madeleine O. Hosli, David J. Howarth, Nicolas Jabko, Pierre Jaillet, Erik Jones, Jean-Claude Juncker, Ilkka Kajaste, Christian Kastrop, Filip Keereman, Jürgen Kröger, Walter Kubista, Thomas Lachs, Patrick Le Galès, Ingo Linsenmann, Ivo Maes, José Marín Arcas, Theodor Martens, Kathleen R. McNamara, Wolfgang Merz, Gabriel Milesi, Carlo Monticelli, Richard Morris, Robert A. Mundell, Xavier Musca, Christiane Nickel, Heikki Oksanen, Tommaso Padoa-Schioppa, Peter Part, Louis W. Pauly, Lucio Pench, Stefan Pflüger, Karl-Otto Pöhl, Peter Praet, Wouter Raab, Klaus Regling, Mark Rhinard, Ad van Riet, Philipp Rother, James Savage, Armin Schäfer, Fritz W. Scharpf, Waltraud Schelkle, Stefan Schönberg, Ludger Schuknecht, Jürgen Stark, Joerg Stefan, Wolfgang Streeck, Bernard ter Haar, Günter Thumann, Hans Tietmeyer, Francisco Torres, Nikos Tsaveas, Carel van den Berg, Jean-Pierre Vidal, Gelsomina Vigliotti, Theodor Waigel, Thomas Weiser, Wolfgang Wessels, Thomas Willett, Guido Wolswijk, Roman Zöller and Hendrik Zorn.

We are heavily indebted to three anonymous referees who accompanied our work during the review process with Cambridge University Press and who provided us with numerous valuable comments and suggestions. We also wish to thank three graduate students of the University of Victoria who gave invaluable research assistance at various stages of this project: Assem Dandashly, Benjamin Gonzalez and Patricia Young. During the publishing process we received invaluable support from the team provided by Cambridge University Press and would like to extend our thanks in particular to Carrie Cheek, John Haslam, Penny Harper, Jamie Hood, Thomas O'Reilly and Carrie Parkinson.

Finally, we wish to present a heartfelt 'thank you' for continued support and understanding to our immediate family: Christine and Wolfgang Heipertz, Zoey, Inez, Yenay, Audrey and Hage Verdun. Without their support and encouragement this book could have not been completed – nor would it have really been worth it. Last and most, we thank our partners, Frances Heipertz and Paul Schure.

Frankfurt and Victoria, 2009

Abbreviations

Art.	Article
BVerfG	*Bundesverfassungsgericht* (German Constitutional Court)
BEPG	Broad Economic Policy Guidelines
CDU	Christian Democratic Union (Germany)
CEC	Commission of the European Communities
COM	Commission
CPE	Comparative Political Economy
CSU	Christian Social Union (Germany)
CTBOIS	Close to Balance or in Surplus
DG Ecfin	Directorate General Economic and Financial Affairs
DNB	De Nederlandsche Bank
EC	European Communities
ECB	European Central Bank
ECJ	European Court of Justice
ECOFIN	Economic and Financial Affairs Council
ECU	European Currency Unit
EDP	Excessive Deficit Procedure
EFC	Economic and Financial Committee
EMI	European Monetary Institute
EMS	European Monetary System
EMU	Economic and Monetary Union
EP	European Parliament
ERM	Exchange Rate Mechanism
ESA	European System of National and Regional Accounts
ESCB	European System of Central Banks
EU	European Union
FTPL	Fiscal Theory of the Price Level
GDP	Gross Domestic Product
IfW	Institut für Weltwirtschaft
IMF	International Monetary Fund
IR	International Relations
MC	Monetary Committee

MTO	Medium-term Budgetary Objective
NCB	National Central Bank
OCA	Optimum Currency Area
OECD	Organisation for Economic Cooperation and Development
OJ	Official Journal
QMV	Qualified Majority Voting
RPR	Rally for the Republic (France)
SGP	Stability and Growth Pact
SPD	Social Democratic Party (Germany)
TEC	Treaty Establishing the European Community
TEU	Treaty on European Union
VAT	Value Added Tax
UK	United Kingdom
USA	United States

1 The politics of the Stability and Growth Pact

On 25 November 2003, the Economics and Financial Affairs Council (ECOFIN)[1] effectively decided to suspend the Stability and Growth Pact (SGP). What had seemed a set of 'boring', or at least technical, European Union (EU) regulations on budgetary policy coordination and surveillance, suddenly made headline news. It did not grab the attention of the world because of 'successful' European integration, but rather, in the eyes of the press, it marked the end of an era of rapid progress in European economic and monetary integration. France and Germany, the two countries that had been the founders of the SGP, were now the ones seen to dismantle it when confronted with procedural steps that – eventually – could have led to sanctions for their persistent failure to respect the deficit limit. Concerned with that prospect, they lobbied enough Member States so that the required qualified majority, needed to adopt the Commission recommendation to take the procedure one step further, could not be reached. According to many commentators, this decision was by no means in line with the spirit of the Pact and it flew in the face of all those who had been led to believe that the underlying intention of the framework was to enshrine budgetary discipline by automatically imposing fines on delinquents.

Some observers, however, were pleased to see the arrangement abandoned. They argued that Europe's single currency would be fine without it. Others were concerned that the procedural 'abeyance' of the SGP's Excessive Deficit Procedure (EDP) might ultimately mean the beginning of the end of the euro and Economic and Monetary Union (EMU). Seeing that the Germans had been adamant about suspending the SGP in 2003, how can one reconcile that situation with the fact that they had been the

---

[1] The Economic and Financial Affairs Council is commonly known as the ECOFIN Council, or simply ECOFIN, and is composed of the Economics and Finance Ministers of the Member States. It meets once a month. Budget Ministers join when budgetary issues are discussed. When the ECOFIN Council deals with issues regarding EMU, the representatives of the Member States whose currency is not in the euro do not take part in the vote of the Council.

1

main advocates of it in 1995–7 when they demanded much firmer rules? Furthermore, if the rules were so politically sensitive and were infringing on crucial elements of national sovereignty, why were they created in the first place? More generally, why does European integration in the area of economic and monetary policy occur in this manner?

Even though the SGP had seemed to be all about rules and to some extent (quasi-)automatic procedures, in July 2004 the European Court of Justice (ECJ) declared that the EU Council of Economic and Financial Affairs was indeed entitled to hold the EDP *de facto* in abeyance by not adopting a recommendation of the Commission to advance the procedure (see Appendix). The Court only annulled the so-called 'conclusions' that the Council had adopted by changing the Commission's recommendations, as in so doing the Council had infringed on the Commission's right of initiative. But it did not admit the plea of the Commission that the Council be forced to adopt a decision in this vein. In the months following the Court judgement, the Commission and the EU Member States underwent a painstaking revision of the legal texts of the SGP, which was concluded in March 2005 (see Appendix). Even though the alleged strengthening of the procedural rules was widely perceived as a weakening of the SGP's substance, not least by the European Central Bank (ECB), the legal nature of the Pact was not substantially altered; it still sought to clarify the EDP of the Maastricht Treaty and impose common rules on the making of national fiscal policies.

Indeed, it is difficult to judge if the reformed SGP will be effective in the long run, particularly given the favourable macroeconomic environment immediately following the reform, in turn replaced by a sudden and dramatic turnaround of the economic climate. Following the reform economic conditions picked up markedly in the latter half of 2005 and especially in 2006, leading to an improvement in the situation of public finances across the EU. The prospect for future growth brightened and the quarrels soon sank into oblivion. In 2007, ten years after the adoption of the SGP at the Amsterdam European Council, none of the euro-area countries were any more in excessive deficit. By 2008, there were only a few Member States falling short of the reference value before the financial crisis worsened in autumn 2008. At the time of writing (2009) the economic outlook was characterised by recession or slow growth in most EU Member States, with the expectation of a few more difficult years to come. As is discussed at some length in Chapter 9, it remains to be seen how the revised SGP will fare in these truly exceptional circumstances.

In this book we do not seek to explore whether the SGP is a useful framework to coordinate fiscal policy, as our primary aim is not to offer a normative value judgement of its merits either in its original or its reformed version. Instead, our aim is to draw lessons from these twelve years of SGP history as an exemplary case for the European integration process more generally. We examine the origins of the SGP, its execution, its crisis and reform, as well as the implementation of the revised framework until Europe slid into recession in 2009. We do so with a view to understanding what factors determine the outcome of each episode and to derive from that theoretical insights of general value. Before closing, in the penultimate chapter, we seek to reflect on the financial and economic crisis and, based on our insights on the SGP until this point, argue what the crisis might mean for the Pact. Our aim is to give a thorough and theoretically rich analysis of the entire SGP case while making the findings relevant for an audience that is interested in European integration more generally. We seek to offer a study that is both empirically well informed but also exploits the insights that can be obtained from the case for integration theory. This study is premised on the understanding that a well-researched case can be examined in a way that is theoretically interesting beyond the special policy problem at hand and, conversely, that theoretical work needs a sound empirical base. After offering an analysis of the origins of the SGP we look at its implementation, explore the reasons behind the SGP crisis in 2003, the reform of 2005, and assess what might lie ahead in light of the financial and economic crisis of 2008–9. Before entering into this intriguing story, let us first turn to a brief description of the SGP.

The Stability and Growth Pact – in short

The SGP contains a set of rules that aim at securing a low budgetary deficit regime. Legally, it belongs to the body of secondary EU legislation and consists of two Council regulations that operationalise Articles 99 and 104, respectively, of the EC Treaty, including the Protocol on the EDP (see Appendix).[2] Both of these regulations were amended in the course of the revision of the SGP in 2005.[3] They are complemented by texts that are not legally binding but are either of political or procedural value: a resolution of the European Council of 1997,[4] a report of the

---

[2] The usual notation for these Articles is 'Article 104 TEC'. We will hereafter drop the term 'TEC' and merely refer to 'Article 104'.

[3] Council Regulation No. 1466/97 of 7 July 1997 on the strengthening of the surveillance of budgetary positions and the surveillance and coordination of economic policies, O. J. 1997, L 209/1 (as amended by Council Regulation No. 1055/2005 of 27 June 2005); and Council Regulation No. 1467/97 on speeding up and clarifying the implementation of the excessive deficit procedure, O. J. L 209/6 (as amended by Council Regulation No. 1056/2005 of 27 June 2005).

[4] Resolution of the European Council on the Stability and Growth Pact, O. J. 1997, C 236/1.

ECOFIN Council to the European Council of 2005,[5] and, finally, a code of conduct.[6]

The SGP stipulates that Member States respect a ceiling on general government budget deficits of 3 per cent of GDP. This 3 per cent reference value was already present in the convergence criteria and in the EDP as laid down in the Maastricht Treaty (Article 104 and the corresponding Protocol).[7] Yet the SGP goes further than putting a permissible maximum on budgetary deficits. It also specifies that Member States should aim for a balanced budget or have budgetary surpluses over the medium term. These objectives are backed up by a multilateral surveillance procedure, the basis of which was also already contained in the Maastricht Treaty (Article 99).

The core of the SGP is the operationalisation of the EDP. It envisages circumstances under which sanctions can be imposed on Member States that are running excessive deficits. From a perspective of European integration theory, the EDP on its own is already puzzling: why would EU Member States agree to sign up to such a far-reaching agreement and limit their sovereignty over budgetary policies? What was the reason for its creation?

The first factor to keep in mind is that the SGP came to the fore in the aftermath of Maastricht. The creation of EMU took place in three stages. Stage I had started prior to the Maastricht Treaty when restrictions on capital markets and financial transactions were lifted, on 1 July 1990. Stage II commenced as soon as the Maastricht Treaty had been ratified, which was on 1 November 1993. It was seen as the preparatory stage in which all legal and institutional arrangements would be set in place for EMU to become operational. Stage III was the irrevocable fixing of the exchange rates of the participating currencies and the transfer of monetary policy-making to the ECB. Stage III was to start any time after 1997 once half of the Member States met the criteria for entry, but no later than 1 January 1999 even if less than half of the Member States qualified.[8] To enter into Stage III, EU Member States needed to meet the so-called

---

[5] 'Improving the implementation of the Stability and Growth Pact' – Annex II to Presidency Conclusions of the European Council of 22 and 23 March 2005 (document number 7619/1/05).

[6] 'Specifications on the implementation of the Stability and Growth Pact and guidelines on the format and content of Stability and Convergence Programmes', Opinion of the Economic and Financial Committee. All legal documents are available on: http://ec.europa.eu/economy_finance/about/activities/sgp/edp_legal_texts_guidelines_en.htm, and the most important documents are reproduced in the appendix to this book.

[7] At the time of writing these Article numbers are the correct ones. However, with the Lisbon Treaty ratified the Article numbers will change. Article 104 will become Article 126, for example.

[8] Strictly speaking, monetary policy in the euro area is conducted by the ECB and the national central banks (NCBs) of the participating Member States, as NCB presidents vote on the ECB Governing Council. The system is formally called the 'Eurosystem',

'convergence criteria' defined in Article 121.[9] In contrast to monetary policy, which was transferred to the ECB, a new supranational institution, fiscal policies were to remain in the hands of national authorities and no final arrangements were incorporated into the Treaty.

During Stage II of the EMU process, the SGP was inspired by a memorandum for an intergovernmental stability treaty, proposed by the German Ministry of Finance under Theo Waigel in November 1995. Waigel used the idea to create a Stability Pact for Europe to fend off domestic political pressures. The other countries initially reacted favourably to the idea to create clearer rules on budgets, which had already been defined as one of the priority areas for the drafting of secondary legislation during Stage II. They were opposed, however, to renegotiating the Maastricht Treaty or to concluding an intergovernmental agreement outside the EU Treaty framework. Therefore, Member States prompted the Commission to propose a solution within the framework of the Treaty.

Negotiations on the possible draft text took place in the Monetary Committee (MC). The MC consists of representatives of NCBs and the Ministries of Finance.[10] In the case of the SGP, the formative discussions took place from January 1996 throughout the remainder of that year. The Commission's draft legislative text turned out much closer to the Maastricht Treaty than to the Waigel proposal. It did not include some of the controversial elements that the Germans had proposed, such as purely automatic fines under the supervision of a newly to be established independent 'Stability Council'. Instead, it reduced the sanctions to a discretionary measure of the ECOFIN Council. The Commission's proposal also included innovations on multilateral surveillance and economic policy

whereas the European System of Central Banks (ESCB) contains the ECB and all NCBs of the EU. In this book we use ECB as shorthand for the more complex functioning of monetary policy within the decentralised 'Eurosystem', consisting of the ECB itself and the national central banks of those EU Member States that have adopted the single currency.

[9] The convergence criteria stipulate entry conditions for Stage III in the form of economic parameters that the Member States needed to comply with. While Article 121 defines the criteria in qualitative terms, a Protocol lays down precise definitions and numerical values, including those for specific reference levels on deficits (3 per cent of GDP) and public debt (60 per cent of GDP). Member States were required to stay below these reference values or show that the levels were continuously declining and coming close to the reference values. These reference values were annexed to the Treaty in a Protocol. The other convergence criteria stated that Member States should have an inflation rate within 1.5 per cent of the three EU countries with the lowest rate. Long-term interest rates had to be within 2 per cent of the three lowest interest rates in the EU. Finally, exchange rates would have to be kept within 'normal' fluctuation margins of the ERM of the EMS. In addition, a legal convergence criterion requires national legislation to be compatible with the TEC, for instance with regard to central bank independence.

[10] With the start of Stage III of EMU, on 1 January 1999, the Monetary Committee was renamed the Economic and Financial Committee (EFC).

coordination. As of then, the SGP has consisted of two parts: a 'dissuasive' or 'corrective' arm, centred on the EDP and Article 104; and a 'surveillance' or 'preventive' arm, centred on the annual submission of so-called 'stability programmes' based on Article 99.

The bulk of the SGP discussions were completed in the MC. Only very few open questions needed to be referred to the political level, i.e. the ECOFIN Council. Yet one issue in particular developed into a major controversy. Germany was isolated in its request for automatic sanctions to be imposed on a Member State with excessive deficits. Waigel demanded nothing less than a GDP contraction of 2 per cent or worse before he would accept an exemption. A political compromise was reached in the morning of 13 December 1996 after dramatic negotiations.

The Maastricht Treaty had provided a restrictive environment for the experts and politicians to operate within. Short of changing the Treaty, it was impossible to alter the functioning of the EDP. For instance, it was legally impossible to replace the political decision-making process on each EDP step with 'automaticity' as demanded by Waigel. The appearance of 'automaticity', which was important domestically for Waigel, was then salvaged through a solemn resolution by which all parties involved subscribed to a self-commitment to apply the EDP in a strict and timely manner. In practice, however, that – not legally binding – resolution turned out to be not very authoritative at all. It was of a purely declaratory nature, as became dramatically clear on 25 November 2003, when the EDP was *de facto* held in abeyance for France and Germany.

It is also noteworthy that sanctions cannot be enforced by legal means. A Member State government or a Community institution can only enforce formal adherence to the sequence of decision-making. It could thereby 'call the bluff' if the Commission or the Council failed to play their part in the process. However, such an appeal for failure to act could not force a positive decision, for instance to initiate sanctions. This happened when the Commission asked the ECJ to review the events of 25 November 2003.[11] The ECJ ruled on 13 July 2004 that the Council had the right *not* to adopt the Commission's recommendation but that it did not have the right to adopt its own conclusions instead of revising the Commission's proposal. Thus the Court ruled the single-handed Council conclusions void – but not the Council's decision not to adopt the Commission recommendations (which, effectively, had placed the EDP in abeyance).

The above discussion shows that the SGP suffers from inherent legal weaknesses. Due to the politicised nature of the EDP, the essence of the

---

[11] On the basis of Article 230.

Pact seems to be not so much a mechanism of 'quasi-automatic sanctions'[12] but rather the institutionalisation of a political pledge to aim for low deficits. Following a period of reflection in 2004, the SGP underwent a painstaking reform until a deal was reached in March 2005. By then, all parties involved were ready to put the quarrelling behind them and make a fresh start. The political leaders in particular were aware that the credibility of the framework could not be overstretched and that it was important to come to an agreement on the revised SGP. Their fate was helped subsequently by a strong economic upturn. In 2006 public finances improved substantially. In fact, during this year most EDP cases could be abrogated and everything seemed in order, with the revised SGP functioning reasonably.

In 2007 the budgetary situation improved further for all countries, but by the autumn of 2007 the fall-out of the subprime mortgage crisis in the USA was starting to affect the market for interbank loans. By autumn 2008, the full crisis reached Europe, activating an adverse feedback loop between the financial and real sectors of the economy. As we shall see in Chapter 9, at the time of writing the SGP is not being implemented in such a way that it restricts Member States to contain their budgetary deficits to 3 per cent of GDP in the midst of the crisis. Deficits above the reference value will, however, trigger the EDP, which means that down the road, once an upturn supersedes the crisis, the SGP may well make headlines again. After all, the SGP will structure the way in which EU Member States will need to work their way out of an era of potentially very large deficits. Throughout its history European integration has been typically a process with ups and downs.

By studying the history of the SGP we hope to draw conclusions that may enable us to learn more about how the general European integration process is to be understood.

Why create the SGP? Various theoretical explanations

If one is to examine the reasons for the creation of the SGP, one could look at a range of explanations, touching on economic, legal and political issues.

Economics literature stresses the fact that EMU could not operate without some degree of coordination in the area of fiscal policy. Member States could perhaps rely on the market as one source of discipline, but the risk would still be that some would benefit ('free-ride') on

---

[12] Waigel introduced the term 'quasi-automatic sanctions' after the Dublin summit, whereas Chirac declared that the compromise entailed no automaticity (*Handelsblatt*, 14 December 1996).

the availability of credit and extend their deficits to the detriment of others. Political leaders and economists have argued that EMU would need either further fiscal and political integration or have reasonably strict rules on budgetary and fiscal policies. The Maastricht Treaty was perceived as having an 'open fiscal flank'.

The legal dimension stresses that the Maastricht Treaty contained Articles and Protocols on the EDP and on economic policy cooperation, but it did not safeguard that Member States would produce the desirable behaviour. Seen that the arrangements were all intricately linked, it would not be possible to make provisions substantially outside the Treaty framework. It was clear that matters could still be decided on details, but stepping outside the existing framework altogether was not an option. It was also not possible to assume that any change to the Treaty text would be acceptable to all Member States.

Political science integration theories focus on the logic of the integration process itself. These approaches deal with issues such as why do states transfer sovereignty? What is their domestic motivation to do so? What is the role of experts in the process of integration? When and how do inter-governmental bargains become crucial? What is the logic behind the creation of European rules? Once they are in place, how are they followed and implemented? How does a crisis build up that can eventually even lead to the suspension of these rules?

In the following we offer an overview of the political science integration theories that offer the most useful possible explanations of European integration in particular regarding the case of the SGP.

Integration theories

For many years studies in the area of European integration have struggled with the question of how to explain European integration phenomena. International relations (IR) scholars typically stress the puzzling fact that national governments give up national sovereignty over policy-making and transfer power to the European level. Through the process of European integration, Member State governments subsequently accept European rules and laws that are enforced by the ECJ. In the case of EMU, for example, they have transferred their monetary sovereignty to a new European supranational institution, the ECB.

Comparative politics and political economy stress that the EU polity increasingly resembles the situation of a nation state (Hix 1994). They argue that one should not overemphasise the transfer of sovereignty. Instead one should look at the specific arrangements that have been made and explain the novel institutional design as well as the policy content. The puzzle is to understand exactly what policy or institution was created and why. They suggest applying theories that are based on domestic factors and political economy and examining differences among Member States.

What do theories of European integration tell us about the causes of integration? Let us turn to a short review of the various integration theories and start with the two traditional approaches, intergovernmentalism and neofunctionalism. Though often discredited as being old-fashioned, they continue to represent polar opposites of the types of explanations given.

Intergovernmentalism (Hoffmann 1966; Moravcsik 1998) stresses that integration occurs when the outcome is in the interest of the Member States. This approach disputes the idea that there is automaticity and some sense of intrinsic direction in the process. Instead, it stresses the importance of the actions of Member State governments, in particular those of the larger Member States. Hoffmann's original intergovernmentalist approach assumed state interests as given. Moravcsik's innovation over Hoffmann's original formulation is that the former offers an explanation of the preferences of national governments, namely that they are determined by domestic economic actors.

Neofunctionalism (Haas 1958, 1964, 1968) expects integration to occur when various domestic actors can no longer solve a particular policy problem at the domestic level and they then turn to the European level for a European solution. In so doing, they prepare to transfer policy-making to supranational actors and transnational elites in order to enable them to work out policy solutions at that level. This process of integration is understood to be the result of spillover, and at the same time the cause for further spillover. The spillover mechanism assumes that integration in one policy area requires progressively more cooperation and ultimately integration in adjacent fields, too. Because of this understanding of the spillover mechanism, one could say that there is a certain degree of automaticity and direction in the integration process according to the neofunctionalist approach. Recent authors have incorporated contemporary criticism and have amended the approach so that the automaticity is not necessarily present all the time (Rosamond 2005; Schmitter 2004).

Besides these two classical theories, the field of European integration has enjoyed a recent upsurge in theoretical developments. However, often the approaches are differently labelled but are not significantly distinct from each other or from one of the two classic approaches. We focus on two further approaches that in substance are distinct from the classical approaches and offer additional insights into the understanding of our case.

Perspectives under the heading of domestic politics stress the importance of domestic actors and structures in influencing the policies that national governments pursue when they bargain for European solutions (Bulmer 1983; Huelshoff 1994; Martin 1995). These approaches also explain why governments sometimes do not aim at a European solution. The domestic situation is the key factor in determining Member State government interests, political actions and timing (including sensitivity to the electoral cycle). Attention is placed on various domestic actors, structures and events.

Approaches focusing on experts and ideas look at the cognitive dimension and stress the role of ideas, paradigms, knowledge and experts for the policy-making process (*inter alia* Marcussen 2000; McNamara 1998; 1999; Radaelli 1995; Risse 2000). These approaches are often referred to as being 'constructivist' (Christiansen *et al.* 1999). They examine more subtle forces behind the formulation of interests (Finnemore 1996) and explain how experts hold certain ideas and formulate policy objectives accordingly. So-called 'epistemic communities', i.e. groups of transnational experts, can be called upon to enable a compromise. They are typically called upon when national governments wish to find an international policy solution to a particular problem (Haas 1992). These epistemic communities do more than merely redefine intergovernmental bargaining. Their own expertise and convictions play a role in framing policy options and driving the process of integration.

There are many more theoretical approaches that are similar in one way or another to the four mentioned above. Some theories seem to be in the same group, roughly speaking, because they share similar notions of the most important actors and mechanisms that determine the outcome of the integration process. For example, the fusion thesis (Wessels 1997), policy networks (Peterson 2003) and advocacy coalitions (Sabatier and Jenkins-Smith 1993) can be seen as close to a functionalist or ideas approach (see also Verdun 2002a, chapter 2).

In recent years, governance approaches have gained in popularity. Multilevel governance (Hooghe and Marks 2001) and other governance approaches (Jachtenfuchs 2001; Kohler-Koch and Eising 1999; Tömmel and Verdun 2009) emphasise the role of state and non-state actors at various levels of governance (i.e. European, national, regional and local as well as in various network settings) as well as the modes of governance used by these actors to coordinate or to create new policies. Given the importance of subnational levels, they emphasise that one can no longer look at integration from a purely IR perspective. One needs to examine the process by looking 'inside' the so-called 'black box' of nation state governments. Governance approaches stress that there is a role to be played for various actors at different levels of governance. Though offering important insights on day-to-day policy-making processes once EU regulations and directives have already been adopted, as well as tools to understand voluntary cooperation, governance approaches do not seek to develop a theory that spells out the conditions, actors and mechanisms that are important for European integration to occur in the first place.

Structure-agency and principal-agent approaches stress the fact that some actors can set the agenda, whereas others just operate within the boundaries of the framework but possess superior information (Kassim and Menon 2003; Pollack 1997; see Savage 2005 for a case study of the Maastricht Treaty that adopts a principal-agent theory and that examines the role of Eurostat in shaping the surveillance procedure and asserting its autonomy). These approaches give us insights into relative power positions of various actors at different points in time. But it does not help us evaluate how certain actors can change their roles depending on their interests or ideas. Some studies focus on the role of leadership for understanding integration. They argue that important people who are persuasive and charismatic can enforce discipline in the ranks and are more capable of forcing through their views. They also stress that these people rise and fall depending on how they can control their immediate surroundings (Drake 1995, 2000).

One could also move away from theories that have already been used to explain some aspects of European integration and instead consider adopting approaches from subfields that discuss other political phenomena. Borrowing from IR, we could consider the insights obtained from regimes theory, dependency school and critical theory. Comparative political economy (CPE) would inform us about the role of interest groups, lobbying, transnational governance, etc. The general field of political science would also offer possible theories about how power is used and which actors have the most influence through various societal structures (e.g. corporatism, pluralism, elitism). However, in most cases these approaches have some overlap with the four integration approaches mentioned above or otherwise we deem them not fully suitable for discussing the case we seek to explain.

For the purpose of this study, we have chosen four European integration theories: two from IR (intergovernmentalism and neofunctionalism) and two from CPE (domestic politics and ideational approaches), because jointly they come closest to providing a complete understanding of the particular policy-making field in European integration in which we are interested, namely that of the creation, demise, reform and future of the

SGP.[13] These approaches explain parts of the questions that IR scholars worry about primarily, namely the question of sovereignty, and the questions that political economists examine, namely the content of policy (see also Caporaso 1996; Risse-Kappen 1996). The IR and CPE approaches chosen differ on the degree to which they focus on state and non-state actors, as illustrated in the table below.

Table 1.1 *Taxonomy of theoretical approaches to European integration*

	International Relations	Political Economy/Comparative Politics
State	Intergovernmentalism	Domestic Politics
Non-state	Neofunctionalism	Experts/Ideas

Methodology

We have selected a different approach for dealing with empirics and theory than is usually adopted. Our aim is to understand as thoroughly as possible the empirical case of the SGP but also to see what insights that case offers into European integration in a wider context. We seek to understand the role of various actors (state actors and non-state actors), that is, national governments, central banks, experts within ministries and central banks, the MC, the European Commission, domestic actors, and experts outside the immediate political domain, such as academics.

In terms of countries, we focus mainly on Germany and France as the most important ones in shaping the history of the SGP. Germany was the initiator of the original Stability Pact and France was the most influential force in opposition. Both countries acted as 'spokesperson' for several others. In the implementation of the SGP as well as for its reform in 2005, again those two countries cover most of the issues in the intergovernmental arena.

In order to 'get the story right', we have based ourselves on a wide range of sources. The study draws on media coverage of the SGP, internal memos of several Ministries of Finance, central banks, the Commission

---

[13] The term Stability and Growth Pact (SGP) will be applied throughout this book, even though that title was only agreed at the Dublin summit in 1996. Before that time the term 'Stability Pact' was mainly used.

and the MC, formal public documents, as well as secondary sources and academic analyses. Over time, we have developed an extensive network of academic and professional experts who are or were very close to the SGP. In part, our own professional activities have involved an intense monitoring and analysis of events unfolding in the context of EMU and the SGP itself.

As part of our personal 'immersion' into the field, we conducted thirty-five face-to-face interviews on the earlier history of the SGP with key informants based on a semi-structured set of ten questions. Furthermore, we did ten additional interviews with key informants discussing the aftermath of the SGP crisis and its reform. Finally, with the onset of the financial crisis and the economic crisis in its wake, we conducted another ten interviews. The persons interviewed included political actors at ministerial and state secretarial level and officials in the Ministries of Finance as well as in the central banks of Germany, France and the Netherlands, officials of the ECB, the European Commission, and former members of the MC as well as present members of the EFC. We also interviewed a number of experts who have been following closely the developments of the SGP without having been involved directly in the decision-making. The average length of an interview was approximately one hundred minutes. We also devised a written questionnaire with forty structured questions which we asked our interview partners to complete. In addition, we sent it out to selected former members of the MC and some current members of the EFC, whom we did not interview, for example MC/EFC members of Austria, Belgium, Finland, Greece, Ireland, Italy, Portugal, Spain, Sweden and the UK, many of whom returned it to us. The list of questions was designed to obtain information about the motivation for and the actual development of the SGP, the support for the various steps of its design, the importance of certain rules and principles, the role of the various actors, the satisfaction with the eventual outcome of the SGP and what its likely future might be.

We began by studying the SGP as a case of European integration in 2001. In the first phase of our research, the interviews as well as the questionnaire served primarily as a source of information on the creation and early implementation of the SGP up to 2004, i.e. a period during which we had not yet been directly involved with the dossier. As of late 2004, hence particularly during the reform of the SGP and the subsequent implementation of the revised framework, we were able to gather first-hand direct experience and knowledge of all relevant issues. In the period 2005 through to early 2009 we kept in regular contact with the dossier and with people close to the SGP. Thus, having had ample access to information about this case, both confidential and in the public domain, we feel in a position to provide here both a case study instructive for European integration theory as well as a complete, authoritative account of the history of the SGP – one of the institutional cornerstones of economic and monetary union in the EU.

The argument

This book examines the above-mentioned four different theoretical approaches to explain the creation of the SGP in 1997, based on extensive empirical material. We then reflect on what the analysis of its origins might teach us about the period in which it was being applied, the 2003 crisis in which the Council temporarily suspended it, the reform of 2005 and subsequent developments up to the onset of the financial and economic crisis in 2008. Following on from there, we briefly speculate about its highly uncertain future as the crisis unfolds. We argue that an eclectic, combined usage of all four theoretical lenses provides a comprehensive appraisal of the SGP. The added value of this exercise goes beyond merely a better understanding of this momentous step in the creation of EMU. It points to potential generalisations of the mechanisms detected in conjunction with the SGP and their usefulness for understanding the politics of EMU. The study pleads for eclecticism rather than singling out one particular theoretical approach to explain this particular instance of European integration.

Starting with intergovernmentalism, we assess to what extent the occurrence and nature of the SGP are due to the fact that it was Germany that demanded an arrangement of this nature. After all, Germany in 1995 was not only the most powerful country in the EU (some would even see it in the position of a 'Eurohegemon'; Rode 1991), but also in the process of monetary unification, it gave up more sovereignty than any other state. For these reasons it was able to set the conditions. Likewise, the alleged demise of the SGP in November 2003 can be explained through an intergovernmentalist lens by the fact that Germany by then had different (economic) interests at stake and saw the SGP no longer as congruent with them.

A domestic politics appraisal of the SGP explains its origins in light of the specific domestic situation of the German government in autumn 1995. The SGP was demanded by Waigel because, within Germany, EMU needed to be defended against growing public resentment. Crucial is the role of the Bundesbank as a powerful domestic actor that not only directly influences the government but enjoys large influence on public opinion in economic matters. It therefore had to be appeased through the SGP. Furthermore, a Stability Pact was called for to pre-empt the social democratic party (SPD), the major domestic opposition party at the time. In a similar vein, French domestic needs and the electoral concerns of the government explain why the word 'Growth' was added to the name of the Stability Pact in Dublin in December 1996. It represents a mere cosmetic concession designed to relieve some of the pressure that the Juppé government experienced in the face of rising unemployment. Finally, as has already been stated, it is German domestic dynamics in the negotiations on structural reforms at the end of 2003 that explain much of the Schröder government's hostility to the SGP as well as its subsequent endorsement by the successor government under Merkel.

From a neofunctionalist perspective, the existing Treaty provided pre-definitions but also clear limitations to the project of designing an SGP, understandable in the form of 'path dependence'. Independently of the legal restrictions, a functional, economic logic implied further institutional solutions to the consequences of monetary union. Placing the centralised and supranational monetary policy *vis-à-vis* a decentralised set of uncoordinated national economic policies was seen as subject to severe risks. Without rules, free-riding on budgetary policy would occur which would risk undermining monetary integration. Therefore, at least a rules-based mechanism was deemed necessary to accompany EMU. It would need to be built on the Treaty provisions in order to arrive at a workable solution between the poles of economic and legal functionalist requirements. In 2005, for the revision of the SGP, we again encounter the workings of economic and legal spillovers, as the framework had to be adjusted to changing political priorities, but in line with the legal basis of the Treaty as well as with the pre-existing structure of the SGP and, not least, on account of a range of economic policy features that had become evident in experiences with the original version of the SGP.

Finally, the actual specifications of the SGP were determined by the authoritative ideas of experts. Specialised experts in the Commission as well as in the Ministries of Finance and central banks of the Member States provided the actual content of the regulations as well as the thinking behind the legal texts. Their cognitive paradigm of economic policy-making was decisive for the factual input into the negotiations. After all, they were asked at the political level to provide expert solutions to a problem that is both of a political and a highly technical nature. Within the frame of the political instructions, first in the MC and later the EFC, experts were free to provide their input according to their ideas and priorities. This situation is not rare in the process of European integration and in the design of EMU. Monetary experts had been similarly influential in the drafting of the ECB statutes and the EMU Articles in the

Maastricht Treaty. Also experts and the evolution in their thinking had a profound impact on the revision of the SGP in 2005.

We argue that these four theoretical lenses provide insights that are not competing but complementary. The book is divided into two parts. The first part consists of four chapters. In each of the chapters of that first part we neatly separate the theoretical insights of each approach and examine the creation of the SGP through each of the four lenses separately (one per chapter). Thus, Chapters 2–5 offer an analysis of the origins of the SGP by examining its creation from one of the four theoretical perspectives. In each of these four cases, the emphasis will be on the part that the respective theoretical approach focuses on, but will also close by stating how that approach is able to explain only part of the case and how in important aspects it falls short of providing a full account.

The second part of the book contains four chapters that offer an account of the events related to the implementation, crisis and reform of the SGP and that complete the account of its history, always in conjunction with an analysis that applies our framework: Chapter 6 examines the SGP implementation in the last half of the 1990s and the early years of the new millennium up until excessive deficits started to emerge; Chapter 7 examines the events leading up to the SGP crisis of November 2003 and the actual event, again followed by a theoretical analysis; Chapter 8 offers an account of the immediate aftermath of the SGP crisis, the legal case that served before the ECJ as well as the revision of the SGP, and again analyses these events. In Chapter 9 we offer an analysis of how the SGP has fared faced with the turbulence of the financial market crisis and we speculate about the policy outlook in a scenario of rapidly rising deficits.

In Chapter 10, the conclusion, we stress the scholarly benefits of an eclectic approach that combines the four theoretical approaches in explaining the creation of the SGP and its aftermath. We argue that such a strategy is useful for overcoming what we see as being counterproductive and artificial boundaries inside the political science discipline by applying different approaches of integration theory in an eclectic manner for empirically rich and complex studies. The understanding of the SGP gained in this way will allow theory-guided speculations about its future as well as some general statements on European integration. By presenting a detailed narrative of the SGP history as well as chapters that provide theoretical analyses that focus on the four theoretical approaches, we hope to provide an enquiry that is informative for readers directly interested in the SGP as well as for a scholarly audience that seeks to obtain a greater understanding of political economy issues and their relationship to theoretical explanations.

Part I

2 States, intergovernmentalism and negotiating the SGP

Presenting intergovernmentalism

Classical European integration theories aimed to explain the phenomenon of integration by focusing on various actors and mechanisms in the integration process. The intergovernmentalist approach formulated in the mid-1960s (Hoffmann 1966) was a realist response to neofunctionalism. Intergovernmentalism argues that national governments are the key actors that determine integration. In other words, whether integration occurs depends on whether or not it is in the interest of national governments. For his theoretical approach Stanley Hoffmann relied on the personality and the euro-sceptic stance of Charles de Gaulle. In the 1960s, the French President had been largely opposed to transferring power to supranational institutions. Thus, Hoffmann concluded, one should look at state interests to explain integration. However, Hoffmann's approach did not clarify how one could identify and enlighten the notion of state interest itself. Twenty-five years later, Moravcsik (1991) opened the 'black box' of the state and incorporated the national economic features and priorities of a country as variables that determine 'national state interests' as far as European integration is concerned. Though Moravcsik was able to make the overall approach subtler, his liberal intergovernmentalist approach still mainly considers state interests and hence interstate bargaining as key to understanding European integration (Moravcsik 1993, 1998).

Because national governments are the most important actors in this view, most of the integration decisions occur in intergovernmental bargaining arenas, such as the European Council Summits, the Meetings of Council of the EU and other similar scenes, primarily intergovernmental conferences and, to a lesser extent, (intergovernmental) committees that prepare the work of the Council. According to intergovernmentalism, the high-level meetings and the involved interstate bargaining are fundamentally more important for the integration process than day-to-day policy-making at working level.

When Member State governments bargain with one another, the largest countries have the greatest influence. Small countries may support each other or large states depending on their national interest. When Member State governments support each other's objectives that are not immediately in their own interest, they will demand 'trade-offs' or 'package deals' so that they receive some form of compensation in return (Moravcsik 1993). Ultimately, relative state power determines the negotiations. If an issue is of extreme importance (i.e. crucial to the national interest) that Member State will be more influential on that subject matter, even if it is not a large country. An example is the importance of financial market legislation for Luxembourg, which exerts its veto in this area as it touches upon a vital national interest. In practice, the combination of power and national interest implies that in most cases the large four Member States (Germany, France, Italy and the UK) are the most influential players whenever an issue is sufficiently important to them.[1]

For intergovermentalism, the main integration mechanism is primarily bargaining and therefore the exertion of pressure by states. As a result of the focus on bargaining, the intergovernmentalist approach disagrees with the idea that there would be any 'automaticity' or inevitable 'direction' in the development of European integration. Contrary to the neofunctionalist proclamation, no explanatory power can be derived from there being any kind of automatic processes (such as spillover). Furthermore, the intergovernmentalist approach also disputes the idea that the socialisation of government leaders or experts would have any explanatory effect, or that there would be an important independent role to be played by supranational bodies, such as the Commission or the ECJ, or that individual people such as the Commission President would have considerable influence in fostering or shaping integration.

Following an intergovernmentalist approach implies focusing on the role of Member State governments and emphasising their aim to secure national interests. When adopting this perspective on the particular case of the bargaining to create the SGP, one could take insights from intergovernmentalist and realist discussions of EMU (Garrett 1994; Grieco 1995; Moravcsik 1998).[2] Such a consideration would identify Germany

---

[1] More recently, Spain and Poland have joined the ranks of 'large' Member States given their voting weight under the Nice Treaty. Note that there is some discussion about the definition of 'large' states as to whether that notion is derived from voting power, the size of the economy, or population (for a discussion, see Maes and Verdun 2005; Schure et al. 2007; Schure and Verdun 2008). As was already referred to, in some instances a Member State can gain in importance (power) if an issue touches on its vital interests. Most academic literature on this topic in fact is rather vague on what determines the relative 'power' of a Member State.

[2] For a two-level game analysis of intergovernmental bargaining of EMU see Hosli (2000).

and France as the two most important actors. Not only are they two large Member States, but their relative power position was increased because they represented the two prevalent different views in the EU on economic and monetary union. Germany was extraordinarily powerful on this issue due to the fact that it was giving up its *de facto* leadership on the monetary policy regime. Once the finalising of an SGP had come to favour the German national interest, there was no longer a question as to whether some kind of Pact would be adopted, only what it would consist of. France, in contrast, can be seen as representing the positions (i.e. reservations) of a number of countries from the south, showing some degree of reticence about a German-inspired fiscal austerity corset.

Thus, according to an intergovernmentalist perspective, Germany and France dominate the negotiations and determine the crucial features of the outcome among themselves. Following Scharpf (1997), one could see the Franco-German exchange as a subset of the multiparty negotiations among the twelve, later fifteen, Member States. By reducing the number of players in the negotiations to two, the Franco-German negotiations decrease the transaction costs for reaching an agreement, which in turn increases the chances of finding a compromise solution among two 'delegated' players that is later on accepted by everyone else.

An intergovernmentalist approach is also well equipped to explain patterns of coalition-building among nation states. They would arrange themselves into two camps, siding either with Germany or France. Their position would be determined by their interests and could be classified according to the principles of 'balancing' or 'bandwagoning' (see Walt 2000). A country with an interest structure similar to that of Germany, for example the Netherlands, would easily bandwagon with Germany. Another one might side with France, for a number of reasons, such as exerting a balancing effect on the German predominance (as in the case of Luxembourg), or be more reserved about a strict rules-based regime (for example, Italy). Each camp delegates its interests to the leading country; any compromise between the two antagonistic leaders is accepted by the entire group.

The mechanism that describes the arbitration of national interests in the EU is an institutionalised form of interstate bargaining. It takes place in various arenas. The requirement for potential compromises is that they still are acceptable in light of the national interest and that they therefore secure a minimum arrangement of what the Member State had originally preferred. The highest level at which state actors meet in the EU arena is the level of the European Councils of the heads of state and government (so-called 'summits'). In the case of the SGP, some of the final political issues were solved at that level – between the respective heads of state and sometimes even in bilateral side-meetings of the leaders of Germany and France. The next highest level is national ministers' meetings in the ECOFIN Council. Most of the formal decisions on the SGP were taken at these meetings. Finally, one could look at the role of national representatives in advisory and preparatory bodies, such as the MC and later the EFC, which were in charge of preparing the ECOFIN meetings and which drafted the legal texts of the SGP. Peripheral arenas and exchange for a outside of the formal EU negotiation process allow the players to exchange views, signal their interests or sound out emerging compromises.

Looking through an intergovernmentalist lens, one can see that the MC was able to provide the major content of the final SGP legislation due to a process of delegated negotiations in which national MC representatives bargain for the positions of their respective governments that in turn provide detailed instructions on how to decide. Importantly, in the intergovernmentalist view of this process, MC members do not bring their own convictions to bear on the outcome. Instead, the approach would expect the deliberations in the committee to be dominated by the powerful countries and to be focused on finding common ground between the prevalent national interests.

Interstate bargaining in the Council, ECOFIN and the MC

As stated above, the intergovernmentalist view of the SGP focuses attention on the bargaining process among Member States and puts particular emphasis on larger ones. In 1995 the EU comprised twelve Member States. Given the voting weights, the size of the economy and population size, four of these could be considered 'large'; the others were medium-sized or small. In 1996 three relatively 'small' Member States joined the EU (Austria, Finland and Sweden). German dominance was due in part to the fact that the Deutschmark had been the anchor currency of the European Monetary System (EMS). Its central bank, the Bundesbank, had been setting monetary policy that effectively functioned as the baseline for all countries participating in the Exchange Rate Mechanism (ERM) of the EMS (Gros and Thygesen 1998; Heipertz 2001). Thus, by joining EMU, Germany would have to transfer real sovereignty to the future ECB. The central banks of the other countries had been shadowing the policies of the Bundesbank and thus had not been exerting their sovereignty in recent years.[3]

---

[3] Under capital mobility, a central bank can either follow an (external) exchange rate target or a (domestic) monetary target – not both (Mundell 1961). Fixing the exchange rate implies following an exchange rate target, which radically reduces the room for

France, the other dominant country, as discussed above, to some extent represented the views of the countries more sceptical about Waigel's proposal. Italy was not strictly opposed to a Stability Pact as long as it did not imply higher barriers to entry into EMU. In fact, in some sense the shift of political emphasis away from the Maastricht debt criterion towards the deficit criterion through the SGP can perhaps even be seen as being in Italy's interest.[4] While no Italian government could have lowered the debt ratio to 60 per cent of GDP in the foreseeable future, a deficit below 3 per cent appeared more feasible. More importantly, the Italian government was in principle not opposed to the SGP as it saw the opportunity for an external commitment (*vincolo esterno*) that would help rectify its traditionally poor record on public finances and price stability (Dyson and Featherstone 1996b). Germany (and the Netherlands) in particular had been indicating uneasiness with the prospect of having Italy join EMU unless its budgetary deficit and public debt were reduced dramatically (Dyson 2002; Radaelli 2002; Verdun 2002b). Hence, subscribing to an SGP would allow Italy to assuage the German apprehensions about its participation in EMU and at the same time provide external support to the required consolidation measures.

Concerning the other large country of potential relevance for an intergovernmentalist interpretation, the UK did not wish to join EMU, having 'opted out' of the EMU clauses in the Maastricht Treaty, and thus was not seen as a core actor. At the same time, it was keen not to be excluded from the policy process and thus sought ways to contribute to decision-making on this issue (Verdun 2000a). In fact, a very important mediation role was played by the British Chairman of the MC, Sir Nigel Wicks, as well as by Kenneth Clarke, then Chancellor of the Exchequer (Finance Minister) who facilitated at several occasions the high-level bargaining between Germany and France. The Dutch held views on monetary policy similar to those of the Germans and as a result were a strong ally of their Eastern neighbour. In consequence, and because reduction is often part of explanation, the countries to be looked at from an intergovernmentalist perspective are limited to two: Germany and France.

Germany

Waigel's initiative can be seen as one particularly complex and insightful case among several instances in which Germany influenced EMU policy

---

manoeuvre of domestic monetary policy. There was a joke among central bankers that the monetary sovereignty of the other countries lasted for ten minutes, i.e. the time that they had to follow an interest rate decision in Frankfurt.

[4] We are grateful to Erik Jones and Roman Zöller for pointing this out to us.

in line with national interest. From an intergovernmentalist point of view, Germany held a strong position, not only because it was giving up *real* monetary sovereignty but also because German GDP represented roughly a third of the combined EU economic output. Because of this strong position, the Kohl government could more easily impose its views about EMU than other Member States.

Nevertheless, economic growth rates slowed down considerably after the reunification boom and even the then relatively sound German public finances deteriorated markedly. Only in 1996 would it become clear that, in 1995, for the first time Germany itself had been unable to respect the Maastricht deficit criterion. In the other countries, however, economic conditions were even less rosy in that year, which also meant that they were not performing well on the 'convergence criteria'. The other countries, including France, felt under higher pressure to still 'pass the EMU exam' than Germany, which added to their weaker bargaining position in EMU matters. This was the case notably for countries such as Belgium, Greece, Ireland, Italy, Portugal and Spain, which tried to toughen up their bargaining positions during the negotiations, predominantly because of the economic downturn at the time. The recession made them realise the potential consequences of signing up to a strict SGP, which would require them to contain budget deficits even in an economic downswing. This, in turn, confirmed the fears of the German critics that some of the future EMU partners had not subscribed reliably to financial stability in the first place. Interestingly, the blow to Waigel of having been unable to achieve a budget deficit below 3 per cent of GDP did little to undermine the German position. Both the government as well as its European partners underestimated the structural problems inherent in the German economy and thought the 1995 case to be of a singular and exceptional nature, still related to the costs of reunification.

The EMU and central bank provisions of the Maastricht Treaty represented an agreement based on the German model. The Stability Pact as proposed by Waigel aimed at strengthening the rules on budgetary deficits so as to enforce the stability culture that Germany had been living up to and was professing as the basis of successful monetary policies. This finding was supported by the respondents to our questionnaire. The vast majority, regardless of their nationality, agreed that 'EMU and the SGP are oriented along the lines of the German model'.

With its initial SGP proposal, the German government attempted even to transgress the EU legal framework by demanding an additional intergovernmental treaty that would not be required to stay within the parameters determined at Maastricht. By signing a new treaty, Germany would not be restricted by the Maastricht Treaty but could propose stricter (e.g. automatic) rules. In so doing, the proposed international treaty would move beyond the stipulations made in the Maastricht Treaty regarding rules on budgets and avoiding excessive deficits.

Why was Germany interested in strengthening the principles of fiscal discipline in EMU by introducing a Stability Pact? From an intergovernmentalist perspective, the fact that Germany had signed up to EMU in the first place makes sense if one sees it in conjunction with Germany's primary foreign policy interest. EMU could be interpreted as a deal to make reunification acceptable to its partners.[5] Additional interests that came to bear on the decision to join EMU might have been of an economic nature. For example, the structure that existed prior to EMU might not have been perceived as sustainable or optimal from the German point of view, which meant that monetary union would offer economic gains, such as reducing transactions costs and the costs of de- or revaluations and the increase in trade due to the greater transparency of prices.[6]

So, the Kohl government was keen on proceeding with EMU but was worried that Member States would slack in their duties of fiscal prudence once they entered into Stage III. In the German view, the project as designed in the Maastricht Treaty still contained risks and costs – especially in the form of potentially undermining monetary stability if Member States with a tradition of unsound policies (especially the Mediterranean countries, it was feared) joined EMU but still pursued

[5] This argument is debatable because the Delors Committee had already proposed a blueprint for EMU in April 1989. The Delors Report was thus published well before the fall of the Wall. However, the personal commitment of Chancellor Kohl to EMU *vis-à-vis* French President Mitterrand dates back to the December 1989 Strasbourg summit, only weeks *after* the fall of the Berlin Wall and in the middle of the struggle to achieve reunification as fast as possible (see van Esch 2007 for an analysis of Kohl's views on these matters). The logic often asserted is that the ultimate support for EMU from the German side at the Maastricht summit in December 1991 was to show to Europe that a united Germany would not pose a threat to Europe but was willing to become a 'European' Germany. For the French it was useful to say that, by having EMU, they were able to rein in Germany (albeit by accepting an EMU based on the German model).

[6] Germany dominated the pre-existing EMS. However, it still pursued policies based on domestic needs. As other countries 'shadowed' German interest rates in order to preserve their exchange rate targets even when the domestic monetary policy stance should have been different, the effect that German interest rates had on other Member States was not always positive. Some analysts have pointed out that German reunification led to a short-term boom and inflationary pressures, which the Bundesbank soon countered by high interest rates. Other Member States which were not experiencing inflationary pressures also raised rates to maintain their exchange rate targets *vis-à-vis* the Deutschmark, even when their economic situation would have militated against higher interest rates. It is almost ironic that, in 2003, the opposite happened, albeit to a lesser degree. In EMU, the ECB sets interest rates for the euro area as a whole, but German inflationary pressures were lower and growth was more sluggish than the euro-area average, which meant for some commentators that Germany would have benefited from having lower interest rates than those set for the euro area as a whole in 2003.

their traditional policies. The optimal strategy of retaining the benefits of EMU while controlling these risks would be to strengthen the existing rules. This strategy would ensure either the exclusion of 'suspicious' countries or enforce their appropriate behaviour once they had entered. Hence, some sort of additional agreement that made EMU more compatible with German requirements was clearly in the national interest.

However, the constellation of political power in 1995 differed significantly from the situation in 1991 when the Maastricht Treaty was adopted. After all, Germany had already signed and ratified the Treaty, including Article 121, which stipulated that Stage III of EMU, if not fixed before, would commence on 1 January 1999 among those countries satisfying the convergence criteria. Because of this rule, on which Mitterrand had insisted in 1991, in 1995 Germany had no legal chance of withdrawing from its EMU commitment, even if, as *ultima ratio*, it could threaten to do so politically. The exit option of not entering into EMU would have entailed breaching an international agreement and thereby undermining the process of European integration at large, which could also not have been in the national interest. Therefore, on balance, the German bargaining position after Maastricht was still strong but weaker than before.

Our interviews and respondents provided further insights into this matter. The questionnaire featured several questions on the position of power that Germany had to block EMU. The findings show mixed results but overall suggest that Germany had some leverage over the process due to that veiled threat. Alternatively, a majority of our interlocutors thought that it could at least have insisted on certain countries not participating in Stage III right from the outset. Although Germany could in theory make such bold steps, the costs of breaching the agreement by exerting the exit option would be very high, not least politically for Kohl, who had come to be seen as the personal sponsor of European integration and EMU in particular. Germany was therefore on the one hand in a position to demand a strict Stability Pact but on the other hand it had to be willing to negotiate a compromise that would include at least some concessions. It could certainly not simply impose a 'dictate', even if the SGP was subsequently portrayed as such in some circles in France (see Chapter 3).

To its European partners Germany presented a Stability Pact which at first was conceived as an ancillary treaty outside the Maastricht framework (a so-called 'fiscal Schengen')[7] that entailed an automatic sanctioning

---

[7] The Schengen Treaty is an international agreement of a majority of EU countries that agreed to open their borders. It was concluded as it had become apparent that no consensus was achievable within the entire union. It was first an international treaty outside the legal framework of the EU, but eventually became incorporated into it.

procedure for fiscal delinquents. It was obvious that Germany was eager to safeguard the rules in EMU Stage III by securing some form of Stability Pact. However, on the issue of a new treaty outside the Maastricht framework, the German government eventually agreed that this request would be out of the question. The actual legal nature of the SGP – Council Regulations rather than a separate treaty – delineates the loss of bargaining power that Germany experienced after having signed up to Maastricht. Prior to 1991, it probably could have demanded substantially more than it could have done four years later. Since a new treaty was clearly against the national interest of France – and most other countries – they could summon legal reasons militating against the German intention. The others convinced Germany that a new treaty would have to be ratified by all participating Member States, which would be difficult to achieve in 1996, at a time in which almost all Member States could not even meet the convergence criteria.

Despite the restrictions imposed by the Maastricht Treaty on what Germany could effectively demand, it retained the notion of automatic sanctions as a policy objective until the last moment. Finally agreeing to not having full automaticity in the SGP was the most substantial concession made by Germany, which for some time still went on describing the sanctions as 'quasi-automatic'. In our analysis, the characteristics of the final SGP have to be compared to the initial interests in order to gauge the power distribution of the players.

France

As said, besides Germany, France was the other powerful player on the intergovernmental scene. It was generally accepted that, without either Germany or France, EMU would not come into being. There was no other country on a par with these two. Even the other two large countries had a weaker position regarding EMU: the UK had marginalised itself by having negotiated an opt-out of EMU, and Italy still had large public debt, poor inflation and exchange rate performance, and issues of governance which made it a less crucial partner for EMU. None of the other Member States would be large enough individually to make a difference. The only country that had a reasonably important role in this regard was the Netherlands as it had the strongest stable currency record *vis-à-vis* Germany, and it was generally seen as at the core of European monetary integration.[8]

---

[8] Note that when the ERM was reformed after the 1992–3 currency crises and the fluctuation bands moved from ±2.25% to ±15%, the only exchange rate that officially stayed within the original band was that between Germany and the Netherlands.

The intergovernmentalist approach would therefore predict that the constellation of preferences and power of Germany and France would determine the outcome of the bargaining. For the most part, other countries did not matter in this case since a compromise agreed between these two players would in principle be backed by them. As France had also voiced strong opposition to the German initiative, the other countries had no major difficulties in delegating to the French the role of brokering a deal with Germany. Those countries in favour of a strict Stability Pact would side with Germany, the others with France.

The negotiations

Intergovernmentalists look at international negotiations from a top-down perspective. They expect issues that are at the heart of national sovereignty, and those that are of a general political nature, to be decided at the level of the European Council by the heads of state and government. However, during our research, we found mixed results on the importance of the European Council. A majority of questionnaire respondents and interview partners recognised its contribution, but only a quarter actually thought that its involvement was crucial throughout the negotiations; rather, it was seen as important on specific issues.

The next negotiating level below the European Council is the ECOFIN Council, which consists of the ministers of finance and economics. It conducts preparatory negotiations on issues that are more economic, monetary or financial in nature and thus require the specific competence of these particular ministers. The level below this is of a mixed nature between political and technical dimensions and deals with the preparation of the ECOFIN meetings as well as the drafting of the relevant texts. In the case of the creation of the SGP and EMU more generally, this task fell to the Monetary Committee (MC), which itself consisted of senior national officials from ministries of finance and, in extended composition, central banks. In Stage III, the MC was renamed the 'Economic and Financial Committee' (EFC). The MC/EFC operates at two levels: one upper layer is staffed with negotiators, ranked one or two steps below the minister of finance and the central bank governor respectively, while a lower file, the so-called MC 'alternates' deal with preparatory issues. The latter are often more of a technical than a political nature. In addition, there is the 'Economic Policy Committee' (EPC), which also reports to the ECOFIN Council. In general, the EPC is regarded as less influential than the MC/EFC, staffed with less senior officials and dealing primarily with technical issues. For the SGP, the EPC would at times have contributed analytical input on certain matters, without, however, negotiating on the drafting of more general legislative texts, which was conducted by the MC. Both the MC/EFC and the EPC can form working groups dedicated to special topics that are subsequently reported to the 'parent committee'.[9]

These empirical insights confirm that the workings of the three levels: European Council–ECOFIN Council–Monetary Committee, are clearly perceived to function according to the hierarchical lines outlined above. The implicit assumption of the EU legislative working method is that a higher level by default agrees with a consensus found on one of the lower levels and only deals with those issues that have not yet been decided. This is possible because each representative at the lower level receives instructions from his or her superior at the higher level. In principle, the more 'political' in nature an issue is, the higher up in the hierarchy it is decided. However, the SGP case also shows that even questions that seem of a purely technical or even trivial nature can become 'political' to the extreme, if they are 'contested' – an example being the lower bound of the definition of what is to count as a 'severe recession' (see Chapters 4 and 5). The deliberations in the MC sometimes progressed beyond 'technical' fields, at least according to ECOFIN, which meant that the MC representatives at times had to restrain themselves so as not to overstep their mandate. The European Council and ECOFIN consist of elected politicians and feel therefore as the more legitimate actors in adopting legislation than the 'technocratic' committee level.

We will discuss the three levels in turn. What follows is largely based on the authors' interviews with finance ministry and central bank officials, on documents released to us, reports in the media and on one particularly useful descriptive account of an important participant observer, i.e. that of Stark (2001).[10] The content of the bargain is interesting to analyse in terms of how the SGP came into being. An intergovernmentalist approach also looks for trade-offs as well as linkages for package deals, including issues outside the SGP dossier and related to EMU projects in the French interest, such as a European initiative on employment policy. The actual features of the outcome are interpreted according to how close the bargained result is to the (inferred) interests of Germany and France.

Negotiating in the European Council

The European Council discussed the SGP for the first time during the Spanish Presidency of the EU at its meeting in Madrid on 15 and 16

---

[9] The role of the EPC became more important after entering Stage III of EMU, when it was charged with a series of technical tasks such as the definition of 'sustainability' indicators to flow into the definition of country-specific medium-term budgetary objectives under the preventive arm of the SGP.

[10] Jürgen Stark is widely seen as having had an important hand in drafting the SGP. His account of the negotiations offers a valuable step-by-step description of the process.

December 1995. The Presidency Conclusions, i.e. the usual public relations document adopted at each European Council meeting, stressed the importance of budgetary discipline for the functioning and public acceptance of a future EMU – besides announcing that the future common currency would be named the 'euro' (European Council 1995). The European Council formally initiated the legislative procedure for the SGP by instructing the ECOFIN Council to report on measures that would ensure budgetary discipline. In this way it played its role of guiding the policy-making process of the EU but not interfering with the actual legislative work.[11]

The European Council received the first ECOFIN report on the SGP at its meeting in Florence on 21 and 22 June 1996. The measures proposed by ECOFIN (see below) were generally endorsed. Beyond that, there was a first instance of disagreement and deliberation on factual issues that had been left open by the MC as well as ECOFIN. At this stage, the European Council had already ceased its constitutional role of initiating and guiding the legislative process rather than actively participating in it. The heads of state and government had to discuss the German desire to frame the sanctioning procedure in such a way that the imposition of fines for breaching the budgetary ceiling would be automatic. They were split on the issue and, unable to resolve it, referred it back to the ECOFIN level for further deliberation. The European Council had to discuss two additional ECOFIN impasses, i.e. the size of the financial sanctions and the question of how to define the so-called 'exceptional circumstances' that would justify a transgression of the 3 per cent of GDP deficit limit. In addition, the European Council at that stage was unclear on the legal nature of the SGP, pondering the question whether and how the Treaty Protocol on the EDP should be replaced instead of issuing the SGP as secondary legislation in the form of Council regulations.

The issues debated in Florence were finally all settled at lower levels, with one exception: what was to constitute a 'severe recession' as a particular

---

[11] Strictly speaking, these institutions are defined as follows: the EU Council (also referred to as Council of the EU or 'Council of Ministers') is an institution of the European Union that is made up of ministers responsible for the matters under consideration. The EU Council meeting in the composition of the ministers of economics and finance is often referred to as the ECOFIN Council. In cases of particular importance, the EU Council can meet in the composition of the Heads of State or Government. Strictly speaking, this EU Council of Heads of State or Government is not the European Council. The latter provides the EU with the necessary impetus for its development and provides general political guidelines. It brings together the Heads of State or Government of the Member States and the President of the European Commission but does not have legislative capacity. In our study we have not differentiated exactly in what legal capacity the Heads of State and Government acted. Suffice to say that the political decision was made at times at the highest level and got translated into the legislative process through the EU Council.

case of 'exceptional circumstances' that would authorise deficits above the 3 per cent level? It was clear that this clause would eventually justify the exertion of political discretion over the application of the core of the SGP, i.e. the EDP, and therefore became the focal point of dissent. The EDP is contained already in the Maastricht Treaty (Article 104 as well as the EDP Protocol) and does foresee political discretion (as confirmed by the ECJ in its 2004 verdict – see Chapter 8). However, the German intention was to reduce that discretion and subject it to as much automaticity as possible under the SGP regulations. The ECOFIN Council on 13 December 1996 in Dublin was unable to define the lower bound of what was to constitute a 'severe recession', and so finally the bargain had to be struck personally between the German Chancellor and the French President. Kohl and Chirac met at 0.75 per cent, right in the middle of the points defended by Waigel and Arthuis in the ECOFIN Council (see below).

From an intergovernmental perspective two things are interesting about the nature of the 0.75 per cent compromise. First, it had little to do with any factual, economic reasoning behind it, since no economist would be willing to propose a strict, numerical definition of what was a 'severe' recession and what was not. However, the issue was of symbolical value and had become 'political', thereby a question of bargaining power rather than economic common sense.

Second, we learned that the deal was struck between Kohl and Chirac only when Kohl said that this was the last chance to proceed with EMU, warning Chirac that the French government would find no successive German chancellor willing to commit his country to this mission. Many observers have indicated to us that Kohl had made EMU and related legislation (such as the SGP) his personal objective. Kohl's bargaining power was based in part on the fact that personally he could completely drain the political support for EMU, which would cause Germany to withdraw from the project and thereby make the whole scheme entirely pointless. Yet it is also clear that many were aware of the political capital he had used to seek to secure EMU, and hence withdrawal of support would only be an extreme option to him if all others had been exhausted.

The Amsterdam summit in June 1997 (after the change of government in France; see Chapter 3) saw the final endorsement of the SGP through the European Council. The preceding solution was again a package deal in which French Prime Minister Jospin accepted the SGP and Kohl agreed to the inclusion of an employment chapter into the Treaty. The fact that the provisions on employment policy are far less substantial than the rules on budgetary policy serves as a good indicator for the power differential between Germany and France in 1997. By this time, it was less than one year to the selection of the first wave of countries to enter EMU and it was understood that a favourable view of Germany on the admission of Italy (whose membership was in the interest of France) would be greatly helped by the European Council having delivered on a substantiated SGP.

Negotiations in the ECOFIN Council

Before the European Council of heads of state and government took notice of the issue, the SGP had already become topical at the ministerial level, in the ECOFIN Council. In several bilateral meetings with his colleagues of the other EU Member States during September 1995, German Finance Minister Theo Waigel hinted at a forthcoming initiative on a Stability Pact. Their response was mixed. There was broad agreement in principle to strengthen the budgetary regime as defined by the Maastricht Treaty. Yet there was firm opposition to the suggestion of a new intergovernmental treaty that would furthermore contain automatic sanctions for those exceeding the budgetary reference value.

Most countries were concerned that in reality the German move was designed to erect additional barriers to entry into monetary union beyond the convergence criteria (Stark 2001). Therefore, at an early stage, Waigel realised the need to concede designing the rules in the form of secondary legislation that would be based on the Maastricht Treaty. In other words, the terms of EMU would not be renegotiated. By dropping one of his initial demands, he obtained in return a general agreement in the Council on initiating secondary legislation along the lines of his proposal. This move away from an international treaty (the original Waigel proposal) in favour of remaining within the framework of the Maastricht Treaty can be seen as an indication of the importance of intergovernmental bargaining in this aspect of the SGP.

The gist of the Waigel proposal was presented publicly for the first time in the budgetary reading of the German Parliament on 7 November 1995 (see Chapter 3). The first formal ECOFIN discussion on the issue took place on 27 November 1995. The Council, based on the deliberations of the MC (see below), received the initiative favourably but without any concrete results.[12] According to Waigel, the Italian Finance Minister was the first to come up to him to express his support in principle of the proposal. The smaller Member States generally endorsed the German plan.[13] Also, France agreed in principle that the move was welcome but made it very explicit that such a Pact would not require or lead to modifications of the Maastricht Treaty.

---

[12] *Agence Europe*: Europe Daily Bulletin No. 6614; *Financial Times*, 28 November 1995.
[13] Two Scandinavian countries, Finland and Sweden, became members of the EU in 1996. They strongly endorsed the German proposal.

Based on progress in the MC, the ECOFIN Council worked towards an interim report to the June 1996 European Council in Florence, defining the 3 per cent reference value of the Maastricht Treaty as an absolute ceiling that was to be secured through sanctions unless 'exceptional circumstances' prevailed. Furthermore, each Member State should aim for budgetary balance in the medium term to allow the functioning of automatic stabilisers without approaching the ceiling. The interim report also announced the design of a preventive surveillance mechanism and resolved to amend the structure of the EDP as laid out in the Treaty with the aim of speeding up the decision-making sequence. Thus, the Council was able to find common ground for the Florence summit, but at the same time the state of the deliberations already pointed towards issues of increasing dissent.

The Florence European Council did not represent a breakthrough on the open questions (see above), and work was back in the hands of ECOFIN and the MC. Waigel tried to break the deadlock by conducting another round of bilateral talks on the need to achieve an SGP if Germany was to proceed with EMU. However, an informal ECOFIN meeting in Dublin on 20–22 September 1996 failed to make substantial progress.[14] Initiated by the Bundesbank, the Council commissioned the MC to report on the question of whether one could reverse the burden of proof for the decision on the existence of an excessive deficit. This decision, which initiates the application of the EDP on a particular country case, is laid out in Article 104.7 of the Maastricht Treaty. Based on a Commission report, the Council decides (with qualified majority voting, not including the Member State in question) on the existence of an excessive deficit. The Bundesbank convinced the German government to lobby for the reverse situation, where a qualified majority would be needed to declare a deficit above the reference value as not being excessive, i.e. in the case of 'exceptional circumstances'. This case illustrates how the negotiating parties tried possible alternative trajectories at different levels of deliberation in order to find common ground for a potential compromise. Three major issues were still unresolved at this point in the proceedings: (1) a mechanism for the 'automatic' imposition of sanctions (without violating the Treaty-based degree of political discretion on this matter); (2) the definition of a 'severe recession' that would constitute an 'exceptional circumstance'; and (3) the size of the financial fines.

The goal set by the European Council at this point was to conclude the negotiations by the end of 1996, and time was running out. An ECOFIN meeting at the beginning of December 1996 brought agreement on the size of the sanctions as well as on the time frame for application of the separate

---

[14] *Financial Times*, 23 September 1996.

procedural steps under the EDP. However, for the remaining issues an emergency meeting of ECOFIN had to be held in parallel with the regular session of the European Council in Dublin, scheduled for 12 and 13 December 1996. This very unusual step had become necessary in order to resolve three important outstanding issues at the last minute.

First, given the degree of political discretion enshrined in the Treaty (and the impossibility of signing a new one), a self-commitment of the political leaders not to avail themselves of that discretion appeared to be the only feasible way of creating at least the impression of what came to be called 'quasi-automatic' sanctions. Second, the ECOFIN Council was called to hammer out finally a definition of a 'severe recession'. Third, France, for domestic reasons, had developed a growing preference for obtaining some concession that could be signalled as avoiding stability at the expense of economic growth (see Chapter 4).

The ECOFIN meeting, which participants experienced as 'historic', began at four o'clock in the afternoon and concluded in the morning hours of the following day. France rather easily obtained the domestically relevant concession of adding the word 'growth' to the title of the Pact. The responses to our questionnaire show that all actors at the time were aware that this result was purely cosmetic to help the domestically embattled Juppé government. At the same time, Germany's position of demanding a strict, numerical definition of 'severe recession' was not reconcilable with Council discretion on the implementation of the EDP as stated in the Treaty – and *vice versa*. The political rather than legal objection to the German claim was that sovereignty should not be eroded further (Stark 2001) – a clear indication that this stand-off has to be interpreted through the lens of intergovernmentalism.

Based on a proposal attributed to Luxembourg's Prime Minister, Jean-Claude Juncker, Germany accepted the self-commitment on 'quasi-automaticity' to be framed in a not legally binding resolution rather than as part of the SGP regulations. However, the German side linked this issue to its demand of a quantitative and unambiguous definition of 'severe recession', which up to that stage had been anathema to France. The talks were interrupted for bilateral meetings between the French and German Ministers of Finance, a fact to confirm the intergovernmentalist expectation that these two countries were decisive. At the very critical stand-off in Dublin, virtually any Franco-German compromise was sure to find acceptance within the entire group of ECOFIN ministers who simply wanted to come to a result.[15]

---

[15] Milesi (1998: 145) quotes a delegation member of the Dublin summit: '*C'est un problème franco-allemand (…) Mettez-vous d'accord entre vous et nous accepterons votre solution*' ('This is a Franco-German problem. See to an agreement between yourselves, and we will accept your solution').

The special ECOFIN meeting had not yet arrived at a solution, when the regular session of the European Council commenced, virtually next door. The German and French ministers together with their deputies were ordered to find a compromise under the mediation of Juncker, who, according to all participants, is judged as having been the broker of the final deal between France and Germany. Interestingly, the UK Chancellor of the Exchequer, Kenneth Clarke, also participated in the session, as a neutral arbiter.

The solution finally adopted for the definition of a 'severe recession' in the political self-commitment of the SGP resolution was to set a 'grey' area in which the ECOFIN Council would have full political discretion. This so-called 'Wicks Box' (named after the influential MC Chairman, who was from the UK Treasury) delineated an area of discretionary assessment between a yet unspecified lower bound of negative growth, below which no excessive deficit would be authorised as having occurred under special circumstances, and an upper bound at or above annual GDP falling by 2 per cent. Hence, a recession at or above negative growth of 2 per cent would by definition qualify as 'severe' and exempt a deficit of 3 per cent or more from being qualified as 'excessive'.

However, ministers were still unable to agree on the quantitative definition of the lower bound, i.e. the lowest possible recession that could in principle be admitted as being 'severe'. The solution lay somewhere between 0.5 per cent (defended by France to make the exemption as lenient as possible) and 1 per cent (for Germany, to set the standard as high as possible). This not even technical but in fact rather trivial issue had become politicised to the utmost, and therefore had to be referred to the heads of state and government. Kohl and Chirac then settled for the middle, 0.75 per cent (see above). Therefore, if a recession occurred whereby growth dropped to between 0 and 0.75 per cent of GDP, this would not qualify as an exception to the 'automatic' application of sanctions. However, if a severe recession occurred with the economy contracting at a rate of 2 per cent of GDP or more, its government would be temporarily exempt from the excessive deficit rules. Within these boundaries the Wicks Box would apply, meaning that it would be left to the Council to decide whether the recession was 'severe' or not. Ironically, this most heatedly debated issue of the entire negotiations turned out to be completely irrelevant in the later history of the SGP, as the clause of 'severe recession' has not been used by any Member State in their request that the procedures be interrupted. As we will see, we expect this situation to change following the financial and economic crisis that Europe is currently experiencing.

After the 'Dublin Marathon', ECOFIN and MC deliberations were dominated by Germany attempting to eliminate as many 'as a rule' statements as possible in the draft texts that the Commission was tabling in the

MC on the basis of the compromise. The German fear was that, for example, a recession of 0.3 per cent that 'as a rule' did not qualify as exceptional would nevertheless be admitted as an excuse to run higher deficits than 3 per cent once this case would have to be decided in practice. In other words, the practical value of painstaking compromises like the Wicks Box was undermined by making them subject to the 'as a rule' provision, which would always allow for exceptions to the exemption, thereby invalidating the legal penetration of any such text. Also still unresolved was the issue of the size of sanctions and a potential upper limit to these payments, as well as a formula for their allocation, Germany insisting that such payments should accrue to the 'virtuous' Member States.

Six months later, barely two weeks before the Amsterdam summit in June 1997, a new French government came to power. During its election campaign it ran on a Keynesian platform favouring fiscal stimulation and, among other things, renouncing the SGP agreement of the Dublin Council in a very outspoken manner (see Chapter 3). The stance of the new French government briefly seemed to put all common ground into question.[16] However, as stated above, the French side was won over in the European Council with yet another package deal, involving the draft of a second resolution, besides the one that contained the 'self-commitment' of Member States, the Council and the Commission to implement the SGP in a strict manner.[17] This resolution on growth and employment was to be passed by the European Council in parallel to the SGP resolution.

Negotiating below and beyond the Council

The MC was the first body to have a substantive discussion on the Waigel proposal. Ten days after the proposal came out in written form, on 20 and 21 November 1995, the MC met and concluded on a generally positive tone. After the kick-off discussions at the political level, especially the European Council on 15 and 16 December 1995, it was in the MC that the actual work started in January 1996.

The deliberations during the first half of 1996 were based on a legislative proposal of the Commission. The negotiations in the MC proved to be long and difficult, dealing with a wide range of issues that were, at least initially, not so much controversial but rather a common advance into unknown territory. Among the topics debated by the experts was, for example, the question of whether an additional deficit target was to be

---

[16] *Le Monde*, 4 June 1997.

[17] In the aftermath of the Amsterdam summit one could hear an insider joke in the corridors: it took Mitterrand ten years to become persuaded of the virtues of fiscal stability, Chirac one year, whereas Jospin only took one week.

introduced below the 3 per cent of GDP reference value. Germany had proposed a 1 per cent target to be aimed at under normal conditions. Most representatives favoured a soft medium-term target – that is, one without a quantitative definition. A related question was whether that target should be common among the EU Member States or whether heterogeneity among the economic conditions should allow country-specific targets, possibly in conjunction with some overarching principles to be adhered to union-wide. Further proposals concerned debt targets, given that the strengthening of the EDP shifted the balance between the deficit and debt references values of the Maastricht Treaty more towards the former. Furthermore, the experts in the MC discussed a wide range of issues concerning the factual basis on which to initiate the EDP as well as criteria for defining the 'exceptional circumstances' that would warrant deficits to exceed 3 per cent without being deemed 'excessive'. It also became clear to MC members that the automatic sanctions desired by Germany were not feasible within a framework based on the Maastricht Treaty.

In its deliberative form, the MC/EFC does not act in line with the intergovernmentalist view. Instead, it functions rather as a group of experts that jointly try to work out the best feasible solution for an objective policy problem. We will return to this 'expertocratic' sort of interaction in Chapter 5. From the perspective of intergovernmentalism, the MC/EFC is of interest as a negotiation forum for contested positions of national interest. This other side of its 'Jekyll and Hyde' nature became relevant whenever any of the issues under discussion turned out to touch upon competing national interests.

For example, immediately before the European Council meeting at Dublin on 12 and 13 December 1996, the MC attempted to formulate a compromise on one of the most controversial issues between Germany and the other countries, i.e. the question of automaticity, as discussed above. The solution was brokered by Juncker in the European Council, but it had already emerged as one possible option in the MC to agree that, instead of an automatic procedure, the relevant institutions as well as the Member States would endorse a resolution in which all parties involved solemnly committed themselves to a strict interpretation of the SGP and a timely imposition of its procedures. One additional option was to determine that the Council would precommit itself to always adopting a Commission recommendation on the initiation of the EDP to a particular country. By testing several variations on this theme, the MC prepared the ground for a political compromise, which subsequently did not contain such a full precommitment but, as discussed above, featured numerous statements that would apply only 'as a rule'.

Of course, the MC could not resolve all issues, which meant that controversial topics would have to be solved at the political level. For example, there was no agreement among the MC negotiators on the imposition of sanctions, so that the Committee only formulated a range of options on this issue and passed it along to the ECOFIN Council to decide. The most prominent issue where the MC failed to achieve a compromise was the question, discussed above, of how to define a 'severe recession'. This case is illustrative in that it clearly shows the range of possibilities discussed in the MC. The Committee narrowed the solution space down to the Wicks Box and handed three different versions over to the ECOFIN Council. ECOFIN settled the numerical definitions of the upper boundary of the Wicks Box but still had to leave the options for the lower bound of the Wicks Box to be decided by Kohl and Chirac.

From an intergovernmentalist perspective, the role of the MC is primarily to structure and in fact reduce the workload of ECOFIN negotiations by allowing issues of minor importance to be decided by dependent, delegated negotiators who receive clear instructions from their governments. The representatives of the most powerful countries dominate the deliberations of the MC and ensure that the interests of their governments are implemented. The members of the MC have a certain degree of control over what issues become the matter of dissent and potentially political conflict. Whenever this boundary is overstepped, they function according to the intergovernmental logic, which essentially boils down to bargaining over national preferences. When this happens one could state that the role of the MC – as one of its members described it – is that of 'financial diplomats', whereas otherwise they operate as a group of experts seeking to find the optimal solution for a collective policy problem.

Besides the formal negotiation fora, there were additional settings of international encounters, like meetings in the context of the G7 or in international economic policy organisations, mainly the Organisation for Economic Cooperation and Development (OECD) and the International Monetary Fund (IMF). Such bodies did not serve as bargaining arenas for the SGP directly but, given their general occupation with macroeconomic policy-making in Europe, developed and advanced their own views on EMU and the fiscal policy framework, thereby contributing to the formation of ideas (to be discussed in Chapter 5). In addition, the corridors of such meetings were often used for an informal exchange of views on SGP-related issues among officials as well as political leaders, especially in times when the negotiation process in Brussels had reached difficult terrain. On such occasions, participants can signal interests as well as sound out potential compromises or room for manoeuvre. The powerful countries here find fora in which they can try out ideas ahead of upcoming ECOFIN negotiations, to pressurise weaker players and to build coalitions.

A special Franco-German exchange, institutionalised through the Elysée Treaty of 1963, represents one forum of peripheral exchange that is of particular interest from an intergovernmentalist perspective. The Franco-German meetings, that take place at least once a year, involve all political levels down from the heads of state and government, the respective ministers of finance and economics and even exchanges at the 'working level' of ministerial officials as well as meetings of parliamentary committees and, more recently, even joint sessions of both Parliaments. The hierarchy of these meetings is complementary to the different levels at which EU legislation is enacted. According to our sources, the intergovernmental meetings between Germany and France, which often took place in the run-up to a European Council, were instrumental in a number of specific breakthroughs on the SGP dossier.

Given the fact that Germany and France represented the opposing camps of the EU Member States on the SGP, as was discussed above, one has to interpret such Franco-German meetings from an intergovernmentalist perspective as prenegotiation fora. Obviously, such exchanges are not aimed at producing concrete results on a dossier formally located in another forum. What the Franco-German meetings did deliver, however, is a regular climate of exchange, trust and cooperation. More than once they prevented the occurrence of a serious rift between the two opponents, particularly exemplified by a meeting between Jospin and Kohl in Poitiers on 13 June 1997, only days before the Amsterdam summit. The new French government having expressed serious reservations about the SGP, this Franco-German summit cleared the way for the compromise that linked the adoption of the Pact to the inclusion of an employment chapter in the Treaty. These Franco-German meetings are purely intergovernmental and form a not very visible but important part of the bargaining process, which supports the applicability of intergovernmentalism to this feature of the SGP case.

Lessons from intergovernmentalism

The above analysis shows that the SGP can indeed be explained partially as the outcome of intergovernmental bargaining. The intergovernmentalist approach offers important insights into the interaction between states. It explains the importance of Germany and France in the creation of the SGP as well as that of other national governments. The approach stresses how and why the European Council interferes in the legislation process on economic and monetary policy-making, which is not normally the case.

A strength of the intergovernmentalist perspective is that it offers a plausible explanation why Member States that were sceptical at first finally accepted detailed rules on budgetary surveillance: ultimately because of

German dominance. In a similar vein, the intergovernmentalist approach can explain that the eventual outcome of the negotiations lay closer to the German demands than to those of France or of any other country; the reason being that Germany had more power over these matters than France or anyone else. This power asymmetry, in turn, is explained by the fact that the future EMU depended on Germany's willingness to continue the project. If the eventual outcome of the SGP negotiations had not been acceptable to Germany, the entire course of EMU would have been endangered. EMU was ultimately not feasible without German participation. At the same time, Germany also needed to make some substantial compromises so as to accommodate the needs of others, such as dropping the insistence on fully automatic sanctions. This need to compromise reflects the fact that dominance in international bargaining is not equivalent to omnipotence. After all, the German government saw EMU as being in its interest (as long as certain conditions were fulfilled) and required France to stay committed as well.

Intergovernmentalism can also explain why there were no more extreme positions on the spectrum of loose versus strict and automatic rules on budgets than those that were represented by France and Germany, respectively. More extreme positions than either those of France or Germany could possibly have been associated with the Netherlands (being even stricter on the SGP) on the one hand, and, almost certainly, with Italy (being even more interested in lenience than France). However, such deviations were submerged by delegating the leadership of the negotiations to France and Germany.

Despite the advantages of this analysis, an intergovernmentalist approach does not, however, offer a complete analysis of the SGP case. Taking national interests as given, it is puzzling that the exceptionally dominant position of Germany did not lead to a bargaining outcome that was identical with or even closer to the German interest and, above all, that was achieved much more swiftly. Could Germany not simply have offered an international treaty in a manner of 'take it or leave it'? The answer of an astonished politician to our question was simply that 'this is not how we deal with each other in Europe'.[18] Intergovernmentalism is obviously ill-suited to explain why the concerns of other countries were taken so seriously and why German negotiators offered them considerable concessions in the process of lengthy negotiations that contained more than pure bargaining. In fact, they had a cognitive dimension to them in the sense that the Germans tried to *convince* their partners through the strength of arguments and not simply by overruling them with power.

---

[18] Interview with the authors, München, 10 December 2003.

Beyond that, the approach falls short of clarifying exactly where national state interests come from. Liberal intergovernmentalism puts strong emphasis on how economic interests would be the driving force behind the formulation of state preferences. But why was Germany in favour of a system of automatic sanctions at a time in which that country itself was already violating the rule of having budgetary deficits no higher than 3 per cent of GDP? Another factor lacking full explanation is the political dimension of state interests. Intergovernmentalism does not explain the dominant role of the Bundesbank or that of public opinion in influencing the German bargaining position. There are more aspects that beg further analytical clarification. Why would countries ever give up sovereignty in the area of budgetary policy for the sake of rules? Perhaps one can argue that Germany's partners had *de facto* already given up sovereignty over monetary policy. This situation had already impinged indirectly also on their discretionary scope for budgetary policy, so adopting further restrictions would only be the logical extension of forgone sovereignty. However, a system of rules that could impose sanctions on countries, including Germany and France, is a bridge too far for intergovernmentalism.

In fact, there are some dimensions of the SGP outcome in 1997 that one can appreciate better by adopting a functionalist approach. One reason why Germany did not succeed in obtaining a new intergovernmental treaty is that rules and arrangements on economic and monetary coordination were already embedded in the Maastricht Treaty. The Germans were asked to stay within that framework rather than adding a new treaty *à la* Schengen. An intergovernmentalist approach that attributes considerable power to Germany does not explain why the Germans would have accepted the limitations of the Treaty. Likewise, once the SGP was approved, it was a very detailed legalistic text containing considerably more than the minimalist Stability Pact that the Germans proposed. In other words, the SGP rules and regulations became firmly embedded in the legal framework set out at Maastricht.

What needs to be spelled out is that most of the content of the SGP, perhaps as much as 95 per cent of the text (estimated by some of our interview partners) was agreed to in the Monetary Committee without further discussion at the political level. As we shall argue in more detail in Chapter 5, the role of experts in creating the SGP cannot be boiled down to a mere bargain between France and Germany.

In summary, the intergovernmental contribution to the general understanding of the SGP is helpful for those elements of the framework that became highly political in the course of interstate bargaining. For the more subtle issues as well as for an understanding of the origins of the Pact, we need to adopt different analytical approaches.

3   Opening the box: A domestic politics approach to the SGP

Presenting the domestic politics approach

Some European integration scholars found intergovernmentalism and its focus on nation state interests on its own insufficient to explain the process of European integration (Bulmer 1983; Webb 1983). Intergovernmentalism was criticised for looking at the state as a 'black box'. Based on comparative politics and political economy approaches, domestic politics scholars stressed that, in order to understand state preferences, one would want to analyse internal dynamics of the state and appreciate the importance of the domestic political context (Huelshoff 1994). National elections, domestic structures, constituencies and sensitivities, later also called 'national identities', were seen to have a crucial impact on the way the EU is perceived by the national government as being an instrument to obtain domestically important objectives. Likewise, the domestic scene may impose a constraint on the national government which then would affect the way it operates at the European level, for example to secure its national interests in negotiations.

Scholars who emphasise the importance of domestic politics argue that there are certain domestic actors that are significant in understanding the outcomes of the European integration process. These actors are: the national government, party leaders, the opposition, the general public, interest groups, corporations, the media and so on.

Not only are the actual actors important, but the domestic institutional setting and the institutional structures in which they operate also play a role. For example, the party-political constellation in which a government has to operate is of influence, as is intra-party competition among political leaders. Furthermore, the debates taking place in the general public affect the way governments, opinion leaders, media and the general public engage with one another. An often-used example of an important structure of this sort is the Danish arrangement of a special parliamentary committee on European integration, limiting the Danish negotiators in European negotiations to a very narrow mandate (Martin 1995). Likewise, the existence (or not) of national referenda on particular European integration policies or treaties is crucial for the empowerment of particular countries or governments as well as for their negotiation positions in the EU. Besides institutions, particular domestic politics events like elections and preceding campaigns obviously have an important impact on European integration. The integration process is also often influenced by what the outgoing government still can do or wants to enshrine upon its successors. The opposite can also happen in the sense that the EU process stalls until a new government has been elected. Sometimes Europe is used for the electoral platform on which parties run. In 1995, for example, the German SPD tested 'euro-sceptic' elements in regional election campaigns, which were not without influence on the origins of the SGP (see below). In all these ways the domestic scene, its institutions and actors, have an impact on European policy-making and integration.

The mechanism by which integration occurs from a domestic politics perspective is a little erratic. Many different issues can come up at different points in time and there is no knowing when they might occur over a longer period. Thus, there is no neat automaticity or continuity of domestic influences on the European integration process. One of the few regular phenomena that to some extent structure domestic issues is the national election cycle, which, in some cases, can become crucial for explaining government behaviour at the European level.

A government facing an election or strong political pressure from the opposition will be guided by what appears to bring electoral victory (which as such does not imply that we could theorise *a priori* whether it would be in favour of integration or against). Again, this process does not explain or even predict when issues emerge, but it at least suggests being sensitive to electoral considerations in the analysis of European integration events.

There are other analyses that emphasise the important role of domestic politics. The 'two-level game' metaphor, for instance, describes how governments may gain bargaining advantage by being bound domestically and how certain domestic actors in turn are empowered to act in such a way (Putnam 1988). Other scholars have looked at how domestic actors have increasingly lobbied EU institutions directly (Bouwen 2002; Mazey and Richardson 1993). There is some evidence that domestic actors have been able to influence agenda-setting and policy-making processes in a direct fashion, although this constellation does not appear relevant in the SGP case.

We will see in the following how domestic politics was able to influence European politics by staging the public arena in which the SGP negotiations were conducted and decisions made and by raising the stakes for governmental actors, sometimes considerably so. The approach consists of scrutinising the domestic situation of the relevant governments, which in the previous chapter have been identified to be mainly Germany and France. In the remainder of this chapter and in the style of other studies that incorporate a domestic politics perspective of EMU (Dyson and Featherstone 1996a; Hallerberg 2004; Martin 1994; McNamara 1994; Sandholtz 1993; Youngs 1999), we develop our view of the domestic politics dimension of the SGP.

On balance, the SGP dossier was and is by its nature the subject of international negotiation and interaction, hence an arena where only a very narrow set of domestic actors can wield strong influence on governments, and where exclusively governmental actors are involved in the actual deliberations and decisions at the European level. Therefore, in the SGP case, the only potentially strong domestic actors are central banks and political parties. To a lesser extent, an important role is also played by specific lobby groups (such as trade unions or banking associations), mainly via their influence on public opinion that in turn bears on the behaviour of parties.

Central banks play a special role in this policy field as they have two channels of influence. They have an indirect one through their influence on the formulation of economic policy, not least via their bearing on public opinion, and a direct one through the fact that their representatives personally participate in the negotiations. For understanding the SGP as an example of economic policy-making at the European level, it is imperative to discuss the role of the Bundesbank in the origins of the Pact and that of the ECB as far as the later developments surrounding the implementation and reform of the SGP are concerned.

Political parties, especially those in opposition, constitute the other set of actors to be looked at for our SGP enquiry. The negotiating government representatives – and indirectly also their envoys to the technical committees – are ultimately dependent on parliamentary and public support of the governing political parties. Therefore, tendencies within these organisations can come to bear on the government's stance on the SGP whenever the issue becomes topical within the ruling coalition or within a party. The influence of the opposition is based on the degree to which it succeeds in utilising the SGP as a policy issue for strengthening its own profile in public. Intra-party influence depends on whether a competitor for leadership uses or engineers a salient issue to exert pressure on the incumbent. In doing so, the opposition or party-internal competitors can initiate a dialectical process by which they first draw public attention to the SGP and then define their own stance, as far as credibly possible, in line with the perceived preferences of the public. To the extent that this strategy is successful, it will inevitably amount to a political challenge to the ruling powers.

By definition, the domestic state of affairs of the government of a representative democracy is strongly contingent on overall swings of public opinion. These increase sharply in importance for the government according to patterns described as 'electoral cycles' (Lohmann 1993). Hence, it is imperative to incorporate important trends of public opinion into the analysis as far as they can be identified as having influenced government and opposition. For the SGP, this requires an analysis of the public perception of both the advancing EMU project and the general situation of the economy and its effects on fiscal policy, to the extent that this was a concern to the government and the public at the time.

The domestic politics approach enlightens the case of the SGP in several ways. It acknowledges the role of national governments, of various domestic actors, of the opposition and of domestic preferences prevalent in public opinion. Mechanisms such as the electoral cycle, two-level situations and the dynamics of domestic political debates influenced the (European) politics of the day.

In what follows, we will trace the origins of the SGP back to an initiative of Theo Waigel, the German Finance Minister in 1995. As we shall see, Waigel's original move was preceded by a domestic overture, staging the German central bank and the opposition as well as competition within Waigel's own party. Also, the French interests in the SGP negotiations in 1997 will be explained by the preferences of domestic actors and their bearing on the government. Taking these two themes in turn will provide the reader with the insights to be gained by following a domestic politics approach in the analysis of the creation of the SGP, before returning to this analytical perspective as part of a comprehensive appraisal of the subsequent implementation and reform of the SGP in later years.

German domestic politics

At the time of the SGP's origination, the German domestic arena was dominated by the powerful central bank, the Bundesbank, and by a political struggle surrounding Chancellor Kohl's commitment to economic and monetary union. We will address both issues in turn.

The Bundesbank was in principle in favour of creating an economic and monetary union in the EU but it had some reservations about the way EMU was designed and incorporated into the Maastricht Treaty. The Bundesbank was concerned that the institutional design was less solid than the system in Germany with its focus on securing price stability. It also felt uneasy about insufficient discipline among the participating Member States in the third and final stage of EMU. Nevertheless, the Bundesbank had accepted the political will of EU Member States to move towards EMU, after having ensured that the ECB statutes were similar to its own.[1] Yet it held a persistent and growing concern that, once operational, the actual EMU might be less stability-oriented than the German regime had been over the past few decades. Its reservations were that some of the Member States with a poorer record, after entering the currency area and transferring monetary policy to the ECB, would not 'behave' as well in terms of fiscal policy as they had prior to joining the club, when they had been under constant pressure by their peers as well as by financial markets to fulfil the convergence criteria. In fact, Ministry of Finance officials and central bankers from several countries, including France and the Netherlands, shared to some extent the Bundesbank's concerns that, once accepted into monetary union, fiscally weak countries would run 'excessive' deficits and thereby push inflation rates (and thus interest rates) up throughout the currency area.[2] The German central bank did not consider the Maastricht Treaty sufficiently equipped with strict rules to secure stability and fiscal prudence once the final stage of EMU had been reached. The Bundesbank was thus exerting pressure to rectify this situation. From this perspective, stricter rules would either prevent the entry of weaker candidates or exert sufficient discipline on them after entry, thereby minimising the damage.

Due to its historically strong standing in Germany, the Bundesbank was in a particularly good position to criticise the EMU project (see also Heipertz 2001). The hyperinflation in the first part of the twentieth century had made Germans sceptical about government interference with monetary policy. Instead, in Germany, an independent central bank was responsible for conducting monetary policy.[3] In comparison with other, less independent, central banks, the Bundesbank had performed well in the four decades before EMU and had achieved relatively low levels of inflation, contributing to a steady appreciation of the German national currency, the Deutschmark, and its gradual ascent as a global reserve currency. The Bundesbank was one of the most respected institutions in Germany. Besides that, there are three concrete reasons why the Bundesbank's criticism of EMU and its demands for stricter rules gained important influence on the German government.

First, its plea needs to be seen in the context of a preceding verdict of the German Constitutional Court (*Bundesverfassungsgericht*), another highly

---

[1] On the influence of the Bundesbank on the design of the future ECB, see Verdun (2000a) and Heipertz (2001).

[2] On the sidelines of some international fora, particularly among central bankers, the fiscally weaker Mediterranean states were sometimes disrespectfully referred to as 'PIGS' (Portugal, Italy, Greece and Spain) or 'Club Med' countries.

[3] For a concise account of the Bundesbank's history, see Kennedy (1991).

authoritative domestic player. The Constitutional Court had decided in 1993 that the German Parliament's ratification of the Maastricht Treaty would only be in line with the country's constitution as long as EMU did not endanger the stability orientation of the economy.[4] Hence, at least hypothetically, the outcome of any renewed attempt to challenge the EMU project before the Constitutional Court (as happened in 1998 on the selection of the participating countries upon entering Stage III of EMU and in 2009 against the Lisbon Treaty) was less likely to be in favour of the single currency if the authoritative Bundesbank had opposed it on the grounds of stability. At least hypothetically, the legal argument could be that, on the ground of the Bundesbank's verdict, the stability orientation of EMU was not or no longer guaranteed and therefore the government would be constitutionally required to withdraw from the project.

Second, even in the absence of a formal judicial confrontation, the political costs for the Kohl government of moving forward with EMU in opposition to the central bank would rise markedly due to the influence that the Bundesbank could bring to bear upon public opinion. Third, the Bundesbank President of course had a seat on the Governing Council of the European Monetary Institute (EMI), which, according to the Maastricht Treaty, was to be consulted on the European Council's selection of countries for Stage III of EMU. There was a risk that a negative vote from the Bundesbank would influence the joint verdict of the central banks in the EMI and thereby undermine the credibility of the entire EMU project right from the start. In short, any attempt to proceed with EMU without at least tacit consent from the Bundesbank would have been unwise if not outright impossible for the Kohl government.

These three considerations shared a large degree of potential and hypothetical – rather than actual – relevance in the actors' minds at the time and should therefore be interpreted as *indirect* levers for the bank's influence on the government. In the extreme case of open conflict, the Bundesbank would have come to bear on the government in the form of an 'informal veto player', limiting the latter's scope for action in the form of a two-level game situation as described by Putnam (1988).

However, the Bundesbank had at its disposal also a *direct* channel of influence, which in practice turned out to be more relevant than the indirect one. As stated above, EU central banks were represented on both the MC and in ECOFIN, bodies in which the preparations for

---

[4] The *Bundesverfassungsgericht* (BVerfG) 89, 155, 148 of 12 October 1993 states: 'The conception of monetary union as a stability community constitutes the base and content of the acceptance law. If the monetary union is unable to further develop the stability achieved at the time of entry into Stage III, it would leave the contractual conception' (authors' translation).

Stage III of EMU were being crafted. The Bundesbank representatives in these fora were therefore able to shape the legislative process directly, both by introducing their *ideas* into the deliberations (see Chapter 5 on the role of experts and ideas) and by influencing concrete decisions. The latter would take place more in a cognitive say on the consensus-building, rather than through clear opposition, since central banks had no formal veto-power in these European fora.

Finally, another direct way of influence is given by the Bundesbank's traditionally good lines of communication to the Ministry of Finance. These exist in the form of regular meetings and informal consultations, for example in the framework of the annual fiscal planning council (*Finanzplanungsrat*). The situation in 1995 was exceptionally close: the President of the Bundesbank at the time, Hans Tietmeyer, had previously been State Secretary under Finance Minister Waigel and, therefore, could rely on a particular basis of trust and cooperation with the ministry. Furthermore, Chancellor Kohl had previously entrusted Tietmeyer as his personal envoy to negotiate intra-German monetary union in 1990.[5] The German central bank thus had close and direct access to government politicians and ministry officials on all issues related to EMU. Hence, not only strategic considerations through its say on the future of EMU, but also direct influence on the German government make the Bundesbank a decisive actor to be studied for understanding the origins of the SGP.

Besides appeasing the Bundesbank, the German government, on the road to EMU, had to confront a particularly pronounced euro-sceptic swing of public opinion in 1995. Obviously, in any important project that a democratically elected government pursues, the wider state of public opinion is crucial. Public opinion and its swings are an important factor influencing political dynamics at the national level and feed into national positions at the European level. Public opinion hence plays a role in the definition of the national interest, including of course a government's preferences and negotiation positions regarding EMU.

We interpret the bearing of public opinion on the German and French governments' approach to EMU as requiring politicians to take a specific, publicly visible stance on the issue of economic and monetary union. This does, notably, not imply that a government succumbs necessarily to a majority view held by the public – it can obviously try to turn and influence opinions over time. Otherwise, the Kohl government in Germany would have been unable to proceed with the EMU project altogether. In the first half of 1995, around 65–7 per cent of the German population was opposed

---

[5] See Heipertz (2001) on the role of the Bundesbank in inner-German monetary union in 1990.

to the single currency (Commission of the European Communities 1995; Allensbacher Archiv 1995). Hence, rather than giving in to this public opposition, the government had to take into account widely shared concerns and preoccupations and do 'something' to alleviate them. According to Luhmann (1990), an issue brought to the fore of public debate can translate into political impetus depending on the urgency, persistence and virulence with which it demands a solution. Because of the fierce competition for votes, a democratic government cannot afford complacency without allowing the political opposition to benefit from such a situation. Given the importance of public opinion, we have to direct our analysis of the impact of domestic politics on the SGP to other influences on public opinion besides that of the Bundesbank.

Another prominent position in German public debates on matters of economic policy was held by the *Sachverständigenrat*, the economic policy advisory board to the federal government. This body had already demanded in 1992 that the provisions of the Maastricht Treaty in the area of budgetary deficits (such as sanctions) be further strengthened and rigidly applied in the third stage of EMU (Sachverständigenrat 1992: 433). By that time, the discussion had already been fuelled by a so-called 'manifesto' of sixty economists, published in several newspapers and arguing against EMU as a rushed and premature project.[6]

The public debate moved on in May 1995, when, following an exchange of views with Bundesbank officials, a federal lobby association of cooperative banks (the *Bundesverband der Volksbanken und Raiffeisenkassen*, BVR) was the first to demand in public an additional treaty on fiscal discipline to be concluded by the future EMU Member States.[7] The Bundesbank, for its part, was content that such public demands were first advanced from within the private sector, even if it was obviously promoting or even initiating them behind the scene. With the BVR demands for an additional treaty on stability, the issues leading up to the conception of the SGP were 'in the air' and prominently present in German public opinion.

The debate on stricter fiscal rules intensified in the course of the year as part of the larger theme of growing public reservations in Germany about EMU.[8] Naturally, the opposition party SPD picked up the topic, both in general terms as regards euro-scepticism and, specifically, by referring to the fiscal weaknesses of the EMU framework. It is notable, however, that, by the time the SGP issue became a major political theme in Germany, the cognitive framework had already been predefined through the formation of preferences and ideas from domestic actors and within European fora

---

[6] *Frankfurter Allgemeine Zeitung*, 11 June 1992.   [7] *Handelsblatt*, 9 May 1995.
[8] For an account of public opinion in Germany on EMU, see Hoekstra *et al.* (2007).

as well as national institutions, above all the Bundesbank (see Chapter 5 on the role of experts and ideas for the SGP).

Turning to party-political dynamics, one has to recognise that the domestic situation of the Kohl government in late 1995 was difficult, especially in the fields of economic and European policies. The reunification boom had worn out and the initially rapid convergence of the Eastern *Länder* had slowed down markedly. German overall growth performance was meagre, while public finances deteriorated quickly due to the burden of reunification. In that situation, it would have been risky to ignore the mounting public hostility to EMU, which, as the flagship project of European integration, was closely associated with Chancellor Kohl personally.

When the SPD sensed the opportunity behind the popular mood in Germany and became critical of EMU, the euro-scepticism of the population grew into being Kohl's weakest spot at the time, even more than the economic disaster of reunification. The SPD, initiated by the then-Prime Minister of Lower Saxony, Gerhard Schröder,[9] quickly became more confident in airing remarks on the dangers to economic stability stemming from EMU. Moulded on the propositions of the Bundesbank, the *Sachverständigenrat* and the BVR, SPD leaders started to demand stricter rules for economic and monetary union. An explicit request for a 'Stability Pact' was put on the agenda of a federal SPD conference to be held in December 1995.[10] The confrontation between the SPD and the government coalition escalated when both sides accused each other of populism. For example, the SPD regional election campaign in Baden-Württemberg was coloured by voices claiming to turn the vote into a 'referendum on monetary union',[11] given the background that the German constitution does not foresee referenda on international treaties.

For the Kohl government, a critical moment arrived in November 1995 with the budgetary debate in Parliament. Traditionally, discussing the annual budgetary law is one of the most prominent occasions for the parliamentary opposition to bundle its criticism of the ruling party – and for the latter to defend its political priorities. By November 1995, SPD party leaders held speeches in Parliament that seemed to reiterate literally some Bundesbank statements. For example, opposition leader Scharping declared:

[The Maastricht Treaty] needs an amendment in the form of a better coordination of budgetary and fiscal policy; it needs a better and lasting assurance of the stability

---

[9] It is not without irony that the SGP was triggered by the same man who contributed to its predicament eight years later.
[10] *Süddeutsche Zeitung*, 2 November 1995.   [11] *Focus Magazin*, 12 February 1996.

criteria than currently provided. It needs this so as not to overburden the European Central Bank.[12]

By then, it had already been decided in Kohl's government that the budgetary debate would be the moment to turn the tide and to regain the lead on the EMU debate. The counter-attack would naturally be led by Finance Minister Theo Waigel, whose political party CSU (Christian Social Union) is the Bavarian sister organisation of the CDU (Christian Democratic Union, the main conservative party in Germany).

At that point in time, Waigel experienced additional pressure within his own camp. Bavarian Prime Minister Edmund Stoiber contended with him on party leadership and attempted also to benefit from the euro-sceptic public sentiments by running on an anti-EMU platform.[13] Some of the actors close to the conceptual origins of the SGP judge that the intra-CSU pressure on Waigel was even more influential than the populist move by the SPD. In principle, the mechanisms by which public opinion can translate into opportunities for the opposition also work within parties and fuel the competition for political leadership. An internal contender will utilise issues of public pre-eminence in order to appear more able to attract votes than the incumbent. This is exactly what Stoiber tried to do in 1995, thereby forcing Waigel (as the incumbent) to take up the issue in a resolute manner.

The combined effect of political pressure from within the CSU and from the SPD opposition had gathered such momentum that the SGP initiative was urgently needed as an excursion for the beleaguered Kohl government and Waigel personally. The domestic escalation explains the speed with which Waigel's experts had to produce the text of his initiative (see also Chapter 5). Deliberations among academics and experts had been going on informally for months. The first memorandum of the German Ministry of Finance, which consisted of ten pages and was still quite vague, had to be conceived within a couple of weeks. At the ECOFIN Council in Valencia on 30 September 1995, Waigel for the first time informed his European partners about the advances in Germany. Finally, a short English version of the proposal had to be produced within hours on the eve of Waigel's appearance in the Bundestag. It was sent out by fax to the other capitals so that Waigel could state in Parliament that his initiative was already on the European table:[14]

---

[12] Deutscher Bundestag, 13th legislative period, meeting 67, minutes p. 5774, authors' translation.
[13] For example, *Frankfurter Allgemeine Zeitung*, 4 November 1995.
[14] Official formerly with the German Ministry of Finance, interview with the authors, June 2003.

You will not teach us about stability. The SPD now wants to discuss a Stability Pact for Europe at its party conference. But I have already back in September proposed such a Pact as a binding self-commitment for participants in Stage III of EMU. (...) Now you have to say: 'Yes, Waigel is right, and we follow him after a couple of years or months.' (...) For such a Stability Pact, we propose the following elements: a Member State's budget deficit must not overstep the limit of 3 per cent, also in economically difficult times. A deficit target of 1 per cent is to be achieved over the medium term under normal economic conditions. Countries with high levels of public debt commit to a more ambitious target. Exceptions are only possible with the consent of the other countries, for example in the event of a natural disaster. Participants will accept a more precise and enhanced mechanism for sanctions. Participants will found a European Stability Council, which will coordinate national fiscal policies and adopt the necessary decisions.[15]

Outlining the details of a concrete, European initiative before the German Parliament, Waigel re-established himself as the authoritative political leader in charge of EMU, taking care of the concerns in the population and keeping the project on track as one of the core themes of the later Kohl era.

As we have seen, the effect of German domestic politics on the SGP was strongest in the origins of the project and kick-started the process of European negotiations. But, obviously, the value of the Pact to the CDU in the domestic debate did not wear off after the inception of the European initiative and was subsequently used repeatedly for public display as the dossier moved on. For example, Helmut Kohl pronounced after the Amsterdam European Council:

The euro will come. The Stability and Growth Pact has been adopted without any trade-off. (...) The conference in Amsterdam has made clear: there is no contradiction between stability and employment.[16]

In a similar vein, the CDU/CSU majority in Parliament used the outcome of the Amsterdam summit in 1997 as an occasion to present its successful quest for stability to the public, and thereby did not fail to overstate the actual result of the negotiations as if the entire set of German demands had been accepted in full, which obviously was not the case:

It is your merit, Federal Minister of Finance, to have enabled the Stability Pact in the first place and to have helped it over the last difficult hurdle in Amsterdam in completely unchanged form.[17]

---

[15] Deutscher Bundestag, 13th legislative period, meeting 66, minutes p. 5672, authors' translation.

[16] Deutscher Bundestag, 27 June 1997, minutes p. 16736, authors' translation.

[17] Deutscher Bundestag, Karl Lamers, foreign policy spokesman of the CDU, 27 June 1997, minutes pp. 16743f, authors' translation.

Finally, in March 1998, after the selection of countries that would enter into Stage III of EMU by 1 January 1999, Waigel continued using the SGP as a way to assuage the fears of the German public about a 'soft euro', given that EMU was now becoming a concrete possibility. He thereby exaggerated the nature of the final agreement as one of 'automatic sanctions', far from the degree of political discretion that remained in the legal texts:

There will be no soft euro. This is guaranteed through the essential elements of the Stability and Growth Pact: the definition of 3 per cent as the upper limit for deficits, the automatically initiated sanctioning procedure when the limit is exceeded and the imposition of sanctions within ten months, if no effective measures have been taken.[18]

Adopting a domestic politics perspective for Germany's approach to the SGP enables us to conclude that the Pact should also be seen in the context of a whole range of – sometimes symbolical – decisions that were related to EMU and that were adopted with regard to the need of the German government to please its hesitant constituency.

In that vein, one should also list the decision to name the future currency 'euro' rather than the 'ecu'. The European Currency Unit (ECU) as unit of account of the EMS had been depreciating over time *vis-à-vis* the Deutschmark and was not held in high regard by the German public, not least because of its 'French'-sounding name and the fact that, in the past, a French currency had circulated under the same title. Furthermore, the decision to have Frankfurt rather than Paris, Brussels or Amsterdam as the seat of the future ECB was a choice geared to relieve the concerns of German domestic opinion (as well as a decision that served the interest of the German government to obtain the seat of one of the most important European institutions). Finally, the nomination of Willem Duisenberg as the first ECB President, rather than Jean-Claude Trichet (who would become his successor), was a concession to German preferences. The Dutch central bank president rather than immediately having a Frenchman at the helm of the ECB served to symbolise the fact that the role of the central bank was independent from politics and in line with the German–Dutch model. Unlike the SGP, these decisions were not as fundamental to the design of EMU, but their high symbolical value made them very visible in the domestic domain and showed the political importance for Kohl of appeasing the euro-sceptic position held by the German public.

Regarding the SGP, the Bundesbank as well as the dynamics between and within political parties and their interaction with public opinion were

---

[18] Deutscher Bundestag, 5 March 1998, minutes p. 20259, authors' translation.

all of crucial importance for the domestic formulation of the German interest, albeit to different degrees. Our questionnaire results confirm a view of the situation as such that public opinion and the Bundesbank were both of paramount importance to the framing of the German position, followed at some distance by the influence of political pressure originating from the SPD and inside the CSU. Maybe surprisingly, people close to the scene only attribute a very small role to actual concerns of domestic economic policy at the time, such as Waigel's fruitless attempts to contain the fiscal effects of reunification and to resolve the *impasse* of fiscal federalism in Germany. After all, his European Stability Pact initiative ran almost parallel with attempts to conclude a domestic Stability Pact on the fiscal constitution of Germany. It is worth recalling that, in addition, 1995 was the first year in which Germany itself overstepped the Maastricht reference value on budgetary deficits of 3 per cent. However, these considerations were considerably less important for Waigel's European initiative than the domestic concerns associated with the Bundesbank, the opposition and public opinion more generally.

To summarise, in order to understand the emergence and timing of Waigel's Stability Pact initiative in November 1995, one needs to place it in the context of the party political dynamics and the broader domestic scene in Germany at the time. It then becomes clear that there were strategic reasons for the German government to address the concerns of the Bundesbank as well as of the wider public with respect to the 'open fiscal flank' of the Maastricht Treaty. The domestic political considerations of a national government define its European interests. The German government turned to amending a European project, EMU, in a way that satisfied domestic needs. By doing so, it aimed at reducing the political pressure in the domestic arena. This was the predominant motive, without excluding but downgrading to some extent other considerations that also stood behind the German interests for concluding an SGP.

French domestic politics

In 1995, while featuring strongly in German domestic debate, creating stricter rules for EMU was not at all an issue in French public opinion. Once the SGP was on the European negotiation table, the French 'external' position was closely aligned with that of the Commission under the Frenchman de Silguy, i.e. cooperating on the elaboration of a Stability Pact while rejecting automatic sanctions and an independent Treaty. Given that it was so far from the core issues of domestic politics at the time, it can be said that the emergence of the SGP dossier and the technical negotiations strengthened monetarist circles in France around the then-Governor of the Banque de France, Jean-Claude Trichet, who welcomed a strengthening of fiscal rules in principle. Only later, and to a lesser degree, did the sway of German domestic politics on the emergence of the SGP find itself paralleled by the influence of French domestic politics on the final SGP negotiations.

One characteristic feature of the French political system is the shared power between the President of the Republic and the Prime Minister, who both hold important leadership functions. Although the President is directly elected, the Prime Minister is appointed by the President, and the chosen candidate is selected from the ranks of the majority coalition in Parliament. If President and Prime Minister have different party affiliations, a particular situation emerges which is referred to as *cohabitation*. Given that the key political players adhere to opposing camps, *cohabitation* is usually perceived as a somewhat awkward constellation. Adopting a domestic politics perspective for understanding the SGP, particular importance should be attached to the French situation surrounding the negotiation and final acceptance of the SGP up to June 1997, which is coloured by dramatic electoral events that occurred in the spring of 1997 as well as by the ensuing *cohabitation* between Jacques Chirac and Lionel Jospin.

In 1995, Jacques Chirac – leader of the Gaullist RPR political party[19] – was elected President on a platform called *une autre politique*, which had in part been designed to fend off competition from within his own party. In the later years of the Mitterrand era, the French public was longing for policies of social welfare and economic prosperity after years of austerity and monetarist discipline, subsumed under the *franc fort* strategy associated with players like Trichet. The *franc fort* course was backed by RPR Prime Minister Eduard Balladur, who had since 1993 been governing in *cohabitation* with Mitterrand. RPR leader Chirac had preferred to refrain from becoming Prime Minister, knowing perfectly well that the unpopular *franc fort* measures were necessary to avoid further depreciation of the franc and to prevent the EMU project from being derailed, especially after the 1994 currency crisis in the EMS.

In order to appeal to the public, Chirac's 1995 presidential campaign on *une autre politique* signalled a relaxation of the *franc fort* policy and distanced him from Balladur, who, as Prime Minister, had developed ambitions for the presidency. Instead, Chirac promised looser reins on fiscal policy, including tax cuts and increased welfare spending. However, once in power, he instructed his new Prime Minister, Alain Juppé, to continue

---

[19] RPR stands for *Rassemblement pour la République*, which can be translated as Rally for the Republic, or Assembly for the Republic.

the unpopular measures, not least in the light of market pressures and the persistent need to fulfil the EMU convergence criteria. The urgency of fiscal austerity became increasingly important in 1997, given that the European Council decision on the set of countries that were to enter Stage III of EMU in 1999 was due in 1998, on the basis of 1997 data. In fact, the *Plan Juppé* involved an increase of income taxes by five percentage points, rather than the decrease promised in Chirac's campaign. Hence, the strategic aim of attaining monetary union with Germany required Chirac to accept the political costs of reneging on earlier election pledges.

Inevitably, the strategy was perceived as treason in the eyes of the public and heavily attacked by the Socialist opposition under Lionel Jospin. Even worse, Juppé's policies did not deliver any immediately observable positive effects. On the contrary, unemployment was rising in a context of continuously low economic growth.[20] Public opinion increasingly identified the conservative government's policies of fiscal consolidation and structural reform as being in part 'dictated' by the German-influenced EMU project. Significantly, the prospects of creating a Stability Pact fuelled such concerns and entered prominently on the stage of domestic political debate. Portraying the government as giving in to a German 'dictate' on reinforced rules for fiscal rectitude became a key theme for the Socialists.

Against this background, Finance Minister Jean Arthuis attempted to weaken the design of the SGP and in particular to link it to a 'Pact on Employment'. As far as the SGP was concerned, his efforts only led to a cosmetic change of the title, when 'Stability Pact' was amended and became 'Stability *and Growth* Pact' – without altering anything in substance. In addition, Arthuis obtained German agreement to the establishment of the so-called Euro-X Council. This precursor to the Eurogroup was presented to the French public as the achievement of some sort of *gouvernement économique* which would ensure that elected politicians rather than unaccountable technocrats would steer economic policy in EMU (Verdun 2003). For the purpose of these two domestic themes – a political counterweight to the ECB and a focus on employment and growth – President Chirac stated before the Dublin summit:

The euro is no end in itself but an instrument in the service of growth. (…) The states adopting the euro have to form a government that clearly shows the ECB its limits and commits it to accountability.'[21]

---

[20] The unemployment rate increased from 11.4 per cent in the first quarter of 1995 to 12 per cent in the third quarter of 1996 (OECD 1996). The disappointing labour market performance was the central theme of the Socialist opposition in France at the time.

[21] In a TV debate before the Dublin summit, quoted in *Handelsblatt*, 31 December 1996, authors' translation.

After the Dublin summit, Chirac declared:

> France wanted the Stability Pact as much as Germany. On the one hand, France wanted a Stability Pact that is also a Growth Pact – which has been accepted by our German friends, who, I have to say, were not opposed to this idea. On the other hand, France did not want automaticity. (…) In reality it is the Council of Ministers and above all the European Council of those countries that introduce the euro who will jointly represent, in yet undefined form, the power opposite the European Central Bank. (…) To put it clearly, the Summit has made the euro an instrument to the service of Europe's future growth, and growth means jobs.[22]

In the French domestic debate on EMU, the term 'economic government' features repeatedly as a vague notion of squaring the Maastricht Treaty's insistence on central bank independence with some desire for *dirigisme* and political leadership in matters of economic policy. One reason why the government of France was frustrated with the governance framework of EMU is that the more explicit coordination of macroeconomic policies other than monetary policy which had been discussed in the preparations for Maastricht gradually disappeared (see Kenen 1995; Howarth 2001 and Dyson and Featherstone 1999 on the French proposals for EMU). The SGP is a disciplinary mechanism of individual countries which entails some degree of coordination but the French were dissatisfied that this mechanism does not give sufficient visibility to the politicians gathered in ECOFIN (cf. Pisani-Ferry 2006). Economic government was presented to the public as 'balancing' to some extent the 'technocratic' power of the independent central bank. The *gouvernement économique* would embody democratic rule over fiscal policy despite the SGP framework and counterbalance the fact that monetary policy was not under political control. However, to the extent that economic policy coordination or even political dominance over the central bank were to be pursued at the European level in some form of economic government, it would by definition involve yet another transfer of sovereignty from the national to the supranational level. Such a further weakening of the nation state, however, would be at conflict with the Neo-Gaullist reflex to defend national sovereignty against integration. Such thinking remains deep-rooted in French political discourse and continues to influence the country's approach to European integration over time. The unavoidable dilemma between transferring a French notion of economic *dirigisme* to EMU on the one hand and retaining sovereignty on the other hand explains the incoherence of successive French proposals for *gouvernement économique* up to this day (Howarth 2005).

---

[22] Press conference after the Dublin summit, quoted in *Handelsblatt*, 14 December 1996, and *Agence Europe*: Europe Daily Bulletin No. 6875, 15 December 1996, authors' translation.

The new title of the SGP as well as the establishment of the Euro-X Council were both decided at the Dublin summit in December 1996 but soon proved unable to assuage public apprehensions in France. Indeed, all our interview partners as well as the respondents to the questionnaires were of the view that France obtained only cosmetic concessions from Germany at the Dublin summit. That insight was probably hard to deny in public, so that domestic opinion was perfectly aware that no fundamental changes to the nature of the framework had in fact occurred.

In the meantime, President Chirac pondered the chances of his camp in the upcoming 1998 parliamentary elections. Even though his policies and thus the government had come under heavy attack, the opposition parties did not appear to be capable of offering a credible alternative election platform that could challenge the ruling coalition. By predating the elections, Chirac saw a chance to obtain a clear mandate from the French citizens for his necessary measures on the road to economic and monetary union and, at the same time, avoid the ballot at a later point in time when the political costs of the reforms would probably be highest. Interestingly, in his situation, the election timetable had to follow the reform timetable, required by the convergence criteria, rather than the usual order of priorities, by which policy measures are subordinated to elections. On balance, the risk had to be taken and elections were called for 1 June 1997, after dissolution of the *Assemblée Nationale*.

Chirac's judgement and that of all political observers (including the opposition parties) at the time was that the Juppé government, although unpopular, was in a good position of being re-elected in face of a disorganised opposition. However, while Chirac may have underestimated resentment in the population, the Socialist party realised that it had nothing to lose and quickly formed a left-wing block with the Communist party, promising, *inter alia*, a reduction of the legal working week to 35 hours. The joint platform also contained the outright claim that a Jospin-led government would not sign up to the SGP that Chirac was negotiating with the Germans.

The unexpected happened: the RPR lost its majority. Although after the elections the RPR still remained the strongest party it lost eight percentage points and thereby only obtained 36.1 per cent of the votes. The Socialists improved their share to 25.7 per cent and were able to form a minority coalition to govern with the Communists and the Green Party, given that the extreme right had won 14.9 per cent. The result of the general elections hence led to a change of government with Lionel Jospin becoming Prime Minister on a platform of reviving growth and boosting employment at the expense of fiscal rigour. By consequence, *cohabitation* was established between Chirac as President and Jospin as Prime Minister.

As far as the SGP was concerned, their respective positions had seemed to represent polar opposites: Chirac had agreed to the Dublin compromise *vis-à-vis* his European partners; and Jospin, in the election campaign, had promised to renegotiate the SGP and to reverse the 'ultraliberal excesses of EMU'.[23] It was completely unclear how France would behave at the forthcoming Amsterdam summit in June 1997, only two weeks after the election.

Pierre Moscovici, incoming Minister for European Affairs, rattled financial markets by hinting at a possible French veto in Amsterdam. It was obviously of ultimate importance to Jospin to obtain some bargaining successes that could be 'sold' domestically to the victorious constituency. German leaders signalled that a veto or substantial demands for changing the SGP agreement would cause a major disruption to the EMU process.

Meanwhile, the new head of the Economics and Finance Ministry, Dominique Strauss-Kahn, was keen to avert a further slide of the French franc against the Deutschmark – after all, the first thing that top-level civil servants used to acquaint an incoming French Minister of Finance with was the Reuters foreign exchange market screen. Aware of the market sensitivities, Strauss-Kahn requested additional time to reconsider the SGP issue:

I don't say that I want to renegotiate the Pact, but neither do I say that I can accept it in its current form.[24]

Also Commissioner de Silguy pressed the seriousness of the situation, not least targeted to the French audience:

On the eve of the third millennium, Europe will be judged in terms of the success of its economic and monetary union. Either EMU is a success and Europe will count in the world, or it fails and Europe will be considered an ageing and rigid continent, with limited growth potential.[25]

Behind the scenes, Chirac was able to convince the new French government that an agreed negotiation package could not be abandoned at the last minute, in particular because he himself, as Head of State, had supported the agreement. As discussed in more detail in Chapter 2, Jospin obtained a number of concessions to be presented to the French public, particularly the employment chapter of the Amsterdam Treaty, in conjunction with the announcement of a special summit on employment. Furthermore, the public presentation of the already agreed Euro-X Council was reinforced as an embryonic version of *gouvernement*

---

[23] *Agence France Presse*, 30 May 1997, authors' translation.
[24] *Financial Times*, 10 June 1997.
[25] *Agence Europe*: Europe Daily Bulletin, No. 6994, 13 June 1997.

économique in light of the domestic considerations referred to above.[26] On the substance of the SGP, however, Jospin acquiesced, realising himself that the election promise of a veto had been unrealistic, made under the impression of a campaign fought against all odds.

Following the Amsterdam summit, Chirac pronounced:

> To safeguard their economic and financial interests, the Fifteen must (...) adopt the Pact for Stability and Growth. But the interest of the single currency also requires a policy for growth, employment and social progress, which explains the resolution adopted on France's initiative.[27]

Jospin obviously also had to present the outcome of the European Council as a success for the new government, in light of its previous election platform. In doing so, he admitted that his room for manoeuvre had been limited by prior commitments of the President. He therefore presented himself as 'having limited the damage' that the SGP could do to the French priorities:

> My government had wanted, in respect of France's commitments and the promise of the President of the Republic, if not to have new areas emerge, at least to insist on a certain number of requirements regarding growth and the fight for employment.[28]

Lessons from domestic politics

Both cases, Germany as well as France, demonstrate that the SGP project was to a considerable extent driven by the domestic considerations of the participating governments. These considerations did not so much have a direct influence on the technical content of the negotiations but rather framed a publicly salient input into the discussion as well as the official interpretation attached to resulting agreements. By way of reduction, public opinion focused on a very limited set of specifications of the future SGP that, partly of more symbolical than actual value, shaped the negotiation less than its presentation. Yet, domestic politics in Germany did have a major impact on pushing the issue to the fore in the first place, and domestic politics in France was a major source of restraint on possible changes to the existing framework as already laid out in the Treaty.

Domestic dynamics determined, more or less unpredictably, which issues on the negotiating table became absolutely vital to the government

---

[26] On the inclusion of the employment chapter in the Amsterdam Treaty, see Schäfer (2002). On the development of the Euro-X Council, now the Eurogroup, see Puetter (2004, 2006).

[27] *Agence Europe*: Europe Daily Bulletin No. 6998, 19 June 1997.

[28] *Agence Europe*: Europe Daily Bulletin No. 6998, 19 June 1997.

in question. When stirred up by the opposition or by internal competition, government representatives had to defend the most salient issues as *conditio sine qua non*. A good example is Waigel's stance on the level of 3 per cent being a *ceiling* rather than a *target* (the public version of which was 'three point nil is three point nil') or Arthuis having to insist on the word 'growth' being added to the name of the Pact. The actual importance that these issues had or did not have in the structure of the SGP is secondary to their symbolical weight in the domestic scene. In these symbolically important areas, the domestic circumstances required that 'something' be achieved that could be 'sold' to the domestic actors.

It was in the interests of Germany to achieve a result that would solve the domestic problem of a population that resented EMU, while at the same time addressing some of the fundamental concerns of the Bundesbank. For the French, the major issue was to reduce the 'damage' that the SGP agreement could bring to the domestic debate on unemployment.

Public statements from French and German political leaders as quoted above seem to refer to very different parts of the agreement and at times appear even to contradict each other. They only make sense next to each other if one takes them as what they were: signals to very different domestic scenes. Politicians of course understand and, up to a point, tolerate each other's urge to please public opinion, so the degree of mutual understanding can be assumed to be very high, as is the willingness to make concessions to a colleague – as long as one's own domestic preoccupations are not jeopardised.[29]

In sum, a domestic politics approach explains a number of important moments in which country-internal dynamics play a crucial role for the SGP. The approach provides tools to examine the domestic actors that influence national government policies and priorities. The perspective identifies the important actors as well as the mechanisms and institutional context that determine the internal dynamics. The approach also shows that simply the fact that national governments obtain a concession in a domestically pertinent area is crucial, not so much the actual content of that concession. In the SGP case, the important actors are the national governments of Germany and France, the Bundesbank, public opinion in both countries and, crucially, the political opposition as well as, at certain times, intra-party competitors to political leaders.

---

[29] This does not prevent the emergence of cultural misunderstandings about the features of EMU, as it is being portrayed differently in countries like France and Germany. In turn, these differences in discourse could be seen to lead to conflicting perceptions of institutional legitimacy, for example that the stability-oriented monetary policy of the ECB might be perceived as welcome in Germany and at the same time find harsh criticism in France.

The domestic politics approach allows us to understand the German motivation and particularly the timing of the origins of the SGP. In light of the German domestic situation, the analysis of the origins of the SGP becomes more sensitive to the fact that the Pact was created along the lines of a *perceived* 'German model'. In France, the domestic situation was such that the government was being pressured into showing economic success in terms of growth and employment. Once Member States were negotiating the final deal on the SGP, the French needed 'something' they could use for the domestic constituency that would prevent the agreement being displayed as counterproductive to the quest for employment.

From a domestic politics perspective, national representatives in the Monetary Committee are dependent representatives of their respective governments. Their personal insights and convictions on any one issue are irrelevant or at least secondary compared to the instructions that they receive from their superiors, who, always with an eye on public opinion, advise them on how to bargain for the domestically framed 'national interest'. Negotiators have to realise which issues are of symbolical value and subsequently have to sometimes defend lines that, to their mind, seem trivial or even counterproductive. This process includes both governments as well as MC members having to anticipate potentially dangerous reactions of the domestic opposition or of important domestic players. As will be discussed in Chapter 5, in reality, MC members (now EFC members) and their alternates are Janus-faced individuals who at times show the side of a negotiator of the domestic interest ('financial diplomat'); at other times – and whenever possible – act as a professional expert deliberating among colleagues on technical issues, which, at home, they try to make palpable to their political masters.

Hence, the domestic politics approach falls short of providing a complete explanation of the SGP case. As has been clarified through the intergovernmentalist perspective, the prominence of Germany and France requires an insight beyond the internal dynamics of domestic politics. The degree to which a domestic issue becomes important at the European level is a function of the (intergovernmental) power of the country *and* the domestic salience of the issue (which includes the relative power of the domestic advocates). Without taking the intergovernmental 'weight' of a certain country for given, the domestic politics approach could not explain why primarily the prerogatives of France and Germany would come into play, rather than, say, those of Greece or Belgium. Similarly, the importance of France as Germany's opponent in the international bargaining is understood rather through the intergovernmental approach than by assessing domestic politics in isolation. Finally, the European Council, which according to the actors interviewed was crucial for resolving specific points of the negotiation dossier, is a purely intergovernmental organ that engages in interstate bargaining. Its functioning requires an explanation that can deal with the intergovernmental nature independently of the fact that the bargaining results are subsequently translated into domestic signals by the actors.

There is more to be said about the SGP. If the logic of negotiations was all geared towards obtaining ostensible and visible bargaining success for topics of domestic salience, then why is the final outcome a sophisticated, rules-based regime for economic governance? Why do we get an elaborate arrangement on the budgetary rules of the Treaty rather than only a minimalist, declaratory document pleasing the German (and French) public, like the resolution of the Amsterdam European Council?

It is evident that, beyond the intergovernmental and domestic approaches, we have to apply additional theoretical perspectives to arrive at a comprehensive assessment and explanation of the SGP. The following chapter will therefore take up the issue that the SGP was a concrete answer to a policy problem, framed as secondary legislation in the context of the Treaty and designed in such a way that it would address in the best attainable manner the perceived shortcomings of the Treaty in view of the economic policy requirements of monetary union in Europe.

4   The functional logic behind the SGP

Presenting neofunctionalism

For many years neofunctionalism was the leading explanatory approach to European integration (Haas 1964; Lindberg and Scheingold 1970, 1971). Based on the 'liberal' or 'idealist' or 'world order' international relations theory that sought to explain regional integration after the Second World War, it became discredited when it was unable to account for the apparent setbacks in the process, i.e. the fact that its automatic mechanisms were evidently unable to account for integration reversals or stagnation.

Intergovernmentalism was the first theory to criticise the functionalist approach (Hoffmann 1966), but even Haas himself eventually agreed it had limitations (Haas 1975, 1976). The previously claimed automaticity of spillover principles could not be observed. However, during the 1990s a considerable number of scholars incorporated parts of the neofunctionalist principles into their theoretical approaches (Corbey 1995; Mutimer 1989; Tranholm-Mikkelsen 1991). The idea that integration in one area of policy-making could necessitate further decisions regained some of its attractiveness (cf. Börzel 2005; Niemann and Schmitter 2009; Risse 2005; Rosamond 2005; Schmitter 2004, 2005, 2009; Stone Sweet and Sandholtz 1998). Adherents to the approach were no longer concerned with the fact that the integrative principles could not *always* be observed and argued instead that the mechanisms they studied worked over longer periods of time, regardless of possible intermediate setbacks in the process of integration.

According to the neofunctionalist approaches, the players that matter most are supranational actors, supranational institutions and transnational elites (Deutsch *et al.* 1957, 1967; Stone Sweet and Sandholtz 1998). Originally Haas (1958, 1964) focused on social groups, trade unions, employers' organisations and other interest groups. These agents were seen to transfer their activities to the European level when, due to transnational interdependence, it was no longer efficient to pursue policies exclusively in isolation at the national level. The arguments were that such organisations, when operating at the European level, acquired an additional edge over the policy-making process and thus, almost involuntarily, contributed to integration.

Furthermore, so-called 'policy entrepreneurs', in particular figures like certain Commission Presidents, are crucial in this view for furthering integration through personal leadership. From this perspective, the integration process is aided significantly by decisions prepared by supranational institutions, EU committees and other elites who have been socialised. The socialisation process has enabled them to have a good sense of which actions and projects may benefit the integration objective.

In neofunctionalism, the spillover mechanism remains probably the most important explanatory component for understanding the advance of integration. Spillover implies that developments in one area of policy-making subsequently necessitate further steps along previous lines or require further developments in adjacent areas of policy-making in order to fulfil the original goal. According to the neofunctionalist logic, negotiations follow the neofunctionalist path when policies follow each other to ensure a successful policy objective. Spillover, according to contemporary scholars, can take place in different domains (functional[1], political, cultivated and geographic; see Tranholm-Mikkelsen 1991).

In recent years neofunctionalism has been revised so as to include the possibility of the integration process being interrupted by a politicised process (Schmitter 2004). However, the fundamental underlying principle still remains that there is a certain path that will be followed and that builds on the previously achieved steps of integration. In that sense, modern neofunctionalism draws on the principle of path dependence (cf. Pierson 1996) and historical institutionalism (cf. Hall and Taylor 1996).

During calm periods, supranational institutions (for example, the European Parliament, the ECJ, the ECB and, the supranational body *par excellence*, the Commission) have an edge over national institutions or even governments in shaping integration and deepening the integration process in those policy areas that are already partly or completely integrated. Recent approaches that are based on neofunctionalist principles no longer primarily talk about 'spillover' but also focus on the importance of 'transactions' which require European-level regulation and the existence of a 'self-sustaining dynamic' (Stone Sweet and Sandholtz 1998). This process in turn is seen to lead to 'supranational governance' (see for instance Burley and Mattli, 1993, who consider the ECJ in this light; see also Cichowski 2007).

---

[1] Tanja Börzel (2005) has called functional spillover 'task expansion'.

The most important actors for a neofunctionalist interpretation of the SGP history are EU supranational institutions and fora. These are the MC, the Commission and, to a lesser degree, the ECOFIN Council. An important difference between an intergovernmental and a neofunctionalist take on these fora is that the former sees the ECOFIN and also the MC (now EFC) as arenas for intergovernmental bargaining, whereas the neofunctionalist approach would stress precisely the fact that ministers act differently when they are in an EU Council setting than if they were just bargaining over their national interests in a random intergovernmental forum (Corbey 1993; Sandholtz 1993; Verdun 2000a). The neofunctionalist perspective assumes that members of a supranational institution incorporate in their interests not only the 'pure' national interest but also some sense of wanting to help build the 'Europe of the future'.[2] It is a matter of debate to which extent the ECOFIN Council and the MC can be seen that way – but if it is true that the SGP deliberations were not exclusively about interest bargaining, then the neofunctionalist approach will be instructive on yet another dimension of the complex SGP dossier.

Indeed, the notion of building Europe jointly becomes apparent when national representatives discuss matters in deliberative committees such as the MC. Socialisation takes place in such a circle and the members get to know each other very well. Being acquainted creates trust and enables them to propose policies that go beyond the lowest common denominator, which is what mere intergovernmental bargaining would expect. The MC is a particularly strong committee in this regard, as has been identified by Westlake (1995); Hanny and Wessels (1998) and Verdun (2000b). The neofunctionalist perspective sees a strong role for transnational elites regardless of their exact forum of deliberation. It is seen that they contribute to a common understanding of the next stage based on the past steps taken and even an idealist aim to 'build Europe'.

Policy entrepreneurs, such as Commissioners, and the Commission President, already mentioned above, also play an important role in the creation and evolution of the SGP.[3] Although Theo Waigel, as a national actor, could be seen as some kind of policy entrepreneur for the SGP initiative, strictly speaking, one should not forget that the SGP dossier itself is embedded in the wider project of EMU, which would be

---

[2] This particular role of making a 'forward' contribution towards European integration is nowadays not often emphasised in the literature on neofunctionalism. However, in the original works of the neofunctionalists (Haas 1958, 1964; Deutsch et al. 1957; Lindberg and Scheingold 1970, 1971) there was an assumption that these supranational actors were actively contributing to furthering the integration objective.

[3] On the role of policy entrepreneurs see Laffan (1997).

completely unthinkable without an illustrious group of 'entrepreneurs' around people like Kohl, Mitterrand, Delors, de Silguy and so on. Although some of these hold national offices, it would do them injustice to interpret their actions as being limited to advancing the national interest. 'Jointly building Europe' should be seen as more than rhetorical lip-service; it was an important part of their underlying motivation.

Turning to the neofunctionalist mechanism for integration – spillover – one could differentiate between functional, political, cultivated and geographical spillover. The cultivated spillover in a sense is socialisation.[4] For the purpose of the SGP the two most important forms of spillover discussed in this chapter are functional and political. The former was prevalent, it can be argued, when the original Stability Pact proposal was revamped within the context of the legal setting of Maastricht, but also in the fact that there was a widely held belief about sound economic reasons that would require EMU to entail strict rules on budgetary deficits. Furthermore, the review of the SGP in 2005 constitutes an important case of functional spillover to the next version of the Pact, as will be discussed in more detail in Chapter 7.

The principle of political spillover was present implicitly. As further integrative phases advance in the area of budgetary policies one should be willing to transfer some sovereignty to a new supranational institution (or, as we shall see, subscribe to rules at the European level). They are complemented by the exchanges among financial experts representing the Member States and discussing policies in a supranational setting. The rules created in the Maastricht Treaty influence the direction and the pace of policy-making in the area of economic and monetary integration. For the success of EMU, it was deemed necessary to have rules on budgets not only to enter Stage III (i.e. the convergence criteria), but also specific rules especially adapted to the functioning of EMU once Member States had entered Stage III. Thus the connection made between EMU and rules on budgets followed a functional logic.

The case of the SGP from the neofunctionalist perspective

From a neofunctionalist perspective, the two prominent supranational actors are the Monetary Committee and the Commission.[5] The MC consisted of representatives of the Member States (Ministries of Finance

---

[4] The concept of socialisation will be discussed in the context of the role of experts; see Chapter 5.

[5] As said before, the ECOFIN Council can also be seen as a supranational body in which more happens than mere intergovernmental bargaining. However, we will restrict our discussion to mainly the MC and the Commission as the core neofunctionalist supranational actors.

and central banks) and two members of the Commission. The details of the SGP were settled in the MC. This committee has a strong collegial feel to it; its members respect each other a great deal. The negotiations that took place in the MC had the character of being discussions amongst peers. Those present were working towards a common goal, namely to derive appropriate rules for the surveillance of fiscal policies in EMU.

The actors participating in the process generally felt that the MC negotiators worked both as representatives dependent on what the national government wanted, yet at the same time they were able to influence their respective government through argumentation and negotiation. The MC, after all, was a body of the EC that was to prepare two Council regulations on macroeconomic policy coordination and the containment of budgetary deficits. As such, it was ready to accept that there are rules in the Treaty that would have to be considered as the authoritative framework within which to operate. They were, so to say, both in the mindset of European integration as well as bargaining over a final agreement based on specific national needs.

The MC Secretariat was located in the European Commission (Directorate General Economic and Financial Affairs, DG Ecfin), which allowed for tight linkages between the MC and the Commission services. The Commission official acting as Secretary to the MC traditionally combined superb access to information and actors with diplomatic skills to sound out compromises that would flow into the drafting of texts. The MC Secretariat would usually produce the main documents under discussion, in particular the drafts of the legislative texts for the SGP regulations. In addition to the Secretariat, a Commission representative also acted as formal MC member. The linkage between the MC and the Commission via the Secretariat and the Commission representative ensured, among other things, that legislative proposals of the Commission were cleared with the MC before they reached higher levels. This reduced the degree of friction between the two bodies to a minimum.

Once it had been politically agreed to base the SGP on the Treaty in the form of secondary legislation, the role of the Commission was considerable. For the phase of its inception, when Germany demanded specific arrangements, the Commission sometimes toned down the actual drafts by convincing the German side that the SGP would have to stay consistent with the Treaty or with other secondary legislation. The Commission also voiced the concern of Member States when Germany favoured solutions that would not be acceptable to everyone. For example, the Commission developed the 'close to balance or in surplus' notion for the medium-term budgetary objective because it aimed at a solution that would strive for a small deficit yet still give Member States more flexibility, whereas the Germans had asked for a strict and numerical 1 per cent deficit rule (Artis and Buti 2000).

The 'close to balance or in surplus' notion (the so-called 'CTBOIS') had already appeared in Commission proposals in October 1996 in early drafts for the two Council regulations, one concerning the EDP (applicable to EMU countries), the other regarding the strengthening of surveillance and coordination of budgetary positions, which would apply to all Member States.[6] It was in particular the representatives of the Nordic states who supported an ambitious target in the text. The Scandinavian countries, who were engaged domestically in highly ambitious fiscal reforms after the crises of the early 1990s (Hauptmeier *et al.* 2006), were concerned that a 1 per cent target might encourage deficits at a time when some countries should be aiming for balanced budgets or even surpluses. At the same time, certain other countries that were already running deficits of 3 per cent or more and had no intention of doing otherwise, were concerned that a mechanical 1 per cent rule would be too strict for them, especially at times of low economic growth. The Commission proposal combined both concerns: the target was more ambitious than 1 per cent (which more than satisfied the German interest), allowed some countries to target balanced budgets or even surpluses, and at the same time gave more flexibility over the cycle, given that it was not numerical. Before being introduced to the SGP negotiations by the Commission, the concept of CTBOIS had already been used in early versions of the Broad Economic Policy Guidelines (BEPGs) for purposes of multilateral surveillance (Costello 2001).

Overall, these examples show that the Commission was highly influential in providing the expertise, offering background reports and calculations (see, for example, its reports: CEC 1996a, 1996b, 1996c)[7] and, above all, acting as an impartial arbiter whenever Member States' interests were pitched against each other. When the Commission released its formal legislative proposal for the SGP regulations on 16 October 1996,[8] it was using its right of initiative to push the discussions in a certain direction. Whenever the EU enacts legislation, the influence of a Commission proposal is that it sets the path for the direction in which the eventual end product develops. The timing, among other things, can be

---

[6] Reproduced in *Agence Europe*: Europe Documents 2010, 6 November 1996 and in O.J. 369 1996, see also O.J. 368 1996.
[7] 'Towards a Stability Pact' (II/11/96-EN dated 10 January 1996); 'A Stability Pact to Ensure Budgetary Discipline in EMU' (II/163/96-EN dated 18 March 1996); 'Ensuring Budgetary Discipline in Stage Three of EMU' (II/409/96-EN dated 19 July 1996).
[8] COM(96)496 1996.

crucial for its success. In the case of the SGP, the Commission put forward its proposal for two Council Regulations before Member States had achieved a comprehensive consensus, when it judged, following the September 1996 ECOFIN Council, that sufficient common ground and momentum had been found (Costello 2001).

By tactically using its right of initiative, the Commission shaped the legislative deliberations of the MC and, thereby, subsequently also that of the ECOFIN Council. Having achieved a political compromise, the Commission again would hold the pen for putting into text form the agreements that had been made. Hence, it once more was able to shape the form and content of the negotiations. For example, the (authoritative) Commission's version of the compromise achieved at Dublin later in December 1996 differed quite significantly from what the German delegation had thought was obtained. However, once the Commission text was on the table, the Germans faced an uphill struggle, for instance to remove the above-mentioned 'as a rule' clauses.

As referred to earlier in the chapter, the role of the MC and the Commission followed the neofunctionalist logic of spillover. These supranational bodies moved the SGP proposal within the Treaty and the path set out before the SGP translated into the negotiation agenda. Staying within the Treaty stood in stark contrast to the original intentions of the most powerful Member State, which had sought to create an international Treaty outside the EC framework. Supranational actors hence are an important part of the explanation and provide added value. Asked to compare the relative importance of all actors involved in the creation of the SGP, our interlocutors on balance even judged the Commission as having had comparatively more influence than the French government. The MC also seems to have on many occasions worked more like an 'old boys club' rather than a 'battlefield', which supports the neofunctionalist thesis that supranational actors and epistemic communities propel integration beyond the mere intergovernmental bargaining that they are superficially engaged in.

Economic spillovers of EMU

Installing a centralised monetary policy for different countries is bound to have strong spillover effects into neighbouring fields of economic policy. Economic spillover effects have been discussed in controversial ways from the viewpoint of the economics discipline (summarised in Heipertz 2003; Heipertz and Verdun 2003). Regardless of what is emerging as the mainstream verdict of professionals and academics now, important for our understanding of the functional logic behind the SGP is a grasp on the thinking in economics, at the time, of how monetary union should be embedded within the overall economic policy framework, primarily to deal with spillover effects.

The three major elements necessary to make EMU viable were seen by officials as well as academic economists to be: (i) precautions against negative externalities; (ii) safeguards for the independence of the ECB; and (iii) institutional provisions for economic policy coordination. There was a widely shared consensus that the Maastricht Treaty was insufficient in all of these respects. In fact, the relevant Treaty Articles themselves contain several references to the need for further legislation, including the legislative procedure by which such specifications would have to be enacted. Some of these clauses even stated that follow-up legislation had to be adopted before 1994.[9] No such legislation had been adopted by 1995, which was in part due to the fact that the Maastricht Treaty only entered into force on 1 November 1993 – as opposed to at the end of 1992, which had been the target date. In this sense, Waigel's initiative met an existing legal requirement to produce additional legislation. To our minds, this need to extend the Maastricht Treaty into secondary legislation along functional lines is an evidence of spillover as proposed by the neofunctionalist approach. We will now address the economic features of that functional logic behind the SGP.

Externalities

From the neofunctionalist point of view, the strongest economic motivation behind the SGP was to address the concern of externality problems related specifically to EMU.[10] Via numerous transmission channels, fiscal policy measures adopted by one country affect the economy of another, and thereby also its public budget. In other words, the budgetary policies of countries participating in monetary union are interdependent. The assumption at the time was that this

---

[9] 'Further provisions relating to the implementation of the procedure described in this Article are set out in the Protocol on the excessive deficit procedure annexed to this Treaty. The Council shall, acting unanimously on a proposal from the Commission and after consulting the European Parliament and the ECB, adopt the appropriate provisions which shall then replace the said Protocol. Subject to the other provisions of this paragraph, the Council shall, before 1 January 1994, acting by a qualified majority on a proposal from the Commission and after consulting the European Parliament, lay down detailed rules and definitions for the application of the provisions of the said Protocol' (Article 104.14).

[10] Negative externalities are welfare or opportunity costs not fully accounted for in the price and market system, usually occurring to a third party not being part of a transaction.

interdependence would grow with integration, and dramatically so with monetary union. In the mid-1990s, strict rules on budgetary deficits were deemed necessary predominantly because of the likely occurrence of negative 'fiscal spillovers' between participating countries, i.e. negative effects of policy errors committed by one country but impinging upon all others. For precisely this reason, the Treaty, in Article 104.2, stipulates that '[the] Commission shall monitor the development of the budgetary situation and of the stock of government debt in the Member States with a view to identifying gross errors'. The notion of 'gross errors' is subsequently associated with the 'Maastricht reference values' of 3 per cent of GDP for general government deficits and 60 per cent of GDP for public debt.

It is noteworthy that the need for limits on debt and budget deficits had already been established years before the conclusion of the Maastricht Treaty in the original EMU blueprint laid out in the 'Delors Report' (Committee for the Study of Economic and Monetary Union 1989). Further justification for limits on budgetary deficits was spelt out by the Commission during the time of the Maastricht negotiations (Commission of the European Communities 1990, 1991).

The most prominent example for the commonly held concerns about 'gross errors' with negative fiscal spillovers assumed the following scenario. A bond-financed increase in government spending would cause the money supply in the euro area to rise, thereby fuelling inflationary pressures. In response, the future ECB would need to increase interest rates, depressing investment and consumption. The higher interest rate would cause the single currency to appreciate and the trade balance to deteriorate. This scenario is in fact based on the concrete policy experience of the early 1990s, when German reunification led to a major fiscal expansion (at a magnitude of around 5 per cent of GDP per year), stimulating exports and thereby aggregate demand in countries closely connected to the German economy – but at the expense of higher inflation and ultimately higher interest rates, stifling growth and reducing employment by the mid-1990s.

During the time of the SGP's inception, such concerns about negative fiscal spillovers from misguided policies were very prominent. However, after the beginning of Stage III of EMU, economists debated whether such worries in fact may not have been exaggerated, given that different types of spillover to a large extent neutralise each other. In the above-mentioned scenario, for example, the financial spillover runs counter the trade spillover, and, it was argued, the net size of fiscal spillovers within the euro area would be rather small under normal conditions (Gros and Hobza 2001).[11] Such insights are model-dependent, and hence the debate has not been completely resolved – but is by now largely absent from the mainstream discussions about economic policy in EMU. Interestingly, it was in the political rather than in the economic debate that the issue resurfaced during the 2003 crisis of the SGP (see Chapter 7). Dutch Finance Minister Gerrit Zalm in December 2003 argued that excessive budgetary deficits in Germany and France would lead to rising inflation in the euro area and penalise the other countries.[12]

Besides fiscal spillovers, another EMU-induced externality effect was seen by economists in the consequences of abandoning national exchange rates by joining monetary union. Before EMU, fiscal profligacy and, eventually, unsustainable debt levels sooner or later would induce the currency of the country in question to depreciate. Close market scrutiny had been taking place in particular in the case of fiscally weaker countries participating in the ERM II of the EMS. As with any depreciation, such indirect effects of lax fiscal policies would contribute to higher rates of domestic inflation and interest. In this manner, financial markets were seen to exert a certain amount of discipline on policy-makers.

After the introduction of the euro, however, this disciplinary effect of financial markets can no longer, in the same way, discriminate between particular governments. Fiscal looseness still translates into higher spreads on government bonds, thereby increasing the cost of debt financing for the government in question. However, until the onset of the financial crisis in 2008 (see Chapter 9), bond spreads were on average smaller than before and no longer contained large risk premia for high levels of debt. To the extent that bond spreads converged to the level of Bunds without improvement in the underlying fundamentals, the disciplining incentive on the initial culprit is reduced commensurately while the negative implications of fiscal profligacy accrue to all countries alike. EMU in this scenario hence aggravates an already existing 'deficit bias', which is imputed to fiscal policy in the public choice literature (Beetsma 1999). Under these conditions, monetary stability and the associated low

---

[11] A model by Gros and Hobza (2001) shows that trade and financial spillovers are rather negligible and neutralise each other to a large extent. This result holds regardless of whether the fiscal expansion takes place in Germany or in different combinations of countries. Negative financial effects are even better mitigated if the ECB follows an inflation target. Furthermore, the relative price level and thereby the domestic inflation rate adjusts as before, further dampening the spillover effect. This would imply that fiscal spillovers may not be a major problem.

[12] *Het Financieele Dagblad*, 5 December 2003.

rates of interest become so-called 'club goods', i.e. commodities within EMU the consumption of which by one country does not depend on the degree to which that country has contributed to the existence of the club good in the first place. Membership of EMU therefore was seen to entail the incentive to free-ride on the provision of stability by other countries. In the mid-1990s, it was feared that Member States would underprovide consolidation and overspend on their budgets.

Similarly to fiscal spillovers, concerns about an EMU-aggravated deficit bias became less prominent in the economic policy debate once Stage III was operational. Most commentators argue that the deficit bias is partially reversed through an increase in the relative price level of the expansionary country. The resulting export loss is seen to reinternalise part of the disciplining incentive. Ex-post, these effects are hard to disentangle.

Nevertheless, it is important for understanding the origins of the SGP to account for the prominence that was assigned to negative externalities associated with EMU prior to entering Stage III. As in any social group where members are unsure about each other's benevolent behaviour, norms are introduced and peer pressure is built up to minimise defections. Also in less formalised settings, group members are threatened with sanctions should they defect nevertheless. Given the 1995 interpretation of certain perverse incentive effects of EMU, the functionalist lens can help to understand the SGP as a norm-setting solution to reinternalise the economic externalities associated with monetary union.

Safeguarding central bank independence

Another major concern that triggered the creation of the SGP was that excessive deficits could undermine the political independence of the ECB, one of the core principles of the stability paradigm. The ECB statutes in the Maastricht Treaty legally guarantee independence of the central bank from political influence. However, a number of commentators and actors at the time were concerned that the Treaty provisions on ECB independence and specifically the 'no-bailout clause' (according to Article 101 TEC, the ECB is not allowed to provide funds for a national government or to buy its bonds), were not credible. The fear was that unsustainable fiscal paths of certain Member States would nevertheless lead to political pressure on the bank – if not to provide funds then at least to ensure low interest rates for public borrowing.

A number of contributions from economic theory supported this fear. A seminal model of debt monetisation, by Sargent and Wallace (1981), argues that an unsustainable fiscal path eventually forces the central bank to buy government bonds. The Fiscal Theory of the Price Level (FTPL, originated by Woodford 1994 and Leeper 1991) makes a similar case. Grossly simplified, the FTPL states that inflation control by the central bank through the interest rate is jeopardised by an excessive fiscal stance that disturbs household expectations and unsettles private sector budget constraints. Public demand substitutes private demand and artificially expands aggregate demand, eventually causing the price level to rise. Hence, monetary independence and the effectiveness and credibility of monetary policy need to be supported through the fiscal regime.

The economic argument that to safeguard central bank independence a fiscal framework was needed (Artis and Winkler 1999) prominently entered the thinking of policy-makers, especially at the Bundesbank, and needs to be seen at the core of the functionalist logic that propelled the SGP. In fact, the almost complete reduction of risk premia on government bonds of high-debt countries in the run-up to Stage III shows that financial markets indeed insufficiently discriminate between high- and low-debt countries, at least until the re-emergence of significant risk premia in 2008. It would be exaggerated to interpret this market view as the anticipation of a bailout. But, long before such an extreme situation the independence and the effectiveness of monetary policy and its very credibility for its function to anchor expectations of price stability require a sound fiscal regime.

Unlike the fading notion of externalities, the functionalist thinking on the need to safeguard central bank independence is still very much at the core of the SGP at the time of writing and explains much of the vigour with which central banks in the EU and the ECB in particular defend the Pact against political attacks. An effective SGP conducive to sound fiscal policies is seen as absolutely essential for the good functioning of monetary union. At the time of writing, with the public debt and budgetary deficit situation deteriorating in many Member States, due to the global financial and economic meltdown, the SGP is seen by many as the decisive institutional requirement. Those who view the SGP as a useful tool anticipate that the SGP may ensure that Member States will not depart too far from a sound adjustment path. Their hope is that the SGP will offer a framework that will assist Member State governments to return to sustainable public finances.

Economic policy coordination

The euro area is not what in economic theory is called an 'optimum currency area' (OCA) (de Grauwe 2007: 88; Kenen 1969; McKinnon 1963; Mundell 1961). According to OCA theory, a single currency is optimal in territories that show the following economic characteristics: wage and price flexibility, factor mobility, openness, regional trade integration, industrial and portfolio diversification, financial integration and fiscal integration (Crowley 2002; McKinnon 1963).

This strand of thought is another important part of the functionalist logic behind the SGP. While externalities and central bank independence do much to explain the 'dissuasive arm' of the Pact (i.e. the EDP), the following considerations should be seen behind the 'surveillance arm', hence those parts of the SGP edifice that define the framework for economic policy coordination and budgetary surveillance. Interestingly, the thinking on dissuasion was most prominent in the Bundesbank, whereas the Commission had from the beginning been keen to address the issues related to policy coordination. These priorities can easily be related to the respective institutional interests of both bodies – the Bundesbank caring most about central bank independence and the Commission being interested in acquiring a prominent role in the running of EMU. These linkages are not detached from what would be seen as 'policy entrepreneurship' from the neofunctionalist angle.

Based on the lack of OCA qualities of the future currency zone, supporters of the 'coronation' view of EMU in the early 1990s had argued that monetary union should be the final, 'crowning' step of economic convergence in the EU (cf. Dyson 1994). The introduction of a common currency would only be justified when the structural heterogeneity of Member States in the Internal Market had sufficiently diminished. (A number of the opponents of EMU hoped that this process would take an indefinite amount of time.)

The contrary argument of the 'monetarist' view was that real convergence would follow monetary integration. EMU would act as a 'locomotive' for integration in other fields of (economic) policy, above all the completion of the Internal Market. Hence, *ex-post* convergence would be achieved precisely due to the functional effects of integrating monetary policy.

Indeed, throughout the 1990s, the Maastricht convergence process showed remarkable results in terms of countries approaching common patterns of cyclical performance, notably in price levels, interest rates and budget deficits – as required by the Treaty for entering Stage III of EMU. The underlying assumption of the current EMU regime was that this process would continue beyond 1999. Some even thought that it could endogenously lead to an OCA (Padoan 1999). However, the convergence record is not due to the fact that the functional need for further integration had been met with institutional answers. It was the result of independent and unilateral measures of individual states trying to meet the convergence criteria. Once the incentive to enter EMU, and thereby the sanction of being excluded, had become defunct because EMU had started (with a large group of members), the externally induced process slowed down. Maastricht convergence seemed to have been replaced by 'Maastricht fatigue' (Fatas and Mihov 2003).

While it would be premature to conclude on a pessimistic view of structural convergence, one has to acknowledge that the forces now at work are much more subtle than the 'top-down' process of Maastricht convergence. Patterns of trade diversification and factor mobility are slow to change, especially in light of the pervasive lack of structural reform in most EU Member States. Given the persistence of structural heterogeneity *vis-à-vis* a common monetary policy, the role for economic policy coordination remains significant and continues to buttress the functional rationale behind the SGP framework and, in a wider sense, also the Lisbon Strategy. Coordinating national economic policies *vis-à-vis* the ECB's monetary stance is hence pertinent for the success of EMU (Begg 2002). Governance of economic and monetary policy-making takes on different forms and shapes. Not all of it is purely hierarchical ('top-down') as other forms of governance also play an important role in this process (Verdun 2009).

The issue as such was perceived at the time when the SGP was proposed and was an important part of particularly the Commission's motivation behind advancing the SGP dossier. However, actors at the time, especially on the German side, saw these considerations as secondary to the concerns they had about externalities and, above all, ECB independence. Nevertheless, the Treaty already contained an economic coordination framework centred on the process of Broad Economic Policy Guidelines (BEPG).[13] According to Article 99, Member States 'regard their economic policies as a matter of common concern'. The BEPG procedure is

---

[13] The Commission recommends guidelines on the orientations and priorities of economic policy for each country. Its draft is put before ECOFIN, which decides by qualified majority. The ECOFIN draft is then put before the European Council of the Heads of State and Government. Based on the European Council conclusions, ECOFIN decides on individual country recommendations, again by qualified majority. Since the recommendations are not backed by sanctions and not legally enforceable, the BEPG procedure is considered as 'soft' coordination. It works on the assumption that the identification of 'best practices' through comparing and ranking groups of countries leads to 'naming and shaming', respectively 'peer pressure' that would then induce the necessary policies at the national level. The jury is open as to whether the BEPG method is insufficient to deal with the challenge of divergence. Its inherent weakness might be that benchmarking processes are effective in the private sector but cannot be transferred into the political sphere. Private companies are steered by hierarchical direction that can swiftly react to opportunities identified as best practices, whereas political decisions are the outcome of majority voting or, in the case of federal systems like the EU, negotiations subjected to multiple veto players.

the cornerstone of a set of so-called 'soft law' policy coordination schemes that, in essence, are not substantially more than annual reporting and discussion cycles, which at the 1999 Lisbon Council were grouped under the heading of 'Open Method of Coordination' (OMC) in the EU's Lisbon Strategy on structural reform.[14]

As originally proposed by Waigel, the SGP was not primarily intended as an instrument for policy coordination. However, the Commission successfully moulded the Pact into a rudimentary device for that purpose, at least transcending the limited scope of the BEPG process while retaining compatibility with it. The crucial advantage of the SGP over the BEPG and other 'soft' processes was to be seen via its 'hard' nature of being backed by sanctions. Although this characterisation does not directly apply to the surveillance arm, the Pact as a whole was associated with this 'harder' notion, at least back then.

As a result, the SGP regulation 1466/97 on the strengthening of the surveillance of budgetary positions and the surveillance and coordination of economic policies commits the euro-area countries to aim for budgetary balance 'over the cycle'. The reporting process of 'stability programmes' belongs to 'soft' coordination, but the Council can exert additional pressure on deviant governments by adopting so-called 'early warnings' on a recommendation by the Commission. These early warnings can be issued when a country risks missing its fiscal targets significantly. However, short of any means to demand specific fiscal policy measures or to enforce budgetary targets, the coordination function of the SGP remains extremely limited and depends on the goodwill of the participating countries.

The 'dissuasive' or 'corrective' arm of the SGP consists of the 'hard' EDP which functions asymmetrically in the sense that it defines a formal procedure for dealing with deficits in excess of 3 per cent of GDP. However, the EDP's focus on maintaining deficits below the limit does not on its own ensure a high quality of fiscal policy. For example, it would still allow countries to adopt a procyclical fiscal stance such as succumbing to the temptation of enacting tax cuts or spending increases in times of buoyant revenues, provided that the deficit stays below the limit. The function of coordinating fiscal policy in a qualitative and more comprehensive manner is vested in the 'surveillance' or 'preventive' arm, which has undergone considerable development as actors gained additional experience and methodological finesse (see Chapter 6).

---

[14] On the Open Method of Coordination and EMU see Hodson and Maher (2001) and Schelkle (2004b). On the OMC and employment policy see Schäfer (2002).

The procedural separation between these two dimensions of preventing fiscal policy mistakes is not fully in line with the functional economic logic. After all, the occurrence of excessive deficits during economic downswings is linked to procyclical laxity during an upswing, where tax cuts or expenditure increases prevent the build-up of 'reserves' or, in SGP terminology, 'safety margins' to the 3 per cent limit. A course of countercyclical restrictions during an upturn also contributes to stabilising the cycle and, at least in theory, prolonging the growth period. In a sense, imposing fiscal rigour through the EDP once large deficits occur virtually comes too late and should only be a measure of last resort. In practice, countries will always argue that the imposition of fiscal restriction during periods of weak or even negative growth would be counterproductive and possibly even procyclical in itself.

This problem highlights the fact that the requirements of functional spillover do not always guide the process of integration towards institutional solutions that are perfectly suited to the occasion. Rather, all kinds of legal and political restrictions are imposed on the range of possible options; the functionalist strand is only one force among many that exerts its influence on the outcome. All in all, the SGP is open to widely different interpretations as to the degree to which it fulfils the functional needs of EMU. The SGP stands for a rudimentary form of policy coordination, asking the decentralised fiscal authorities to 'keep their house in order' (Issing 2002) rather than strategising fiscal policy in a top-down manner from the European level. As a piece of secondary legislation, the SGP can in fact not be expected to transgress the Treaty itself and its limitations in terms of institutional development towards 'political integration'. From the viewpoint of neofunctionalism, the rules on the SGP were primarily created to counter free-rider incentives related to negative externality effects of monetary union, not to advance into the direction of closer integration.

Legal spillover

As soon as Germany had dropped its initial request to conclude the SGP in the form of an international treaty and accepted having it based on the Maastricht Treaty instead, a whole series of legal consequences ensued that can best be grasped by the concept of functional spillover in the legal domain.[15]

---

[15] On the role of law in neofunctionalism, see also de Búrca (2005).

Title VII of the TEC contains the Articles that form the legal basis of EMU. It defines economic and monetary policy as one of the policies of the Community. Besides employment, trade, social policy, etc., the Treaty stipulations on EMU in general are partial and ambivalent, which is due to the fact that the text was a political compromise. Exceptional in its coherence are the statutes of the ECB (see Chapter 5). However, the ECB statutes and the Treaty provisions on monetary policy are only one side of the coin. Other fields of economic policy, especially fiscal policy, were underdeveloped, partially because the negotiating parties were unable to agree on the form of a political union in addition to economic and monetary union.

The Maastricht Treaty is hence from the very outset an incomplete contract as far as rules on EMU are concerned (see also Schure and Verdun 2008). In the area of fiscal policy, the Treaty and its Protocols are limited to rather loose stipulations on the EDP and budgetary surveillance; most concepts being derived from the budgetary reference values laid down in the convergence criteria. Despite these obvious shortcomings, both the Commission and France insisted that the SGP would have to be based entirely on the Maastricht Treaty. From the French perspective, it was paramount not to touch or to supplement international law that committed Germany to EMU. From the Commission perspective, it was equally important to prevent the emergence of a parallel framework under an intergovernmental 'Stability Council', in which it would play no role (see also Chapter 3).

Retaining the Treaty as the legal basis of the SGP implied designing the entire framework as a piece of secondary Community law. By definition, secondary legislation has to be consistent with primary law. Legal spillover spells out the details of what it meant that the SGP followed from the Treaty. This relationship should in fact be seen as one of 'path dependence' (Pierson 1996). The concept of path dependence explains the political reasons why suboptimal institutional solutions persist over time. Apart from 'critical junctions', the development of institutions is contingent on historical features and occurs in a very piecemeal or incremental fashion. Applied to the SGP, path dependences capture the notion that, given the limitations provided by the Treaty, the functional consequences of EMU in the economic domain cannot be ideally solved. For example, the Council regulation operationalising the EDP by definition cannot qualitatively change the nature of the procedure to also deal with procyclical policy mistakes during economic upswings, as discussed above. By flowing from the principles defined by Article 104 and the EDP Protocol, the SGP in this area is limited to a much more narrow and, possibly, not ideal function. Similarly, without changing the Treaty, regulation 1467/97 could simply not deliver the political, 'quasi-automatic' EDP decision-making process desired by Waigel.

However, legal spillover is not only a restricting factor in the sense of path dependency. The SGP has indeed delivered some 'added value' to the TEC and went some way towards fulfilling what was perceived as the requirements of economic functionalism and legal clarity. For example, it has shortened the timeline of the decision sequence, defined the distribution of possible fines among the 'virtuous' Member States, clarified the notion of 'exceptional' and 'temporary' deficits as exemptions from sanctions, introduced an urgency procedure and defined the conditions under which the EDP can be held in abeyance. It has also increased transparency: the Council has committed itself to always making its recommendations public as well as the voting of Member States.

In sum, the two functional dynamics coming to bear on the initiation and negotiation of the SGP, one economic and the other legal, work in part in seemingly opposite directions. In all respects that the SGP addresses economic functional features, it is bound to stay within the limits of the legal functional logic of the Treaty. In its legal weakness (especially compared to the original German demands), the SGP is clearly path dependent on Articles 99 (ex 103) and 104 (ex 104c).

At the time that the SGP was proposed there was broad consensus on the economic rationale behind strict rules on fiscal policy in EMU. The first reason was the perceived need for consolidating public finances across Europe. This requirement applies generally and is not directly related to EMU. The other three arguments stem from the peculiarities of installing a centralised monetary policy whilst having a decentralised set of national fiscal policies. They concern negative externalities in the form of fiscal spillovers, the need to protect the independence of the ECB, and the requirement to provide minimum provisions for the coordination of fiscal policies.

At the core of the neofunctionalist approach to integration lies the concept of 'political spillover'. As integration takes hold in a specific policy field, the functional requirements of this field interacting with others (for example, trade and external relations) exert a certain pressure towards integration in the neighbouring field. Applied to EMU, the argument would be that, by integrating monetary policy, functional pressures emerge that militate for integration of fiscal or economic policy more widely. Waigel's original proposal for a 'Stability Council' to implement the SGP would be the case in point. Following this line of reasoning, one could argue that the fact that, to date, EMU has not led to a transfer of fiscal policy to the supranational level could be seen as lack of evidence of the principle of political spillover.

However, the implicit assumption of a functional requirement for integrating fiscal policy is not convincing. Given the above-mentioned heterogeneity of the currency zone, it could actually make perfect sense to leave responsibility over fiscal policy at the national and subnational levels of government at this point in time. Furthermore, no European body today would have the democratic legitimacy to tinker with the very core of what parliamentary democracies are concerned with, i.e. the levying of taxes and the spending of public budgets. In both respects, the EU's 'subsidiarity principle' may militate against fiscal centralisation at the European level.

Yet, some elements of political spillover are reflected even in the current set-up of EMU. While leaving fiscal policy entirely in the hands of national authorities, their actions have become subject to common *rules*. It is rules rather than an institutional body that cater to the pressures triggered by functional spillover. In this way, EMU in general, and the SGP in particular, is an experiment of governing by rules rather than through institutional bodies. This is why we have chosen *Ruling Europe* as the book title. Nevertheless, rules-based governance also requires institutionalised fora rather than only networks and decentralised action. The rudimentary attempts of further institutionalising common approaches to economic policy-making through the Eurogroup (the informal meeting of euro-area Ministers of Economy and Finance, see, for example, Puetter 2006) shows some signs of political spillover in that respect.

The neofunctionalist approach would not predict spillovers to translate quickly into foreseeable forms of integration. It explains, however, some underlying, logical principles that shape the course of direction whenever change occurs and pre-existing institutional structures come into stress or even crisis. An institutional crisis in fact results from the combination of suboptimal institutional structures in the face of severe policy problems.

Given that the effects of the several forms of spillover (we have focused on functional and legal ones) can be contingent on each other, radical change and fully developed solutions cannot be expected. Therefore, it is far too early to look for substantial occurrences of political spillover in the fiscal domain. However, over time, conditions could become more permissive and some more developed layer of supranational fiscal governance may take hold on top of the existing national and subnational layers. The SGP does not represent a large step in that direction. However, it shows clear signs of following the functional logic implied by economic and legal spillovers. Moreover, one could argue that the SGP is not disconnected from some sort of 'cultural spillover': after all, it is primarily thanks to the SGP that, across the euro area, citizens are nowadays more aware of the need to conduct prudent and sustainable fiscal policies in the interest of growth and stability.

Lessons from neofunctionalism

Applying the neofunctionalist approach enables us to appreciate the importance of the Commission and of the MC in the creation of the SGP. The detailed rules as well as larger decisions about the contents of the framework were prepared by the MC, in which the Commission played an important role. The neofunctionalist approach also helps us understand the direction of policy-making through the notion of the functional logic or – as the First Commission President Walter Hallstein has called it – *Sachlogik* (Hallstein 1979).

We identified two dimensions of functionalist spillover: an economic and a legal dimension. The economic dimension explains the policy problem perceived by the MC as well as possible solution concepts. The legal dimension encompassed the Maastricht Treaty and the secondary legislation that limited the legal options open to the MC.

Hence, the neofunctionalist approach helps us explain important elements in Waigel's initial proposal and especially why and how the Commission advanced the framework for multilateral surveillance and further specifications on the Broad Economic Policy Guidelines. It also explains why Member States that had accepted the rules on budgetary deficits and convergence criteria with reference values already in the Delors Committee and the Maastricht Treaty then logically continued on that strand, developing a 'regime' that would naturally flow from the existing structures.

However, the neofunctionalist approach does not explain why Germany had an exceptionally strong bargaining position in the creation of the SGP nor would it clarify the position of any of the other national governments (those of France or the Netherlands, for example). A neofunctionalist explanation also does not deal well with the struggles within the European Council when it interfered in the legislation process. A neofunctionalist approach is also unable to appreciate the importance of domestic factors that gave rise to the behaviour of Member State governments. For example, in order to understand the urgency of Waigel's proposal one needs to look at the importance of domestic German actors, as we did in Chapter 3.

Another question that is left unanswered is why the neofunctionalist logic did not transform fiscal policy further. Why, for example, does the process so far fail to create a supranational body that can deal with a European budgetary policy? One might argue that the legal dimension of the functionalist logic trumps the economic dimension. That is, the authors of the Maastricht Treaty could not agree on the need for such a body and subsequently it is not in that Treaty. Given that the Treaty is taken as the basis, there is no 'push' for it. Also in other fields of economic policy, for example employment, we find only the very first steps towards integration. At this point, an intergovernmentalist or domestic politics approach or even a more careful look into the paradigm held by the experts involved in the dossier might give us more insights into this matter.

In fact, the role of experts needs to be considered in detail. Neofunctionalism talks about 'socialisation' and thus it is argued that experts may be contributing positively to European integration. However, we need analytical tools to understand exactly how experts derive proposals and suggestions for collaboration. We need to appreciate how important it is that they hold on to a common paradigm. It is also important to understand the shared cognitive basis from which they draw causal inferences about economic policy-making. Seeing that most of the content of the SGP was discussed in the MC in a group that consisted of high-level *experts* means that we should try to find out more about exactly how that process of decision-making took place.

5 The role of experts and ideas

Introducing an expertocratic approach

European integration theories have been strongly influenced by the emergence of ideas-focused or knowledge-based approaches (Richardson 2001; Risse 2004; Waever 2004). Various scholars stressed the role of experts and the prominence of certain ideas in the formation of policies and integration more generally (Jacobsen 1995; Lequesne and Rivaud 2003; Parsons 2002; Radaelli 1999). The debates sometimes centred on the dichotomy between rationalist and constructivist approaches (Checkel 1998, 2001; Pollack 2001). The former would encompass all IR approaches that assume that states can identify their interests. A constructivist approach would seek to 'scratch the surface' and see what interests consist of and how they are formulated (Christiansen *et al.* 1999). Incorporating the importance of norms, rules and paradigms is at the core of this approach.

In order to enhance our understanding of European integration we propose to organise this multitude of 'approaches' in a systematic manner. We adopt from these approaches the importance of experts, expertise, policy learning, socialisation, expert communities, ideas and paradigms. We label this composite perspective that focuses on individuals at the 'working level' of policy-making an 'expertocratic approach'. 'Expertocracy' literally means the 'rule of experts' and, interestingly, the word 'expert' derives from the Latin term for 'trying out'. Thus this term captures nicely what we want to look at: those who 'rule' backstage are the ones who are testing out various ideas and who can bring their professional experience to a policy problem.

The terms used in our analysis are defined as follows. An expert is a person who has 'expertise' over the subject in question, which usually contains complex and technical matters. We differentiate between 'actor experts', and 'non-actor experts'. The former participate personally in the policy formulation process and typically work as economists or lawyers in those institutions that are responsible for the SGP dossier, i.e. finance ministries, central banks or the Commission. Non-actor experts are part of a more diverse group that includes academics, journalists and officials working in international organisations who follow the developments of the Pact from an informed but detached perspective without direct access to decision-making procedures.

'Expertise' is subject knowledge in a particular policy field at a 'high' level, resulting from an academic background and professional experience. By their very nature, finance ministries and particularly central banks require a specialised, technical understanding of economics and economic policy. The professional experience of experts, as generated in such institutions, accrues over time through analysis but also 'trial and error' in the policy-making domain. This process has been referred to in the literature as 'policy learning'. When experts collaborate with one another in a professional setting, they become socialised. This 'socialisation' process is a constitutive part and has a cognitive dimension that leads to a smaller set of acceptable ideas and behaviour than outside the institution. This socialisation also occurs across different institutions and makes for small and exclusive 'expert communities' that develop a certain *esprit de corps*. Within these communities experts have privileged access to information, which perpetuates existing group structures and partially explains the dependence of political actors on experts.

In general, information on at times highly complex policy issues is processed and simplified through the incorporation of certain 'paradigms' and 'ideas'. 'Paradigms' contain fundamental principles that are upheld over a longer period of time and form the world view of the experts in their domain. The paradigm makes up a certain way of seeing the (economic) world; it is a mentally constructed model of reality. These paradigms are widely shared among actor experts. An example of such a paradigm is the notion of 'stability'. Smaller fluctuations that remain within the paradigm but differ along political preferences or priorities are represented by the concept of 'ideas'. We use the term 'ideas' to describe the variety of ways in which one can 'translate' the paradigm into practice and apply it to a specific policy problem. Note that we envisage that there can be a multitude of ideas on a continuum of possible variations, for example the exact, legal framing for allowing deficits above the reference value in the case of severe economic downturns. Furthermore, important examples of competing ideas in the case of the SGP are whether or not to have automaticity in the application of sanctions.

With the help of our questionnaire, we learned that experts, while they may differ on specific ideas, still share the more general paradigm. Examples include the view that 'rules on budgets are important' and, specifically, that 'rules on budgets are even more important in a monetary union' as well as that 'rules have to be backed by sanctions'. Also, all experts that we encountered rejected the statement that 'political decisions on the budget should not be limited by rules'. However, on specific ideas, there can be disagreement among experts in the sense that they support either one of two conflicting statements: 'budget rules should be explicit (3 per cent) but flexible' versus 'budget rules should be explicit (3 per cent) and strict'. By contrast, none of those who returned the questionnaire thought that 'budget rules should be general and flexible'.

Expert ideas can differ along cultural or national lines. In the case of the SGP, these differences are visible – for example in 1995 as a split along the lines of German experts supporting automatic sanctions and non-German experts strongly resisting that notion. These findings suggest that the importance of budgetary rules is part of the overall stability paradigm that is generally shared, whereas there are different ideas regarding the issue of automaticity and the degree of strictness. From the viewpoint of an expertocratic approach, the SGP negotiations should therefore also be seen as a cognitive process of ideational convergence.

As alluded to above, experts operate within a legitimised community that grants privileged access to information. Given this asymmetric information, and given the background of the professional experience of experts, this situation gives rise to an interdependent relationship between experts and politicians. This relationship could be characterised as a principal-agent relationship in which the principal (the politician) defines the goal for the agent (the expert), but where the agent benefits from his/her informational advantage, and can therefore deviate somewhat from the goal or shape certain features of the outcome without the principal noticing this change. We found out that, in the creation of the Pact as well as during its reform, actors at the political level gave considerable leeway to their experts whom they saw as very capable and reliable for the provision of 'expert content' to the 'political container' that they had set up.

In an expertocratic approach, the ideas carried by experts become crucial for understanding the integration process. The actual 'interests' and therefore the 'policy proposals' that are being negotiated should be seen in the light of how they were constructed at working level. What paradigm and which ideas supported those particular interests? Which experts influenced the formulation of these interests? Experts (actor and non-actor experts) as well as politicians jointly determine the process, building on each others' input. The actor experts provide the politicians with ideas that he/she can use for political purposes. The politician can also ask the actor expert to work on a particular policy proposal that will serve the interests of the politician. There is a constant dialectical process going on between actor experts and politicians. Seeing that the politician does not have the same expertise and information as the actor experts, he/she will in a certain way be dependent on these actor experts. The actor expert can influence the politician and vice versa. This influence is particularly strong in the context of the MC, where experts usually had a wide margin of discretion to reach consensus within certain bounds defined by the politicians and could then, in turn, influence their political masters.

Different mechanisms are at work. One of these, already briefly touched upon in the previous chapter, is the use of so-called 'epistemic communities' for the purpose of international bargaining. Epistemic communities are called upon to find a compromise among states that need to come to an international agreement (Verdun 1999). Four principles define the existence of an epistemic community, following Haas (1992: 3). First, they share beliefs for a value-based rationale of social action. Second, they share causal beliefs, which are derived from their analyses of problems that in turn serve as the basis for understanding the linkages between policy actions and desired outcomes. Third, they have shared notions of validity – that is, intersubjective understandings that help them weigh ideas within their area of competence. Fourth, they have a common policy enterprise and common practices and methodologies associated with a set of problems to which their competence is directed. The literature on epistemic communities suggests that a group of experts is often called upon when national governments are divided on intergovernmental collaboration. The MC is an ideal group to ask for advice as its members can wear double hats. The members of the MC, later renamed the EFC, act as independent experts yet are fully aware of the political issues at stake.

Another mechanism is the exchange of ideas in expert communities. Experts influence each other at a more subtle level than mere power bargaining. They are able to mediate between power political bargaining and the arrangements that one could find if political considerations did not play a role. A dialectic process takes place both horizontally and vertically between governments and experts to determine interests and strategies for policy-making that, by consequence, shape the process of integration. Experts influence politicians; the latter in turn provide guidance to experts on what is politically acceptable. Experts inform each other of their respective political boundaries as well as of their professional thinking and try to mediate between expert options and political feasibility. In doing so, experts draw on their longer historical experience, benefiting from institutional memory and policy learning from similar situations and problems that occurred in the past.

Commission officials are socialised whilst being in office and do not necessarily have fixed preferences; their identities and interests are created, so to say, 'on the job' (Hooghe 2002). Hierarchical institutions enforce concepts and preferences on the individuals who work for them (Scharpf 1997). However, the causality runs both ways: the same experts collectively define the positions and policies of their institutions, even if final decisions are adopted through hierarchical lines. In that sense, an expert's 'experience' is a good proxy for the degree to which he or she is able to influence decisions at his or her hierarchical level in an institution.

An expertocratic approach applied to the SGP

From an expertocratic view the most important actors for our subject are the experts involved in drafting and implementing the SGP, working on a wide range of related issues and preparatory documents for the decision-making of the competent bodies. As stated before, the approach differentiates between actor experts and non-actor experts. The former have direct influence on the policy-making process. The latter can exert indirect influence through their writings (policy papers, academic writing, or publications in the wider media), which contribute to the formation of ideas and paradigms that are shared by the actor experts. Of course actor and non-actor experts communicate frequently with each other and hence share and mutually enrich their expertise. Actor experts defend national proposals, work on their own possible compromises when their original national proposal meets with opposition, and argue with peers to find a possible solution. They do not merely negotiate on behalf of their respective governments but they also have their own capacity to introduce insights and possible solutions.

In the case of the SGP, the actor experts are the officials in the Ministries of Finance (in some cases Ministries of Economy), the officials in the central banks, and Commission officials. More precisely, these experts are located in the respective departments of economics and/or European affairs of these institutions. In the case of the Commission, our concept of experts applies to the staff of the Directorate General Economic and Financial Affairs (DG Ecfin) entrusted with the preparation of decisions related to the design and implementation of the SGP.

The most relevant experts for our analysis are those representatives that met in the context of the MC[1] and their subordinates who were tasked with preparing the MC dossiers. As they were in constant touch with their colleagues from the other Member States, these individuals were at the core of the search for solutions which they could support in line with their

---

[1] Since the start of Stage III of EMU in 1999 renamed the Economic and Financial Committee (EFC).

expertise and, above all, which were acceptable in light of the positions held by their respective institutions.

Non-actor experts are academics, journalists, researchers of corporate banks and officials in important international organisations, such as the IMF, the OECD and so on. In the SGP case, non-actor experts are not directly involved in the policy-making process but are still held in high esteem by the actor experts. It is not rare for experts to switch roles from non-actors to actors and back as international organisations and academic bodies are sometimes staffed from ministries or central banks and vice versa so that, in the course of an 'expert' career, one might work in a similar field from a different perspective.

Several mechanisms are involved. A paradigm supported by experts is subject to long-term trends. Hence, the stability paradigm underlying the SGP changed slightly over time and continues to do so.[2] Dyson and Featherstone have stressed the fact that the German rules-based model was seen as a successful archetype. It was thus left to the appropriate technical experts to negotiate a sound, durable EMU. Any EMU agreement had to be based on *Sachverstand* (expertise; Dyson and Featherstone 1999). Also, ideologies play a role and may influence experts in the sense that different policy options stem from ideological differences that are not imposed but are deeply incorporated into beliefs. Furthermore, in the case of the MC as in similar committees, socialisation occurs through participation (Verdun 2000b). Members get to know each other personally and find informal fora and even social events to exchange their views. A newcomer is admitted to the 'club' if he/she respects the pre-existing frame of mind.

We were given the example of the brief appearance in 1998 and 1999 of German State Secretary Heiner Flaßbeck under Minister Oskar Lafontaine, both adhering to very different views than the ones prominent with the MC. His approach in the MC has been referred to as entirely counterproductive mainly (it was argued) because Flaßbeck failed to show respect and modesty towards the vested knowledge of his colleagues. Had he first been respectful of the committee members, then the MC might have been willing to listen to him, even if his ideas were out of line with those prevailing in the committee.

---

[2] A number of authors have written about how EMU has been dominated by a neoliberal paradigm, *inter alia* Gill (2001) and Wylie (2002). Note, however, that those who are in support of EMU rarely talk about neoliberalism in this way. In other words, neoliberalism tends to be used with a negative connotation and as a vehicle to criticise the paradigm, which is even the case (albeit to a lesser extent) in McNamara (1998) and Marcussen (2000).

Another important mechanism, policy learning, was prevalent in the MC in the form of lessons learnt over the years of exchange rate cooperation in the context of the EMS and the long and winding path of creating EMU. After all, the MC had been involved extensively in the drafting of the Maastricht Treaty and thereby knew precisely the economic and legal considerations that had flowed in the basis of primary law for the SGP.

The SGP dossier involved national and transnational experts as well as specialists outside the institutions. The MC provides again a special case in so far as it consists of national actors (officials from the Ministries of Finance) and domestic representatives (from the central banks). However, MC representatives can also be seen as transnational, European actors. The socialisation process that occurs in the course of the successive meetings leads to a double identity, where national interests feature next to the requirements of making EMU workable as an end in itself.

The importance of experts for the creation of the SGP cannot be overestimated. All substantial input to the deliberations of the higher levels and all legislative drafts were written by experts in the MC, the Commission and the services of the Council. Their professional thinking flowed into the drafts at least to the same extent as the political objectives that they had to incorporate.

We find experts to be central at all stages of the SGP genesis and its subsequent history. For example, the Bundesbank and the BVR in 1995 jointly coordinated and engineered an initiative to launch a public debate on stricter rules in EMU (see Chapter 3). The speeches of this initiative were written by an economist after consultation with the experts of the Bundesbank. The Waigel proposal was the result of strong indirect influence of non-actor experts (see Chapter 3). Finally, the Commission proposals, which represented the base for the legislative deliberations in the MC and at the ECOFIN level, were all written by experts of DG Ecfin, assisted by experts from the Council Secretariat. We will subsequently look at these issues in more detail, beginning with a discussion of the 'paradigm' that is at the ideational base of the Pact.

Experts and their SGP

The stability paradigm

Given its size and complexity, any understanding of 'the economy' is bound to involve a great deal of simplification and short-cutting or, in technical terms, modelling. For instance, with regard to concrete questions about economic policy, one is required to have a certain understanding of how an economy works and how it can be influenced. These simplifications can take the form of a 'world view', 'ideology', 'paradigm', a 'model', 'economic or political mechanisms', 'transmission channels', etc. Rather than being 'rational' – in the sense of possessing perfect information and the capacities to carry out strategic computations on utility maximisation – the economic (and political) agent will adopt these simplifications as long as they serve him or her well (March 1986). For the purpose of managing the economy politically, a whole host of different paradigms have been *en vogue*, varying over time and space.

There is one set of economic paradigms that have diffused gradually but with growing success after the Second World War: the paradigms of 'Keynesianism', 'neoliberalism', 'monetarism' (Johnson 1998) and, in its expressive form for the management of economic policy (Henning 1994), the paradigm of 'stability' (Artis and Winkler 1999) or 'sound money' (Dyson 2000; Dyson and Featherstone 1999; Marcussen 2000; McNamara 1998).

Again, as stated, despite global success in economic theory as well as practice, paradigms remain just specific ways of seeing the world. These paradigms receive support in varying degrees from different groups of actors in various parts of the world. One can identify periods in which one paradigm has more support, followed by periods where it loses support and another receives more. Often the rise and fall in the support of a paradigm can be correlated to its perceived success or failure in producing tangible results. For example, the Keynesian paradigm lost support in the mid-1970s when the phenomenon of 'stagflation' appeared. Increasing inflation did not improve growth. The paradigm of monetarism then seemed to offer a possible alternative and, for example, the Bundesbank as a 'monetarist' institution was seen as being better able to contain inflation and support growth than any Keynesian settings. Governments adjusted to such changing dominance of paradigms and increasingly started to instruct their central banks to keep inflation under control, ultimately by establishing central bank independence.

One aspect of monetarism was to focus on the importance of price stability. With it came an emphasis on the value of predictable low inflation. Due to the success of German monetary policies and their emphasis on the 'stability paradigm', its language and terminology ('price stability', 'consolidation', 'trust', 'sustainability', etc.) became increasingly prominent. These concepts form the actor experts' understanding of economic policy and structure the economic discourse. The stability paradigm took on the form of what Goldstein and Keohane (1993) call a 'causal belief'. As such the stability paradigm reduces uncertainty and enables the decision in favour of a certain institutional model and policy choices under that model.

To clarify what the stability paradigm refers to in practice we identify four core principles: first, the overarching economic parameter to be attained is 'price stability', i.e. low rates of inflation. Second, price stability is a precondition for growth, not its trade-off, the reason being that growth at the expense of price stability only translates into inflation. Third, price stability is ensured by a central bank that sets interest rates independently of the (opportunistic, time-inconsistent) political process. Fourth, and crucial for the SGP, the central bank can only fulfil its mandate if other fields of economic policy do not run counter, e.g. in the form of excessive wage bargains (wage policy) or high levels of public debt (fiscal policy).

Supporters of the paradigm can be classified into three 'layers' of experts. The core is represented by central bankers – a group of actor experts who back its principles in the form of a professional ethos and, not least, by institutional interest. A second layer of actor experts can be found among Ministry of Finance officials who, in many cases, are in frequent contact with central banks. These officials also adhere to the paradigm in principle, but variations exist. The third layer consists of non-actor experts and has provided the origins and theoretic foundations of the paradigm. Scientific economists in academia but also in research departments of central banks and international organisations have gradually developed the theoretical base of the stability paradigm, which has replaced Keynesian views of monetary policy as the mainstream of economic thought (Beetsma 2001; Brunila *et al.* 2001).[3] Their work was also foundational for neighbouring paradigms such as neoliberalism. Interestingly, the stability paradigm is linked to national culture to some extent – giving rise to the question of whether institutions like the Bundesbank shape *Stabilitätskultur* or vice versa.

Strictly speaking, the stability paradigm prescribes only a certain monetary policy and its institutional set-up. However, under the presence of transmission channels between fiscal and monetary policy, the mandate of the central bank cannot be seen in isolation from the behaviour of the budgetary authorities. Hence, the paradigm implicitly includes a doctrine of fiscal discipline so that it facilitates the success of monetary policy in maintaining price stability (see Chapter 4).

Policy learning

Why and in what sense do experts in a Ministry of Finance subscribe to the stability paradigm? Within each national administration, the Ministry of

---

[3] On Keynesianism in economic policy in Western Europe see Hall (1989); on the changeover from Keynesianism to monetarism see *inter alia* Hall (1992).

Finance plays a special role. It collects the funds for the government, mainly through taxes (but also by taking on debt and engaging in privatisation measures) and pays its expenses. These go to servicing the refinancing costs of public debt (now often around a fifth of a national budget) and to the 'spending ministries'. Those in charge of spending ministries have an incentive to maximise their budget in order to fulfil their function and please their constituencies. In aggregate, the public sector shows a 'deficit bias' (Alesina and Drazen 1991; Alt and Lowry 1994; Balassone and Giordano 2001).

Unlike his/her colleagues, the Finance Minister neither has a constituency nor an intrinsic interest in running a deficit, i.e. paying more government expenses than collecting public income. As long as it does not politically endanger his/her hold on the office, he/she will favour any measure that restrains the spending ministries. The EDP and its strengthening through the SGP were therefore perceived by the actor experts within some Ministries of Finance as welcome external constraints that enhance their position in the domestic confrontation with spending ministries.[4]

By the mid-1990s, the thinking in most Ministries of Finance had converged to accept in principle the notion of a general need for consolidation – with and without EMU (Verdun 2000a). The need is seen to stem from the expansionary stance of fiscal policy in most of the OECD countries since the 'golden age' of Keynesianism and welfare-state expansion (Scharpf and Schmidt 2000; Tanzi and Schuknecht 2000). According to this understanding, soaring interest rates, which had been the result of the high inflation rates at the time, had reduced investment and contributed to weak growth and underemployment. Governments had found themselves redirecting an increasing portion of their revenue into debt servicing. Furthermore, ageing populations in Europe implied that maintaining generous welfare states would be increasingly expensive and would require a fundamental reallocation of public spending (Beetsma and Oksanen 2007; Commission of the European Communities 2007; Dudek and Omtzigt 2001; UNDP 1998). An additional factor in this light is that the implicit debt of the public sector (mainly through obligations for future pensions and the future liabilities of pay-as-you-go welfare schemes) was much larger than the nominal debt – for EU Member States often as much as 200 per cent and more of GDP (Kotlikoff and Raffelhüschen 1999).

---

[4] However, these experts would only support the imposition of financial sanctions as long as they were convinced that these would not have to be applied to their country and that would thereby hurt the Finance Ministry directly.

The need to restore the sanity of public finance and to correct the presently unsustainable paths is now generally accepted among most experts. Further considerations also address the requirement to improve the quality of government budgets, principally in the sense of shifting expenditure from consumption towards investment, which has a superior impact on the growth performance of the economy. The same holds for retrenchment measures, which are more lasting and even beneficial to medium-term growth prospects if they cut into consumptive spending instead of reducing public investment (Hauptmeier *et al.* 2006).

The drafting of the SGP by officials in the German Ministry of Finance provides an insightful case into the linkage between non-actor experts and actor experts. In the wider context of the debate on EMU after the start of Stage II, the *Institut für Weltwirtschaft* (IfW) in Kiel, an academic institution staffed by non-actor experts, published a discussion paper on how to make the Maastricht stipulations workable through a complementary contractual agreement (Lehment and Scheide 1995). The IfW proposal suggested automatic, interest-free deposits with the ECB for countries exceeding 3 per cent that should be paid back as soon as the excessive deficit was removed. The paper was prominently discussed in the *Frankfurter Allgemeine Zeitung* (12 October 1995) and was seconded by positive comments of the Bundesbank.[5] The IfW paper was used as a direct input for drafting a proposal in the Ministry.[6] The actor experts were under time pressure, given that Waigel urgently needed 'something' to pre-empt the opposition (see Chapter 3). On the same day that the IfW paper was presented to the public[7], the authors received a call from the Ministry, asking for a copy of the paper to be faxed.[8] One week later, an official called at the IfW and posed detailed questions on the proposal. Actor experts in the Ministry obviously used the work of academic non-actor experts for drafting their policy initiative. Four weeks later (7 and 10 November 1995), Waigel announced 'his' version of a Stability Pact (Bundesministerium der Finanzen 1995) to the public and to his European partners during the second reading of the 1996 budget (Waigel 1995a, 1995b).

In Europe, the stability paradigm was most firmly rooted in Germany in the form of *Stabilitätskultur*. German *Stabilitätskultur* was the lesson of a hyperinflation in 1922–3 and a currency reform in 1948. In both cases, ordinary citizens saw their savings wiped out virtually overnight and

---

[5] *Frankfurter Allgemeine Zeitung*, 15 October 1995.
[6] Interview with the authors, Bundesbank official, 4 July 2003.
[7] *Frankfurter Allgemeine Zeitung*, 12 October 1995.
[8] Authors' correspondence with IfW, 3 November 2003.

subsequently became ardent supporters of the 'sound money' paradigm in principle. Under US guidance, the paradigm was institutionally enshrined in the legendary Bundesbank, which was then called *Bank Deutscher Länder*. After the demise of the global fixed-exchange regime Bretton Woods in August 1971, years of reliable, sturdy Bundesbank policy lifted the Deutschmark *nolens volens* into the league of reserve currencies, with the result that it steadily appreciated against other European currencies.

The 1970s saw attempts to cushion the loss of stable exchange rates at least among European currencies. In a policy-learning fashion of trial and error, a regime called 'the snake' was created, which was a system of fixed but adjustable exchange rates in which most but not all EC Member States (and sometimes a few non-EC Member States) participated. The snake was not very successful as there were frequent realignments and the currencies of various countries, notably France, dropped out a number of times (Tsoukalis 1977).

Policy learning led to the EMS, which was designed around a currency basket called the ECU (Ludlow 1982). National currencies floated within bounds around their ECU conversion rates. Germany represented more than a third of the aggregated GDP in the EC. The Deutschmark was the strongest and most 'stable' currency in the EMS (it never once needed to be devalued). Other countries, for example France, tried to keep its currency stable within the EMS framework by fixing the franc to the Deutschmark. As the inflation differentials led to pressures for devaluations, the strategy became to follow German monetary policies closely. As a result these countries 'imported' low levels of inflation by fixing their currencies to the Deutschmark within the EMS framework, even though this *de facto* meant the loss of monetary sovereignty. Thus over the course of the 1980s the Bundesbank set the monetary policy for countries that participated in the ERM of the EMS.[9] It was demonstrated that one of the important institutional characteristics of the Bundesbank was its independence. This institutional feature became the basis for the ECB. In 1988 at the Hanover European Council meeting the heads of state and government asked the then-President of the Commission, Jacques Delors, to chair an ad hoc committee of predominantly central bankers to draft a blueprint for EMU. Their notion of an ECB clearly followed that of the Bundesbank, the central bank which was to be replaced by a European one. It is highly relevant for the expertocratic approach to European integration that the EMU blueprint and the design of a future central banking system

---

[9] During the 1980s the UK stayed out of the ERM, but was part of the EMS. For that reason the British refer to participation in the 'ERM' rather than talking about the usual term 'EMS'.

in monetary union were drafted by the experts, the central bankers themselves.[10]

Cooperation in the context of the EMS had implied that most monetary authorities had contributed to convergence in monetary policy with the *de facto* fixing of exchange rates as its result (Giavazzi and Giovannini 1989). Monetary authorities of the ERM countries had been 'shadowing' Bundesbank policies (Dyson 1994). The resulting convergence meant that monetary authorities had learnt lessons about economic and monetary governance. The important outcome of the diffusion of the German model is that central bankers across the EC became convinced of the sound money paradigm and, through their close professional contacts, merged into an 'epistemic community' (Kaelberer 2003).

In the form of the 'Delors Committee', built on the regular gathering of EC central bank governors with a Secretariat in Basel, this epistemic community of European central bankers and two EC Commissioners was able to influence decisively the economic principles of EMU (Verdun 1999). The ECB statutes are a striking example of the results of policy learning through decades of central banking being guided by the stability paradigm.

The workings of the Monetary Committee

The MC (since 1999 it has been known as the Economic and Financial Committee, or EFC) is responsible for preparing ECOFIN Council meetings. It is also asked for consultation on EU policies in this policy domain when they need adjustment. At the time when EMU was being negotiated the committee provided various options. For example it produced the exact definition of the convergence criteria (Italianer 1993).[11] During the past three decades it has also dealt with exchange rate issues, devaluations and revaluations of the ERM (which was for example highly politically

---

[10] A former participant of the ECOFIN Council said that the then Bundesbank President Karl-Otto Pöhl was most surprised when he first heard about the central bank governors' participation in the writing of the EMU blueprint. He was quoted as having said to his Dutch counterpart, Willem Duisenberg: 'Have you heard what those idiots [the Heads of State and Government at the European Council Meeting] in Hanover decided? They want us to help think about EMU!' Duisenberg's answer apparently was: 'Can you imagine what they would come up with without us?' (interview with the authors 10 December 2003).

[11] Monetary Committee official, interviews with the authors, autumn 1996 and 17 June 2003. In an interview held on 1 December 2003 a Dutch official of the Ministry of Finance who attended the Maastricht negotiations in the capacity of an MC member, clarified that there had been the options of 3 or 4 per cent. The Germans and Dutch were advocating 3 per cent. A French official of the Banque de France suggested in an interview with the authors on 30 September 2003 that the French could agree to the 3 per cent rule as this target had been used in France in 1983 after Mitterrand had changed the course of his policy and abandoned large-scale fiscal expansion.

charged during the ERM crisis).[12] It has given recommendations on the use of Broad Economic Policy Guidelines and on the convergence performance in the run-up to EMU. The members of the MC were the core actors in determining the actual provisions of the SGP. The political choices were formally made at the level of the ECOFIN Council and a very small number of them at the European Council level.

Before 1 January 1999 (i.e. before the start of Stage III) the MC consisted of two members per Member State and two members from the Commission. The Member States had one member representing the Ministry of Finance; the other represented the central bank. The MC representatives were typically the 'number two' in each of these organisations, i.e. the Vice-President of the central bank and a State Secretary from the Ministry of Finance. Each of these members had a vote on the Committee, although the MC almost never (if ever) voted.[13] In addition all members of the MC have an alternate. These alternates also take on a role in the MC. In the case of the SGP they worked on technical details. The work on the SGP in the MC was also further supported by the services of the Commission (DG Ecfin) and of the legal services of the Council.

The MC became involved in the SGP through the request for draft legislation. When the Waigel initiative to create a 'Stability Pact for Europe' formally came to the ECOFIN Council in December 1995, the European Council subsequently initiated legislation. The Commission (which has the right of initiative) presented a proposal to 'ensure budgetary discipline and co-ordination in the monetary union in accordance with procedures and principles of the Treaty' (European Council conclusions, quoted in Costello, 2001: 107). The Commission does not draft such a text completely on its own, but addresses the MC alternates to bounce off ideas before it puts forward its proposal for formal approval by the MC and subsequent submission to ECOFIN.[14]

MC meetings were generally based on frank interaction. After a *tour de table* members were informed of each others' starting points. Discussion and exchange of opinions would be heard, and mutual adjustment of the respective positions would take place in this process. At the end there would be fewer options to choose from, and in some cases it became

---

[12] On the ERM crisis see for example Busch (1994).

[13] Interviews with the authors, Monetary Committee officials 1996, 13 June 2003 and 17 June 2003.

[14] 'Towards a Stability Pact' (II/11/96-EN dated 10 January 1996); 'A Stability Pact to Ensure Budgetary Discipline in EMU' (II/163/96-EN dated 18 March 1996); 'Ensuring Budgetary Discipline in Stage Three of EMU' (II/409/96-EN dated 19 July 1996).

immediately clear what the consensus solution was. As stated before, the MC aimed for decisions by consensus, which required ideational convergence as well as 'package' deals.

The MC was the arena where all ideas and proposals were shared. The Commission stressed the need to stay within the Treaty, which eventually happened. As stated before, the Germans had at first wanted an international treaty outside the Maastricht Treaty. They had sought the advice of legal experts of the Ministry of Finance and the Ministry of Economics as well as from academia, who had backed up that proposal. But it soon became clear that such an arrangement would not fit with the general principles of policy-making and treaty provisions of the EU (and as we saw in Chapter 2, the Germans became wary of having to obtain ratification in all participating Member States if a new treaty was created). The legal experts of the Commission and Council services had pressed through their point. Having decided to design the Pact as secondary legislation, the MC worked out the main structure of the SGP by March 1996. Yet it took the financial experts the rest of the year to work out the more complicated details (although a formal Commission proposal was released on 16 October 1996 (COM(96)496), see Chapter 4).

A number of issues were discussed in the MC with important differences of opinion among the experts. In most cases the Commission had a different stance on the matter compared to Germany. One issue concerned the medium-term deficit target (Artis and Buti 2001). Waigel's original proposal suggested a target of 1 per cent, which would be clear, transparent and easily verifiable. The Commission argued that individual Member States might need different targets at specific times. Most Member States agreed with the Commission (albeit for different reasons). The result was the formulation of 'close to balance or in surplus' (see Chapter 4). They also briefly discussed whether to specify a time period by which Member States would be expected to reach the medium-term deficit target, as advocated by the Commission. In the end it was decided not to include language to that effect in the regulation, but the understanding at the time was that Member States would have to adjust within the timeframe of the stability programmes, which is three years. Furthermore the question emerged whether the deficit target required additional targets in other areas of economic policy, such as spending. The Commission was seeking far-reaching arrangements on this matter, which the Member States did not accept. In the end only a loose text was adopted: 'The Council shall furthermore examine whether the contents of the stability/convergence programme facilitate the closer cooperation of economic policies.'[15]

Another set of issues was related to how the rules would determine excessive deficits. As stated in the neofunctionalist chapter, the point of departure for the experts was the aim to avoid 'gross errors' in the development of Member States' budgets and public debt (Article 104.2 TEC). The notion of 'gross errors' narrowed down to one of 'excessive deficits'. Subsequently, the relevant questions were whether the definition of an excessive deficit had to take into consideration public debt or only budgetary deficits. Other questions came up, such as: should the deficit be nominal or structural? (In the end it was decided, supported by the Commission services, that the nominal deficit ceiling was sufficient.) The reasoning was that the public debt-to-GDP ratio would diminish anyway if deficits stayed 'close to balance or in surplus' in the medium term and that a position of budgetary balance would allow fixing a nominal ceiling for the deficit without endangering the use of automatic stabilisers (which are deducted in the calculation of the structural deficit). The other aspect was that the convergence criterion requiring public debt to stay below the reference value of 60 per cent or to diminish sufficiently and approach the reference value remained in the Treaty also beyond the beginning of Stage III.

Discussions also concerned the issue of how to calculate the deficit. Debates took place on whether investment expenditure should not be considered in a different way as consumptive expenditure. There were long debates on this issue as it was clear that there were different views on what would be best for the economy, for the different economic policies that various countries would pursue and the fact that the rule was supposed to be simple, transparent and accountable. In the end it was decided not to differentiate between investment and consumptive expenditure as a departure from the European System of Regional and National Accounts (ESA) appeared not to be possible and would have led to different calculations in the Member States, which in turn would have made it pointless to apply one rule to all (the example often given was how to deal with expenses for education or for health; would they be consumptive or investment?).[16]

Another debate dealt with creating a sanctioning mechanism in conjunction with a system of 'early warning'. It was clear that although coordination and monitoring procedures of macroeconomic policies already featured in the Treaty, the discussions about the SGP would have major implications on the existing arrangements. They would have to be upgraded. The Commission made a number of proposals regarding

[15] Article 5.1 Council Regulation (EC) 1466/97 on budgetary surveillance.
[16] Interviews with the authors, June, July and September 2003. Note that revisions of the ESA system were being finalised in parallel with the ongoing work on the SGP.

the timeframe of the submission of annual budget proposals. The Member States agreed with most of them but were sceptical about a short timeframe. A compromise was to aim for the end of the year but no later than March of the following year.

Experts in the MC had to propose some form of linking the early warning system to the EDP, which was achieved in the form of recitals of both Regulations in the Resolution of the European Council (Costello 2001: 119). Furthermore, one had to decide on how to deal with those members who were not in EMU (the so-called 'pre-ins' or 'non-participating countries'). From the outset the idea was that the SGP should cover all Member States. In the end it was the general macroeconomic policy coordination (convergence programmes) that would apply to all, the argument being that if a country has an external exchange rate it can still be subject to market reactions (Costello 2001).[17] The EDP applies also to 'outs', but it cannot lead to sanctions.

Until that point, discussions were not confrontational. A number of issues, however, led to contentious debates. For example, the idea of sanctions was already incorporated in the EDP of the Maastricht Treaty but had not been operationalised. The SGP represented the missing secondary legislation that developed the mechanism. It was a fundamentally different instrument than any other instrument used thus far in the EU. If a sanction were to be imposed on the Member States that had an excessive deficit it could eventually amount to substantial sums.[18] Of course the idea had been to have the possibility of sanctions inserted in the SGP to enforce that Member States 'play by the rules'. It was clear, though, that if sanctions were ever applied they would have unprecedented and undesirable effects on the Member State and on the perception of the public on the role of governance in the EU. Therefore the sanctions were embedded in a layered set of steps to be taken before they would actually be applied. Furthermore both the EDP sequence as well as the definition of 'excessive deficit' effectively contain escape clauses and leave the Member States room for manoeuvre.

The automaticity of this process was a very touchy topic. It is one thing to threaten to impose sanctions; it is another if the impression could be given that an EU Member State could face very steep sanctions without any political authority having to decide whether that would be appropriate.

---

[17] Costello (2001) notes that the convergence programmes are almost identical to the stability programmes. For a further discussion of the stability and convergence programmes see Fischer and Giudice (2001).

[18] The sanctions first take the form of a non-interest-bearing deposit with the Commission of 0.2 per cent of GDP plus a variable component linked to the size of the deficit. Subsequently, the deposit is converted into a fine if the excessive deficit has not been corrected after two years.

In fact, the Commission and most Member States advocated more flexibility and discretion. They stressed that the Maastricht Treaty would not allow for completely automatic sanctions. However, the Germans wanted maximum credibility of the threat of sanctions (so that Member States would take the rules seriously) and hence sought the strictest possible arrangement that would still stay within the limits of the Treaty. Eventually the arrangements were designed so as to balance the two. Costello (2001) points to three legislative solutions that were found by the experts: (i) clear definitions of the key provisions in the EDP; (ii) strong language about the actions that the Commission and Council would need to take during the various steps; (iii) regarding the excessive deficit, once it is identified as being excessive, the burden of proof is reversed. It would be up to the respective Member State to make a case for the need of the exemption clause.

Here, one of the more disputed issues became the definition of cases that would represent an exemption from sanctions even if the deficit went beyond 3 per cent. The discussions focused on whether a political escape clause would be desirable. The experts realised that the more political leverage was built into the text the less powerful the pact would become. Yet it was also clear that having too strict a Pact might undermine the regime altogether once that it would actually have to be applied.[19] A balance had to be struck. The compromise solution between expert-based knowledge about a tight pact and the political leverage that most Member States (and the Commission) wanted was to have the escape clause only apply to a situation in which an exceptional and temporary deficit occurred and the budget was close to the 3 per cent reference value. Then the question of course became: what is exceptional and temporary?[20]

An exceptional overshoot of the 3 per cent line was granted in the case of an unusual event (like natural disasters) or a 'severe economic downturn'. The most politically sensitive issue turned out to be the question of how to define a 'severe economic downturn'. This term incorporated the situation where a country would be inevitably allowed to run a deficit above 3 per cent. The Germans wanted negative real growth in four consecutive past quarters compared with the respective preceding quarters, or negative real growth rate of GDP in a fiscal calendar year exceeding 2 per cent. The Commission and various Member States wanted to stay away from a

---

[19] This is one interpretation of the events in November 2003, see Chapter 7.

[20] The MC also needed to define 'temporary'; Costello (2001). The definition applied at the time was that the deficit needed to be forecast to fall below the 3 per cent line within twelve months. Both conditions need to be fulfilled – temporality and exceptionality – for a deficit above 3 per cent not to be excessive.

numerical definition of a severe economic downturn. Instead, each case should be assessed on its own and with discretionary leeway. The Commission stressed the importance of the output gap (two years of zero growth would lead to an output gap of 4 per cent of GDP; Costello 2001). The Germans and the Commission each showed calculations about how often the respective situations had actually occurred in the past. The Germans insisted on their proposed formula as those situations had occurred much less often than the ones based on the Commission's calculation. The compromise already mentioned above was eventually proposed by the chairman of the MC, Sir Nigel Wicks, who suggested the 'Wicks box'. A recession in which the economy contracts by 2 per cent of GDP or more would be automatically considered a severe economic downturn, but there would be a grey zone of political discretion below that level. The lower boundary of the Wicks box, as discussed, became the most contentious issue of all after it was clear that automaticity was only achieved in the form of a non-binding self-commitment. The lower boundary is part of that self-commitment and therefore the linchpin of political discretion over the sanctioning mechanism. The issue was neither resolved at the level of the MC nor through ECOFIN. Eventually it had to be referred to the Dublin European Council, which settled at 0.75 per cent (see Chapter 2).

Insights from an expertocratic approach

From our interviews we received confirmation that the MC was the arena in which almost all the important issues surrounding the creation of the SGP were dealt with exhaustively. We highlighted in Chapter 4 that the MC played a double role. On the one hand it is seen as a club of professional experts who share a common understanding of EMU. On the other hand its members were a group of dependent negotiators who bargained for the positions of their governments.

The results of the questionnaire and the interviews show that there was a strong support for a stability paradigm. There were common principles that were adhered to, which included the basic design of EMU (independent central bank, price stability, the need for rules on budgets). There was support for the principle that EMU would need to be backed by rules on budgets.[21] There was also unanimous support that 'Political decisions

---

[21] All respondents answered 'true' to the following question: 'Rules on budgets are important.' The next question had three possible answers. 'Budget rules should be ...' A majority (roughly 60 per cent) chose the following statement: 'explicit (3 per cent) but flexible'; a minority (roughly 40 per cent) chose this answer: 'explicit (3 per cent) but

on the budget should be limited by rules.'[22] Furthermore, all but one of the respondents agreed that EMU and the SGP are oriented along the lines of the German model. The interviewees also agreed that the Maastricht Treaty did not supply sufficient provisions to deal with EMU in Stage III. This became more urgent when it became clear that EMU might start off including the Southern countries, rather than only a small group in the core.

A number of less likely findings are perhaps worth stressing as well. When asking respondents whether there was conflict within their organisation about the SGP all but one responded 'no'. We asked respondents whether they thought the rules on budgets should be backed up by sanctions, the respondents (all but one) answered 'true'. However, when asking if sanctions should be automatic three-quarters answered 'false', whilst the remainder answered 'true'.

We also sought to trace the effect of the change in political orientation of the governments since 1997. The results show that the experts were divided as to whether these political changes affected the overall consensus. On the question 'The political changes after 1997 (from conservative to social-democratic dominance in Europe) have challenged the underlying consensus that enabled the SGP', the experts were 50–50 split on the issue (i.e. half chose 'agree', half chose 'disagree'). However, three-quarters felt that 'The views of politicians are unstable but the position of experts (central bankers, Commission officials, journalists, academics …) on the SGP has not changed substantially.' Finally, we asked respondents to comment on the following question: 'How would EMU run today without the SGP?', and they all answered 'worse'.

Our interpretation of these results is that the experts are a reasonably closely knit community. They share common notions of validity and general beliefs. As such their views influence the outcome beyond mere intergovernmental bargaining. Nevertheless, actor experts have to balance political requests with their expert knowledge. The political dimension becomes more dominant in the case that the experts hold a variety of ideas about the possible options to consider.

An expertocratic approach to the creation of the SGP explains the importance of 'actor experts' sharing a common paradigm, and the mechanisms that facilitated their role in the decision-making process. This approach offers insights in the particular role of experts, expertise, policy learning, socialisation, expert communities, ideas and paradigms in order

---

strict'. None of the respondents picked the 'general and flexible'. Finally, regarding rules on budgets, all respondents answered 'true' to this question: 'Rules on budgets are even more important in a monetary union.'

[22] The question was phrased as a negative, Q15: 'Political decisions on the budget should not be limited by rules'; all respondents ticked 'false'.

to grasp the process. The so-called actor experts involved in the discussions of the SGP were those that participated in the MC, as well as those in the national Ministries of Finances, the Commission and the central banks. Actor experts draft what politicians see as their interests but incorporate their own insights as to what is economically sound and feasible. They deliver explicit definitions for broad concepts according to their world view (such as the successively ever more refined definition of 'excessive deficits' in the SGP, starting from the broad notion of 'gross errors' in Article 104.2). Non-actor experts (academics, journalists and persons working in other international organisations, such as the IMF, OECD, etc.) are also influential, as they determine the overall economic policy debate that the actor experts consider to define the realm of the possible.

An expertocratic approach stresses the importance of a paradigm that we see to mean a view of how to conduct economic policy. The actor experts try to shape the functionalist logic to comply with their paradigm. An example of this mechanism is that the need for structural reform is relabelled as a (functional) consequence of monetary union (see also Verdun 2000a). Whether or not an expert agrees with this logic depends on his or her ideological preference. The difference here is between ideology and paradigm. Even though there is a stability paradigm, there are ideological preferences (size of the welfare state, the degree of competition, reduction of inequality, for example). There can be a common paradigm and still differences of opinion among experts.

The role of actor experts also offers part of the explanation for the fact that the SGP was chosen to stay within the Maastricht Treaty. Beyond that, it offers an explanation why the SGP is accompanied by a whole wealth of further secondary legislation, official communication and formal documentation (such as internal working documents, a Code of Conduct, etc.). The multitude of rules and practices regarding the processing of Broad Economic Policy Guidelines and Multilateral Surveillance is a related example.

The socialisation principle explains why actor experts in the Ministries of Finance, the Commission and central banks (convening chiefly in the MC) have become used to pursuing economic and monetary policies in line with previous decisions (such as the rules on budgets as set out in the Delors Committee and the Maastricht Treaty, convergence criteria, etc.) These actor experts will then logically keep accepting the policies within the framework of how policies and rules are made in the EU.

An expertocratic approach does not explain the prominence that Germany and other national governments nevertheless had on the eventual process. It was clear that German experts had some degree of leverage over the others as they represented the largest Member State and a country that at that time was still associated with a relatively successful model, and which could thus wield authority over the design of rules for Europe. The actual outcome still lay closer to German proposals than to that of the French and one should incorporate German inter-governmental bargaining and overall German power in the analysis.

Another phenomenon was that the European Council at times inter-fered in the legislation process. This interference happened when the actor experts and ECOFIN felt unable to take a political decision. An expertocratic approach does not clarify any part of that process.

The significance of domestic German actors in the behaviour of the German government is obviously not addressed by this approach either. We need a domestic politics approach to understand the German motivation for wanting the SGP in the first place. (The latter becomes particularly puzzling once Germany itself fails to meet 3 per cent). An expertocratic approach also does not address fully the strength of the Bundesbank or the linkage with German public opinion.

Finally, the limit of 'functional' versus 'expert knowledge' needs further elaboration. An expertocratic approach does not explain the predomi-nance of legal functionalism (path dependence) over economic function-alism, which can be explained through the neofunctionalist lens, as previously done.

Conclusion of Part I: an analysis of the SGP origins

We began the introduction of this book asking why states agreed to limit their sovereignty over budgetary policies. Why did they create an SGP that would restrict their freedom to run deficits? More pre-cisely, why did the Pact take on the form it did? To answer these questions, we examined four theoretical approaches. Each of them offered a partial explanation. In the introduction we suggested that the SGP has various dimensions, which we analysed through four theoretical lenses subsequently discussed in Chapters 2–5. The final section of this chapter sets out to make that linkage more explicit. Now we offer a synthesis of the analysis developed in the four preceding chapters.

The origins of the SGP can be traced back to a functional need for additional policies and institutional provisions for Stage III of EMU. According to the understanding of the actors at the time, the existing framework of the Maastricht Treaty was insufficiently developed in the area of economic governance and lacked in particular precautions against overly lax fiscal policy and arrangements for fiscal policy cooperation. The ensuing design of secondary law amounted to further advancing the state of integration, driven by a functional logic.

The analytical concept of spillover provides us with a tool to clarify this functional mechanism. In Chapter 4 we proposed to divide up functional spillover along economic and legal lines. Under economic spillover, we subsume the economic reasoning behind the creation of the SGP. The notion of political spillover explains the boundaries set by the Maastricht Treaty, within which the SGP was to be embedded.

The actual spark to ignite the debate was Theo Waigel's proposal in late 1995 for a 'Stability Pact for Europe', laid out in the form of an ancillary Treaty outside the Maastricht framework. The timing and content of this initiative can only be understood if one appreciates the domestic politics of Germany in that period. A sceptical Bundesbank, unfavourable public opinion, and opposition parties as well as internal competitors that were all becoming increasingly negative about EMU forced the German Minister of Finance to step up his efforts and prove his leadership in this area. Waigel was under domestic political pressure to show that EMU would not imply a weakening of the stability culture that had been built in Germany. There had of course already been some informal discussions (among MC members as well as within the Bundesbank and the German Ministry of Finance), but before November 1995 there was not enough momentum for an EU proposal on this matter. It is not very likely that any EU policies would have been proposed in 1996 had it not been for Waigel's initiative.

The subsequent, concrete genesis of the SGP demands an expertocratic explanation. It was experts in the German Ministry of Finance who drafted the Waigel proposal, using at times input from academic 'non-actor' experts as well. In the process of deliberating on the issue and writing the proposal, the Ministry of Finance officials expressed their view of what remedies the lacunae in the Treaty of Maastricht required in order to make Stage III of EMU viable. For this intellectual exercise, they relied on specific ideas of how EMU should function and in what sense it should be based on existing models, including the German one. These ideas were contained in the stability paradigm that they subscribed to.

Experts of the Commission subsequently provided the legislative draft of the SGP. They held somewhat different views and saw other priorities compared to the experts in the German Ministry of Finance. Above all, they were aware of the functional implications of the Treaty in the legal domain and saw an institutional interest in retaining that Treaty base. They incorporated the two competing functional strands, the legal as well as the economic one, into one single draft text that again was based on ideas flowing from the stability paradigm. Their attempt at squaring the circle (i.e. staying within the Treaty but expanding its functionality) explains the most important features of the final SGP – the political discretion of ECOFIN in the application of the SGP procedures, the addition of an additional surveillance mechanism that represents a rudimentary device for economic policy coordination and the attempt to make the sanctions more credible and thereby effective in maintaining fiscal discipline in Stage III of EMU.

The Commission input in different stages was fed repeatedly into the intergovernmental negotiation process in a bottom-up manner. The vast majority of issues was settled in a collegial manner by the experts of the MC. The so-called 'MC alternates' solved predominantly technical questions, whereas the regular members of the MC paved the way for political compromises on conflicting issues. In doing so, they managed jointly to keep all but the most controversial subjects in their hands and solved them within the MC. Once the MC had agreed on a subject, it was closed and sent to the higher level, ECOFIN, for approval. We would argue that, from the drafting of texts in the Commission up to an agreed compromise in the MC, a combined view through the neofunctionalist and expertocratic 'lenses' on the SGP explain the results observed.

Controversial discussions that were not solved in the MC, however, and hence a number of important elements of the SGP compromise can only be explained through bargaining and interstate negotiation, adopting an intergovernmental perspective. The negotiation process was structured in a bottom-up manner. MC members wear two hats (see Chapters 3 and 5). As financial experts, they broadly agree and provide jointly endorsed solutions for the political level. As 'financial diplomats', they receive instructions from their superiors to achieve a certain kind of solution on a specific issue.

The interstate bargaining begins at this level in the MC. If a consensus is achieved, it passes on in the same manner as a non-conflicting agreement. If a majority vote had to be called (which, as we noted before, very rarely happens – if at all), or if no decision can be taken, the issue is discussed by ECOFIN Ministers, at the necessary level of detail. Ministers would define their positions in line with the political priorities of the heads of state and government, which meant that eventually even the European Council had to solve the remaining open questions. This happened for two kinds of reasons: one occurred when the Ministers felt unable to take a political decision because of the feeling that they lacked legitimacy, such as deciding on the name of the future currency.[23] The other reason was that even ECOFIN could not produce a consensus. The latter has occurred on only one issue, i.e. the question of what constituted the lowest admissible level of a recession that would exempt the ECOFIN from its self-commitment to declare a deficit of over 3 per cent as 'excessive'.

Other decisions taken by the European Council concerned the general impetus for the legislative process in the sense of politically guiding the deliberations of the lower levels. Proceedings at the highest political level also follow the logic of intergovernmental bargains. This includes issue linkage in the form of a package solution for adopting the SGP in Amsterdam in conjunction with an employment chapter in the Treaty. These deals were struck at a highly personal level between the leaders of France and Germany. The fact that other countries play virtually no (or only a mediating) role is understandable only on the basis of assessing the power-political constellation prevalent in that situation. Similarly, the ultimate weight that Germany carried in these negotiations shows in the overall result. The SGP *does* represent a compromise, yet the meeting point often was not in the middle of two preference points but somewhat leaning more towards the German side. This phenomenon can only be explained by the fact that all deliberations and negotiations in the context of EMU took place 'in the shadow' of Germany's dominant position (see Genberg 1990).

In summary, a combination of intergovernmental, domestic politics, functional and expertocratic approaches to European integration enables us to understand the process that led to the creation of the SGP in the period 1995–7. We shall now apply this framework in the second part of this book to the history of the Pact up until the time of writing in 2009.

---

[23] Naming the future currency was one of the symbolic decisions in the context of EMU, as was the nomination of the future ECB President and the seat of the central bank. These were taken at the highest political level. One of the functions of the SGP, that is the symbolical effect that it was designed to carry to the German electorate, can be seen in this context (see Chapter 3). Rather than a question of legitimacy, a reason for taking these decisions at the level of the European Council is the intended result that the public effect is maximised.

Part II

6 Implementation of the SGP in good and in bad times

Introduction

Ever since the SGP had been conceptualised it was clear that the proof of the pudding lay in the eating – i.e. the real policy implementation of the framework was key, not the political noise surrounding its inception. Would Member States conduct their fiscal policies in a cooperative way, conducive to sound public finances and monetary stability – or would the fiscal dimension of EMU put either the Member States or the Pact itself under stress? The first years of the implementation of the SGP put the scheme under some pressure right away, but serious difficulties only occurred a few years into its implementation, after the macroeconomic environment had progressively darkened.

This part of the book offers an analysis of the first nine years of the implementation period, from 1999 until late 2008. It is structured as follows. The first section of Chapter 6 offers a narrative of the SGP implementation in the period 1999–2002. The second section of this chapter analyses this first implementation period by choosing from our theoretical framework and combining the thrust of the domestic and intergovernmental approaches that best suit this episode. The next two chapters assess respectively the SGP crisis in 2003 and the reform period up to 2005 – again providing analytical assessments informed by the four approaches developed in Part I of the book. Chapter 9 presents an account of the developments up to the end of the year 2008, when the financial and economic crisis put renewed stress upon the SGP framework. Chapter 10 contains a conclusion of our findings and their implications for European integration theory.

SGP implementation – the first three years

When the SGP was agreed upon in 1997, it was not clear at all how it might be implemented in the years to come. For one, EMU had not yet entered into its final stage. On 2 May 1998, the heads of state and government unanimously decided that eleven countries fulfilled the conditions to enter Stage III of EMU, and thus to adopt the euro as of 1 January 1999: Austria, Belgium, Finland, France, Germany, Ireland, Italy, Luxembourg, the Netherlands, Portugal and Spain. To many observers it came as a surprise that EMU started off with such a large group of countries. Greece joined in 2001, and Slovenia was the thirteenth country to join in 2007, followed by Cyprus and Malta in 2008 and Slovakia in 2009. During the mid-1990s, one had assumed only a small group would proceed with Stage III of EMU at the end of the decade, but convergence in the meantime had been more rapid and wide than expected.

In addition, during the final years of the 1990s a shift in political orientation had occurred across Europe. Many EU Member States (including Germany) were now ruled by left-wing governments that, in many cases, held different views on the virtues of fiscal discipline compared to their conservative predecessors. The strengthened European left signalled to the ECB that it wanted monetary policy to focus not only on price stability but to take growth equally into account.[1] The German Minister of Finance Oskar Lafontaine called on the ECB to cut interest rates and thereby fuelled concerns about the independence of the young central bank.[2]

Also, the SGP came under political fire very early on. Mario Monti, Internal Market Commissioner at the time, was one of many politicians to ask for changes to the new rules, demanding that investment spending should be deducted from the deficit evaluation.[3] Incoming German Chancellor Gerhard Schröder called for an employment pact to complement the SGP.[4]

Despite economic and financial crises in Russia and East Asia in 1997–98 as well as bleak economic forecasts in late 1998, growth rates slowly picked up throughout Europe in 1999. However, the political will to use unexpected government revenues (so-called 'windfalls') for building up fiscal reserves or reducing debt was not present from the start. It soon became clear that most governments were not serious about aiming for the SGP's medium-term objective (MTO) of bringing budgets 'close to balance or in surplus', although they all included that aim in their forecasts, i.e. claiming to achieve it at some future point in time.

---

[1] *Frankfurter Allgemeine Zeitung*, 2 January 1999.
[2] *Frankfurter Allgemeine Zeitung*, 4 January 1999.
[3] *Financial Times*, 24 October 1998.
[4] *Financial Times*, 27 October 1998. The 'Cologne Process' or 'macroeconomic dialogue' that was installed under the German Presidency is the only reminiscence of that initiative; social partners twice a year exchange views with governments and ECB representatives.

Instead of prudently implementing fiscal restraint during the economic upswing, throughout 1999 and 2000, major European economies conducted mildly procyclical policies or at least considerably reduced their ambition to continue the consolidation effort. 'Maastricht fatigue' was widespread and growing (Fatas and Mihov 2003) – only the annual stability and convergence programmes (SCPs) submitted under the preventive arm of the Pact paid lip service to good fiscal intentions, forecasting balanced budgets and falling debt.[5] It became obvious that the SGP regime was unable to contain the political incentives for fiscal profligacy in upturns. The 'blind eye' that Article 104 and regulation 1467/97 turn to fiscal behaviour in upswings allowed loosening the reins during that period without immediately and openly breaking the rules.

Lafontaine's sudden departure from the German Ministry of Finance in 1999 resulted in a temporary shift of the emphasis of economic policy in Germany. His successor, Hans Eichel, committed to fiscal consolidation and was soon dubbed *Sparhans* ('Thrifty Hans') by the German public. His new course seemed to be backed by Chancellor Schröder, who now positioned himself closer to Tony Blair's liberal market, supply-side version of social democracy than to traditional demand-side policy. Germany, the UK and Spain agreed to concentrate on labour-market flexibilisation. This move provoked a rearguard action from France and Italy, renewing calls for a Keynesian-type employment pact that would boost public investment and would include a 3 per cent target rate for economic growth.[6]

Eichel professed an increased consolidation effort for the year 2000 and used the SGP requirements as a justification in the domestic debate.[7] In fact, on 23 June, the German government approved budget cuts to the magnitude of €15.3 billion, spending being reduced predominantly in the areas of employment and social policies, but also in the fields of education, research and foreign aid. The expected deficit for 2000 was revised down to 1.5 per cent instead of 2 per cent. On 26 August 1999, the cabinet decided on a controversial package of further spending cuts and pension reforms that, however, had no chance of passing both houses of parliament untouched.

Despite the German turnaround, the first serious and visible setback to the SGP framework occurred as early as 25 May 1999, when Giuliano Amato, Italy's newly appointed Treasury Minister, convinced the ECOFIN Council to relax his country's 2 per cent deficit target in the BEPG,

---

[5] Germany's 1999 Stability Programme under Lafontaine envisaged the deficit to fall to 1 per cent of GDP and debt to be reduced below 60 per cent by 2002 (*Financial Times* and *Frankfurter Allgemeine Zeitung*, 7 January 1999).

[6] *Financial Times*, 21 April 1999.   [7] *Frankfurter Allgemeine Zeitung*, 9 May 1999.

which is the wider economic-policy coordination framework based on Article 99 of the Treaty.[8] Following an emotional intervention by Amato in the ECOFIN Council, his fifteen colleagues accepted that Italy's deficit could increase to 2.4 per cent of GDP if the allegedly adverse economic conditions prevailed for the country. The Commission was appalled at the move that, by touching on the wider BEPG process of Article 99, also openly put into question the preventive arm of the SGP (i.e. regulation 1466/97), which is based on the same Treaty Article. Amid warnings from ECB President Willem Duisenberg, the euro's external value slid down to a record low of US\$1.05. However, early in 2000, it became clear that the actual value of Italy's deficit in 1999 had turned out to be only 1.9 per cent – even below the original target. The misjudgement of the Italian situation is just one example that shows to what extent the growth pick-up of 1999–2000 had arrived unexpectedly and contributed to a sizeable improvement in public finances.

Much stronger than projected, the year 2000 brought robust growth but marked a further shift towards expansionary fiscal policy, especially in the larger Member States. The move was largely unnoticeable in the nominal development of budgetary figures as the cyclical upturn was continuously easing the nominal situation of public finances and masking the lack of structural improvement. Government revenues were further strengthened in a number of countries due to significant windfall gains from auctioning licences for third-generation mobile communication frequencies. In fact, the sale of these so-called 'UMTS' licences propelled a number of state budgets into surplus. Overall, the euro area's combined budgetary deficit had fallen from 2 per cent in 1998 to 1.2 per cent in 1999. However, 0.5 per cent of the overall reduction was due to lower interest payments, and only 0.3 per cent accounted for a structural improvement of the primary position.[9]

The worth of nominal budget targets showed its limits in that first economic upturn of monetary union. The ECB was critical of this development and commented that 'it is not clear whether the actual fiscal policy stance in the respective countries is sufficiently stringent' (ECB 2000: 41). However, governments were able to point the public to their 'performance' in reducing nominal budget deficits and stated with some justice that they were fulfilling the terms of the SGP – despite partially increasing government expenditure. In other words, the Pact even became an excuse during the economic upswing, allowing governments to benefit rhetorically from purely cyclical improvements in their financial positions that served to fulfil outdated budgetary targets.

---

[8] *Financial Times*, 26 May 1999.   [9] *Financial Times*, 28 March 2000.

Most notably, the German government conducted yet another turnaround and suddenly pressed ahead with bold tax-cutting plans, initiating a European-wide round of tax cuts. This move was orchestrated by the Chancellery and the Ministry of Economics rather than by Eichel's Ministry of Finance and aimed to reduce corporate taxes in 2001 to 25 per cent from 40 per cent and the bottom income tax rate to 15 per cent in 2005 from 23.9 per cent in 2004. The Commission was sceptical and warned Germany in February 2000 to implement its planned tax reforms with great caution 'in order not to risk a lasting deterioration in the structural government deficit'.[10] It noted that the German government expected its deficit to rise to 1.5 per cent of GDP in 2001, compared with the 1 per cent target set under the SGP.

France's Socialist-led government followed suit and also unveiled the framework for a series of tax cuts. Christian Sautter, having succeeded Dominique Strauss-Kahn as Minister of Finance in November 1999, announced that up to €6.5 billion would be cut each year in taxes over the next three years, starting in the 2001 budget. These tax cuts would aim to bring down the fiscal burden from the record high in 1999 of 45.3 per cent of GDP to 43.7 per cent, a level comparable to that of the time when the Socialist government had taken office in 1997. In September 2000, Laurent Fabius, who had taken over the French Ministry of Finance in April, presented the draft 2001 budget. It was tailored to suit election purposes and featured further tax cuts besides increases in public sector employment and, by consequence, only a very modest deficit reduction. Fabius' ECOFIN colleagues and the Commission warned in vain that insufficient effort was being made to curb public sector spending and stated that the official growth projections looked over optimistic.

The implicit thinking behind fiscal policy in that period seemed to be that elevated growth rates could be taken almost for granted in the 'new economy', allowing for permanently higher expenditure, lower taxes and less consolidation effort, which in turn would facilitate the political process of implementing structural reforms. With the benefit of hindsight, it can be said that the major misjudgement was to assume temporary revenue windfalls to be permanent increases in the revenue level, giving rise to structural increases in public spending. Hence, the structural position of public finances deteriorated fundamentally, while headline figures still improved as long as revenue outgrew expenditure.

---

[10] *Financial Times*, 17 February 2000.

The Irish warning

Similar to most other euro-area countries at the end of 2000, the government of Ireland decided to cut taxes and to increase public spending. From a budgetary point of view, Dublin was in a comfortable position to do so, boasting a surplus of nearly 5 per cent and a debt level approaching only 25 per cent of GDP, benefiting from one of the most remarkable expenditure reform successes in the 1980s and 1990s (Hauptmeier *et al.* 2006). Ireland was still catching up economically with the richer nations in the EU, exhibiting fast growth and inflation. The country represented the textbook case for tightening fiscal policy in order to offset the inflationary effects of rising wages during fast growth. However, politically, the government was willing to accept an overheating of the economy in order to appease the trade unions, whose wage restraint had been instrumental to the growth performance.

At that juncture, the Prodi Commission and particularly DG Ecfin (under Director-General Klaus Regling, reporting to ECOFIN Commissioner Pedro Solbes)[11] were becoming more assertive at managing economic policy coordination in the euro area. Solbes stated that it was 'clearly necessary to increase the use of informal coordination in the Eurogroup and peer group pressure'.[12] The Irish case was chosen to set a precedent. On 24 January 2001, when adopting its recommendation for a Council opinion on Ireland in the context of the BEPG progress (which, like the preventive arm of the SGP, is based on Article 99), the Commission strongly advised Dublin to tighten its stance on fiscal policy in order to keep inflation under control. Already in the previous year, the Commission had stated that, without fiscal tightening, Ireland would no longer be in keeping with the BEPGs adopted by EU leaders in the summer of 1999.[13] The Commission's harsh criticism met with strong resentment in Ireland. A successful, small country meeting every standard of fiscal sustainability saw itself as being reprimanded by larger Member States faring less well on all grounds of public finance. The parallel silence in Brussels with respect to promises for tax cuts made by Silvio Berlusconi, running for general elections in Italy, further strengthened the impression that the rules were applied rigorously

---

[11] Regling had previously been a senior official in the German Ministry of Finance closely involved with the SGP policy initiative in 1995.
[12] *Financial Times*, 25 January 2001.   [13] *Financial Times*, 19 January 2000.

only to small Member States.[14] Dublin stiffened immediately and Irish Deputy Prime Minister Mary Harney denied inflationary risks for the economy and insisted on the fact that the Irish budget had outperformed most other euro-area countries on the SGP requirements.[15] Nonetheless, the ECOFIN Council issued a recommendation to Ireland and asked it to tighten the budget by 0.5 per cent of GDP. Instead, Irish Minister of Finance Charlie McGreevy ensured that the budget was adopted as planned. Peer pressure had dramatically failed. While not directly concerning the SGP, the incident discredited the BEPG process and was perceived as a second and even more serious blow to the rules-based regime of EMU after the gentlemen's agreement of changing the Italian deficit target in 1999.

Entering the downturn

By 2001 it became clear that the growth effects expected from the ubiquitous tax cuts failed to materialise in most countries. Excessive wage bargains and over-investment had further reduced the prospects for growth and employment. In addition, external conditions deteriorated sharply during 2001. The downward trend became even steeper in the aftermath of the terrorist attacks in Washington and New York and due to the bursting of the stock market bubble that had built up to staggering heights in the previous year. Government revenues started to turn in lower than expected and public finances began deteriorating in most EU Member States. Portugal was the first country to approach the 3 per cent of GDP reference value for the deficit.

Also Germany was already in spring 2001 set to exceed its budgetary commitments, due to lower than expected growth and associated tax shortfalls. However, with general elections due to be held in 2002, the government was determined to maintain its overall level of public expenditure and continued to display optimism about the state of the economy. In June 2001, Eichel tried to use his consolidation commitments made under the SGP in order to ease domestic pressure on his budget. At the same time, the intra-German fiscal transfer framework (*Länderfinanzausgleich*) was

---

[14] The suspected application of different standards to small countries by the larger Member States was being evoked even twice with the election of Berlusconi in Italy. Not only did he seem poised to decide budgetary measures that by all standards (of direction and magnitude) were far more serious than the Irish ones, but also did he form a government coalition with the post-fascist *Allianza Nazionale*. Another small country, Austria, had earlier been treated with official isolation for including the right-wing Freedom Party in its ruling coalition.

[15] *Financial Times*, 5 February 2001.

being renegotiated in the context of the need for continued federal subsidies towards the development of the Eastern *Länder*. The negotiations were concluded partly at the expense of the federal budget, while the government officially maintained the SGP aim to reach general budgetary balance by 2006.

On 11 September 2001, hours before the terrorist attacks, Eichel admitted that the central government budget target of reducing the deficit to €21.1 billion would not be met in the coming year because of the apparent growth slowdown. Following the attacks, most governments quickly resolved to increase spending on defence and home security measures and to support industry sectors hit particularly strongly by the effects of the attacks, such as airlines. Within ten days of the terrorist attacks, Germany decided on surprise tax increases, predominantly on tobacco, in order to raise an additional €1.5 billion for anti-terrorist measures without further weakening its budgetary commitments. Meanwhile, close cooperation among central banks and the prompt provision of large amounts of liquidity kept financial markets intact.

The Eurogroup informal discussions agreed to leave the SGP untouched, but the following ECOFIN meeting on 22–3 September 2001 produced somewhat mixed results. French Minister of Finance Laurent Fabius argued that nothing should impede the free functioning of automatic stabilisers, whereas the Commission argued that France, Germany, Italy and Portugal should, in the worst case, restrict their stabilisers partially. After all, these countries had previously failed to bring their budgets close to balance or in surplus, which would have created the necessary room for manoeuvring the downswing without approaching the reference value. However, the European Council, convening for a special meeting on the same day in Brussels, resolved the debate and declared that 'efforts made to consolidate public finances have provided the necessary room for manoeuvre to enable automatic stabilisers to come into play'. When Council President and Belgian Prime Minister Guy Verhofstadt in a press conference described the Pact as 'our bible', Commission President Prodi interjected with the words 'almost our bible', only to earn the rebuke: 'No. Our bible. Full stop.'[16]

At a Franco-German summit in Paris, Jospin lobbied the German government to soften its opposition to relaxing the SGP. Schröder and Jospin agreed that the EU needed a coordinated response but the German Chancellor still insisted on adhering to the budgetary targets. Jospin, facing presidential and parliamentary elections in the coming year, argued

---

[16] *Financial Times*, 24 September 2001.

that France had no intention of undermining the Pact but that he would closely monitor the further developments. Earlier during that week he had stated: 'If necessary we are willing to do more to sustain the French economy on the path to growth and lower unemployment.'[17]

With the beginning of the US-led anti-terrorist offensive in Afghanistan, the German stance on the SGP also began to change. At a G7 meeting in Washington on 6 October, Eichel stated that the German deficit would probably be closer to 2 per cent rather than the targeted 1.5 per cent. He advocated a postponement of the consolidation effort. Higher deficits should be accepted in 2001, without this implying a general shift away from consolidation.[18] In the following weeks, official growth forecasts for Germany and France had to be revised downwards significantly – a recessionary or even deflationary scenario was looming on the horizon. European leaders showed impatience with the ECB, demanding further cuts in interest rates, and voiced ideas of increasing the fiscal stimulus through additional tax cuts. Still, the European Council of 19 October produced orthodox language on budgetary rigour and structural economic reforms, accepting that the ECB would only have scope for a significant easing of monetary policy if inflation fell by more than already expected. Reviewing Europe's economic slowdown since the terrorist attacks in the USA, European leaders also pledged to uphold the SGP and accelerate structural reforms.

German economists called for a considerably more expansive fiscal policy stance in the autumn of 2001 in the face of the most severe economic downturn in a decade. The government confirmed a €9.8 billion tax shortfall, €2.7 billion more than expected, because of the slowing economy. Eichel still wished to meet his deficit targets (€21.1 billion in 2002, €22.3 billion in 2003, a balanced budget by 2006) and reinforced privatisation measures to increase government revenues. However, the receipts from privatisation were quickly marginalised by the Chancellor's decision to predate tax cuts originally foreseen for 2003 by one year.

Respect for the SGP boundaries was sliding, not only in Germany, but all across Europe. The new official parlance on the SGP gradually adopted by EU leaders was that the Pact provided all the flexibility required to ride through the economic slump with the help of automatic stabilisers. The shift of emphasis away from budgetary targets under the preventive arm and focusing on respecting the deficit ceiling of the corrective arm of the Pact gave additional breathing space, implying that a postponement of

[17] *Financial Times*, 6 October 2001.
[18] *Frankfurter Allgemeine Sonntagszeitung*, 7 October 2001.

the targets was acceptable as long as countries kept their deficits at a certain distance from the 3 per cent reference value.

However, in early 2002, new figures confirmed that the German fiscal position continued to deteriorate, the deficit widening to 2.6 per cent for 2001, 1.1 percentage points higher than expected. The Commission was beginning to consider issuing an early warning to Berlin as the government seemed to be steadily approaching the 3 per cent reference value. Yet Finance Minister Eichel tried to alleviate concerns that Germany was in danger of exceeding the reference value in 2002: 'We will be clearly below. (...) We will not exceed the limit; that is already clear.'[19]

Preventing the preventive arm

The fiscal stance of Germany posed several political difficulties for the Commission. While highlighting Germany's deficit problem for procedural reasons, Commisioner Solbes was *de facto* in support of the economic substance of Eichel's policies. Germany was trying to play by the rules and even allowed a limitation in the functioning of its automatic stabilisers by raising taxes on tobacco and insurances in order to control the deficit. Solbes agreed that Germany would be wrong to raise taxes even further or to cut public spending at a time of apparent recession. Yet, the Commission risked weakening the SGP in favour of a large Member State if it failed to act, having rebuked Ireland in the previous year on yet weaker grounds.

The upcoming general elections in Germany in September 2002 made the situation even more salient politically. Presenting Germany with an early warning was bound to provoke a strong reaction from Chancellor Gerhard Schröder. But Commission officials in cooperation with the German Ministry of Finance tried to frame such a warning in a constructive manner that would strengthen Eichel's fiscal strategy internally and reinforce the government's opposition to bold wage demands by Germany's trade unions. The early warning under the preventive arm of the SGP (i.e. on the basis of regulation 1466/97) would allow Solbes to demonstrate the effectiveness of the SGP also in times of economic slowdown, while reinforcing Eichel's position in Berlin. The error in that calculation was to ignore the Chancellery, however.

On 30 January 2002, the Commission publicly expressed support for Eichel's policies and at the same time recommended the ECOFIN Council to decide on formal early warnings to Germany and Portugal,

---

[19] *Financial Times*, 18 January 2002.

which was in a similar position of approaching the reference value. Side-stepping the Ministry of Finance, the Chancellery in Berlin attempted at the last minute to convince the Commission of only adopting a critical recommendation for a Council opinion on Germany's stability pro-gramme while refraining from the more significant early warning. The domestic situation of Chancellor Schröder, facing an uphill struggle in the beginning of the election campaign, was such that he could not afford an early warning from Brussels, given that it would provide ammunition to the opposition campaign. At one point, Schröder even accused the Commission indirectly of trying to support the CDU opposition.[20] Obviously, the faltering economy had become the main issue of the electoral debate, granting a head start to Edmund Stoiber, the CDU/CSU candidate for Chancellorship. Stoiber, promoting the envied eco-nomic success of Bavaria within Germany, successfully positioned himself as more able to solve Germany's economic problems than Schröder. Schröder did not wish to have additional trouble stemming from interfer-ence by Brussels.

A Eurogroup meeting in the evening before the ECOFIN of 12 February 2002 found a compromise that prevented a vote on the issue. The Commission would have been sure to lose a vote as Germany and Portugal needed only one additional large Member State to constitute a blocking minority (France, Italy and the UK all being more than ready to vote against the early warning). In the face of these circumstances, the Commission could only try to save its face by withdrawing its recommen-dation for an early warning in exchange for declaratory but legally empty commitments of Germany and Portugal to control their deficits.

Solbes declared that the compromise fulfilled the Commission's objec-tives and proved the effectiveness of the SGP procedures which could be invoked again, whereas Eichel renewed his aim to reach budgetary bal-ance in 2004 through substantial spending cuts, praising the unanimous agreement of the fifteen EU countries as a 'clear strengthening of the Stability and Growth Pact'.[21] These statements did not prevent that, in the public eye, the credibility of the Pact was severely damaged. However, financial markets did not react; only the rating agency Standard and Poor's contemplated that Germany's triple A credit rating was not a 'birth right'.[22]

---

[20] Schröder implied that the Commission had 'other than economic' reasons for preparing an early warning (*Financial Times*, 5 February 2002). This allegation was widely under-stood to refer to DG Ecfin's Director-General Klaus Regling, who had been a close collaborator of the former CSU Finance Minister Waigel.

[21] *Financial Times*, 13 February 2002.   [22] *Financial Times*, 6 March 2002.

In the following weeks, while the German draft budget for 2003 was being negotiated in the cabinet, Eichel tried to turn the European commitments into domestic policy practice but, like Waigel ten years earlier, failed to enlist the *Länder* into a substantial national stability package. This obstruction circumvented the government's efforts to contain the general deficit. The federal budget was only partially responsible for the widening gap between public revenue and expenditure, the latter being heavily influenced by the regional governments and the social insurances. The Finance Ministry largely blamed the *Länder* for the sharp reverse in Germany's general budget deficit in 2001, which, after all, Eichel was being held accountable for in Brussels. While the federal government's deficit had increased only moderately from 1.19 per cent of GDP to 1.34 per cent, the shortfall among the states had been far more serious, growing from 0.4 per cent to 1.24 per cent. The *Länder* Prime Ministers, by contrast, replied that their revenues had fallen so dramatically because of the federal government's tax cuts, given that the states had very little control over their revenues. The 'National Stability Pact' that in the end was concluded only contained a political commitment from the *Länder* Prime Ministers to aim for balanced budgets. The federal government for its part committed to reduce its spending by 0.5 per cent in 2003 and 2004, whereas the *Länder* and communalities vowed to restrict spending increases to 1 per cent over the same period. Neither of these good intentions were kept during the aggravating downswing, nor did they help to fix the public impression of a mounting fiscal *dérapage*. For most commentators, the SGP had not been respected at the first serious instance when the underlying political commitment saw its 'baptism of fire' and had floundered immediately.

An analysis of the first three years of SGP implementation

The first three years of the implementation of the SGP seem above all to be a tale of domestic politics and, to a lesser extent, one of intergovernmentalism. There were no reasons to suggest changes to the framework from a neofunctionalist point of view. The role of experts did not change either, nor did we witness a major shift in the underlying ideas. Thus, the analysis focuses on a domestic politics approach with some ingredients from the intergovernmentalist strand towards the end of the period under consideration.

Many of the events that occurred in these first three years from 1999 to 2002 were responding to the domestic setting in which fiscal policies continued to operate. To focus just on a few countries – Germany, France, Ireland and Italy – we find in each of these cases that governments sought, for domestic political reasons, to reduce tax rates and to increase spending. In so doing, they were willing to bend the rules of the SGP as well as of the BEPG framework. Hence, for very rational reasons, they preferred meeting domestic electoral objectives rather than incurring political costs for respecting the European fiscal rules.

In Germany a new SPD Finance Minister, Oskar Lafontaine, entered office in 1998. Lafontaine had very different views about macroeconomic policy-making and European integration compared to his predecessor. He sought to influence the ECB, asking it to cut interest rates so as to boost economic growth and thereby increase employment, very much according to Keynesian thinking. Incoming Chancellor Gerhard Schröder was also focusing on employment rather than inflation. However, when Eichel replaced Lafontaine as Finance Minister in April 1999, German politics reoriented once again to fiscal consolidation. Indeed, Eichel used the SGP in domestic debates to justify his policies, with Schröder in tacit support during that time. However, in 2001 Germany cut taxes further, which increased the deficit when the period of strong economic growth ended. In France, reducing the fiscal burden had been an electoral commitment that was to be honoured even though the budget was not in surplus (unlike Germany, which benefited from very significant UMTS receipts). The government resorted to unfunded tax cuts. In Italy two years earlier, Amato had responded to domestic priorities by granting himself a more relaxed deficit target than that which had originally been agreed at the European level.

In the much discussed Irish case (see also Hodson 2004; Hodson and Maher 2004), the government was running a budgetary surplus, but when it started to reduce taxes the Commission judged in January 2001 that it was not meeting the requirements of the BEPGs. For domestic reasons too, the Irish government was not pleased with the negative Council opinion adopted at the recommendation of the Commission. In the public eye, Brussels was seen to be picking on a small country that was growing fast and outperforming other Member States in terms of economic growth and fiscal consolidation. The functional reasoning of the Commission of cautioning against procyclical policies during an upswing did not resonate with the public at large. In light of how Italy had been treated favourably in 1999, the Irish government felt comfortable in disregarding the BEPG commitment and focusing on what was necessary from a domestic politics perspective. Although strictly speaking the Irish case was not based on the SGP, its actions discredited the entire class of rules-based frameworks for economic governance in Europe.

When the downturn commenced in late 2001, Member States did not seriously consider the requirements of the SGP but rather focused on what might be the most urgent reaction for domestic political reasons. In

Germany, during the autumn of 2001, economists were calling for more expansive fiscal policies. The Commission found a German Chancellery unwilling to accept the early warning as the country was heading for an election in September 2002. Indeed, there was a power struggle domestically between the Minister of Finance and the Chancellor as to whether to accept the early warning. Predictably, the Chancellor trumped his Minister of Finance.

The intergovernmentalist interaction during this period can be identified as activities in the Council and between Member States that were flowing logically from these domestic considerations. Since no government had yet overstepped the 3 per cent of GDP deficit reference value, the interaction between Member States and the Commission at the European level concerned exclusively the preventive arm of the SGP and, in the case of Ireland, the BEPG process – both of which are based on Article 99. Economic policy coordination under that regime is considered 'soft law' and relies on consensus-based cooperation, at maximum subject to 'peer pressure'.

All experiences made with that regime under stress – Italy, Ireland, Portugal and Germany – confirm that peer pressure is insufficient to counter strong, domestically motivated preferences of national governments in case of conflict. The relevant European institutions, i.e. the Council and above all the Commission, habitually have to retreat through face-saving, rearguard actions whenever the national interest of a country trumps the requirements of an unenforceable consensus hitherto agreed at the European level.

In concrete terms, Italy's insistence on relaxing the deficit target had to be accepted by its partners. There was no legal means of preventing Rome from simply ignoring the European objective in the pursuit of its national policies. In the face of such resistance, the European bodies, primarily the Commission, can at most 'call the bluff' or acquiesce. In the case of Italy, it decided to acquiesce and accept a new budget target.

The Irish case is a different variation of the same theme. Presented with a government unwilling to translate European peer pressure into domestic action, Brussels was forced to choose between appeasement and defeat. Maybe on the basis of a miscalculation, this time, it opted for defeat – learning that national disrespect of a cause jointly supported by the Commission and the Council can even earn a government respect from its domestic, euro-sceptic constituency.

Yet again, Brussels chose to acquiesce. The Commission was concerned about the almost certain prospect of failure if it tried to issue early warnings to Germany and Portugal. Two features are of particular interest in this case. First, the likely failure of the Council to adopt a Commission recommendation on issuing an early warning became apparent in the intergovernmental setting of the Eurogroup, where Germany and Portugal were able to muster a sufficient blocking minority (even majority) by enlisting potential allies. This constellation was to be repeated under different auspices in 2003, when Germany and France engineered a similar blocking minority under the EDP (see the following chapter).

Second, faced with the compelling logic of the intergovernmental dynamics, the Commission knew it would be fighting a losing battle. However, unlike later in 2003, it decided to give in, withdrew its recommendation and agreed to a political commitment by Germany and Portugal, the sole purpose of which was to save the Commission's face. One year later, under the EDP, it decided to pick the fight and lose. Apparently, in 2002, the underlying strategy was not to escalate further and to contain the damage wrought to the credibility of the SGP.

The Commission and the Council were keen to portray the result of the 2002 confrontation with Germany and Portugal as proof of the 'flexibility' of the Pact as well as of the 'pragmatic' approach of the Commission for implementing it. In a legal sense, this approach was correct, since the 'bite' of the entire framework is not any automatic application but ultimately the political will to sustain prior self-commitments for the sake of prudent fiscal policy. The domestic politics approach explains why such a commitment cannot be taken for granted and intergovernmentalism explains how shifting domestic priorities translate into European dynamics that can bear little resemblance to previous declarations.

In a similar vein, we will now turn to the more serious events that unfolded under the corrective arm of the Pact once governments had overstepped the budgetary reference value.

7   From bad times to crisis

This chapter deals with the SGP crisis of 25 November 2003 and the period running up to that dramatic ECOFIN Council. It contains two main sections. The first offers an account of the events; the second an analysis drawing on a composite version of our methodological apparatus, in particular the domestic and intergovernmental approaches with some ingredients of the other two perspectives.

The initiation of EDPs

In April 2002, a centre-right coalition came into power in Portugal. The new government under José Manuel Durão Barroso not only accepted the Commission's critical stance on the budgetary situation but, stating that the socialists had 'left the country in rags', Barroso went a step further and asked the nation to 'make a patriotic effort to save'.[1] The 2002 budget was revised and austerity measures were adopted, including a 2 per cent increase of the VAT rate and a postponement of planned corporate tax cuts besides efforts to reduce public expenditure. Barroso successfully employed the SGP framework and accepted in particular the placing of his fiscal policies under the EDP regime. Portugal was the first country to be found in excessive deficit in 2003 and its government used the SGP as an external constraint for making the consolidation course domestically acceptable (see below). This strategy implied close cooperation between the government and the Commission. The measures over time did not fail to produce the desired effects and the Barroso government was eventually able to correct the excessive deficit under the EDP.

Before the autumn of 2002, general elections were held not only in Portugal but also in France, Germany and Italy. These four countries were also those that experienced the greatest difficulties in disciplining their public finances. The coincidence of the domestic electoral calendar

---

[1] *Financial Times*, 2 May 2002.

and world economic conditions implied additional strain on the SGP, which materialised especially in France and Germany.

French President Jacques Chirac was determined to keep the promised tax cuts, having learnt in 1997 that the electorate does not easily forget reneging behaviour on the part of the government. More importantly, as opposed to 1997, in Stage III of EMU there was no Maastricht convergence criterion to meet and hence less external pressure to contain the deficit. This different approach already indicated that the original intention of the German SGP proposal in 1995, i.e. perpetuating the disciplining pressure of the budgetary convergence criterion, could not be achieved by the SGP. Having won the presidential election, Chirac refused to back down on planned tax cuts and higher security spending in the run-up to the June general election. He further postponed the target date of reaching the MTO of CTBOIS to 2007. European Ministers of Finance, above all those from small Member States, were highly critical about what they saw as a further undermining of the credibility of the SGP. Target dates for reaching budgetary balance were generally based on optimistic growth expectations and it became frequent practice to postpone these 'moving targets' when fiscal developments failed to turn out as projected. A centre-right coalition won the French general election in June 2002, terminating the undesired *cohabitation* with Jospin and rendering parliamentary and presidential control to Chirac.

After the French election, the ECOFIN Council of 20 June 2002 was scheduled to address the issue of setting new budgetary targets under the preventive arm of the SGP and the BEPG. A deal was eventually struck by the ECOFIN Ministers in the morning hours of a highly controversial meeting where the smaller Member States fought in vain for a strict reading of the BEPG documents. The compromise text on the BEPG for France replaced the zero deficit set for 2004 with the aim of a deficit 'close to balance' (which Commissioner Solbes interpreted as containing up to half a percentage point) and made the 2003 and 2004 targets conditional on the unlikely event of growth performing at least at 3 per cent of GDP. The provisions had thereby lost most of their commitment value, since already in August the French government had hinted that 3 per cent growth would not be achievable.[2] The Ministers also toned down the text of the BEPGs for the UK, Italy and Portugal. Most countries insisted on the fact that their commitments would be invalidated if economic growth turned out lower than expected.

---

[2] This episode shows similarity with the developments in 2007, when incoming President Nicolas Sarkozy again based the budgetary targets on rather unrealistic economic growth assumptions.

The Italian government immediately used the opportunity to advance tax cuts and increase spending on unemployment benefits, both measures being electoral promises that Berlusconi still had to honour. Italian officials greeted the BEPG compromise as a shift to 'a political approach to the stability pact'[3] and joined the British Chancellor of the Exchequer, Gordon Brown, in highlighting the fact that Finance Ministers at the ECOFIN Council were dealing with the SGP in a more flexible and pragmatic manner than the Commission. Giulio Tremonti, Italian Minister of Finance, even asserted a shift of power from the Commission to ECOFIN, which for him represented a 'move from technocracy to democracy' that would enable a 'reinterpretation' of the SGP, altering the focus from stability to growth and flexibility.[4] He demanded the exclusion of government spending on infrastructure, defence, structural reforms and overseas aid from the definition of the 'Maastricht' deficit.

In the meantime, on 19 June 2002, the German government had approved its draft budget for 2003. It was drawn up to display superficially a firm commitment to the SGP requirements, including the target to reach budgetary balance by 2004. Federal government spending was planned to fall by 0.5 per cent of GDP in 2003 and a further 0.2 per cent in 2004; the deficit was estimated to drop from 2.7 per cent of GDP in 2001 to 2.5 per cent in 2002 and 1.5 per cent in 2003. However, the fact that the draft budget was of a provisional nature and would only be adopted by Parliament after the September general election reduced the reliability of these announcements. In addition, the targets were rightfully criticised for being based on unrealistic growth assumptions, as was the case in most other Member States. Indeed, the Finance Ministry announced in July that nominal tax revenues of the first half of 2002 had turned out to be 5.2 per cent lower than in the previous year, pointing to further fiscal imbalances.

In a speech on 9 July 2002, Commissioner Solbes reacted to the mounting criticism and outlined a more flexible interpretation of the rules. At an ECOFIN meeting three days later, he announced 'common standards' which should apply exclusively to countries with balanced budgets, low levels of public debt and low pension liabilities. The latter issue and the theme of fiscal sustainability more generally had in the meantime acquired the growing attention of fiscal experts who sought to introduce related concepts to the SGP surveillance framework. According to Solbes, countries who had reached their MTO in structural terms and who displayed sustainable fiscal positions could be authorised to run higher deficits in order to fund public investment and reforms as long as

---

[3] *Financial Times*, 24 June 2002.   [4] *Financial Times*, 25 June 2002.

they stayed below 3 per cent. Conversely, countries such as Greece or Italy, with high levels of national debt and high implicit liabilities, would be given only minimal room for manoeuvre. In line with the academic debate on economic policy, the Commission argued that, for a given budget volume, the 'quality of public spending' should be raised by making expenditure both more effective and efficient – for example, by increasing the proportion of growth-enhancing spending, such as investment, over consumptive expenditure. Also, on the revenue side, the Commission sought to promote 'quality', for example by encouraging Member States to shift from direct to indirect taxes. The guiding principle was, however, that these rules could only come into operation once the requirements of the corrective arm of the Pact were fulfilled and, specifically, after any excessive deficit had been corrected. In other words, Solbes was trying to add some 'carrots' to the 'sticks' of the SGP, by aiming to increase the incentives for Member States in the preventive arm to abide by the rules of the corrective arm.

On 10 July 2002 French Minister of Finance Francis Mer won cabinet approval for his revised 2002 budget. Government spending for law and order was increased as a reaction to the surprising success of the extreme right under Jean-Marie Le Pen in the presidential elections. At the same time, the rate of personal income tax was cut by 5 per cent as promised by Chirac in the election campaign. The new 2002 deficit estimate stood at 2.6 per cent of GDP, which meant that France was also approaching the 3 per cent limit. Meanwhile, Italy announced tax cuts for low and middle incomes as well as for corporations. Ignoring the SGP commitments made a few weeks earlier, Tremonti announced a deficit of 0.8 per cent for 2003 which was equivalent to admitting that he would no longer aim for a 'close to balance' budget with a deficit target of 0.5 per cent. At the same time, the official growth forecast was reduced by an entire percentage point to 1.3 per cent of GDP, which experts still deemed over optimistic.

On 25 July 2002, Portugal presented an upward revision of its 2001 budget deficit to 4.1 per cent of GDP, which meant that the reference value had already been overstepped prior to the retrenchment efforts of the Barroso government (see above). The Commission announced that an EDP would immediately be initiated, with the first step being taken in September, namely the preparation of a report under Article 104.3. The government continued to cooperate and was confident that the existing, and if necessary additional, austerity measures would rein in the deficit before sanctions would have to be applied. Finance Minister Manuela Ferreira Leite reiterated the government's commitment to reaching budgetary balance by the end of 2004.

On 6 September 2002, the Eurogroup assembled on the eve of the ECOFIN Council in Copenhagen to debate the growing strain on the

SGP against the background of an increasingly worrying economic outlook. The weak recovery was expected to put further pressure on the
already critical deficits of Portugal, Germany, France and Italy. The
meeting fuelled speculation that the four countries would fail to fulfil
their BEPG commitments in the light of drastic downward revisions of
forecasts for growth and government revenues. Germany, France and
Italy ran the risk of joining Portugal in exceeding the 3 per cent limit. At
the same time, pressure was coming from Italy, and to a lesser extent
France, for a looser reinterpretation of the SGP, whereas the German
government reiterated its commitment to the Pact and Portugal was seen
to cooperate with the Commission. Small Member States were particularly opposed to any talk of reforming the framework. However, around
the same time that Schröder very narrowly won the general election on
22 September, it became clear that Germany would breach the deficit
limit of 3 per cent in 2002. It was also obviously unrealistic to cling to the
goal of achieving a 'close to balance' budget in 2004. The official deficit
forecast for 2002 of which the Commission was notified in September –
after the election – still stayed narrowly below 3 per cent, but it was seen as
likely that the reference value would be overstepped with the final notification of 2002 data, expected in spring 2003.

Following a request by Commission President Prodi, on 24 September,
Solbes contended that the 2004 target for balanced budgets had to be
extended for a number of countries. The Commission tried to engineer an
EU-wide postponement of the target to 2006 as a one-off tactical retreat,
stressing the ability of the SGP to adapt flexibly to changed circumstances.
The Commission, referring to the new 'common standards' that were
being prepared for the application of the SGP, also announced that more
emphasis would be put on *structural* balances in order to assess the underlying stance of fiscal policy and increase the 'economic rationale' of the
Pact.[5] Member States showing a lack of will to play by the rules would be
encouraged to cut their structural deficits by 0.5 percentage points each
year, a figure that was to reappear as a common benchmark in future
applications of the EDP and for the 'adjustment path' to the MTO. The
small Member States were dismayed, arguing that in practice a different
set of rules was used for the large countries. The Commission argued that
the 2004 target would quickly have become impossible to defend against the
lack of ability and willingness of the laggard countries to endorse it in practice.

---

[5] Structural deficit figures are calculated from the nominal values while controlling for the
effects of the economic cycle and deducting one-off and temporary measures. The calculation
of the cyclical component of a deficit is contentious, depending inter alia on competing
methodologies as well as assumptions about the potential growth rate of an economy.

The Commission was particularly concerned about the political priorities of France and Italy who, compared to Germany and particularly Portugal, showed less willingness and determination to reduce their deficits. Solbes was seen as trying to support Hans Eichel, just reappointed as German Minister of Finance, in his domestic quest for budgetary discipline. In the negotiations of forming the new 'red-green' governing coalition in Germany, Eichel was even said to have threatened to resign if the course of consolidation was not kept and the budget not drawn up as required by the SGP. The Commission hoped to divide the front of its two main critics – France and Italy – by isolating Italy and making France move towards Eichel's restrictive stance.

However, on 25 September 2002 the French government passed a 2003 budget that, above all, implemented Chirac's promises of a further 1 per cent cut in the income tax and yet another reduction in corporate taxation. At the same time the government significantly increased the military budget as well as spending on justice and domestic security. After a sizeable decline in popularity, Prime Minister Raffarin tried to regain the initiative by enacting a series of policy measures in the areas of health and employment. These, in turn, had implications for budgetary policy and pointed to a further increase in public spending and in the deficit. The only significant cuts occured in the areas of cultural policy and research. The decision to suspend the process of deficit reduction was explained by the problems of other partner countries and the generally weak economic climate. The deficit projection for 2003 of 2.6 per cent of GDP, holding constant the expected 2002 level, was again based on highly optimistic growth forecasts. The target of coming close to budgetary balance by the end of 2004 was officially dropped. Finance Minister Francis Mer even suggested that the deficit was there to stay beyond 2006, which straight away undermined the credibility of the postponement offered by the Commission.

Commissioner Solbes criticised the French budget sharply and hinted at the possibility of an early warning. At a Eurogroup meeting on 7 October 2002, Mer refused to amend his budget and triggered a heated exchange, which was considered the most serious rift in the group since the launch of the euro. All Ministers except Mer agreed on Council conclusions stressing the need for further cutting deficits. Germany, Italy and Portugal committed to annual reductions of their structural deficits by 0.5 percentage points, whereas Mer insisted that France would not start doing so before 2004. The ECOFIN meeting of the following day saw very outspoken criticism from ECB President Duisenberg directed at France but also at Germany and Italy for failing to bring their public finances under control. Mer was outvoted on the text of the Council conclusions and retorted: 'We have decided there were other priorities in France – for instance increasing military spending. Other countries have not taken this kind of decision, but we are still in a Europe where budgetary policy and political decisions are still under national control.'[6]

Portugal, by contrast, approved a 2003 budget at the beginning of October 2002 that was geared towards bringing the deficit down to below 3 per cent. Planned government spending was cut significantly by 10 per cent, leaving the projected deficit at 2.4 per cent of GDP despite mounting domestic opposition to the austerity measures. These were proving effective and the 2002 deficit was on its way to coming down to 2.8 per cent. Unlike France and Italy, Prime Minister Barroso had broken promises on tax cuts made in the election campaign and had not made use of the extended 2006 deadline for bringing the budget close to balance. The government kept its course despite continuing protests throughout 2002, including a general strike in December of that year .

The German government, in the domestic context of negotiations on the relaunch of the red-green coalition during the first half of October following the election, softened the deficit reduction targets on the adjustment path to reaching the MTO by the end of 2006, postponing much of the consolidation effort. This softening was a defeat for Eichel who had tried to push for additional spending cuts and for front-loading the adjustment effort, in line with the strategy laid out in the stability programme. Observers noted that the French attitude not to honour European commitments seemed increasingly to influence a number of German actors, who became more used to the idea of relaxing the course of budgetary consolidation. However, both political parties stated that they were committed to honouring the ultimate 3 per cent limit of the SGP and, indeed, decided on 14 October 2002 to implement spending cuts (predominantly in the area of subsidies) and *de facto* tax rises (through reducing tax expenditures and closing 'loopholes', i.e. expanding the tax base, in particular for corporate and private income taxes). This move was conceived as a strong signal to the public, the Commission and, above all, to the ECB that the government was still intending to honour the SGP. Nevertheless, the more substantial elements of the package were subsequently blocked by the CDU opposition-dominated *Länder* representation, the *Bundesrat*, and hence failed to materialise.

On 16 October 2002, the domestic blocking of the consolidation package induced Eichel to admit that the German deficit for 2002 would

---

[6] *Financial Times*, 10 October 2002.

breach the 3 per cent reference value. Having defended a near miss of 2.9 per cent in the election campaign, the new government finally had to present the facts. While preparing the launch of an EDP for Germany, Commissioner Solbes nevertheless made clear that the German government had decided on strict measures to bring the deficit back down below 3 per cent of GDP. It was therefore to be expected that the Commission would pursue the EDP with leniency as long as Germany cooperated, as was the case with Portugal. Without a change of government, however, Eichel found it more difficult than the Portuguese government to explain how the excessive deficit had materialised right after the election.

On 17 October 2002, Commission President Prodi declared in an interview that the SGP was 'stupid, like all rigid decisions'.[7] He stated that the Commission was trying to interpret the rules more flexibly and intelligently but that it lacked the authority for enforcement. Prodi's widely quoted remark on the *Pacte de Stupidité*, as it became known in a jocular fashion, was welcomed by the critics of the framework, notably France. Other governments, trying hard to implement the requirements of the SGP to their domestic audiences, felt betrayed and reacted strongly against the position taken by the Commission President. Defending his remark, Prodi stated that he had wanted to open up the public debate, arguing that strict rules were needed to underpin the euro but that they should be interpreted flexibly.[8] He hinted at desirable changes, such as a strengthened role of the Commission, which should be entitled to issue early warnings and declare deficits to be excessive on its own account and without the need to obtain ECOFIN approval.

In the meantime, Eichel assured the Commission that Berlin would accept the launch of an EDP against Germany. This was becoming increasingly likely, as a preliminary Commission projection in late October showed Germany's budgetary deficit at 3.7 per cent of GDP for 2002 (based on an estimated shortfall in government revenue of around €14 billion) and 3.2 per cent for 2003. Hence, a deficit in excess of the reference value was to be expected for at least two consecutive years. Reducing the deficit below 3 per cent would imply a retrenchment effort even harder than the already decided €11.6 billion package of tax rises and spending cuts that had just been blocked by the opposition, and it was unclear how Eichel would circumvent this domestic political hurdle in the federal chamber, the *Bundesrat*.

On 13 November 2002, the Commission officially revised downwards its growth forecasts for France and Germany, revealing expected deficits

---

[7] *Le Monde*, 17 October 2002.   [8] *Financial Times*, 22 October 2002.

of 3.8 per cent for Germany in 2002 and 2.9 per cent for France in the following year. On that occasion, Solbes initiated an EDP in the case of Germany and an early warning to France. Three days later the Commission collegiate approved Solbes' move and formally issued the respective Commission recommendations to the ECOFIN Council. Eichel and Mer both signalled cooperation; Eichel stating that the 2003 budget would be back below 3 per cent, and Mer announcing that 'we don't need to modify the Pact because it is our responsibility to succeed in controlling deficits'.[9] Meanwhile, the Italian government imposed a curb on public spending with the exception of debt servicing and pension handouts. The move was intended to prevent Italy from joining the ranks of Portugal, Germany and France.

At the end of November 2002, the Commission launched an ambitious reform programme for the SGP. Prodi proposed a twin-track strategy to apply 'more intelligence and authority'[10] to economic governance, providing more flexibility to countries that had already achieved sound public finances while retaining a strict stance towards those with notoriously large levels of debt. Incorporating debt levels to a greater extent into the evaluation of a country's situation would allow those states with low debt levels to incur higher deficits for public investment and structural reforms. Debt inclusion had repeatedly been demanded by the UK Treasury under Gordon Brown, who was seeking to mould the SGP along domestic lines and more in the way of the 'golden rule' approach followed in the UK, by which investment spending is deducted from the deficit ceiling. Portugal, Germany, France and likely also Italy, however, would still be required under the new approach and in light of their budgetary situation to reduce their structural deficit by 0.5 percentage points of GDP each year in order to regain and undercut the reference value by a generous safety margin. Countries with very high levels of public debt (predominantly Belgium, Italy and Greece with figures over 100 per cent of GDP) would be required to lay out ambitious consolidation plans, backed up by a sanctioning scheme. In addition, the Commission proposed an enhanced role for itself, such as the issuance of early warnings on its own account (i.e. without requiring Council approval) in cases where countries failed to cut their deficits in times of economic growth. The reforms would be proposed for approval by the spring 2003 European Council in Brussels, following discussions by ECOFIN Ministers over the months to come.

---

[9] *Financial Times*, 20 November 2002.   [10] *Financial Times*, 28 November 2002.

At the end of 2002, the Portuguese government claimed to have achieved 'victory' over its budgetary deficit, which had been brought down from 4.1 per cent of GDP in 2001 to 2.8 per cent in 2002, thanks to extensive austerity measures. The stability programme submitted to Brussels envisaged further reducing the deficit to 2.4 per cent of GDP in 2003 on the way to coming close to balance in 2006. Growth was expected to rise from 0.7 per cent per annum in 2002 to 1.3 per cent and 3.5 per cent in the subsequent years, well above the euro-area average. Prime Minister Barroso admitted that the deficit reduction was partially generated by one-off measures but was able to point to successful structural reforms underlying the improvement in public spending. Finance Minister Manuela Ferriera Leite commented on the SGP positively: 'The big advantage of the Pact is that it imposes a sustainable containment of public spending that encourages structural reform.'[11] In early 2003, Barroso even lauded the Pact of living up to the ingenuity of Ulysses: 'The Pact helps a government to tie itself to the mast and resist the sirens who are trying to lure us to destruction with seductive songs of more state spending and bigger bureaucracies'[12] (see also Dyson et al., 1995, who had made a similar comparison about disciplinary mechanisms in central banking).

At the beginning of 2003, the Commission reacted strongly to the stability programmes of France, Italy and particularly Germany. Commissioner Solbes warned that Berlin and Paris could surpass the 3 per cent limit in 2003, which would be the second consecutive year in the German case, and that Italy could break the limit in 2004. He urged the three largest euro-area countries to take immediate measures to contain their deficits and accused them of relying on systematically over-optimistic growth forecasts.

A Eurogroup meeting on the eve of the ECOFIN of 21 January 2003 brought agreement to issue an early warning to France as well as a request to reduce the structural deficit by 0.5 percentage points. Finance Minister Mer was isolated in trying to prevent that outcome. The decision to open an EDP in the case of Germany was endorsed without debate. At the ECOFIN, Mer abstained as his fourteen colleagues approved the early warning, which was the first instance of EU Finance Ministers taking a vote in the context of the SGP framework. He threatened not to obey the prescriptions on France's budgetary policy due to his country's economic problems. Solbes dismissed the French position, arguing that 'France, being a member of the Union, cannot ignore the obligations of the Treaty (…) otherwise we will have a credibility problem. France's budgetary

[11] *Financial Times*, 27 December 2002.   [12] *Financial Times*, 29 January 2002.

problems will not go away by simply ignoring them.'[13] Mer, in turn, criticised the rigidity of the Pact and, referring to the USA, stated that the EU's demands for a reduction in public expenditure at a time of slow economic growth would be counterproductive. The EDP on Germany was, by contrast, initiated unanimously. Solbes found particularly vocal support for his staunch line among several smaller Member States, above all Austria, the Netherlands, Luxembourg and Finland.

In early February 2003 the updated statistics suggested that the French deficit for 2002 would be 2.9 per cent or exactly 3 per cent of GDP, which the Commission saw as a vindication for its stern course. Later in the month, Prime Minister Raffarin admitted, however, that the limit had already been overshot in 2002 and that this was likely to happen again in 2003. At the same time he rejected austerity measures or a postponement of tax cuts. The definite figure for the 2002 deficit was reported in early March 2003 and turned out to be exactly 3.038 per cent of GDP. Mer stated that this was sufficiently close to 3 per cent as not to warrant the initiation of an EDP. However, the deficit for 2003 was already projected to be 3.4 per cent.

In early March 2003, the Eurogroup and ECOFIN discussed the development of the French deficit as well as the Commission's reform plans for the SGP. These issues were linked – a number of countries were highly critical of the French *nonchalance* about the common rules. Because they saw some degree of weakening in the Commission's reform proposals, they also opposed any changes to the Pact, although another set of countries strongly encouraged the Commission in its new course, notably the UK, France and Germany. Ministers only agreed on a minimal solution, mainly the principle of taking into account country-specific circumstances as well as the quality of public finances when evaluating the budgetary situation of a Member State for a report under Article 104.3. A new, informal rule for countries with high deficits was envisaged, consisting of a self-commitment to reduce the structural deficit by half a percentage point each year. The UK was explicitly exempted from this agreement.

In early April 2003, the Commission issued its recommendation for a decision on the existence of an excessive deficit in France. It stated that France risked breaking the deficit limit again unless urgent action was taken, which implied once more that President Chirac would face the choice of reneging on his European commitments or his electoral promises. With ongoing sensitive negotiations between the government and

[13] *Financial Times*, 22 January 2002.

public sector unions on pension reforms, the domestic situation appeared unfavourable to further retrenchment measures. The spring forecasts of the Commission further reduced the growth outlook for the euro area and also highlighted the danger that Italy could be facing a deficit in excess of 3 per cent by the end of 2004.

Early in May, the Commission publicly called on the French government to cut spending or raise taxes before October 2003 in order to start bringing down its budget deficit below 3 per cent by 2004. The use of comparatively strong language reflected the belief in Brussels that most of France's budget problems were home-grown and due to tax cuts and increased spending rather than external circumstances. French Prime Minister Raffarin promised to curb public spending in 2004 but found himself domestically in an increasingly heated stand-off with public sector employees over the persisting issue of pension reform. At the same time, quarterly growth performance had turned negative for the first time since 1991.

On 11 May, the German government officially dropped its aim of reaching budgetary balance by 2006 when it released the spring estimate of the 2003 tax revenues. 'A balanced budget by 2006 would require growth rates that I cannot realistically expect,' stated Schröder. 'And if achieving this aim meant cutting spending as much as revenues are falling, or giving up the 2005 step of the tax reform, I would not be ready for it.'[14] The Commission pointed out that the move did not imply that Germany would fail in its commitments under the SGP, specifically the task of reducing the deficit below 3 per cent and to continuously trim down the structural deficit by half a percentage point each year.

The question of how to deal with the French deficit remained highly controversial. Francis Mer won a period of nearly twelve months before the government would be obliged to get the problem under control. The Commission had no choice but to acknowledge the existing budgetary plan for 2003 in the French stability programme (entailing a deficit of 3.4 per cent) and, while obtaining the launch of an EDP on 3 June 2003, had to accept the postponement of retrenchment measures. In exchange, the French government committed to starting a process of budgetary consolidation in 2004 that would include reductions in public expenditure and smaller than planned tax cuts. The French solution was in stark contrast to the course taken by Germany and Portugal – these two countries had pledged to reduce their deficits in the same year in which the EDP was opened, as implied by the SGP. However, Germany would not

[14] *Tagesspiegel*, 11 May 2003.

be required to impose additional measures if growth turned out even lower than expected. Over the following months, the Commission visibly distinguished between the cooperative attitude of Germany and Portugal on the one hand and the more aggressive stance of France on the other, which met with a less conciliatory approach from Brussels.

Heading for crisis

In July 2003, the German government decided to press ahead in 2004 with income tax cuts that had originally been planned for 2005, admitting that, as a result, Germany could record a deficit above the reference value for a third consecutive year in 2004. The aim to respect the 3 per cent reference value had been based on an unrealistic growth expectation of 2 per cent for 2004 and over optimistic privatisation plans. In addition, a large proportion of the saving measures already accounted for in Eichel's budgetary planning was likely to be vetoed by the opposition in the *Bundesrat*, the upper chamber of Parliament in which the *Länder* are represented. A number of smaller EU Member States joined the Commission in criticising the course of the German government. France, by contrast, praised the German strategy of using tax cuts in order to revive economic growth. Schröder, for his part, increased the verbal pressure on the ECB to deliver a cut in interest rates, warning that his country could slip into recession if not deflation otherwise. The ECB, for its part, repeated that it had contributed its share for creating growth-inducing conditions by providing price stability and anchoring expectations of a low-inflationary environment. Meanwhile, Italy confidently presented a four-year programme with the intention to maintain the deficit well below the threshold level of 3 per cent. About two-thirds of the containment was, however, to be achieved through one-off measures such as tax amnesties and the securitisation of future revenues from state property.

On 14 July, the French national day, President Chirac demanded a 'provisional formula' and a 'political interpretation' of the SGP to make it more flexible and to help stimulate depressed growth. This request for changes, as of yet the most forceful one, was immediately rebuffed by the Commission, with Solbes arguing that the Pact did not need to be modified.[15] Chirac's remarks led to a serious dispute in the Eurogroup. The smaller Member States were highly critical of the lack of respect of the common rules on the part of France. Austrian Minister of Finance Grasser even broke the Eurogroup's code of secrecy and infuriated

[15] *Financial Times*, 15 July 2003.

French civil servants by announcing that France's Finance Minister Mer had admitted over dinner to be heading deliberately for another year of excessive deficit in 2004. Grasser in turn was accused by French sources of trying to 'kill the Eurogroup'.[16]

Towards the end of the month, the French government scaled back its plans to cut public sector employment, showing the underlying difficulties of Prime Minister Raffarin in addressing the vested interests behind the persistently high levels of state expenditure. The militancy of the public sector trade unions had taken the government by surprise. At that time, Nikos Christodoulakis, Greek Finance Minister, accused the large Member States of threatening the economies of smaller euro-area countries by calling the SGP into question. He reproached some of his colleagues about 'demonising' the SGP,[17] thereby seeking to undermine its rules on government borrowing. Austria, Finland, Greece, Ireland, the Netherlands and Spain each sent strong signals that they expected the Commission to defend and enforce the Pact against France and Germany.

In mid-August, the Commission became increasingly critical also of Germany and gradually gave up treating Paris and Berlin differently. The German government had made a deficit reduction dependent on the opposition signing up to the refinancing package of cutting subsidies in order to facilitate tax cuts. To the degree that the Christian Democrats withheld their support, Germany was bound even to increase its deficit rather than reduce it back down to 3 per cent. Eichel was turning to Brussels, showing that his hands were tied by domestic circumstances. In light of this development, Solbes hinted at the initiation of the next step of the EDP: 'If Germany breaches the Stability Pact's 3 per cent ceiling next year, we will present ECOFIN with a new recommendation. It is our duty.'[18] A recommendation under Article 104.8 (stating that the measures taken were not sufficient) could even be brought forward as early as November, depending on the autumn forecasts of the Commission. The Bundesbank immediately joined the Commission in warning that a third consecutive breach of the SGP limit was a concrete possibility.

At the end of August 2003, it became clear that France would breach the 3 per cent limit in the current as well as the coming year. The deficit estimates for 2003 moved between 3.7 per cent and 3.9 per cent of GDP. In a meeting with Commission President Prodi, Prime Minister Raffarin pleaded for an easing of the SGP's application, arguing that weaker than expected growth had rendered the initial projections obsolete. Prodi, however, stated publicly that the Commission had no choice but to initiate

[16] *Financial Times*, 30 July 2003   [17] *Financial Times*, 30 July 2003.
[18] *Financial Times*, 18 August 2003.

the sanctioning mechanism of the EDP in the cases of France and Germany if both countries recorded deficits above the reference value for three consecutive years. He declared that the Pact was already being applied with maximum flexibility but that eventually the rules had to be upheld: 'Let there be no misunderstanding, the Commission must and will apply the Treaty for the common good.'[19] This stance was strongly endorsed by the small Member States, including some of the accession countries that were to join the EU in 2004. A spokesman for the Slovak Finance Ministry declared: 'We are doing everything we can to fulfil the EU's criteria so we can get into the eurozone. The pressure on candidate countries is enormous. The rules should be valid for all countries.'[20] There was also widespread apprehension that it would be detrimental to distinguish between large and small Member States in the application of the Pact. The impression that a different set of rules applied to large and small Member States was seen to have contributed to a 'no' vote in the Swedish referendum on adopting the single currency in September 2003.

Suspending the EDPs

Meanwhile, Germany sided more clearly with France and abandoned the course of cooperation with the Commission. Chancellor Schröder perceived a growing alliance of EU Member States willing to risk a confrontation with the Commission on the SGP: 'We don't want to leave the Stability Pact but we want to interpret it in an economically sensible way. It is my impression that this is the view of many countries, and will become the view of others.'[21] This change in communication contributed to rapidly worsening relations between Germany and the Commission as well as between larger and smaller Member States. Schröder clearly stated that Germany's position was 'shared by the French government and I haven't seen Italy taking a different position'.[22] The Franco-German tandem, normally seen to support European integration, seemed to have regained the highest levels of mutual understanding, trust and cooperation – this time in opposing the SGP. Both leaders, Chirac and Schröder, demonstrated their good relations and even personal friendship to one another. Their alliance was reinforced simultaneously in the field of foreign policy (by jointly opposing the US-led intervention in Iraq) and in the area of European economic policy (by joining forces to prevent a strict implementation of the SGP).

[19] *Financial Times*, 28 August 2003.   [20] *Financial Times*, 28 August 2003.
[21] *Financial Times*, 29 August 2003.   [22] *Financial Times*, 29 August 2003.

Behind the scenes it was understood that the Commission was trying to convince the French and German governments to acquiesce in the implementation of Article 104.9, while leaving the recommended measures sufficiently vague as to allow maximum flexibility in its application, which would not lead to sanctions in the foreseeable future. This move would uphold the impression that the Pact was being rigidly applied while allowing significant room for manoeuvre – without undermining the credibility of the framework even further. France, in principle, was willing to accept that deal. Yet the German Chancellery had developed a categorical resistance to activating Article 104.9 and would rather have accepted more stringent measures to be proposed in a new recommendation under Article 104.7 – which obviously would not have had the same force as recommendations under Article 104.9 that would at least hypothetically be backed by sanctions.

The underlying reasoning in Berlin was twofold. First, control over budgetary policy had under no circumstance to be relinquished to Brussels – but the regime of Article 104.9 would at least have implied quarterly reports on budgetary measures to Brussels. Second, it was completely unacceptable to the Chancellor that the question of converting a 'stability deposit' into a 'fine' could potentially arise in the year of a general election, 2006, even if the Commission tacitly promised not to proceed with sanctions – both sides knowing perfectly well that the 'quasi-automaticity' announced back in 1995 did not exist in reality. Realising that Germany would not move and rather risk a head-on collision with the Commission, France abandoned its comparatively conciliatory attitude and joined forces with Berlin. In the following weeks, Germany and France mustered the coalition for a blocking minority against Council decisions on Articles 104.8 and 104.9.

The Commission tried to continue its tactic of 'divide and rule', publicly singling out France as the main culprit for the culminating crisis. Whereas Germany and especially Portugal were lauded for doing everything possible to comply with the Pact, France was accused by a Commission spokesman of having let its budgetary policy 'run off the rails'.[23] This statement came as a reaction to yet another upward revision of the French 2003 deficit in early September, at the time projected at exactly 4 per cent of GDP. The Commission even held France responsible for having caused the aggregated euro-area budgetary deficit to exceed 3 per cent in 2003. The symbolic importance of the Commission speaking out against France drew out the stark contrast between the performance of

---

[23] *Financial Times*, 3 September 2003.

that country on the one hand and that of the small and medium-sized Member States on the other hand. France, for its part, felt unjustly treated – the feeling was that it took the blame for simply being more honest about its budgetary reality than Germany, which *de facto* was in a similarly precarious situation.

On 4 September 2003, the French government set the stage for a showdown with the Commission, announcing a 3 per cent cut in its income tax, which made it certain that the deficit reference value would be exceeded in 2004 yet again. Economists cautioned that, based on realistic growth assumptions, the deficit could expand even to 4.5 per cent of GDP in 2004 as a result. Prime Minister Raffarin polemically declared on television: 'My first duty is to employment and not to solving accounting equations and mathematical problems until some office or other in some country or other is satisfied.'[24] Finland spearheaded the counteraction of the small Member States, urging the Commission to apply the Pact strictly. Chancellor Gerhard Schröder, by contrast, supported Chirac and declared after a Franco-German summit in Dresden that France and Germany agreed on 'the rejection of a dogmatic focus on one aim in the Pact'.[25]

The ECOFIN Council assembled in Stresa, Italy, on 12 September and featured very outspoken criticism of France from most Member States. According to rumours, a compromise floated around in which the loophole of 'special circumstances', delineated in the resolution of the European Council of June 1997 on the SGP, could be applied in exchange for a French 2004 draft budget (due to be presented at the end of the month) that entailed a significant reduction of the deficit. But Gerrit Zalm, Minister of Finance of the Netherlands, raised the stakes and threatened to take the Commission to the ECJ should it fail to propose recommendations for decisions on Articles 104.8 and 104.9. Zalm himself had to impose significant spending cuts on his 2004 budget and was using the SGP as an external framework by which to contain the mounting pressures in his own country. In early November, Austrian Minister of Finance Grasser also signalled his readiness to sue the Commission should it fail to initiate sanctions against France.

France unveiled its 2004 budget plan without any clear signals on further efforts at consolidation – rather to the contrary, the level of public debt was permitted to rise above the reference value of 60 per cent of GDP. The expected deficit in 2004 was 3.6 per cent. Chirac defended the deliberate violation of the SGP as a conscientious choice for growth and employment. The plan was to reach a deficit figure of 2.9 per cent in 2005, again based on rather unrealistic growth expectations. The Commission

---

[24] Television française 1, 5 September 2003.   [25] *Financial Times*, 5 September 2003.

indicated that it would be prepared to launch an enforcement action under Articles 104.8 and 104.9 in response to the draft budget. The deadline of 3 October passed without France having presented a plan for deficit reduction as demanded by ECOFIN.

After an ECOFIN meeting on 7 October 2003, the situation seemed salvageable with France committing to extra measures and a clear promise to regain a deficit level below 3 per cent in 2005. Having gained an extra year, the French government still seemed to be willing to accept the additional measures being framed within the procedure of Article 104.9. The requested measures were expected to amount to a tightening of the structural deficit by 1 per cent of GDP in 2004 plus a further 0.5 per cent in 2005 and the implementation of structural reforms. Only Austria, Finland and the Netherlands at that moment were still prepared to adopt a hard line against France and to request the deficit to be reduced below 3 per cent in 2004. The compromise appeared to be possible particularly due to Francis Mer's more conciliatory stance, assuaging the demands of previously hawkish countries like Spain.

However, after the ECOFIN meeting Germany reduced its growth forecast for 2003 down to a mere 0.25 per cent. New figures towards the end of the month did not exclude a zero growth performance, which implied that Germany would also breach the Pact in the following year. A supplementary budget was being prepared for 2003 in order to cover for tax shortfalls by increased borrowing in the record magnitude of around €40 billion. On 21 October it also became clear that France would not deliver a full percentage point cut of its structural deficit in 2004 – compared to the 0.6 per cent reduction already planned. The government stated that any additional reduction would have a destabilising effect on the cycle. With Germany and Italy already in recession, the French government accused the Commission of forcing France to pull down the entire euro area.

By the end of October, the Commission had begun to draft its recommendations for Council decisions on Articles 104.8 and 104.9 for the cases of France and Germany, i.e. a move that would entail the initiation of a sequence that, hypothetically, could lead up to the sanctioning component of the EDP. At the same time, the two countries concerned were enlisting a blocking minority, likely consisting of Italy, Portugal and either Belgium or Luxembourg. Outgoing ECB President Duisenberg warned that these governments were tampering with the hard-earned confidence of the populations and the markets in the single currency.

On 3 November 2003, the Eurogroup assembled in order to discuss the pending sanctioning procedure against France. Officials described the development as the most serious situation so far for the functioning of

the institutional framework underpinning the euro. The highly contentious meeting cemented Germany and France into an alliance to prevent
even the hypothetical possibility of sanctions. Germany again proposed to
'scale back' the procedure by issuing new recommendations under Article
104.7 rather than taking a decision on Article 104.8 on the basis of the
existing recommendations. This compromise was not endorsed by the
Commission or the hardline block of countries, led by Austria and
the Netherlands. These countries, particularly the Netherlands, felt
betrayed by what they perceived as a fundamental shift of German policy
away from formerly jointly held beliefs.[26] Hence the gathering of the twelve
euro-area Ministers of Finance ended in a stalemate, as did the ensuing
ECOFIN assembly. In order to take the heat off the discussion, decision-
making by qualified majority voting was postponed to 25 November.

In the aftermath of the meeting, Eichel proposed as a general guideline
for the reading of the Pact that 'cooperating countries' should be exempted from the sanctioning procedure, regardless of the success of their
retrenchment measures. According to Eichel, the point of the sanctions
was not to worsen the situation of a country in fiscal difficulties but to
enforce cooperation in case of a deliberate violation of the rules. By
consequence, the instrument of sanctions would not be applicable to
Germany and France since both countries did their utmost to comply
with the Pact. The incoming President of the ECB, Jean-Claude Trichet,
stated at his first press conference that the Commission was already
applying the SGP with the greatest possible flexibility, implying that it
would be impossible to bend the rules even further.[27] Commissioner
Solbes also rejected the German idea, stating that 'it would be a different
kind of Pact if it was sufficient for a country to sit down at a table for a
discussion of its budgetary policy in order to be called cooperative and
thereby avoid sanctions'.[28]

In mid-November, the Commission adopted its recommendations
for ECOFIN decisions in accordance with Articles 104.8 and 104.9 also
in the case of Germany, due to be decided jointly with the case of France
at the end of the month. The texts would have requested Germany to
reduce the deficit by 0.8 per cent of GDP in 2004, equivalent to additional
spending cuts of around €4 billion. In return, Germany (like France) would
have gained one additional year for reducing the deficit below 3 per cent.

---

[26] One Dutch official stated with respect to the sentiment *vis-à-vis* Germany as the traditional guardian of stability: 'We have lost our ally.' Interview, Dutch Ministry of Finance,
1 December 2003.
[27] *Frankfurter Allgemeine Zeitung*, 7 November 2003.
[28] *Frankfurter Allgemeine Zeitung*, 18 November 2003, authors' translation.

Eichel categorically rejected reducing the structural deficit by more than the already agreed 0.5 percentage point annual reduction. The German Minister of Finance and senior officials were appalled and felt unjustly treated alike, although from their point of view Germany did everything possible to comply, more so than France.[29] Solbes was optimistic that a qualified majority could be assembled by the ECOFIN Council to adopt recommendations for France and Germany as recommended by the Commission. However, Luxembourg under Prime Minister Juncker was already signalling that it would join Italy and Portugal in siding with the two countries in question in order to form a blocking minority in the Council against the Commission recommendations. A few days later, Eichel linked the aim to regain the 3 per cent reference value in 2005 to growth rate of 2 per cent in 2004. Similar to the French approach, Berlin refused to define concrete, additional spending cuts as demanded by the Commission. Some reason for this lack of committment was represented by the ongoing negotiations in the mediation committee between the two houses of Parliament, the *Bundestag* being dominated by the governing SPD-Green coalition, the *Bundesrat* being controlled by the opposition. Reforms in the area of taxation and structural policy as well as a reduction of government expenditure had to be approved by both houses, and the negotiations did not allow more room for manoeuvre.

The culmination point of the crisis arrived on 24 and 25 November 2003. After a heated exchange of views in the Eurogroup, the 25 November ECOFIN meeting eventually resorted to voting. First it took a vote on the Commission's recommendation for a Council decision under Article 104.8, stating that France had not implemented sufficient measures to correct its excessive deficit. With only Denmark, Spain, Belgium, Sweden, Austria, the Netherlands, Finland and Greece voting in favour, there was no qualified majority and the decision hence was not adopted.[30] Similarly, the countries of the euro area voted on the Commission's recommendation for a Council recommendation under Article 104.9, prescribing more stringent measures to be implemented by France and a stricter and more direct supervision of these measures through the Commission, under the final, hypothetical threat of sanctions. With only Spain, Belgium, the Netherlands, Austria, Finland and Greece voting in favour, this recommendation likewise was not adopted.[31] The play was subsequently repeated for Germany.

---

[29] Telephone conversation with German Ministry of Finance official, 10 December 2003.
[30] The country in question has no right to vote on Articles 104.8 and 104.9.
[31] Only countries that have adopted the euro vote on Article 104.9, without the country concerned.

After not adopting the decisions recommended by the Commission, the Council adopted 'conclusions' on its own initiative, i.e. legally not binding political declarations that effectively changed the text of the original Commission recommendations. These Council conclusions were endorsed by a qualified majority, comprising the votes of Germany (respectively France on the conclusions for Germany), Italy, Greece, Belgium, Portugal, Luxembourg and Ireland under the voting rules of Article 104.9. The EDP for both countries was declared to be 'held in abeyance', evoking Article 9 of regulation 1467/97 of the SGP. The conclusions effectively replaced the EDP with political pledges of the two countries, which promised to deliver a deficit below 3 per cent of GDP in 2005, provided certain growth conditions were met, and to reduce their structural deficits as foreseen in the national budget plans (i.e. by 0.8 percentage points in 2004 and 0.6 percentage points in 2005 in the case of France, and by 0.6 percentage points in 2004 and 0.5 percentage points in 2005 in the case of Germany).

The outvoted small Member States were infuriated at what they saw as the large Member States playing at will with their interests and thereby abusing European law. The Commission entered the following statement into the Council minutes:

The Commission deeply regrets that the Council has not followed the spirit and the rules of the Treaty and the Stability and Growth Pact that were agreed unanimously by all Member States. Only a rule-based system can guarantee that commitments are enforced and that all Member States are treated equally. The Commission will continue to apply the Treaty and reserves the right to examine the implications of these Council conclusions and decide on possible subsequent actions. (Council Document 14492/03)

The possibility of bringing a court case before the ECJ was immediately alluded to after the meeting. The General Council of the ECB stated after a telephone conference that the ECOFIN Council had violated the SGP and that this amounted to a grave danger to the single currency. To the surprise of some observers (cf. Leblond 2006), however, the financial markets showed hardly any reaction to the events, with the exception of a temporary and mild slide of the euro against the dollar.

The outcome of the vote contributed significantly to souring relations between the two camps in the Council and did not bode well for the negotiations over a future Treaty Establishing a Constitution for Europe that were to be concluded in Rome in December 2003. As a result of the SGP crisis, smaller countries were even more determined to maximise their hold over power in the new Constitution – exemplified by the issues of voting weights and the right for each country to nominate one

Commissioner in Brussels. Indeed, failure to reach agreement on the Constitution in December was to a great part caused by the reluctance of small and medium-sized Member States to relinquish control over voted decisions.

An analysis of the SGP crisis

The crisis of 25 November 2003 and the run-up to that event are best analysed by applying two of our four theoretical lenses – the domestic politics and intergovernmentalist approaches – although there was also some degree of expert involvement when the Commission tried to react to functional requirements that became clearer in the actual implementation of the SGP. Let us focus again on the behaviour of a few selected governments (those of Germany, France and, by contrast, Portugal) but also on the emerging antagonism between small and large Member States. As we shall see in the next chapter, the expertocratic and functional lenses are particularly useful in examining the reform period, which was largely fed by experts' experiences in the run-up to the crisis as well as by their lessons drawn from the first implementation phase of the framework.

In Portugal, a centre-right coalition under Barroso had come to power and sought to address the country's fiscal difficulties by embracing the SGP as a source of external discipline. Barroso implemented a fiscal austerity programme and restored some degree of control over the deficit. Nevertheless, after important statistical revisions, it became clear that Portugal had effectively already been in excessive deficit and thereby was to become the first country subjected to the EDP regime. By way of contrast, in the cases of France and Germany this degree of fiscal restraint never materialised, for different reasons which are best understood from a domestic politics perspective.

In the case of Germany, there were difficulties between Finance Minister Eichel and Chancellor Schröder of the SPD-led government on the one hand, and, more fundamentally, also between the federal government and the *Länder* on the other. The *Länder* co-legislate in the second chamber of Parliament and, under the leadership of the CDU/CSU, were in a position to block the consolidation course proposed by the federal government. In that constellation, Eichel's attempts at disciplining fiscal policy were to a large part frustrated by the opposition, whereas Schröder prevented any more active embracement of the SGP as an external source of discipline, judging that this would likely backfire during elections.

The French case is different as neither Finance Minister Francis Mer nor President Jacques Chirac were convinced of the SGP regime and hence were from the beginning not willing to subject themselves to its discipline. The SGP was perceived as a tedious interference from Brussels, limiting the pursuit of fiscal policy. For that reason, Mer presented more openly and proactively than Eichel the increasing divergence of his budget from the requirements under the SGP. The focus of the Finance Minister was one of changing the rules or at least interpreting them with maximum flexibility. This more aggressive approach in turn affected the way the Commission treated the French government, up to the time when it could no longer avoid also presenting Germany with the prospect of further measures under the EDP. As domestic conditions allowed Portugal to cooperate, while very different domestic restrictions and priorities pointed Germany and France in the direction of conflict with the Commission, an intergovernmentalist approach is best suited to explaining the dynamics at the European level in the run-up to the crisis as well as during the crisis itself.

At the heart of the events surrounding the 25 November 2003 meeting lay a power struggle between France and Germany on the one hand and a coalition of small Member States and the Commission on the other.[32] In particular, the French contest with the Commission had been building up and ultimately came to a head in the fall of 2003. The German case could give the impression that the relations only worsened in autumn 2005. In reality, problems had already started to emerge in September 2003, but stayed below the surface. When the French were openly heading for a collision course, the Germans closed ranks with them and followed this line right through to the Council meeting of 25 November. In fact, according to our information, both the French and the German courses reinforced each other to the extent that the 'seriousness' of Berlin's opposition to Brussels became clear to Paris and vice versa, which again points to the very strong intergovernmental mechanics at play.

The additional, small-versus-large Member State struggle had been lingering in the background ever since the Irish BEPG case. Such antagonism about the SGP became part of a wider theme among small Member States who felt they were being 'bossed around' by a *directoire* of the larger countries and which manifested itself most notably in the deadlock over constitutional reform in the EU which continues up to this day, even if the final ratification of the Lisbon Treaty plasters over those decisions superficially. The picture that emerged more generally was one of small Member States accepting the imposition of European

---

[32] Paul Schure and Amy Verdun (2008) offer a formal model to explain the power struggle between large, medium-sized and small Member States, using the case of the SGP as an illustrative example.

norms and in particular the SGP framework as one of predictability and equal treatment against the arbitrariness of power politics seen in the behaviour of the large countries (Buti and Pench 2004; Schure and Verdun 2007, 2008). Fitting that mould, Portugal accepted the EDP and other small countries defended the Commission as well as the SGP against what they saw as a high-handed and arrogant, destructive approach of the large Member States – Germany and France in particular.

Italy and the UK, the other two large Member States, adopted a wait-and-see attitude in that *mêlée*. Italy, given its fiscal problems, had only to gain from the Franco-German attacks on the Commission, while the UK was positioned more distantly anyway, enjoying its EMU opt-out and domestically following a 'golden rule' in its fiscal policy rather than allegiance to the SGP. This did of course not prevent those two countries from lending their votes to the Franco-German cause in the Council, facilitating the formation of the anti-SGP coalition.

What happened on 25 November then simply followed the intergovernmental logic of the 'large-versus-small countries' constellation in the Council. That in turn was determined by the voting arithmetic for Articles 104.8 and 104.9, which is laid down in Article 104.13 and requires a two-thirds majority to adopt a decision, based on the voting weights determined under Article 205 and excluding the votes of the country concerned. Accordingly, a decision on Germany or France under Article 104.8, where all EU Member States (except the country concerned) have the right to vote, requires at least fifty-two votes whereas a blocking minority consists of at least twenty-five votes. Either Germany (for the decision on France) or France (for the decision on Germany) already had their own ten votes and knew that Italy and the UK, with their ten votes each, would be sufficient to block the decision. In the event, the large countries were even supported by Ireland, Luxembourg and Portugal and were thereby able to in fact form a blocking majority of forty votes. The Commission was only supported by Austria, Belgium, Denmark, Finland, Greece, the Netherlands, Spain and Sweden (thirty-seven votes). A similar behaviour occurred in the decisions on Article 104.9, albeit without the votes of the countries that had not adopted the euro. Hence, Sweden dropped out of the pro-SGP coalition and the UK left the anti-SGP coalition, leading to a 30–30 draw and hence a situation where this decision could not be adopted either.

It would be going too far to explain the national interests behind the voting behaviour of Ireland, Luxembourg and Portugal, but it is not hard to speculate that Ireland sought a reprisal for its BEPG trauma and that Portugal's adherence to the EDP did not go as far as supporting the activation of further measures than those contained in Article 104.7.

The case of Luxembourg is harder to understand, given that its two votes did not change the outcome and were of rather symbolical value.

The two Luxembourg votes, however, mattered significantly in the ensuing adoption of Council 'conclusions'[33] that were voted on under Article 104.9 with the votes of Germany (respectively France for the 'conclusions' on Germany), Belgium, Greece, Ireland, Italy, Luxembourg and Portugal. The two-thirds majority (forty votes) was reached exactly and hence Luxembourg was decisive in obtaining it. It is possible that Mr Juncker, Prime and Finance Minister of Luxembourg, wanted to vote consistently with Germany and France (unlike Belgium and Greece), but the voting behaviour of one of the architects of the SGP in 1997 is still remarkable and open to intergovernmentalist speculation about 'bandwagoning' of the smallest EU Member State situated between the two largest ones.

The behaviour of the Commission is even harder to understand. It was guided either by a miscalculation of the voting behaviour of one of the large Member States (possibly the UK) or, which we deem more probable, by the desire no longer to twist the rules (for example by accepting the issuance of new recommendations under Article 104.7) but rather 'calling the bluff' of the Council. Based on our interviews with decision-makers at the time, we are led to believe that the Commission sought to salvage the credibility of the SGP by advancing the application of the EDP to France and Germany to Articles 104.8 and 104.9. It gave less importance to the actual content of such recommendations, i.e. the specific budgetary targets and requirements that would be set – provided that the procedural intensification would be imposed. This was, however, anathema to Paris and, particularly, Berlin which would happily accept new and even more ambitious targets under paragraph 7 but were ready to prevent at any cost an escalation of the EDP to paragraphs 8 and 9.

So far, the story of the SGP's major crisis in late 2003 has been a purely domestic and intergovernmental one. The fact that the DG Ecfin in the Commission had, as of 2002, worked intensely on proposals of how to improve the implementation of the SGP was hardly noticed and indeed overshadowed by the dramatic events on the intergovernmental stage. Nevertheless, fiscal experts in the Commission as well as in the national Ministries of Finance and central banks constantly reflected on experiences with the SGP framework since 1999. Thus ideas evolved on how to translate into practice certain shortcomings and restrictions of a functional nature. Some of the Commission's reform proposals were aired in

---

[33] The ECJ later annulled these 'conclusions', which is discussed in more detail in the next chapter.

the run-up to the 2003 events in order to defuse the crisis, obviously without success. But these proposals indicated developments in the underlying thinking at expert level and resurfaced in 2004 and 2005 during the reform of the SGP, which we will address as part of the next chapter. Before that, however, the positions that had hardened in conflict and finally clashed on 25 November 2003 required legal clarification in front of the European Court of Justice (ECJ), to which we now turn.

8 The SGP before the European Court of Justice

This chapter deals with the aftermath of the SGP crisis of 25 November 2003, which led to a legal contest between the Commission and the Council and subsequently a so-called 'review' of the SGP. Following the memorable ECOFIN meeting, a case served before the ECJ in July 2004, which unearthed the dual nature of the SGP. The court decision triggered the perceived need for a revision of the SGP, which took place in spring 2005.

The structure of this chapter is as follows. The first section offers an account of these events. The second section provides an analysis, again using our theoretical framework to understand the developments. The events will become understandable mainly from a functional and experto-cratic perspective, even though towards the end of the argument we also benefit from the intergovernmentalist and domestic politics lenses once more.

The court case

Commissioner Solbes had evoked the possibility of taking legal action against the Council immediately after the 25 November 2003 crisis. The Commission's legal services reported to him in early January 2004 on the chances of winning before the ECJ. Thus, Solbes felt sufficiently confident when he went public and labelled the Council 'conclusions' illegal.[1] The main argument of the Commission was that the Council could not legally have adopted 'conclusions' on the basis of Article 104.9 after having failed to come to a decision on the recommendation under Article 104.8. Article 104.8 stipulates that the Council needs to decide based on a recommendation by the Commission, whether the Member State concerned had – or had not – undertaken sufficient action to remedy the situation of excessive deficit. Failure to adopt such a decision, according to the Commission, would not provide the basis for then issuing

[1] *Financial Times*, 8 January 2004.

'conclusions' pretending to be based on the provisions and voting modalities of paragraph 9. By consequence, the Council statement on the commitments of France and Germany was placed in a legal void; outside of the realm of the Treaty. The Commission therefore argued that the Council had violated both its institutional role as well as the procedural integrity of the Treaty.

Its desire to seek legal clarification through the ECJ in Luxembourg was shared by most commentators, given that this case represented an important precedent about the functioning of the EDP as well as on the roles and responsibilities of the two institutions asked to implement the procedure, i.e. the Commission and the Council. On 13 January 2004 after internal deliberations and without paying heed to certain warnings about the risks of such a step, the Commissioners decided to file a legal action and to request an urgency procedure, given the immediate need to restore clarity. Solbes' spokesman was quoted with the words: 'It had to be done. It's our role as guardian of the Treaty to make sure the Treaty is upheld.'[2]

The Commission's move was presented as part of a dual-track strategy, consisting of seeking legal clarity on the one hand, and preparing a reform proposal for the SGP on the other. Brussels was pressing for reform measures under the auspices of the existing composition of the Commission, whose term was ending in November 2004. As stated in the previous chapter, the run-up to the crisis had already provided ample occasion for the Commission experts to develop ideas on possible reforms and changes to the framework.

For the interim period, until the eventual Court ruling, the Commission considered the state of affairs to continue to be defined by the EDP and the recommendations adopted on the basis of Article 104.7. It therefore examined the stability and convergence programmes (SCPs) of the EU countries in a 'business as usual' manner during spring 2004. Italy, the Netherlands, Spain, Portugal, Estonia and Poland publicly backed the course of the Commission to proceed with the examination of the programmes and denied that there was a need for changing the rules. The Bundesbank explicitly warned against any reform of the framework.

In early February, ECOFIN Ministers decided to postpone a possible reform debate until the following year. Their intention was to continue with the effectively suspended EDP for the time being and undergo a 'cooling off' period during 2004. They preferred to start afresh with a new

---

[2] *Financial Times*, 14 January 2004.

Commission and under the Luxemburg Presidency in the first half of 2005, anticipating that the ECJ ruling would be known at that time, and also hoping for improved economic conditions. In addition, the incoming Luxembourg Presidency was seen by all parties as well placed to broker a compromise on how to proceed after the ruling of the ECJ.

At the end of January 2004, in its pursuit of evaluating Member States' SCPs in a 'business as usual' manner, the Commission released a highly critical assessment of the French stability programme, voicing concern that, without countermeasures, Paris would violate the 3 per cent threshold for the foreseeable future and would in any case require until 2007 to build up a safety margin that would, under normal circumstances, prevent the budget from exceeding the reference value. Solbes also voiced concern at the budgetary situation of the UK and the Netherlands, as both countries were approaching the 3 per cent reference value. The UK situation, however, was characterised by sufficient room for manoeuvre, thanks to the comparatively low level of public debt at that time. The Italian government was criticised for not providing information on how it was intending to return to budgetary balance. An ECOFIN meeting in early February approved the Commission recommendations on the first set of stability programmes. The Council confirmed that the UK's likely transgression of the reference value in 2003 would be treated as an 'excessive deficit' but that the situation was not particularly worrying. By contrast, France was warned that, under any 'plausible' assumptions, its deficit was going to exceed 3 per cent in 2005, contrary to the renewed commitment made on 25 November 2003.

Eichel submitted a stability programme to Brussels that envisaged a deficit of below 3 per cent of GDP by the end of 2005. Even before its official release, Solbes was doubtful about that target and requested additional consolidation efforts. The German government projected a deficit of 4 per cent of GDP in 2003 and a reduction down to 3¼ per cent in 2004. Like France, Germany would hence violate the deficit criterion for a third consecutive year in 2004 but, assuming a real growth rate of 2¼ per cent for 2005, was projected to stay below the 3 per cent threshold in that year with an estimated deficit of 2½ per cent of GDP.[3] Solbes' scepticism about these projections was mainly based on his assessment that Germany was insufficiently improving its structural position, i.e. the budgetary balance net of one-off and temporary measures, given the continued practice of large-scale privatisations underlying budgetary

---

[3] The German practice of submitting rounded fractions rather than decimal figures in its budgetary projections is a traditional cause for complaint by the Commission as well as by the ECB for lacking transparency.

targets. The Bundesbank also voiced considerable doubt about the chances of the German deficit being reduced to 3 per cent in 2005. In addition, it pointed out that the public debt level would rise significantly and thus would lastingly exceed the reference value of 60 per cent of GDP, regardless of the development of the budgetary deficit.

The Commission draft of the Council opinion on the German stability programme in mid-February called into doubt Germany's claim that the deficit was under control and that its economy was growing sufficiently to reach the consolidation targets announced by the government. The Commission saw the underlying forecast as unrealistic and itself projected that the deficit reference value would be violated for a fourth successive year in 2005. Furthermore, it criticised the fact that Germany had openly given up the aim of balancing the budget in the medium term: Berlin projected a deficit of 1 per cent in 2007, at the end of the forecasting period – thereby nonchalantly dropping the MTO. Nevertheless, Brussels welcomed the government's 'agenda 2010' structural reform package for employment policy, pensions and the health sector.

In April, the Commission adopted a recommendation for a Council decision giving an 'early warning' to Italy, based also on the assessment that the Berlusconi government continued to rely heavily on one-off measures, such as the securitisation of government asset sales and a tax amnesty. The move had domestic political ramifications as it occurred only weeks before the European election. Berlusconi accused Prodi of abusing his position as Commission President to pave the way for his return to Italian politics in the general election of May 2006. As was to be expected, the Commission recommendation was not endorsed by ECOFIN, repeating the 2002 experiences in the cases of Germany and Portugal. In addition to the early warning on Italy, the Commission had also announced that it was going to initiate an EDP in the case of the Netherlands. With Greece and the UK also approaching a 3 per cent deficit, six out of the fifteen EU countries were now above or close to the 3 per cent budgetary deficit reference value.

Early in May 2004, days after the celebrations of EU 'Eastern' enlargement from fifteen to twenty-five Member States, the German government downgraded its growth forecast to the lower end of the projected range between 1½ and 2 per cent and called a halt to further spending cuts. It deliberately accepted a continuing breach of the SGP. Finance Minister Hans Eichel stated: 'Without growth there can be no consolidation.'[4] In another interview, Foreign Minister Joseph Martin Fischer (usually

---

[4] *Financial Times*, 3 May 2004, quoting *Bild Zeitung*.

referred to as 'Joschka' Fischer) declared that for 'a limited period, the economic recovery must take priority. We won't get the growth we need by just saving and cutting.'[5] The alleged policy shift in Berlin was partially seen as a result of regional election defeats for the ruling Social Democrats and geared to address the weakness in private consumption, which was generally seen as the main reason of Germany's growth malaise amidst booming export performance. During the following days, the government withdrew its position and assured that the consolidation effort would be continued – only to be criticised for incoherence by the opposition. The government retorted that results from the spring forecast on tax revenues had to be awaited before deciding on the future course of fiscal policy.[6]

During May, prominent members of the governing coalition became increasingly sceptical about the chances or even the desirability of budgetary commitments. SPD chairman Franz Müntefering was among the most outspoken advocates of relaxing the SGP rules in favour of increased spending on research and innovation, which featured among the aims of the EU's Lisbon Agenda and, according to Müntefering, should not fall prey to adverse macroeconomic conditions. His remarks laid open a controversy within the government between Müntefering and Eichel. Pinpointing the requirements of the SGP versus those of the Lisbon Agenda, Chancellor Schröder replied elusively to the question of whether he thought that 3 per cent of GDP should be spent on research and innovation rather than the deficit being contained at below 3 per cent: 'What is more important for a good harvest – sun or rain?'[7] Ahead of the spring forecast on government revenues, Berlin decided to compensate the expected tax shortfall for 2004 with a corrective budget and higher debt rather than spending cuts. The revenue projections were released on 13 May and showed an €8.3 billion shortfall for 2004, rising to €15.2 billion in 2005. These figures confirmed that Germany would breach the 3 per cent threshold for a fourth consecutive year in 2005. Eichel attacked the CDU opposition for having blocked cuts in subsidies in the order of magnitude of €9.5 billion in the *Bundesrat*.

The new French Minister of Finance (and later President), Nicolas Sarkozy, in turn, promised to rein in public spending. He set out to target

[5] *Financial Times*, 6 May 2004, quoting *Der Spiegel* of 5 May 2004.
[6] Twice a year, experts from the federal Ministry of Finance as well as regional finance ministries, the Bundesbank and academics project general government tax revenues in Germany, on the basis of a government macroeconomic growth forecast. The revenue projections subsequently provide the basis for budgetary planning by the national and regional authorities.
[7] *Frankfurter Allgemeine Zeitung*, 12 May 2004.

tax loopholes and declared that the tax cuts promised by Chirac could only be realised through improved growth. Unlike his German counterpart, the Frenchman also vowed to keep to the promised budget deficit of below 3 per cent in 2005. French Prime Minister Jean-Pierre Raffarin sent letters to all ministries calling for tight controls of public spending in the 2005 budget. The letters followed a heated exchange of views between former Foreign Minister and current Interior Minister Dominique de Villepin and Finance Minister Sarkozy during a meeting on the budgetary strategy for 2005. Sarkozy had even taken on President Jacques Chirac by announcing reductions in defence spending, which was quickly overruled by Chirac who was determined to keep his electoral promise of increasing the defence budget to 2 per cent of GDP. Each ministry had to prepare its budget proposals by 10 June, so that Raffarin could take the final decision by the end of July. Sarkozy's tactics at the Ministry of Finance were seen as being part of his ambitions to run for the Presidency in 2007. He was positioning himself as the man who would bring the budget deficit under control, trying to copy the success of UK Chancellor of the Exchequer Gordon Brown at the time.

As the negotiations on a European Constitution were drawing to a close in June 2004, Germany, Greece, Italy and Poland jointly prevented a shift of power from the ECOFIN Council to the Commission in the application of the SGP. The draft text of the Constitutional Convention foresaw Commission 'proposals' to initiate all procedural steps under the EDP, rather than 'recommendations' as per the Maastricht Treaty (Article 250). The difference would have been that, for amending a Commission 'proposal' for a Council decision (against the Commission's will), the Council would have required unanimity. By contrast, a Commission 'recommendation' can be changed by a qualified majority in the Council. Therefore, moving from Commission recommendations to proposals in the entire EDP sequence as part of the new (but now hypothetical) Constitution would have significantly strengthened the Commission *vis-à-vis* the Council and, depending on the Commission's attitude, could have led to a much stricter implementation of the SGP. It would, for example, have become more difficult for the Council to extend deadlines for correcting an excessive deficit. It was therefore not a surprise when the Foreign Ministers of the four above-mentioned countries, led by Germany's Joschka Fischer, insisted on the Council retaining effective control over the SGP and preventing the introduction of Commission proposals other than for the very first step of the EDP, i.e. the initial decision on the existence of an excessive deficit in accordance with Article 104.6. The existing set-up was preserved, where the initiation of subsequent steps, in particular those according to Articles 104.7 and 104.9, takes the form of a Commission recommendation, which can be amended by a qualified majority in the Council. This also remained the legal form of the EDP in the Lisbon Treaty.

An EDP based on Commission recommendations rather than proposals was incorporated into the final text of the Constitution at the concluding meeting of the European Council in 2004. The role of the ECJ was also cut down in comparison to the Convention draft at the insistence of a number of countries, including Germany. Germany and the Netherlands proposed a rather vague and legally not binding annex to the Constitution in order to reduce the impression that the EDP effectively remained in the hands of the Council. The declaration states that EU governments would commit to strengthening their efforts at fiscal consolidation in periods of robust economic growth, aiming for budgetary surpluses. Finally, the package deal also included an increase in the number of seats in the European Parliament for smaller Member States, while Germany agreed to have its number of deputies reduced by three.

On 2 May 2004, the case of Commission versus Council finally served before the ECJ (case C-27/04).[8] To recap, the 25 November ECOFIN Council had failed to adopt the Commission recommendations on Germany and France in accordance with Articles 104.8 and 104.9. According to 104.9, the Council 'may' decide to give notice to the Member State in question. Instead, the Council had issued separate 'conclusions', also based on the voting rules applicable to Article 104.9. De facto, the EDP was thereby suspended and replaced by consolidation commitments in the form of not legally binding conclusions.[9] The provision of Articles 104.8 and 104.9 whereby the Council 'may' decide granted room for a political decision at the discretion of the Council. The judges had to decide whether the Council had used this appropriately.

In a heavily attended session, the Court listened attentively to the pleas made by the lawyers representing the Commission and the Council. In

---

[8] There has been a lot of interest in this Court case from the general public, the media, academics (lawyers, political scientists and economists alike) and the Member States. As it was open to the public, we also attended the court hearing. A few excellent summaries have been made of the case, in particular Doukas (2006). See also Dutzler and Hable (2005).

[9] It is a common misunderstanding, frequently made in the media and in academic writings, that the Council decided to hold the EDP in abeyance. Strictly speaking this depiction of the situation is incorrect. What happened is that the Council did not move to the next step as the EDP sequence requires. Thus it de facto held the EDP in abeyance by not acting. In its conclusions the Council uses the terminology of 'abeyance' but it did not follow the official procedures that could have held the SGP in abeyance. Thus, as the Council did not adopt the formal procedures for holding the EDP in abeyance, which also exist under the SGP Regulations, one can only refer to the Council as having de facto held the EDP in abeyance.

formal terms, the Commission brought an action for annulment against the Council. The Commission explained why it was challenging the Council acts of 25 November 2003 as steps that were not in line with the Treaty. The Commission's case was twofold. First, it challenged the Council decision not to adopt the recommendations, and second, the adoption of separate Council 'conclusions' in so far as they involved suspending the sequence of the EDP and modifying the earlier recommendations of the Commission. The lawyer for the Council argued passionately that it was the right of the Council not to adopt Commission recommendations and, furthermore, to adopt its own 'conclusions'. He defended the 'conclusions' by stating that the less favourable economic conditions had led to changing the earlier Commission recommendations. In formal terms, the Council asked the Court to declare the Commission's case inadmissible on both accounts.

On 13 July 2004, the ECJ pronounced its verdict on the case (see the summary of the ruling in the Appendix). It declared inadmissible the Commission challenge against the Council *not* adopting the Commission recommendations on Articles 104.8 and 104.9. The Court explained that, just because deadlines were expiring, this situation did not mean that the Council had to adopt Commission recommendations under the EDP. It also did not preclude the Council from adopting acts recommended at a later stage (see also Doukas 2006) or, for that matter, repeating steps under the EDP, on the basis of new Commission recommendations (Beetsma and Oksanen 2007, 2008). Making that latter point explicit and stipulating a procedure for repeating, for example, the issuance of Council recommendations to countries in excessive deficit (in accordance with Article 104.7) became an important ingredient of the SGP review later on but had already been implicitly possible under the original SGP, according to the ECJ ruling (paragraph 92).

The Court, however, declared admissible the Commission challenge of the Council's 'conclusions'. The Court disagreed with the Council that it had merely recorded the situation. Instead, it ruled that the Council had used 'conclusions' to adopt measures to be taken by France and Germany. In so doing, the Council moved outside the procedures by using 'conclusions' to modify earlier recommendations by the Commission and thereby changing the deadlines for correcting the deficit as well as the measures required by the two countries. The Court ruled that the responsibility for enforcing budgetary discipline indeed lay with the Council, but that the EDP was a procedure in stages. In each stage the Commission recommends and the Council considers whether Member States have complied with the obligations set out in recommendations previously adopted by the Council. The Court underlined the discretion that the Council possesses to modify measures recommended by the Commission (following the voting rules set out in the respective Articles) if it assesses differently the relevant economic data, measures taken and the relevant timetable (Doukas 2006). However, it stressed that under no circumstances may the Council ignore the rules of the procedures laid down in Article 104 or Regulation 1467/97 and resort to an alternative procedure (as it had done by adopting the 'conclusions' in the 25 November 2003 Council meeting).

Thus, while acknowledging that the Council could *de facto* hold the EDP in abeyance by not adopting Commission recommendations, the Court effectively nullified the ECOFIN 'conclusions' and ruled that decisions under the EDP required a recommendation by the Commission. Whether or not they are amended or adopted is at the discretion of the ECOFIN Council, as long as it follows the procedures. Hence the Council can hold the procedure *de facto* in abeyance, even if explicit abeyance under Regulation 1467/97 is only foreseen in cases where a Member State fulfils its obligations. However, the Commission retains a right of initiative because ECOFIN recommendations have to be taken (or changed) on the basis of Commission recommendations and cannot be framed and reformulated in the form of independent 'conclusions' initiated by the Council. Furthermore, the ECJ called on the Council and the Commission to cooperate in the implementation of the SGP.

Both the Commission and the Council reacted positively to the Court ruling. The Commission stated: 'The European Commission welcomes today's judgments by the European Court of Justice and confirms the Commission's view as to the respective roles of the Commission and the Council in the application of the Stability and Growth Pact' (Commission press release 13 July 2004). The Council stated: 'The Council welcomes the clarification rendered on the interpretation of both the provisions of the Treaty on the Excessive Deficit Procedure (Article 104) and the Stability and Growth Pact, clarifying the respective roles of the Commission and the Council' (Council press release 13 July 2004).

Thus ends the history of the 'old' SGP. The ECJ ruling of July 2004 marked its end, and all parties involved expressed their satisfaction with the decision of the judges. Behind the scenes, the Commission had already started to prepare the reform of the SGP, not least based on its mixed five-year experience with SGP implementation.

Towards SGP 'reform'

Despite the Court ruling, the sense of crisis did not disappear. Tensions resurfaced when Greece announced having revised substantially its public finance figures in 2004, showing that deficit ratios in excess of 3 per cent had even existed at the time of Greece's euro-area accession in 2001. This meant that, had the correct data been the basis for judgement, Greece would not have even qualified to join the euro area! The data revisions led to an intensification of the already ongoing EDP for Greece. For the first time the Council decided to 'give notice' under Article 104.9 of the Treaty. Six of the new Member States were also found to be in excessive deficit. Among these was Hungary. This country had now already twice been declared to have taken ineffective action in accordance with Article 104.8.[10]

In parallel with the ongoing EDPs and in the aftermath of the legal confrontation, it was widely perceived that the SGP had to be reviewed and likely reformed in the course of 2005. Unlike in 2002, when the first group of countries was subjected to the EDP, it was now deemed necessary by the Commission and the Council to amend the SGP regulations. Fearing a weakening of the Pact, the central banking community, most vocally the ECB and the Bundesbank, saw no need for a reform, while a plethora of academic proposals circulated on how to create a better SGP. Speculating on the intentions of the Commission and the Council, it is probably fair to say that the political motivation for a 'restart' after the Court ruling was probably the strongest driver behind reform: Reviewing the Pact would indirectly demonstrate a lack of appropriateness of the existing system and thereby at least in part exculpate both institutions from their 'sins' committed thus far. Nevertheless, one cannot exclude that the existing and growing body of proposals for improvement, which in part had also accumulated within the Commission, found a natural moment for serious deliberation after the fresh start enabled by the Court ruling.

The reform discussions in many ways were a repetition of the procedures that led to the creation of the Pact in 1996 (with the exception of there not being an intense domestic policy debate about the SGP in Germany this time; and, as we shall see, a more general change in its role and preferences). Discussions took place in 2004 and 2005 in the Economic and Financial Committee (EFC), the successor to the MC, and in the ECOFIN Council. The ECOFIN Council meeting of 7–8 March 2005 did not produce an agreement on the reform of the SGP (Council of the EU Press release, 8 March 2005), while the ECB, in a public statement on 21 March, declared that it was 'seriously concerned' about the proposed changes (ECB 2005a).

---

[10] The EDP stages of 'giving notice' (Article 104.9) and potential sanctions (Article 104.11) do not apply to Member States who have not adopted the euro. It would, however, in principle be possible partially to suspend Cohesion Fund payments, which was part of the discussion on Hungary for some time.

Similar to the original negotiation of the Pact, technical discussions and most of the decisions took place at the senior expert level in the EFC. Only a limited number of contentious points had to be referred to the ECOFIN Council. The debate included the traditionally controversial issue of whether and how to relax the definition of an excessive deficit via an easing of the conditions for possible exemptions, above all the specification of the economic circumstances under which a deficit above 3 per cent of GDP would not be deemed excessive. Further issues in the discussions concerned the possibility of repeating certain steps of the EDP and extending deadlines as well as the formal conditions for such judgemental decisions. The idea of a 'minimum fiscal effort' of consolidating the structural balance by at least 0.5 per cent of GDP per year was taken up but not made obligatory. It became a benchmark for the adjustment path to the changed, country-specific MTO, which has replaced the universal 'close to balance or in surplus' rule of the old SGP.

Highly controversial was a list specifying the notion of the hitherto undefined 'other relevant factors' that were already referred to in the original SGP as special circumstances. These factors can be taken into account in the decision on the existence of an excessive deficit as well as in the application of the EDP. Some governments proposed to make explicit a whole range of such possible factors, including expenses related to (German) reunification and net contributions to the EU budget. In the end, such an extensive list of factors was taken on board, but its application was limited by the double condition that the excess over the reference value be, in the view of the Council, temporary and that the deficit stay close to the reference value of 3 per cent of GDP. If the Council judges otherwise, such special circumstances cannot be used as an argument to run deficits above the reference value.

Another major difference in the negotiations for the reformed Pact was that Germany, under the Schröder government, had changed sides and was now among the most fervent supporters of a permissive design of the SGP. The restrictive position was mainly represented by smaller Member States (particularly the Netherlands, but also Austria and Finland). The Dutch, with Finance Minister Gerrit Zalm at the helm, were especially keen to keep as much as possible of the old SGP intact. Fully accepting the EDP obligations imposed on the Netherlands, Zalm also put his money where his mouth was and provided a textbook example of how to address an excessive deficit under the SGP. Together with his Austrian and Finnish colleagues, he sought to enlist as many other Member States as possible against any changes towards a more lenient Pact, but they found many partners unwilling to support the Dutch stance, as it meant being in opposition to the Franco-German position.[11]

In this period there were also many calls for reforms, mostly by academics. Many of them called for a more fundamental revision, others did not see the need for a complete overhaul (more drastic changes were advocated e.g. by Begg and Schelkle 2004; Blanchard and Giavazzi 2004; Buiter and Grafe 2002; Collignon 2004; Enderlein 2004 and Hodson 2004; less drastic ones by Buti *et al.* 2003 and Hallerberg 2004. For an overview of the many different types of proposals see Savage and Verdun 2007 and Fischer *et al.* 2006). Many commentators discussed alternative ways to ensure fiscal discipline. Some of these proposals included abandoning the SGP altogether. For example Enderlein (2004) suggested abolishing the SGP and instead emphasised Member States' responsibility in coordinating their fiscal policies. Furthermore, he proposed to rely on the soft fiscal coordination present in the creation of the BEPG and the surveillance process provided for in the Maastricht Treaty's Article 99, rather than the EDP of Article 104.

Schelkle (2004a and 2005) as well as Begg and Schelkle (2004) also proposed to rely on soft rather than hard coordination. Their idea was to encourage Member State learning and experimentation by relying on the creation of individual fiscal sustainability plans that would be developed through negotiation with the Commission. They suggested creating new economic policy indicators to determine compliance, relying on reputational sanctions and the potential loss of rights at the EU level, such as voting on issues related to the euro area.

Hallerberg (2004) proposed to keep the SGP as is, but to ensure enforcement by strengthening domestic budgetary institutions. The institutions whose role should be strengthened in particular would be the domestic ministries of finance. He also advocated encouraging coalition governments to create domestic 'fiscal contracts' to reinforce their compliance with the SGP.

Ubide (2004) made a case for reinforcing the Commission as an enforcer of the SGP. In addition to this change in the final authority for enforcing the Pact, Ubide proposed to move to a system of political rather than financial penalties for noncompliance. Political penalties could include requiring finance ministers to justify their policies before their own parliaments if the Commission issued an excessive deficit warning or recommendation against a Member State.

---

[11] Officials of De Nederlandsche Bank, interviews with the authors, Amsterdam, 24 August 2006.

Fatas *et al.* (2003) put forward the idea of creating an independent Sustainability Council not dissimilar to the original Waigel proposal from 1995. They envisaged this Council to report to the European Parliament, and to be charged with ensuring the sustainability of Member State finances. The Council would assess the fiscal condition of the Member States, particularly the size of their public debt, and provide a flexible alternative to the defunct rules. Member States would have to submit fiscal plans to the Council, which would have the authority to veto these plans. The Council would rely upon reputational and political sanctions derived from public support for the Council's rulings, rather than financial sanctions on the Member States. This design was modelled on the successful functioning of the Central Planning Office in the Netherlands.

In 2006 and following the review of the SGP, Commission research staff compiled a group of 101 proposals that had been presented as possible answers to the question as to how to reform the SGP framework (Fischer *et al.* 2006). This Commission research paper offers a fine example of how ideas of non-actor experts permeate into the realm of thinking by actor experts (as discussed above in Chapter 5). Here, too, the consensus was that rules were necessary in order to avoid excessive deficits. However, actor experts, identifying at least about four schools of thought as to how one could coordinate fiscal policies, were forced to prioritise their reform options not only on economic theory but mainly according to legal and, above all, political feasibility.

Many of these proposals had in common that the implementation of the SGP could include a stronger role of independent fiscal agencies. Rather than considering some form of independent forecasting and budget framing, Member States were seen to rely most on self-commitment that was backed up by hypothetical sanctions. Most of these accounts agreed to establish economic policy coordination in light of the fact that there was no single supranational body that could set budgetary and fiscal policies for the EU. Thus, one needed to rely on some mechanism for coordinated fiscal policy. At the same time, one could advocate the strengthening of domestic fiscal institutions and rules, possibly including the setting-up of fiscal agencies at the national level.

Even though there was a widespread discussion of the possible reform of the SGP (such as the discussion launched by the Commission in late 2004 and early 2005), in practice, these academic contributions on how to reform the SGP seemed to have had little impact on the specific contents of the debates taking place in the ECOFIN Council or in the EFC. They did, however, impact the overall environment in which the reform discussions were taking place, particularly in the Commission itself, which was collecting input and working towards its own, authoritative proposal.

Actual negotiations were determined much more by the political positions of the various Member States and their specific national preferences. The role of outside expert advice was limited. Seeing that experts agreed on the need to have rules in principle but that they had no uniform, clear-cut view on what precise rules should be preferred, enabled governments to table their own proposals that were more pragmatic in nature and geared towards addressing their tactical concerns primarily. In particular France and Germany were vocal in seeking to have a more flexible interpretation of the SGP and advanced numerous proposals to that effect.

After lengthy consultations, the ECOFIN Council reached a political compromise at yet another special meeting on 20 March 2005 and issued a report to the European Council, entitled 'Improving the Implementation of the Stability and Growth Pact', which was subsequently incorporated into the Presidency Conclusions of the European Council of 22 and 23 March 2005. By June 2005, the Council finalised the formal review of the SGP also in legal terms and adopted Regulations amending the original SGP Regulations.[12] In October, the Council also endorsed a revised Code of Conduct, which legally is an opinion by the EFC. Technical work on procedural and methodological issues continued in the Commission and the EFC throughout 2005 and into 2006. In order to summarise the reforms of the SGP, we could characterise the changes as follows, in turn addressing its preventive and corrective arms.[13]

There were three main changes to the preventive arm. The first one concerns the definition of the MTO. Rather than being required to be CTBOIS, each Member State now presents its own country-specific MTO in the SCP. The country-specific MTO should take into account economic characteristics of each Member State, such as the debt-to-GDP ratio and potential growth as well as, for example, tax elasticities and the size of automatic stabilisers.[14] As part of the SCP review process under Article 99, these MTOs are subsequently assessed by the Council in the

---

[12] The original regulations are: Council Regulation (EC) No. 1466/97 of 7 July 1997 and Council Regulation (EC) No. 1467/97 of 7 July 1997. The new regulations build on the old ones and amend them. They are Council Regulation No. 1055/2005 of 27 June 2005 on strengthening of the surveillance of budgetary positions and the surveillance and coordination of economic policies and Council Regulation (EC) No. 1056/2005 of 27 June 2005 on speeding up and clarifying the implementation of the excessive deficit procedure. Part of the revised SGP is usually also considered the Council Report to the European Council (2007) 'Improving the implementation of the Stability and Growth Pact' 7619/1/05 REV1 Annex II (pp. 1–18).

[13] Good summaries of the reform of the Pact can be found in Doukas (2005), ECB (2005b) and Morris et al. (2006).

[14] Later work in the Economic Policy Committee (EPC) dealt with the development of indicators for the long-term sustainability of public finances, which were to flow into the definition of country-specific MTOs.

form of Council opinions that are drafted by the Commission and submitted to the Council as recommendations. The new emphasis on country specificity was seen to address one major criticism of the 'old' SGP,
which was its so-called 'one-size-fits-all' fiscal policy approach to the in
fact very different macroeconomic situations of the Member States.

The second change introduced to the preventive arm of the Pact
referred to the adjustment path that countries would follow in order to
reach their MTO. If a Member State has not yet achieved its MTO it is
expected to apply a fiscal policy that approaches the target over the cycle.
As a benchmark, the adjustment effort should be an improvement in the
structural balance (i.e. the cyclically adjusted budget balance corrected for
temporary and one-off measures) by 0.5 percentage points of GDP per
year.[15] Furthermore, adjustment should be greater in good economic
times than in bad ones. If Member States do not follow the adjustment
path they need to explain their reasons in their SCP update.

Third, the preventive arm of the revised Pact takes into account structural reforms. Under the new Pact, Member States may be allowed to
deviate from the MTO or the adjustment path if they implement structural reforms (such as pension reforms introducing a funded pillar).
However, only long-term cost-saving effects will be taken into account
and a safety margin with respect to the 3 per cent reference value will have
to be preserved at all times. Furthermore, discounting the budgetary
effects of introducing funded pension schemes is subject to degressive
weighting. The inclusion of pension reforms had become of particular
interest for a number of Central and Eastern European countries during
the reform negotiations.

With regard to the corrective arm of the revised Pact, we can also
distinguish three major changes. First, the definition of 'exceptional economic circumstances' was relaxed. A deficit above 3 per cent is not necessarily considered excessive if it can be shown that the breach is 'exceptional
and temporary'. As before a 'severe economic downturn' could be one such
reason, albeit at a much more lenient definition than the one contained in
the 1997 Amsterdam resolution of the European Council. Under the
revised Pact, any negative growth or even a period of positive but very low
growth could be considered as an exceptional circumstance.

Second, 'other relevant factors' were specified, largely in line with the
'wish lists' of a number of finance ministers, above all Eichel and Sarkozy.
According to the Treaty, in the first step of the EDP, the Commission
should take into account 'all other relevant factors, including the medium-

---

[15] Both the MTOs and the adjustment path are defined in structural terms.

term economic and budgetary position of the Member State'. However, neither the Treaty nor the original SGP regulations spelt out what these factors were. The revised version, however, does so in surprising detail. The medium-term economic position now includes potential growth, the prevailing cyclical conditions, the implementation of the Lisbon Agenda, and the policies to foster research and development and innovation. Furthermore, relevant developments also include fiscal consolidation efforts in 'good times', debt sustainability, public investment, the overall quality of public finances and, literally,

> any other factors that, in the opinion of the Member State concerned, are relevant in order to comprehensively assess in qualitative terms the excess over the reference value (...). In that context, special consideration shall be given to budgetary efforts towards increasing or maintaining at a high level financial contributions to fostering international solidarity and to achieving European policy goals, notably the unification of Europe ...

This already-mentioned list of 'other relevant factors', originally tabled by Germany, reappears as an element to be considered at several stages in the EDP and explicitly shows the large degree of discretion that the Council can wield over the implementation of the revised Pact. However, it is understood that such factors can only be taken into consideration to the extent that the excess over the reference value is temporary and that the deficit remains 'close to' the reference value.

A third, major change to the corrective arm regarded the deadlines for correcting excessive deficits. A number of procedural deadlines were extended. The deadline for correcting an excessive deficit remains 'the year following its identification unless there are special circumstances'. These circumstances could occur if any of the above-mentioned 'relevant factors' are at bay. Furthermore, if effective action has been taken in compliance with a recommendation under Article 104.7 or a notice under Article 104.9 and there are unexpected adverse events with financial consequences, the Council may decide, upon recommendation from the Commission, to issue a revised recommendation or notice which could also extend the deadline for the correction of the excessive deficit. This had been one of the major requests of Germany during the 2003 confrontations, now translated into law.

An analysis of the SGP review

Most commentators have considered the review of the SGP to imply at least a moderate weakening of the EU budgetary framework. The new version of the SGP in essence makes the already very large degree of

Council discretion explicit. It thereby provides in-built political legiti-macy to the Council when it avails itself of the flexibility enshrined in the rules. In other words, the institutional balance between rules and discretion has remained broadly unchanged in purely legal terms.[16]

What has been reduced, however, is the *reputation cost* to the Council members of using that discretion. Under the new SGP, the Council faces less *normative* obstacles when exerting its discretion, since a lot of the reasoning that can be employed against a strict implementation of the EDP is now part of the legal texts themselves. Even more than under the old SGP, a successful implementation therefore hinges on the Council making responsible and wise use of the flexibility at its disposal.

The political motivation behind the SGP reform as well as the first instances of 'test cases' with EDP decisions on Germany, France and Italy at the turn of 2005–6 already gave rise to serious concerns. At the same time, the renewed responsibility that the Council assumed with the SGP reform and its share in the ultimate responsibility for the viability of EMU were seen as possibly having the effect of inducing more compliance and so-called 'ownership' of the SGP. Moreover, policy learning since the mid-1990s was expected to support a stronger commitment to sound budgetary policies. It is also worth noting that the Commission was not necessarily in a weaker position than before but would in fact be able to engage the Council into more substantial and enlightened deliberations on more cognitive and factual rather than just legalistic or formal grounds.

Similar to the historic experience with the EMS after widening the fluctuation bands of the ERM, the success of the reformed SGP seemed to depend on two conditions. First, the actors would have to internalise the norms of the system (i.e. above all the deficit reference value). The 'political capital' invested in the reform of the Pact in this sense was seen as instrumental. After all, the SGP could no longer be described as the German 'dictate' of 1995–7, but was a jointly agreed framework for budgetary policy of 2005, finding strong support (indeed the key advo-cates) among a number of smaller Member States. Second, the actors needed to operate within an appropriate incentive structure that would make them perceive norm-respecting behaviour as their rational strategy. Ultimately, only the need to safeguard the viability of EMU could provide a sufficiently strong collective incentive to resist the short-term individual temptation of free-riding on the deficit bias under the slack reins of an essentially lax political framework.

---

[16] The authors thank Theo Martens for clarifying this point.

The decision to reform the SGP in March 2005 with the revised regulations as adopted in June 2005 is an interesting case to analyse by looking at the process through the four theoretical lenses, as we did when examining the origins of the SGP earlier in the book. Contrary to the SGP implementation and crisis, for which we relied mostly on domestic politics and intergovernmentalism, the SGP reform can be analysed in part by examining it through all four lenses, the expertocratic and functional ones, as well as from a perspective of domestic politics and intergovernmentalism.

In a number of ways, these reforms signal that ideational consensus still existed on the need to have some kind of SGP, but that the compromise solution was to grant the Council even more explicit room for availing itself of the already large discretionary margin that it could wield within the framework. It is clear that the domestic politics had changed compared to the origins of the SGP, in particular with Germany being no longer supportive of strict rules. The fact that the Franco-German axis had been at the core of the November 2003 events was also crucial for the conduct and outcome of the reform. Many have observed that no other single country or pair of countries would likely have been able to 'get away with' not moving to the next step of EDP, let alone subsequently requesting a redrafting of the rules! It is understandable that, in light of this development, the smaller Member States have put centre stage the notion of 'equal treatment'. Once Germany and France were sponsoring legal changes, the question had become to what degree the other side could preserve the core principles of the Pact. In many ways, the compromises sought along these lines consisted essentially of spelling out in minute detail many of the more broad-based stipulations of the 'old' Pact.

However, a radical departure from the existing framework did not take place. Our explanation is that a more moderate reform was chosen over a fundamental one mainly because (i) the ideational consensus among experts to have rules had not disappeared; and (ii), because there was a blocking coalition of smaller Member States against radical change (such as a full-blown incorporation of the list of 'other relevant factors'), in other words there were intergovernmental struggles at play besides the conservatism of experts. Both factors enabled the existing framework (iii) to stay within the institutional path of the SGP origins and development, in line with a functional approach; and, finally, (iv) a domestic politics approach provides insights into the stances taken by the various governments and thus highlights some of the reasons behind positions taken by their representatives in the intergovernmental deliberations.

Let us focus on these four explanations in turn. The ideational consensus stayed more or less intact. While 'policy learning' and 'lesson drawing' had of course been going on and intensified after 1999, it did not lead to fundamental changes in the ideas of actor experts in the EFC. The work of non-actor experts, in particular academics, which talked about the need to find a different regime of fiscal rules, did not undermine the idea that fiscal rules were necessary in the first place. In other words, the overall paradigm remained unchanged. Furthermore, the views of academics were sometimes a lot more distant from the existing state of affairs than those of the experts closer to the decision-making in the EFC. There was no one in the political realm advocating an abandonment of the regime altogether.

In functional terms, radical change was prevented by the fact that the Member States saw the importance of having rules that were more or less in line with those already in place, so as not to upset the legal framework. In terms of legal spillover, the Maastricht Treaty as well as the existing body of secondary law provided clear restrictions. After all, the reviewed SGP would take the form of *amending* the existing regulations, not replacing them. There was no functionally inspired desire to change the Treaty or the fundamental, institutional set-up of the rules. Thus, the scope of the reform was restricted to options that would build incrementally on the existing legal framework.

The reform episode also shows an intergovernmental component. Amending regulation 1467/97 required unanimity and amending regulation 1466/97 required a qualified majority in the Council. The delicate reform exercise overall was driven by the desire to achieve consensus, not least with regard to the need of coherently communicating the intended outcome as a negotiating success for all parties involved. The discussions were therefore conducted under a partly formal, partly informal unanimity requirement and hence subject to the possible veto of any one Member State. This implied that the scope of the review was limited from the outset to the solution space of the 'common denominator' of all parties involved. Furthermore, any more radical departure from the existing framework would have required a Treaty change (which would have been necessary, for example, if the EDP were to be abandoned altogether). Any Treaty change, in turn, would not only have required a unanimous approval by heads of states or governments, but also ratification of a new Treaty. Seeing that both Treaty change and ratification were extremely difficult (viz. the difficulty surrounding the signing and ratification of the Treaty Establishing a Constitution for Europe and subsequently the Lisbon Treaty), a Treaty change was by no means considered a viable option. It was entirely unthinkable to conduct yet another intergovernmental conference, which would have been necessary for touching the text of Articles 99 and 104 (not, however, for changing the Protocol on the EDP, which would have required Council unanimity but not a new intergovernmental procedure). Hence, any more far-reaching move was out of the question. In other words, the intergovernmental power base of countries such as Germany and France was significantly weaker compared to the situation ten years earlier. There was sufficient support from Member States to make moderate changes, but any more radical change met with opposition in particular from the small Member States. They felt the need to keep as much of the SGP intact as possible, as they were still concerned that the basic reason for the reform was to accommodate France and Germany. In particular the Netherlands was advocating the least possible change because they felt that no pair of smaller states would have been able to first bend and then change the rules, and thus that the reform should be kept to a minimum.

Finally, the domestic politics approach is able to explain another relevant part of the reform process, namely the respective positions of the different governments. The French and German governments were still seeking ways to accommodate their domestic budgetary problems and saw the reform of the Pact as part of their tactics to cope with electoral promises. Good examples are to be found in the above-mentioned 'wish lists' on 'other relevant factors', where a whole range of domestic policy requirements were reflected, including continued high transfers to subsidise East Germany. However, such domestic considerations, given the weaker intergovernmental position of their sponsors, were no longer in a situation where they could interfere too much with the actual changes to the Pact.

Given the reporting in the media in November 2003 following the ECOFIN Council of 25 November 2003, it seemed that the SGP was only moderately reformed. Although alarmist notes had circulated in the wake of those events that the SGP was 'dead', the process of integration once again seemed in part to be firmly embedded not only in intergovernmental struggles and domestic needs but also in functional patterns and determined by experts.

Following the adoption of the revised SGP regulations, all institutions involved, including the ECB, agreed that the key to better fiscal policy coordination in EMU would now lie in the correct implementation of the revised Pact. In fact, the macroeconomic environment was benign to a new start: economic growth picked up substantially by 2006, leading to buoyant government revenues – well beyond expectation. Ongoing cases under the EDP were closed, and the SGP disappeared from the headlines as budgetary balances started to improve. Only few commentators remarked that, back in 1999 and 2000, the 'old' Pact had also started off in such blissful times.

9   The SGP in times of financial turbulence and economic crisis

Introduction

The review of the SGP in 2005 was followed by a period of unexpectedly strong economic growth. So much so that most observers were adamant that it was not possible to assess the usefulness of the reformed SGP, given the 'good times' and the absence of a 'bad-weather test'. The situation changed dramatically in the fourth quarter of 2008 when the financial fall-out of the subprime crisis hit home. In less than a few weeks the economic outlook changed from favourable to dire. In other words, as far as the SGP was concerned, the economic circumstances were to move onto uncharted terrain, putting the revised SGP to the test.

This chapter offers an overview and an analysis of the period following the review of the SGP up to the financial and economic crisis that came to the fore in the last quarter of 2008. The chapter also offers tentative reflections on possible scenarios for the ongoing developments in 2009. It is structured as follows. The next section contains a concise narrative of the SGP's implementation in the period from 2005 to 2007. The third section summarises the main events of the financial and economic crisis in 2007 and 2008. The fourth section presents an overview of the initial, political response by EU leaders and the Commission by the end of 2008 as well as possible implications for fiscal policy in the EU and thereby for the SGP. It also offers an analysis of these developments, as far as they were known at the time of writing in early 2009, by examining the events through the various theoretical lenses adopted throughout this book, leading to a tentative outlook about what the financial and economic crisis might mean for the future of the SGP.

Implementing the reviewed SGP (2005–2007)

During the first years following the review of the SGP, the implementation of the revised framework benefited from increasingly favourable economic circumstances and was conducted in a mainly cooperative and consensual manner.

In 2005, the year of the reform, public finances throughout the euro area still showed little progress towards the commonly agreed medium-term objectives (MTOs). In addition, the number of individual countries with deficit ratios above the reference ratio continued to grow. France, Germany, Greece, Italy and Portugal were euro-area countries still with excessive deficits, together with a further eight EU Member States among the 'outs'. Only the EDP for the Netherlands was abrogated (in June 2005). Public finances deteriorated particularly sharply in Hungary, so that the ECOFIN Council adopted a decision in accordance with Article 104.8 on 8 November 2005, stating that the action taken by Hungary was inadequate to correct the excessive deficit. Nevertheless, all in all the euro area recorded a limited degree of fiscal tightening in an environment of moderate economic growth, and its aggregate general deficit ratio decreased below the 3 per cent reference value. In 2006, economic growth picked up further and led to a relatively favourable development of public finances across the EU. Public revenues increased more than expected and government deficits continued declining – in a number of cases also helped by temporary measures. However, only Cyprus achieved a deficit level at which the EDP could be abrogated (in June 2006), while the UK joined the ranks of countries that were still found to be in excessive deficit.

Two episodes in 2006 are of particular interest. In March, the ECOFIN Council adopted a decision in accordance with Article 104.9, giving notice to Germany to correct its excessive deficit in 2007. This decision was taken without much controversy and took place barely a year after the reform of the SGP and not even three years after the heated confrontation between France and Germany on the one hand and the Commission on the other, over precisely the same procedural step in the EDP. This time, however, Germany submitted to the revised rules and agreed to enter the tight surveillance regime imposed by paragraph 9 and the corrective arm of the SGP – which included, for example, the obligation to supply quarterly progress reports to Brussels.

An eclectic approach to European integration theories can help to explain why Germany accepted a notice under Article 104.9 in 2006, having fought it so bitterly in 2003 and 2004. First, a major change had occurred domestically. A grand coalition between the social democratic party, SPD, and the centrist party, CDU, under Chancellor Angela Merkel had succeeded the Schröder government in 2005. Peer Steinbrück, a social democrat who had replaced Hans Eichel at the helm in the Ministry of Finance, embarked on a revenue-driven consolidation course backed by Merkel. Most importantly, this strategy included an increase of the main VAT rate from 16 to 19 per cent – a contested move domestically. A tight rein from Brussels and demonstration of full compliance with the revised SGP was perceived as useful domestically and explains much of Germany's willingness to accept the Council notice. In addition, elements of a functional and expertocratic explanation would point to the fact that the SGP rules, even if adapted, remained in place fundamentally to govern the surveillance of national fiscal policies at the European level. Experts in all involved institutions, including the German Ministry of Finance, not only saw them as the only relevant point of reference for the fiscal policy discourse in Brussels but, following the clashes in 2003 and 2004, also were eager to demonstrate the effectiveness of the revised SGP in this very prominent case. At the same time, it was clear to all participants that the implementation of paragraph 9 would not confront Germany with sanctions in accordance with paragraph 11. This understanding has never been explicit but lay at the core of Germany's willingness to accept the implementation of Article 104.9. In addition, experts both in Berlin and Brussels were aware that Steinbrück's revenue projection was cautious and that, most likely, Germany would easily be able to comply with the deadline for correcting its excessive deficit.

The second significant EDP episode in 2006 relates to Hungary, where public finances continued to deteriorate further. Not being a member of the eurozone, Hungary could not be subjected to a Council notice under Article 104.9, as had been the case for Germany. Instead, the Council repeated the procedural steps of adopting decisions in accordance with Article 104.8, declaring that Hungary had not respected its commitments under the previous recommendations issued in accordance with Article 104.7. In addition, on several occasions the Council issued revised recommendations – an option that had become easier to use since the SGP reform, and in so doing could extend the deadline for correcting an excessive deficit. Nevertheless, the situation in Hungary continued to spiral from bad to worse – the deficit was approaching 7 per cent of GDP and was expected by some commentators to hit 10 per cent – while the procedural steps taken under the SGP had little effect.

Again, an eclectic approach sheds light on this case, in particular in comparison to the German experience of the same year. The domestic political situation in Hungary was one of plain crisis and many feared a general loss of stability. Street riots broke out in September when Prime Minister Ferenc Gyurcsány admitted publicly that he had lied about the state of the economy during the election campaigns in April 2006. Public finances ran out of control and led to severe turbulence in the domestic financial markets as well as in the forint exchange rate until, in 2007, the government finally mustered the political will to embark seriously on a course of consolidation. During the 2006 crisis, however, the functional and expertocratic logic behind the SGP framework was unable to contain such powerful domestic dynamics and prevent public finances from degrading further. Also the ECOFIN Council with its intergovernmental mode of operation saw its influence greatly limited, particularly on a country outside the euro area.

The unsuccessful attempt at implementing the revised SGP in the Hungarian case, expressly going against domestic dynamics, contrasts starkly with the success of implementing it in the case of Germany, where a permissive domestic climate existed. In sum, the SGP continued to be implemented according to the functional logic and expertocratic reasoning that had not changed fundamentally since the reform or even before that time. However, the intergovernmental constellation implicitly assured that sanctions would not come into play in the case of Germany. The degree of influence associated with the SGP in both cases depended decisively on the respective – and very different – domestic conditions. We think that the existence of a permissive domestic constellation can be seen as a necessary (but not sufficient) condition for a successful implementation of the revised SGP. Hence the sway that the European framework holds over national fiscal policies hinges upon the political will, leadership and opportunities within the Member State concerned.

The ECOFIN Council decided in accordance with Article 104.8 also in the case of Poland that actions taken were inadequate to resolve the excessive deficit. However, none of the other EDP cases gave rise to additional procedural steps in 2006. In January 2007, the ECOFIN Council abrogated the EDP for France. Strong economic growth caused relatively favourable fiscal policy developments in 2007 and a number of countries were successful in adjusting towards their MTOs. In the euro area, the average general government deficit declined below 1 per cent of GDP and, for the first time since 2000, no country recorded a deficit above the 3 per cent of GDP reference value. The EDP was abrogated for Germany and Greece in June 2007. Outside the eurozone, developments were more heterogeneous but also improved overall and benefited from better-than-expected fiscal policy outcomes in 2006. Among the 'outs', the Czech Republic, Hungary, Poland and Slovakia were still subject to an EDP in 2007, while the EDP was abrogated in the cases of Malta and the UK. The situation in Hungary improved and was seen to be in line with the latest recommendations, but the Czech Republic was found to have taken no sufficient action, leading to an ECOFIN Council decision in accordance with Article 104.8 and a new set of recommendations in accordance with Article 104.7.

In summary, the period between 2005 and 2007 was characterised by renewed cooperation between the Member States, the Commission and the ECOFIN Council in managing fiscal governance under the SGP rules. Notwithstanding the exceptions of Hungary and the Czech Republic, a climate of consensus and peer support gained ground in the deliberations and permeated the implementation of the EDP as countries grew out of their deficits in line with increasing rates of economic growth and buoyant public revenues.

The Commission took stock of the 2005 review of the SGP (Commission of the European Communities 2007) and concluded that the Pact's corrective arm, i.e. the EDP framework, had regained credibility. It also noted that this achievement had been made possible by the good economic times and pointed to the need to improve the implementation of the preventive arm, i.e. the medium-term budgetary coordination framework based on the adjustment to country-specific MTOs. In October 2007, the ECOFIN Council discussed a range of proposals tabled by the Commission and concluded that countries should speed up their adjustment to the MTOs by using unexpected revenues for faster consolidation. It was also planned to work on a methodology for including indicators of long-term fiscal sustainability in the definition of MTOs. All in all, even after having been described as 'dead' by many commentators in 2003–4, the SGP framework was alive and well after its reform. Of course, it benefited from an increasingly benign economic environment. But this is not the only reason why all policy actors operated within the SGP system. Politicians and senior bureaucrats alike had incorporated the SGP rules as an important reference for their domestic fiscal policy discourse, working with the medium-term objectives and other elements of the framework to structure the supranational orchestration of their national fiscal policies.

The onset of the financial turbulence

The outlook for 2008 was still benign and all but two EDP cases were abrogated – Hungary and the UK (Hungary had been in excessive deficit continuously since 2004; the UK re-entered a situation of excessive deficit in July 2008). Five EDPs were abrogated in 2008, following the five (including the UK) that were abrogated in 2007.[1] Budgetary balances in general continued improving and a number of countries recorded deficits at levels last seen in the 1970s – but by mid-year it was becoming clear that the good economic times would soon be over. The Commission adopted a Communication on 24 June 2008, stating that '[while] European economies are relatively well placed to withstand the fallout from the credit crisis and the surge in commodity prices, (...) the euro area and the EU as a whole will not be immune to the US economic slowdown and the inflationary context.'

[1] See   http://ec.europa.eu/economy_finance/sg_pact_fiscal_policy/excessive_deficit9109_en. htm. Note that in February 2008 France still posed some difficulties, too (Euractiv, 10 February 2008 (Euractiv 2008a)).

(Commission of the European Communities 2008a). In retrospect, this assessment looks far too optimistic. The financial turmoil that had started in the summer of 2007 following the bursting of the US mortgage bubble worsened dramatically in September of that year and had turned into a full-blown global financial crisis by autumn 2008. This financial and credit crisis was the epicentre of what would turn out to become a global economic crisis, likely the worst one in the post-war era.[2]

The global financial crisis was caused by a combination of several factors: the competitive lowering of credit standards in the USA for so-called 'subprime' mortgages; the erosion of market discipline among all participants dealing with the selling, packaging and securitisation of such loans; the failures and complacency in the rating of the related, highly complex credit derivatives in conjunction with faulty risk management practices of financial institutions; and a generally low degree of effectiveness among governmental supervisory agencies (Hellwig 2008). Some commentators argue that the low interest rate policy of the US Federal Reserve System, after the bursting of the New Economy bubble in 2001, had prepared the ground for the housing bubble in the USA, which subsequently attracted much of the ample liquidity and almost all of the rapidly rising private debt in the US economy (Siebert 2008). A sharp increase in demand drove up house prices and private consumption, sped up in turn by financial innovation, aggressive marketing and new forms of securitisation. Importantly, none of the actors involved at the time judged it to be in their interest to withdraw from what was perceived as a virtuous circle: house buyers, mortgage institutions (which, to some extent, were affiliated with political parties), banks, rating agencies, supervisory agencies and, least of all, the political leadership that had professed the virtues of increased house ownership in the first place. To overseas investors, these markets promised a high rate of return, which kept growing in comparison to more conservative investments in a low interest rate scenario and attracted numerous financial players, including many European private banks such as Bradford & Bingley, Fortis, Northern Rock, the Royal Bank of Scotland, and even state banks, such as some German *Landesbanken*, for example Sachsen LB and West LB. Many if not most of the final customers however were not aware of the sheer size of the risks associated with the underlying subprime mortgages in the USA to which they had become exposed.

---

[2] We speak about a 'global financial crisis' to refer to the period that started with the 15 September 2008 collapse of Lehman Brothers through to the end of December 2008 (an artificial breakpoint). During this period many banks faced critical liquidity shortages, and stock exchanges across the globe lost anywhere between 30–50 per cent of their value. We speak about 'economic crisis' in the sense of a period of low growth of the real economy (recession or even depression) thereafter.

The housing bubble in the USA burst as a result of the successive interest rate increases by the Fed, which had been raising rates since 2003, also causing a gradual rise of mortgage interest. The ensuing recession in the housing market deepened in 2007 and coincided with a growing number of defaults of borrowers on their subprime mortgages, turning the previously virtuous circle into a vicious one. Many of the related, asset-backed commercial papers experienced refinancing problems and had to take recourse to bank credit lines. This caused a massive loss of trust among banks, which led to an almost complete drying-up of money markets and interbank lending, coupled with massive write-downs on banks' balance sheets, which in turn contributed to the global stock market downturn. Several banks came close to failure and had to ask for state assistance or shut down investment funds. A dramatic climax was reached in September 2008 when the US government had to nationalise the mortgage institutions Fannie Mae and Freddie Mac, triggering a panic on financial markets amidst fears of a liquidity crisis and the collapse of the investment bank Lehman Brothers.

Faced with the imminent danger of a system-wide financial meltdown after the fall of Lehman, governments on both sides of the Atlantic quickly drew up rescue packages for their national banking systems, involving state guarantees of deposits, partial nationalisation of banks and massive capital injections. The financial system was saved for the time being, but by the end of 2008 it became clear that the real economy would inevitably be pushed into a global recession as a consequence of the financial crisis. Private consumption in the USA collapsed and economic activity started falling rapidly during late 2008 in an adverse feedback loop between the financial and real sectors of the economy. Governments reacted with at times drastic loosening of fiscal policies, in conjunction with continued monetary easing by central banks that, in the case of the Fed, even involved a zero interest rate policy and the use of so-called 'quantitative easing'. Forecasts in early 2009 assumed a fiscal package in the USA of some 5½ per cent of GDP over two years and at least 1½ per cent in the EU (Commission of the European Communities 2009), while governments were still finalising their plans regarding a fiscal policy reaction to the economic deterioration – in most cases a combination of higher public spending and tax cuts or lower social security contributions.

As this book is going to press, the actual size of the fiscal stimuli and their effects on national budgets are still far from clear. Many of the measures adopted to address, as one would hope, a temporary crisis, are of a permanent nature and difficult to reverse. They could contribute to a further degradation of the long-term sustainability of public finances. In addition to these discretionary measures and depending on the magnitude of the recession, budgets will also reflect the functioning of automatic stabilisers, in particular a reversal of past revenue windfalls. The overall effect of discretionary measures and automatic stabilisers in the EU is currently expected to amount to around 4 per cent of GDP over 2009 and 2010, with the general government deficit to more than double in 2009 to 4½ of GDP while the US deficit is expected to even reach 10 per cent in 2009 (Commission of the European Communities 2009).

Among the euro-area countries, France, Greece, Ireland, Italy, Portugal, Slovenia and Spain are expected to breach the 3 per cent of GDP reference value in 2009 and will not see their budgetary deficit return to below the reference value (see Table 9.1 and 9.2 which provide the forecast information current as of 19 January 2009). As can be seen from these tables, budgetary positions are expected to worsen further in 2010 at which time ten of the sixteen euro-area countries are expected to exceed the reference value. For instance, Austria, Belgium, Germany and Slovakia are expected to join the ranks of new EDP countries. Public debt is growing as a result of the increase in net government borrowing. The average euro-area public debt is forecast to rise from 69 per cent in 2008 to 72 per cent in 2009 up to 76 per cent in 2010, which even masks substantially more rapid increases in individual countries. This outlook is obviously associated with major uncertainties – but it is already evident that a new chapter in the history of the SGP has been opened.

The European economy in crisis

With the sudden worsening of the global financial crisis in September 2008, a turbulent period started in Europe and Member States increasingly became aware that the financial crisis, which in the first instance had been US-based, was contagious. Sooner rather than later it hit Europe and the rest of the world – thereby becoming a global problem.

The EU finance ministers had been meeting on the eve of the Lehman bankruptcy to see if a US-style crisis could be avoided in the EU, among other things by harmonising the way in which banks report their financial results (planning a harmonisation of standards is due to come into effect by 2010).[3] The next day the European Central Bank responded quickly to the fall-out by making funds available, while stock exchanges plunged sharply.[4] By the end of the week EU Commissioner Joaquín Almunia stated that there would not be the same type of capital injections in banks as had been the case in the USA. Furthermore, he called upon the

---

[3] EUObserver, 16 September 2008 (EUObserver 2008a).
[4] EUObserver, 17 September 2008 (EUObserver 2008b).

Table 9.1 *General government net lending (+) or borrowing (-) (as a % of GDP) (1)*

	5-year averages		2002–6	2004	2005	2006	2007	Estimates 2008	Forecasts 2009	Scenario unchanged policies 2010	
	1992–6	1997–01									
BE	-5.4	-0.6	-0.5	-0.2	-2.6	0.3	-0.3	-0.9	-3.0	-4.3	BE
DE	-3.0	-1.6	-3.3	-3.8	-3.3	-1.5	-0.2	-0.1	-2.9	-4.2	DE
IE	-1.7	2.4	1.2	1.4	1.7	3.0	0.2	-6.3	-11.0	-13.0	IE
EL	-9.8	-4.2	-5.2	-7.5	-5.1	-2.8	-3.5	-3.4	-3.7	-4.2	EL
ES	-5.6	-1.9	0.4	-0.3	1.0	2.0	2.2	-3.4	-6.2	-5.7	ES
FR	-4.9	-2.1	-3.2	-3.6	-2.9	-2.4	-2.7	-3.2	-5.4	-5.0	FR
IT	-8.3	-2.2	-3.5	-3.5	-4.3	-3.4	-1.6	-2.8	-3.8	-3.7	IT
CY	–	–	-3.7	-4.1	-2.4	-1.2	3.4	1.0	-0.6	-1.0	CY
LU	1.6	4.5	0.5	-1.2	-0.1	1.3	3.2	3.0	0.4	-1.4	LU
MT	–	-7.6	-5.0	-4.7	-2.8	-2.3	-1.8	-3.5	-2.6	-2.5	MT
NL	-3.3	0.0	-1.3	-1.7	-0.3	0.6	0.3	1.1	-1.4	-2.7	NL
AT	-4.1	-1.6	-1.9	-4.4	-1.5	-1.5	-0.4	-0.6	-3.0	-3.6	AT
PT	-4.7	-3.4	-3.8	-3.4	-6.1	-3.9	-2.6	-2.2	-4.6	-4.4	PT
SI	–	-2.9	-2.0	-2.2	-1.4	-1.2	0.5	-0.9	-3.2	-2.8	SI
SK	–	-7.6	-3.9	-2.3	-2.8	-3.5	-1.9	-2.2	-2.8	-3.6	SK

FI	-5.8	2.8	3.2	2.4	2.9	4.1	5.3	4.5	2.0	0.5	FI
€ area	-5.0	-1.6	-2.5	-2.9	-2.5	-1.3	-0.6	-1.7	-4.0	-4.4	€ area
BG	–	1.4	1.1	1.6	1.9	3.0	0.1	3.2	2.0	2.0	BG
CZ	–	-4.4	-4.5	-3.0	-3.6	-2.7	-1.0	-1.2	-2.5	-2.3	CZ
DK	-2.5	1.0	2.6	2.0	5.2	5.2	4.5	3.1	-0.3	-1.5	DK
EE	–	-0.5	1.6	1.7	1.5	2.9	2.7	-2.0	-3.2	-3.2	EE
LV	–	-1.5	-1.1	-1.0	-0.4	-0.2	0.1	-3.5	-6.3	-7.4	LV
LT	–	-4.9	-1.1	-1.5	-0.5	-0.4	-1.2	-2.9	-3.0	-3.4	LT
HU	–	-5.3	-7.9	-6.4	-7.8	-9.3	-5.0	-3.3	-2.8	-3.0	HU
PL	–	-3.9	-5.0	-5.7	-4.3	-3.8	-2.0	-2.5	-3.6	-3.5	PL
RO	–	–	-1.6	-1.2	-1.2	-2.2	-2.5	-5.2	-7.5	-7.9	RO
SE	-7.7	1.2	0.7	0.8	2.4	2.3	3.6	2.3	-1.3	-1.4	SE
UK	-6.0	0.6	-3.1	-3.7	-3.4	-2.7	-2.7	-4.6	-8.8	-9.6	UK
EU	–	-1.4	-2.5	-2.9	-2.4	-1.4	-0.9	-2.0	-4.4	-4.8	EU

(1) The net lending (borrowing) includes in 2000–5 one-off proceeds regarding UMTS licences.
Source: European Commission (2009).

Table 9.2 *General government gross debt (as a % of GDP)*

	2001	2002	2003	2004	2005	2006	2007	Estimates 2008	Forecasts 2009	Scenario unchanged policies 2010	
BE	106.5	103.4	98.6	94.3	92.1	87.8	83.9	88.3	91.2	94.0	BE
DE	58.8	60.3	63.8	65.6	67.8	67.6	65.1	65.6	69.6	72.3	DE
IE	35.5	32.2	31.1	29.4	27.3	24.7	24.8	40.8	54.8	68.2	IE
EL	102.9	101.5	97.8	98.6	98.8	95.9	94.8	94.0	96.2	98.4	EL
ES	55.5	52.5	48.7	46.2	43.0	39.6	36.2	39.8	46.9	53.0	ES
FR	56.2	58.2	62.9	64.9	66.4	63.6	63.9	67.1	72.4	76.0	FR
IT	108.8	105.7	104.4	103.8	105.9	106.9	104.1	105.7	109.3	110.3	IT
CY	60.7	64.6	68.9	70.2	69.1	64.6	59.4	48.1	46.7	45.7	CY
LU	6.5	6.5	6.2	6.3	6.1	6.6	7.0	14.4	15.0	15.1	LU
MT	62.1	60.1	69.3	72.1	69.8	63.8	61.9	63.3	64.0	64.2	MT
NL	50.7	50.5	52.0	52.4	51.8	47.4	45.7	57.3	53.2	55.2	NL
AT	67.0	66.4	65.4	64.8	63.7	62.0	59.5	59.4	62.3	64.7	AT
PT	52.9	55.5	56.9	58.3	63.6	64.7	63.6	64.6	68.2	71.7	PT
SI	27.4	28.1	27.5	27.2	27.0	26.7	23.4	22.1	24.8	25.8	SI

SK	48.9	43.4	42.4	41.4	34.2	30.4	29.4	28.6	30.0	31.9	SK
FI	42.3	41.3	44.3	44.1	41.3	39.2	35.1	32.8	34.5	26.1	FI
€ area	68.0	67.8	69.1	69.5	70.0	68.3	66.1	68.7	72.7	75.8	€ area
BG	67.3	53.6	45.9	37.9	29.2	22.7	18.2	13.8	12.2	10.7	BG
CZ	25.1	28.5	30.1	30.4	29.8	29.6	28.9	27.9	29.4	30.6	CZ
DK	47.4	46.8	45.8	43.8	36.4	30.7	26.3	30.3	28.4	27.0	DK
EE	4.8	5.6	5.5	5.0	4.5	4.3	3.5	4.3	6.1	7.6	EE
LV	14.0	13.5	14.6	14.9	12.4	10.7	9.5	16.0	30.4	42.9	LV
LT	23.1	22.3	21.1	19.4	18.4	18.0	17.0	17.1	20.0	23.3	LT
HU	52.1	55.8	58.1	59.4	61.7	65.6	65.8	71.9	73.8	74.0	HU
PL	37.6	42.2	47.1	45.7	47.1	47.7	44.9	45.5	47.7	49.7	PL
RO	26.0	24.9	21.5	18.7	15.8	12.4	12.7	15.2	21.1	26.8	RO
SE	54.4	52.6	52.3	51.2	50.9	45.9	40.6	34.8	36.2	36.0	SE
UK	37.7	37.5	38.7	40.6	42.3	43.4	44.1	50.1	62.6	71.0	UK
EU	60.8	60.2	61.8	62.2	62.7	61.3	58.7	60.6	67.4	70.9	EU

Source: European Commission (2009).

governments of the EU and in the euro area in particular to collaborate and resort to joint action ('US-style "financial socialism" not an option for Europe').[5] After the weekend, voices could be heard talking about collaboration and the need to improve a European response. The British and German governments advocated that a new international system regulating the financial world would have to be constructed in order to prevent the repeat of a global banking crisis in the future, floating the idea of 'an international authority that will make the traffic rules for financial markets'.[6] On 24 September 2008 French President Sarkozy (during the French EU Presidency) responded and proclaimed the need for capitalism to be more regulated and less opaque.[7] On 25 September, Sarkozy suggested that '"laissez-faire" capitalism is finished'.[8] Nevertheless, at this time Almunia was still optimistic that interventions would not be necessary. On 24 September he told the European Parliament: 'The situation we face here in Europe is less acute and Member States do not at this point consider that a US-style plan is needed' (AFP 2008).

By 29 September the global financial crisis in Europe took on an entirely different meaning when the Belgium-Dutch bank Fortis all but went under.[9] The response by the Benelux governments was to nationalise part of the bank. Simultaneously, emergency discussions between German banks and domestic authorities were taking place regarding the German lender Hypo Real Estate.[10] At this date, it was beyond doubt that the European market would also be affected.[11] European authorities in Brussels, Frankfurt and at EU Member State level scrambled to save the continent's financial system after bank stocks plunged when the US House of Representatives rejected a $700 billion bailout of Wall Street on Monday 29 September. During this week the US stock exchange saw dramatic falls, including a drop of 777 points on 30 September – the largest single-day loss ever reported. At this time, the Icelandic government also announced that it had to nationalise a bank (Glitner), triggering fears (which would soon materialise) of an overall collapse in the Icelandic banking sector. In fact, four months later, on 29 January 2009, the Icelandic government fell due to the financial crisis.

---

[5] Euractiv, 19 September 2008 (Euractiv 2008b).
[6] EUObserver, 22 September 2008 (EUObserver 2008c).
[7] EUObserver, 24 September 2008 (EUObserver 2008d).
[8] EUObserver, 26 September 2008 (EUObserver 2008e).
[9] EUObserver, 29 September 2008 (EUObserver 2008f).
[10] EUObserver, 29 September 2008 (EUObserver 2008f).
[11] EUObserver, 30 September 2008 (EUObserver 2008g).

The European countries experiencing the largest difficulties following the onset of the financial crisis were those that had a formidable banking sector and large financial institutions that in turn were exposed to risks in the USA: the Benelux countries, Germany, Ireland and the UK. Following the dramatic events of the last two weeks of September, European leaders felt the need to respond collectively but often found themselves confronted by the speed of events, the sheer size and complexity of the problem and the lack of clarity as to what collective action could achieve. Under these circumstances they often resorted to unilateral action.

The first player to go out of step was the Irish government. On 30 September it announced a unilateral decision to safeguard all deposits in Irish banks and building societies for a period of two years. Given that the Irish economy is closely connected to that of the UK and the rest of the euro area, this move was heavily criticised by other EU Member States, notably by the UK and Germany, as being against the spirit of European integration, which in these turbulent times would require a joint response rather than a 'beggar thy neighbour' approach. In fact, soon after the announcement there were indications that capital was moving from the UK to Ireland, in order to benefit from the new regime there.

The first attempt at a joint action came on 4 October when Nicolas Sarkozy, again in his capacity as holding the rotating Presidency of the EU, invited the leaders of the four largest EU economies (France, Germany, Italy and the UK) to meet in Paris and to discuss possible options. The invitation was not well received in Berlin and London, where it was felt that a truly collective response was needed. The meeting ended badly as France and Germany disagreed over whether to consider the radical idea of an EU-wide bailout fund as proposed by France.[12] Not even twenty-four hours later, Germany became the second Member State to announce unilateral measures, rescuing the major property lender Hypo Real Estate and securing bank deposits – thereby taking an action similar to that of Ireland, which the German government had so heavily criticised only a few days earlier. At the same time, a deal over the Belgium-Dutch bank Fortis unravelled and the Dutch government decided to nationalise fully its part of the bank, joining the ranks of governments taking unilateral action to solve the domestic problems resulting from the financial crisis.

Despite these unilateral actions, there was some concerted effort within the EU context. On 7 October 2008 the ECOFIN Council agreed to a joint action plan for dealing with the financial crisis, but most observers and the markets doubted its effectiveness. A day later the ECB and the

---

[12] *Financial Times*, 13 October 2008, p. 3.

central banks of Canada, Switzerland, Sweden, the UK and the USA announced a coordinated half-percentage interest rate cut, albeit also without a sustained effect on the markets. The week of 6–10 October was characterised by major plunges in stock markets and attacks on bank stocks, despite the multitude of measures adopted by individual governments.

At the time of writing, it is beyond doubt that the crisis is serious and is hitting all economies of the euro area, the EU at large and especially also the outer ring of Europe (besides Iceland, the Baltic countries as well as Central and Eastern European countries, including Belarus and Ukraine, have entered into serious financial difficulties). Several EU and non-EU countries have already had to take recourse to emergency lending from the IMF in order to avert a sovereign default. The EU seeks to coordinate but does not itself have the legal competence to enact measures such as bailouts for banks, companies or even states, as some fear. Thus the Member State governments remain in charge and decide in a self-interested manner on matters regarding the immediate short term. How do these developments impact on our subject, the Stability and Growth Pact?

On various occasions Member States were quick to ask for a suspension of the SGP in light of the paramount problems imposed by the crisis. A first request came with the Summit of the European G8 members held at the Palais de l'Elysée on 4 October 2008 (Presidency of the European Union 2008a). The heads of state or government of the four largest Member States recommended that the 'exceptional circumstances' clause of the SGP be invoked: 'The four heads of government also concluded that the European economy was facing "exceptional circumstances" and asked for the application of the Stability and Growth Pact – the eurozone rules requiring that national budget deficits be limited to 3% of their GDP – to "reflect" this situation.'[13]

However, the subsequent European Council conclusions stipulated clearly that the rules of the revised Stability and Growth Pact must be maintained. The Council conclusions stated literally: 'Budget policies must continue to be in line with the revised Stability and Growth Pact, which should also be applied in a manner which reflects the current exceptional circumstances, as provided for in its rules' (Presidency conclusions – Brussels, 15 and 16 October 2008, p. 5). In other words, this could be understood as a pledge that the SGP would continue to apply and EDPs would be started against Member States – but no penalties would be envisaged during times in which the situation is exceptional.

---

[13] Euractiv, 6 October 2008 (Euractiv 2008c).

The Commission also strongly advocated the continuing application of the SGP as an overall framework, not least as a source of policy guidance once the financial and economic crisis would recede. In its Communication of 29 October it suggested a strong European response to the crisis that called for bold action but was nevertheless portrayed as respecting the parameters set by the Stability and Growth Pact (Commission of the European Communities 2008b). In the following days EU officials publicly defended the SGP and pointed to both its flexibility and its limits. For example, Commissioner Almunia stated in early November that Member States 'should use the room for manoeuvre they have to cushion the impact' but he also said 'we have red lines, we cannot put an excessive burden on the next generation. (…) Given that inflationary pressures are now easing, monetary and fiscal policy can contribute to supporting demand. (…) Member States can now use the room for manoeuvre they have created.'[14]

The European Council of 15 and 16 October affirmed the need for the Commission to also take action and instructed it to develop a European response to the crisis. By the end of November 2008 the Commission provided details of a package that it designed in order to support 'growth and jobs' (Commission of the European Communities 2008c). Its 'European Economic Recovery Plan' inevitably contained many of the national measures that Member States had already adopted and also reflected the limited budgetary resources of the EU itself.[15] Again, the reference to the SGP was one in which the rules would apply but, during the period of crisis, the flexibility within the Pact would be used. When the heads of state and government met on 11 and 12 December they approved a smaller version of the Commission package, trying to show some concerted effort on the part of the EU. Nevertheless, the overall approach remained one of pronounced national action and limited European coordination, the communication of which bordered on the meaningless. The real value of statements such as the following conclusions of the ECOFIN Council will have to be seen in the near future:

While budget deficits will increase in many Member States in the short run, and a number of Member States will temporarily exceed the deficit reference value, we remain fully committed to sound and sustainable public finances. The Stability and Growth Pact provides adequate flexibility to deal with these exceptional situations. The adjustment path and recommendations will take into account this exceptional situation, as well as differences in fiscal space. These procedures should be seen as an instrument for constructive peer pressure, helping to return to

---

[14] *New Europe*, 3 November 2008.
[15] Some net contributors to the EU budget, above all Germany, prevented the channelling of unused funds from 2008 into additional measures.

sustainable public finances. We are all committed to return to our consolidation path towards medium-term budgetary targets as soon as possible, keeping pace with the economic recovery. The coordinated fiscal stimulus will thus be followed by a coordinated budget consolidation.[16]

Analysis and tentative outlook

Given the criticism of the SGP before and after its reform in 2005, it is without doubt remarkable that it stayed intact – at least for the time being – as the financial crisis unfolded. Another factor that is noteworthy is that the Commission has interpreted the SGP framework as being implemented during and even despite the truly exceptional circumstances. In its official communication, it argued that the European Economic Recovery Programme would be 'anchored' in the SGP. From the look of it, the Commission would also have been able to put the SGP to the side and not apply the EDP to those Member States that are experiencing difficulties. But, in fact, EDPs are being opened for all countries that fail to show that their excessive deficit is 'temporary' and is not exceeding the 3 per cent reference value by very much. The EDP recommendations under preparation at the time of writing make reference to the 'special circumstances' of the crisis and assign long deadlines for the correction of the excessive deficits. They speak of all but a flexible and pragmatic implementation of the SGP, which appears to explain to a large extent why it is no longer under explicit pressure and why nobody, least the Commission, now demands its suspension or adaptation – for the time being.

However, there are first indications that the framework is being applied not only in a pragmatic but almost in a casual way that departs further from the originally promised practice and also from the rhetoric surrounding the review of the Pact. For example, the Commission's recommendations for Council opinions on countries' stability and convergence programmes, as well as the first set of Commission Reports in accordance with Article 104.3 of the EDP, shed doubt on the sincerity with which the SGP is being implemented. In these most recent documents at the time of writing, the Commission establishes the stipulations of its European Economic Recovery Programme as a quasi-formal requirement for loosening fiscal policy. At the same time, pursuit of a country's medium-term objective has largely been removed from the Commission assessments. The SGP procedures hence seem to be hijacked, at least currently and to some extent, by the Commission's urge to orchestrate national crisis policies. How can we

---

[16] ECOFIN Council Conclusions, January 2009.

understand the current situation? Let us turn to the four theoretical lenses to see if and how each of them is able to shed light on these events.

First, it seems that an intergovernmental approach is not well suited to provide insights into these developments. After all, if a country wanted to protect its sovereignty and room for manoeuvre in the future, knowing that rules will be applied under the SGP once growth picks up, Member States would have likely lobbied for the rules not to apply for a period of time. This has not happened extensively and we now only have evidence of Member State governments asking that the rules be applied flexibly, not for their abandonment or a suspension of the SGP. An intergovernmental approach would assume at least some Member States would seek to secure maximum flexibility over the rules rather than lack of clarity as to whether and when the Pact might 'bite' in the future. Given the large uncertainty surrounding the ongoing crisis, an intergovernmentalist perspective would expect that at least some Member States would challenge an approach of keeping rules in place that might affect them in the future. In the absence of such moves, the intergovernmentalist element seems to have little effect on the current outcomes.

A similar verdict applies to the domestic politics approach, which looks at important domestic actors and institutions and examines which of those request or use a particular set of rules or not. Again, in this context we do not see domestic actors or institutions playing a strong role either in favour or against the application of the SGP. Domestic actors are overwhelmed with competing priorities of addressing their respective, national manifestations of the global crisis – and the SGP is likely to be the least of their worries. Hence, thus far we would also not be able to benefit from a domestic politics perspective on the SGP implementation at the current juncture. However, this might change when the implications of the financial and economic crisis for public finances become more apparent.

The other two approaches, the functional and the expertocratic, seem to be better suited for explaining the current events. The way in which the rules are applied assume that implementation of the framework will at least continue formally. This functional logic also seems to be incorporated by governments. While the SGP has little to zero effect on current measures of crisis management, there are chances that it might become relevant again for the formulation of fiscal policy once (and if) growth picks up and the economic tide turns. In that case, the Commission might change its focus back onto the SGP and confront any 'bad performers' with the rules. Given the amount of uncertainty, potentially any Member State could be in that position, which lends support to the thesis that the mechanism relied on is very much a functional one.

The expertocratic approach is also comparatively well suited to provide us with insights for the ongoing developments. Despite the current focus on crisis policy and the Commission's urge to place its European Economic Recovery Programme centre stage, there is continued support for the SGP paradigm among the fiscal policy community, which continues to believe in the existing set of rules as the appropriate instrument to rein in the potential budgetary profligacy of Member States. For better or for worse, the revised Pact is more explicit about its in-built flexibility, which is now being used. While embracing that increased dimension of flexibility, practitioners still seem to agree not to revert to a situation in which rules are absent. In other words, the experts behind the scene remain broadly supportive of having the rules continue to apply. And seeing that there are no other rules that could offer any better coordinative device, the present SGP system of rules holds for now – even if it is at least momentarily overshadowed by measures geared to address the current crisis.

Our last set of interviews in Brussels to check whether these principles had been incorporated into the day-to-day thinking of bureaucrats and other experts close to these issues confirmed that Member States over the past years had indeed almost fully incorporated parameters like the MTOs or the balanced budget target.[17] It is now too early to judge if the current departure signals a temporary deviation or a structural break. In a similar vein, finance ministries of the Member States have come to realise that, in the long run, fiscal sustainability has to be maintained in light of the demographic challenges ahead for their social security schemes. They have by and large also come to link this insight to the SGP as the appropriate policy framework to deal with the problem. Thus the basic ideas behind the Pact, while changing, still amount to broad support. The rationale behind the half-hearted implementation of the Pact during the crisis might be that applying the rules today will not bind the hands of the government of the day but they will to some extent bind the government of the future, once the crisis period is over.

The events unfolding, as this book is going to press, have mind-numbing ramifications for public finances all across Europe. They will undoubtedly shape Member States' fiscal governance in EMU, as laid out in the SGP. The growing number of countries with deficits above the 3 per cent of GDP reference value will mean a resurgence of EDPs, hence an activation of the corrective arm of the Pact. It cannot be excluded that old confrontations between different groups of Member States and with the

---

[17] Commission officials, interview with the authors, Brussels, 18 December 2008.

Commission might resurface. Furthermore, the truly special circumstances implied by the magnitude of the financial and economic crisis cannot fail to have a bearing on the way in which the rules will be implemented.

However, looking back at more than twelve years of SGP politics, we would argue that the SGP will likely continue to exist and will continue playing its part in shaping Member States' fiscal policies as well as their common discourse in Brussels. Informed by our eclectic approach drawing on European integration theories, we believe that one can lay out a number of stipulations about how rules-based governance will likely play out under the SGP, as Member States attempt to address the ongoing crisis through their fiscal policies.

We would expect the Commission to take account of country specificities when carrying out fiscal surveillance. For example, it might point out the more favourable fiscal positions of those Member States that, prior to the crisis, had attentively implemented the preventive arm of the SGP. Budgetary positions that had been in line with MTOs at the outset of the downturn can be portrayed as a more robust starting point for dealing with the crisis.

As the crisis unfolds, we would expect the corrective arm of the SGP, in particular the implementation of the EDP, to do little by way of containing even sharp increases in budgetary deficits. The activation of the corrective arm in itself is positive but should not be overestimated. On the one hand, the revised rules could have been used as an excuse for treating deficits above the 3 per cent of GDP reference value as not excessive, in light of the indeed special circumstances of the crisis. This in turn would have allowed the ECOFIN Council to refrain from applying the EDP. On the other hand, the opening of an EDP could be argued to matter only as much as the country concerned would receive a strict deadline for correcting its excessive deficit. Determination to do so is currently not perceivable on behalf of the policy actors.

Nevertheless, the fact that the option of ignoring the corrective arm has deliberately not been chosen and that, to the contrary, all deficits above the reference value are being treated as excessive by a unanimous ECOFIN, to us suggests at least two things. First, no Member State any longer perceives the corrective arm of the SGP to be a sanction-equipped threat to their fiscal sovereignty. To the contrary, the very faint prospect of sanctions in the past is now even less likely, following the 2005 SGP review as well as the severity of the economic crisis. Second, at least some players and especially the fiscal policy community have come to endorse positively the SGP framework and to see it as beneficial for themselves, even when – and possibly precisely because – they find themselves in excessive deficit. Hence, the SGP is not going to prevent the emergence of large or even very large deficits. However, on the assumption that the crisis will reach its climax at some point and that the recession will come to an end, we would expect the EDP framework to structure the path in which countries can work their way out of excessive deficit. In an optimistic scenario, we would expect budgetary coordination by the Commission and the ECOFIN, based on the SGP, to some extent to coordinate Member States' efforts to limit and drive back the momentous increase in public debt that they currently are building up (in great part 'below the line', such as rescue operations for financial institutions, and possibly to an extent far larger than the cumulative effect of successive deficits 'above the line').

The exact way in which this process might play out of course cannot be predicted. However, we would suggest looking at individual country cases once more through the four lenses of the European integration theories that we have applied so far. Domestic politics will be crucial for determining the political will to contain deficits (or not) and to improve fiscal balances (or not) as economic growth picks up. These invariably different attitudes of different Member States will meet with the functional and expertocratic tendencies to stick to the SGP framework and to apply it pragmatically to individual countries with the aim to support and, if necessary, pressure them into regaining the course of consolidation. Ultimately, the intergovernmental dimension of SGP politics will determine the degree to which the SGP might be applied with force to possible renegade countries. As we have seen in 2003 and 2004, it will be close to impossible to exert meaningful influence and fiscal discipline on one or several large Member States if these, for domestic reasons, should fall short of a sufficient path of adjustment. Conversely, we would expect relatively stronger persuasion and possibly even the activation of further procedural steps under the EDP in the case of smaller countries being found profligate by their larger peers.

The implicit understanding of these expected dynamics might indeed be the underlying reason why the Commission has activated the corrective arm of the SGP right at the beginning of the downturn. In light of the truly stupendous burden that some countries are placing upon their public finances, some governments might seek to self-commit as well as to bind their successors to limit the fiscal damage and to undertake steps against further undermining long-term sustainability. In addition, some Member States might already have an interest in ensuring that they can avail themselves of the SGP in the future, as it is currently the only available framework for exerting pressure over their peers, to the extent possible, should they embark on a course of fiscal policy that bears negative externalities for others or even endangers the cohesion of the currency area at large.

We have described our take of an optimistic scenario for SGP governance once the recession comes to an end. Of course, other scenarios are thinkable. Should the economic situation worsen indefinitely, it might ultimately lead to solvency problems for one or several Member States beyond what can be fended off by emergency lending. It is hard to think that such a situation would be without serious repercussions on the current SGP set of rules or, for that matter, the institutional edifice of EMU at large.

Even short of that extreme, the Commission's current departure from a strict implementation of the SGP towards emphasis on some European Economic Recovery Programme might spell more lasting damage for the SGP than we currently expect. The more the Commission argues in favour of loose fiscal policies, the harder it might find it to regain a discourse of consolidation even after the economy might have turned. More drastically speaking, the Commission is at some risk of harming its role as guardian of the Treaty by exaggerating its ambition to be a 'policy entrepreneur' in times of crisis.

Another scenario could be that the current crisis, like others before it, creates momentum for far-reaching institutional change and innovation in the EU. Calls for more stringent forms of economic cooperation and even a *gouvernement éonomique* have never fully ceased (e.g. Hodson 2009; Howarth 2005; Pisani-Ferry 2006; Verdun 2003) and might resurface in full swing. However, in the absence of integrationist ambition at the level of even the Lisbon Treaty (which preserves the existing SGP framework), we would stick to our above-mentioned scenario as being the more likely one. Falling short of a new Treaty, even changes to the SGP regulations would require a qualified majority in the Council, which currently clearly has other preoccupations than yet again changing the legal basis for a framework that is widely deemed appropriate. It may not be the best conceivable way of 'ruling Europe' and possibly even falls short of a second-best solution to fiscal governance in monetary union – but the SGP does seem to be as good as it gets when it comes to common European rules for different national fiscal policies. As such, it has become an indispensable building block for EMU and, for that matter, European integration at large. With the momentously growing fiscal implications of Member States' attempts to address the global financial and economic crisis, it is from this perspective that one can gauge what is now at risk.

10 Conclusion: The past, present and future of the SGP and implications for European integration theory

This study of the Stability and Growth Pact has sought to provide an in-depth analysis of the SGP case while at the same time it aimed to use integration theories to make sense of the empirical findings. Many EU studies are either empirically well informed but fall short of exploiting the theoretical insights that could be obtained, or, alternatively, are strictly interested in improving the theory while resting on thin empirics. This chapter seeks to bring together the insights from more than a dozen years of SGP history with our take on how better to use theories of European integration for understanding integration phenomena.

The SGP has already attracted more attention than its founders ever thought it would during its entire existence. It has proven to be a Pact caught up in politics, both domestic and international, and firmly embedded in the functional framework of the EU with a large role played by experts and the existing paradigm on economic policy-making.

This study sought to trace the origins of the Stability and Growth Pact, its implementation, its institutional crisis and reform and its implementation in the midst of a global economic crisis – all with a view to understanding what factors determine the outcomes we observe. Reflecting briefly on the financial crisis we speculated on what it might mean for the SGP. In this book we adopted an innovative approach by having parts of the Pact's genesis be analysed by different theoretical approaches, which we argue are complementary in their power to explain the outcome. No single approach can explain what national positions were chosen and the creation of the SGP. In studying the period of implementation we felt a domestic politics approach was best able to explain the behaviour of Member State governments. The SGP crisis in turn is above all an intergovernmentalist story, although some domestic politics explain the formation of national positions on the SGP as well as why the issue stayed salient in the international scene. The period of reform is once again a process best understood by adopting the four theoretical approaches together, with an emphasis on the role played by experts operating within functional strands. Finally, the period of implementation following the reform of the SGP and the financial and economic crises are best understood from a functional and expertocratic perspective.

Theoretical explanations of the SGP

Besides giving a detailed overview of why the SGP was created and what function it fulfils in the EMU edifice, our aim was to reflect on the SGP as a showcase through which better to understand the wider question of a well-known puzzle – how do we explain European integration phenomena? Taking up this challenge requires a theoretical exercise in a scientific field that is split over the choice of explanatory variables, such as levels of analysis as well as the choice of actors and mechanisms to focus on (see Sadeh and Verdun 2009 for an overview of the literature of EMU on these matters).

The SGP seems very well suited for the task of furthering a more general understanding of integration, and it does so for the following reasons. First of all, it is applicable to a range of theoretical explanations that are generally seen to be competing.[1] The literature on European integration theories often seek to show that one approach is superior in explaining integration to another. It is not rare that the scope of the subject under study is sufficiently minimised so as to be able to use a certain approach more effectively.

Second, the creation of the SGP is located at the focal point of integration in the 1990s, namely that of preparing monetary union in the EU. Its implementation turned out to be at the heart of the actual day-to-day business of EMU – besides the setting of monetary policy by the ECB. The difficulties surrounding the SGP crisis in 2003 brought to the fore how at its core it is an instrument of European integration that shows the power politics at stake in the enlarged EU (power struggles within the Council between small and large Member States, and between the Commission and Council). The reform showed that, ultimately, the functional logic within the European integration process is a strong driving force for stability and continuity of rules and regimes. Also the role of experts and ideas (paradigms) remains at the heart of the process of integration. To date the analysis of the SGP in the aftermath of the financial crisis and the onset of the economic crisis further supports this finding.

Third, the policy-making process behind the creation of the SGP, its implementation and its reform, took place at various levels and involved a multitude of national as well as supranational actors. Once the SGP had been created and was put at risk in November 2003, the number of key

---

[1] Note that various authors have suggested the need to merge theories, be eclectic or combine the best of different approaches; see *inter alia* (Verdun 2000a, 2002a; van Esch 2002; Wolf 2002).

players even increased with the ECJ getting involved in determining how the Pact had to be applied.

Fourth, the case shows several aspects of integration, perhaps even a comprehensive range of the important features, involving both high politics and technical issues, intergovernmental bargaining as well as domestic policy concerns, negotiation versus mutual adjustment of different positions, and law-making as well as law implementation.

Nothing speaks against picking more narrow cases that focus on a single aspect of the above list, or to choose to concentrate on a single theoretical explanation. The depth of the understanding gained will likely be more profound, but it would probably imply a lesser understanding of the wider integration phenomena of which the narrow case is a part. We therefore consciously made the choice for a research design that represented a 'messy situation' and would require the use of various theories, and without the result of arriving at a fully satisfactory account. Some questions will necessarily have remained open. We have offered a number of explanations of why the SGP was created, its implementation path, its reform and why it to date has withstood the pressures of the financial crisis. We do not claim to have found *the* explanation. But we have given a set of explanations that seem most plausible to us and that are backed by our understanding of the empirical material we collected and the information that we have access to.

We found the theoretical approaches we chose to be suitable to explain particular, albeit limited, aspects of the case. We think that this suitability also applies to other phenomena of European integration, but also that there will not be just *one* theory suitable to explain a specific policy. The exercise presented in this study should therefore be seen as a proposal of how one could fruitfully examine cases of European integration in political science more generally.

What is characteristic of this approach? Above all, it is *eclectic*. The methodological premise assumes from the outset that any theoretical approach has limitations. Rather than trying to fit the empirics into the theory, thereby building a new theory or advancing an existing one, we chose to apply different theories to explain different aspects of the empirics.

The analytical focus is at the level of national governments as well as below and above. While appreciating the importance of national governments in our analysis, we see the need to transcend the intergovernmental perspective, stating that the domestic scene needs to be fully accounted for in order to understand governmental behaviour. In our view the analysis should go beyond a discussion of economic actors and interests but incorporate the importance of party politics and the role of domestic institutions. Furthermore, non-state actors are influential irrespective of the level at which decisions are taken (domestic, national, transnational or supranational) – experts contribute to the policy-making process in a separate arena that is not fully grasped by the notion of the state but represents a dimension of its own. What was the outcome?

Applying an intergovernmental approach, the analysis showed how Member State governments determine the negotiations in light of their interests. They succeed in doing so depending on their power and on how credibly they convey their determination to achieve a result close to their interests. We found this to be true in so far as the SGP, either in its original form in 1997 or in its reformed shape in 2005, is the outcome of a bargain between sovereign states. Those instances that were of highly controversial nature and became 'political' had to be bargained, and the result often enough reflected the power constellation behind national interests.

From the perspective of a domestic politics approach we learnt how the domestic situation of a government plays an important role in the creation and implementation of the SGP. Indeed, the German government's motivation to create a Stability Pact can be traced back to the need to sell monetary union to an increasingly EMU-sceptic domestic audience and to appease the Bundesbank. The French government obtained cosmetic concessions in order to calm its domestic constituency. Likewise, the suspension of the SGP in November 2003 can be traced back to domestic considerations of the German and French governments. Hence domestic politics often explain the timing of political initiatives and the degree of salience that is attached to them, i.e. the level to which the issue becomes 'political'. Also the implementation period was influenced by domestic politics considerations and to a lesser extent the nature of the reform of the SGP in 2005 can be traced back to issues in the domestic realm.

A neofunctionalist view stressed how the functional implications of EMU require further economic coordination. Conversely, the Maastricht Treaty entails legal restrictions on integration in this area, which makes a rules-based approach most attractive. We found indeed evidence for the presence of this type of tension between two opposing functional logics. It was no surprise to any informed actor at the time that some kind of policy initiative in this field would come after Stage II of EMU had started. Hence, neofunctionalism explains the type of policy initiative as well as its framework and direction given the policy problem that it originated from. Looking through a functionalist lens also helps us understand why, amidst so much criticism about the SGP, the reformed Pact was still firmly based on both the Treaty and the previous Pact. During the financial crisis we saw once again that functional pressures were at work to keep the (reformed) SGP operational and not have its basis questioned.

Finally, focusing on ideas and experts provided a better understanding as to how the realm of acceptable solutions is predetermined by the ideas of experts, who in turn subscribe to a dominant paradigm on economic policy. Changes in these ideas occur through policy learning and exchanges while the principles of the paradigm remain untouched. Our empirical results, based on a broad range of interviews, a questionnaire and direct access to the relevant information, strongly confirm this expectation. Experts and ideas explain the actual content of the policy-making process. Even when the SGP was going through great turmoil, the actor experts (for example those in the EFC) did not abandon the underlying principles. The more radical proposals from non-actor experts (academics) to reform the Pact did not influence significantly those experts who are involved in the policy-making process. The 2005 reform of the SGP was modest, rather than a fully fledged one whereby the regime was altered altogether. Functionalism and the expertocratic approach jointly explain why this was the case. Also the analysis of the SGP in times of financial crisis suggests that experts remained in favour of the ideas underlying the Pact, thereby giving further ammunition to this type of explanation of how the SGP has fared in the first months following the collapse of Lehman Brothers.

The results presented in this book are based on the study of one case, the SGP, over a time period of now almost fifteen years. Despite the long observation period, the 'n=1' situation can therefore not be excluded from being idiosyncratic. The causal relations inferred from our approach might relate only to the aspects of the case that we actually explained. However, we believe this uniqueness of the case to be unlikely. We see the causality to be based on the acting subjects and mechanisms of the policy-making process (e.g. governments, domestic actors, experts, spillover, institutions), not the object (i.e. the SGP). We are confident that one could study another policy in the area of European integration with this approach. We believe that some of what we have discovered about this policy process is of a systematic nature and therefore likely to reappear in different policy areas and for different policy problems, as well as for the same case over time. We therefore postulate a modest degree of generalisability from our study, both to the future of the SGP and, more importantly, to other cases of European integration.

Broadening the theoretical horizon

Our study has shown how four theories contributed not to a comprehensive, but to a profound understanding of the SGP, its origins, implementation and reform. At this point we would like to reflect on the explanatory range of our approach, and see if the method can act as a heuristic device. We argue that it works well to clarify the politics of the functional logic and domestic political origins, the role of experts in its creation, and the inter-governmental bargaining that took place among Member States on the basis of domestically defined economic preferences. We saw that this approach was effective in explaining both the origins as well as the revision of the Pact and its implementation in highly variable economic circumstances.

Though we have by no means checked all aspects of economic and monetary integration in Europe, it seems that this eclectic approach might be helpful for understanding EMU-related issues in a wider context. We would be keen to see a more systematic analysis of the whole EMU area but also how this approach might be applicable to other areas of integration. EMU is a macro-level integration phenomenon. One might ask whether similar large-scale areas could be explained by such an eclectic approach, for example the other pillars of the Maastricht Treaty (e.g. Common Foreign and Security Policy and Justice and Home Affairs and their transmission through subsequent Treaty revisions). Let us speculate about how such an application might work.

If one adopted this approach for the Common Foreign and Security Policy (and European Security and Defence Policy), one would examine the most important Member States in that policy area (i.e. the UK, France and Germany). If one drew the full parallel, one could imagine the domestic politics in one of these countries to be forcing the issue on the agenda. There would have been a felt need for a European policy through the functionalist logic. It would then be subsequently supported at the level of Council and the European Council, with the details to be worked out by military and security experts. Our approach would stress that each of these domains could be viewed through the lenses of the respective approaches. Likewise, matters regarding Justice, Freedom and Security and the creation of common policies at the EU level in this area, could be studied in the same way. We would *a priori* not exclude our approach from being helpful to examine these more complex macro-level integration processes of which the important factors include domestic, functional, expertocratic and intergovernmental bargaining dimensions.

In light of ongoing discussions in the political science discipline about the usefulness of theories, we would want to suggest that one should be pragmatic rather than dogmatic about the choice of theories especially when dealing with an in-depth case study. One should try to find the most suitable approach or approaches for the case at hand. If the case is of a 'macro' nature, in that there are various and highly complex dimensions to the issue under consideration, and that covers a longer period of time, then one should proceed in such an eclectic manner. Arguing instead against the insights obtained through another approach would not be help-ful: it is not likely that one single approach will give the answer to how exactly the process occurred. Indeed, the macro-type integration studies often seek to understand the *process* rather than merely the *outcome*. Although a more narrowly focused approach might be beneficial to adopt in a study that focuses on a particular causal effect, it might be difficult to draw inferences of that specific relationship to a case that takes place in various domains, and in which more actors and mechanisms are important.

The limits of an eclectic approach can also be easily spotted. Given that it encompasses integration phenomena that are complex and involve the interaction between domestic, international and supranational actors and experts, one can imagine that an eclectic approach might be less helpful in cases where European integration is top-down. An example would be the narrow transposition of European law into national law, which is another important dimension of the European integration process. This so-called legal 'implementation' is a process where a Council directive needs to be implemented into national law. The work of Falkner *et al.* (2005) shows that significant divergence occurs in how national laws are adopted (in light of existing national laws and practice) as well as the speed with which that happens. It is clear that the domestic politics dimension would be very important in that aspect of the European integration process, but perhaps at this point the other factors no longer play a large role (intergovernmental bargaining has already taken place, and the functional approach would have little to offer, even though domestic experts would play a role). If there are fundamental problems with the implementation process, the Member States may send the directive back to the negotiating table. But those cases should be considered to be occurring infrequently and thus would be an exception to the rule. In other words, when studying legislative implemen-tation, a more narrow theoretical scope would appear suitable.

Likewise, the micro-relationships that we observe as important but take as given in our approach could be studied more carefully. To do so, one might adopt a quantitative approach that may or may not include formal modelling. Take for example our claim that an issue that is heavily supported by domestic actors, and which has the capacity to undermine the government, can be used in European intergovernmental bargaining (we traced the origins of the SGP, and also the November 2003 crisis back to this situation, see also Schure and Verdun 2007 and 2008). In order to investigate this relationship further, one could collect data on numerous cases that resemble these and examine if they under all circumstances are fought out at the European level and what the results would be. In other words, one could provide a model explaining what domestic cir-cumstances could lead to a domestic issue obtaining salience and thus the government 'going to Europe' to find a solution demanded by the domestic context. Another example of such a micro-relationship would be whether ECOFIN always adopts the decisions supported unanimously in the Monetary Committee (now the Economic and Finance Committee). If these decisions turn out not always to be rubber-stamped, one could examine under what circumstances ECOFIN enforces its own political view on the issues under study.

In summary, the Stability and Growth Pact represents an interesting case in which domestic budgetary policy is subjected to European integration rules. Several factors together form the explanation: intergovernmental bargaining, domestic politics, a functional logic and the role of experts and ideas. It has offered us an opportunity to think about these matters in a broader perspective, thereby being eclectic. The SGP is indicative of the current practice of European governance: using rules when institutional bodies at the supranational level are unattainable. 'Ruling Europe' has become the name of the game – which is becoming more, rather than less, pervasive after the failed referenda on the Constitution and in the new Treaty. In the absence of a qualitatively new stage of European integration, we would expect governance by rules to stay the norm of EU politics. The SGP has provided us with, we think, the prime example of how rules-based governance works, and what problems it poses in terms of setting, implementing and adapting rules.

As concerns our case of observation, its future remains to be seen. We do not intend to predict whether or not the revised SGP will work well once EU Member States have entered a possibly seminal economic recession with indeed very far reaching implications for public finances. The experience of implementing the 'old' SGP has made clear beyond any doubt that fiscal policy in EMU remains the prerogative of Member States. Governing by rules does not lend itself to much more than orchestrating and deliberating at the supranational level what essentially remain *national* policies.

However, we would feel comfortable in pointing to a number of important indicators to monitor in the ongoing saga of the SGP: The fact that the Merkel government, when succeeding Schröder in Germany in 2005, placed great domestic emphasis on the consolidation of public finances had, for a moment, radically changed Germany's position *vis-à-vis* the SGP. This approach has been abandoned temporarily in light of the global economic crisis – but the SGP might possibly help that consolidation is not forgotten in Germany. Maybe we will see the new German government supporting the revised SGP framework as a useful disciplining device once the economic crisis has passed. As such, Germany might have regained its old role of sponsoring fiscal discipline in Europe. Much will hinge on whether, given its own structural problems, this position can be guarded under much more challenging macroeconomic circumstances. The 2003 experience has shown that, on its own, the Commission cannot defend the SGP against the national interests of Germany and France. Any possible repetition of frictions with France (or Italy, as another 'large' country case) would crucially be influenced by whether Germany would side with the Commission or not. This, in turn, would depend on what the German government sees as its domestic priorities in the years to come.

Other than for a renewed conflict on the revised SGP (once the economic crisis has passed and macroeconomic conditions improve but with a legacy of budgetary deficits and public debt), it seems that the implementation of the revised Pact is still on route to happening – although it has never been a Pact that 'bites' during the downturn of the economy.

It was not the purpose of this study to form an opinion on the SGP's ability to achieve fiscal coordination in the 'right' way. Hence, we are not stating to what extent it is conducive to Member States obtaining sound fiscal policies in line with monetary stability and sustainable growth and employment creation. Rather, we sought to understand the political process that led to its origin, its implementation and its reform, and even speculate about its likely future in hard times. We hope that we have contributed to the ongoing debates in the literature of how to understand European integration and provided theoretical building blocks for the further development of the rich literature on European integration. We appreciate that the prospect for the SGP might be grim, depending on how the economic crisis shakes up the institutional structure of economic governance in the EU. But to date we have noted how EU leaders and EU institutions, for now, have supported the SGP rules. Thus, based on our analysis in this book, we expect that the SGP may well be able to weather this storm. But then again, at the time of writing the worst of the storm may not be over, which means that change could well be around the corner. In order to understand that change, we hope to have provided some useful analytical tools to continue the evaluation of the SGP.

Appendix

Primary Law (Articles 99, 104 and EDP Protocol)

Article 99 (ex Article 103)

1. Member States shall regard their economic policies as a matter of common concern and shall coordinate them within the Council, in accordance with the provisions of Article 98.
2. The Council shall, acting by a qualified majority on a recommendation from the Commission, formulate a draft for the broad guide-lines of the economic policies of the Member States and of the Community, and shall report its findings to the European Council.

   The European Council shall, acting on the basis of the report from the Council, discuss a conclusion on the broad guidelines of the economic policies of the Member States and of the Community.

   On the basis of this conclusion, the Council shall, acting by a qualified majority, adopt a recommendation setting out these broad guidelines. The Council shall inform the European Parliament of its recommendation.
3. In order to ensure closer coordination of economic policies and sustained convergence of the economic performances of the Member States, the Council shall, on the basis of reports submitted by the Commission, monitor economic developments in each of the Member States and in the Community as well as the consistency of economic policies with the broad guidelines referred to in paragraph 2, and regularly carry out an overall assessment.

   For the purpose of this multilateral surveillance, Member States shall forward information to the Commission about important measures taken by them in the field of their economic policy and such other information as they deem necessary.
4. Where it is established, under the procedure referred to in paragraph 3, that the economic policies of a Member State are not consistent with the

broad guidelines referred to in paragraph 2 or that they risk jeopardising the proper functioning of economic and monetary union, the Council may, acting by a qualified majority on a recommendation from the Commission, make the necessary recommendations to the Member State concerned. The Council may, acting by a qualified majority on a proposal from the Commission, decide to make its recommendations public.

The President of the Council and the Commission shall report to the European Parliament on the results of multilateral surveillance. The President of the Council may be invited to appear before the competent committee of the European Parliament if the Council has made its recommendations public.

5. The Council, acting in accordance with the procedure referred to in Article 252, may adopt detailed rules for the multilateral surveillance procedure referred to in paragraphs 3 and 4 of this Article.

Article 104 (ex Article 104c)

1. Member States shall avoid excessive government deficits.
2. The Commission shall monitor the development of the budgetary situation and of the stock of government debt in the Member States with a view to identifying gross errors. In particular it shall examine compliance with budgetary discipline on the basis of the following two criteria:
   (a) whether the ratio of the planned or actual government deficit to gross domestic product exceeds a reference value, unless:
      - either the ratio has declined substantially and continuously and reached a level that comes close to the reference value;
      - or, alternatively, the excess over the reference value is only exceptional and temporary and the ratio remains close to the reference value;
   (b) whether the ratio of government debt to gross domestic product exceeds a reference value, unless the ratio is sufficiently diminishing and approaching the reference value at a satisfactory pace.

   The reference values are specified in the Protocol on the excessive deficit procedure annexed to this Treaty.
3. If a Member State does not fulfil the requirements under one or both of these criteria, the Commission shall prepare a report. The report of the Commission shall also take into account whether the government deficit exceeds government investment expenditure and take into account all other relevant factors, including the medium-term economic and budgetary position of the Member State.

The Commission may also prepare a report if, notwithstanding the fulfilment of the requirements under the criteria, it is of the opinion that there is a risk of an excessive deficit in a Member State.

4. The Committee provided for in Article 114 shall formulate an opinion on the report of the Commission.

5. If the Commission considers that an excessive deficit in a Member State exists or may occur, the Commission shall address an opinion to the Council.

6. The Council shall, acting by a qualified majority on a recommendation from the Commission, and having considered any observations which the Member State concerned may wish to make, decide after an overall assessment whether an excessive deficit exists.

7. Where the existence of an excessive deficit is decided according to paragraph 6, the Council shall make recommendations to the Member State concerned with a view to bringing that situation to an end within a given period. Subject to the provisions of paragraph 8, these recommendations shall not be made public.

8. Where it establishes that there has been no effective action in response to its recommendations within the period laid down, the Council may make its recommendations public.

9. If a Member State persists in failing to put into practice the recommendations of the Council, the Council may decide to give notice to the Member State to take, within a specified time-limit, measures for the deficit reduction which is judged necessary by the Council in order to remedy the situation.

   In such a case, the Council may request the Member State concerned to submit reports in accordance with a specific timetable in order to examine the adjustment efforts of that Member State.

10. The rights to bring actions provided for in Articles 226 and 227 may not be exercised within the framework of paragraphs 1 to 9 of this Article.

11. As long as a Member State fails to comply with a decision taken in accordance with paragraph 9, the Council may decide to apply or, as the case may be, intensify one or more of the following measures:

    • to require the Member State concerned to publish additional information, to be specified by the Council, before issuing bonds and securities;

    • to invite the European Investment Bank to reconsider its lending policy towards the Member State concerned;

    • to require the Member State concerned to make a non-interest bearing deposit of an appropriate size with the Community until the excessive deficit has, in the view of the Council, been corrected;

- to impose fines of an appropriate size.

The President of the Council shall inform the European Parliament of the decisions taken.

12. The Council shall abrogate some or all of its decisions referred to in paragraphs 6 to 9 and 11 to the extent that the excessive deficit in the Member State concerned has, in the view of the Council, been corrected. If the Council has previously made public recommendations, it shall, as soon as the decision under paragraph 8 has been abrogated, make a public statement that an excessive deficit in the Member State concerned no longer exists.

13. When taking the decisions referred to in paragraphs 7 to 9, 11 and 12, the Council shall act on a recommendation from the Commission by a majority of two thirds of the votes of its members weighted in accordance with Article 205(2), excluding the votes of the representative of the Member State concerned.

14. Further provisions relating to the implementation of the procedure described in this Article are set out in the Protocol on the excessive deficit procedure annexed to this Treaty.

The Council shall, acting unanimously on a proposal from the Commission and after consulting the European Parliament and the ECB, adopt the appropriate provisions which shall then replace the said Protocol.

Subject to the other provisions of this paragraph, the Council shall, before 1 January 1994, acting by a qualified majority on a proposal from the Commission and after consulting the European Parliament, lay down detailed rules and definitions for the application of the provisions of the said Protocol.[1]

Protocol on the Excessive Deficit Procedure (EDP)[2]

Origin: Treaty of Maastricht.

Protocol annexed to the Treaty establishing the European Community.

THE HIGH CONTRACTING PARTIES,

DESIRING to lay down the details of the excessive deficit procedure referred to in Article 104 of the Treaty establishing the European Community,

---

[1] http://europa.eu/eur-lex/en/treaties/selected/livre223.html#anArt6.
[2] http://europa.eu/eur-lex/en/treaties/selected/livre335.html.

HAVE AGREED upon the following provisions, which shall be annexed to the Treaty establishing the European Community.

Article 1

The reference values referred to in Article 104(2) of this Treaty are:

- 3% for the ratio of the planned or actual government deficit to gross domestic product at market prices;
- 60% for the ratio of government debt to gross domestic product at market prices.

Article 2

In Article 104 of this Treaty and in this Protocol:

- government means general government, that is central government, regional or local government and social security funds, to the exclusion of commercial operations, as defined in the European System of Integrated Economic Accounts;
- deficit means net borrowing as defined in the European System of Integrated Economic Accounts;
- investment means gross fixed capital formation as defined in the European System of Integrated Economic Accounts;
- debt means total gross debt at nominal value outstanding at the end of the year and consolidated between and within the sectors of general government as defined in the first indent.

Article 3

In order to ensure the effectiveness of the excessive deficit procedure, the governments of the Member States shall be responsible under this procedure for the deficits of general government as defined in the first indent of Article 2. The Member States shall ensure that national procedures in the budgetary area enable them to meet their obligations in this area deriving from this Treaty. The Member States shall report their planned and actual deficits and the levels of their debt promptly and regularly to the Commission.

Article 4

The statistical data to be used for the application of this Protocol shall be provided by the Commission.

Secondary Laws (Regulations 1466/97 and 1467/97)

**Council Regulation (EC) No 1466/97 of 7 July 1997
on the strengthening of the surveillance of budgetary
positions and the surveillance and coordination
of economic policies**

Official Journal L 209 , 02/08/1997 P. 0001 – 0005

THE COUNCIL OF THE EUROPEAN UNION,

Having regard to the Treaty establishing the European Community, and in particular Article 103 (5) thereof,

Having regard to the proposal from the Commission[1],

Acting in accordance with the procedure referred to in Article 189c of the Treaty[2],

(1) Whereas the Stability and Growth Pact is based on the objective of sound government finances as a means of strengthening the conditions for price stability and for strong sustainable growth conducive to employment creation;

(2) Whereas the Stability and Growth Pact consists of this Regulation which aims to strengthen the surveillance of budgetary positions and the surveillance and coordination of economic policies, of Council Regulation (EC) No 1467/97[3] which aims to speed up and to clarify the implementation of the excessive deficit procedure and of the Resolution of the European Council of 17 June 1997 on the Stability and Growth Pact[4], in which, in accordance with Article D of the Treaty on European Union, firm political guidelines are issued in order to implement the Stability and Growth Pact in a strict and timely manner and in particular to adhere to the medium term objective of budgetary positions of close to balance or in surplus, to which all Member States are committed, and to take the corrective budgetary action they deem necessary to meet the objectives of their stability and convergence programmes, whenever they have information indicating actual or expected significant divergence from the medium-term budgetary objective;

(3) Whereas in stage three of Economic and Monetary Union (EMU) the Member States are, according to Article 104c of the Treaty, under a

---

[1] OJ No C 368, 6. 12. 1996, p. 9.
[2] Opinion of the European Parliament of 28 November 1996 (OJ No C 380, 16. 12. 1996, p. 28), Council Common Position of 14 April 1997 (OJ No C 146, 30. 5. 1997, p. 26) and Decision of the European Parliament of 29 May 1997 (OJ No C 182, 16. 6. 1997).
[3] See p. 6 of this Official Journal.   [4] OJ No C 236, 2. 8. 1997, p. 1.

clear Treaty obligation to avoid excessive general government deficits; whereas under Article 5 of Protocol (No 11) on certain provisions relating to the United Kingdom of Great Britain and Northern Ireland to the Treaty, Article 104c(1) does not apply to the United Kingdom unless it moves to the third stage; whereas the obligation under Article 109e(4) to endeavour to avoid excessive deficits will continue to apply to the United Kingdom;

(4) Whereas adherence to the medium-term objective of budgetary positions close to balance or in surplus will allow Member States to deal with normal cyclical fluctuations while keeping the government deficit within the 3 % of GDP reference value;

(5) Whereas it is appropriate to complement the multilateral surveillance procedure of Article 103 (3) and (4) with an early warning system, under which the Council will alert a Member State at an early stage to the need to take the necessary budgetary corrective action in order to prevent a government deficit becoming excessive;

(6) Whereas the multilateral surveillance procedure of Article 103 (3) and (4) should furthermore continue to monitor the full range of economic developments in each of the Member States and in the Community as well as the consistency of economic policies with the broad economic guidelines referred to in Article 103 (2); whereas for the monitoring of these developments, the presentation of information in the form of stability and convergence programmes is appropriate;

(7) Whereas there is a need to build upon the useful experience gained during the first two stages of economic and monetary union with convergence programmes;

(8) Whereas the Member States adopting the single currency, hereafter referred to as 'participating Member States', will, in accordance with Article 109j, have achieved a high degree of sustainable convergence and in particular a sustainable government financial position; whereas the maintenance of sound budgetary positions in these Member States will be necessary to support price stability and to strengthen the conditions for the sustained growth of output and employment; whereas it is necessary that participating Member States submit medium-term programmes, hereafter referred to as 'stability programmes'; whereas it is necessary to define the principal contents of such programmes;

(9) Whereas the Member States not adopting the single currency, hereafter referred to as 'non-participating Member States', will need to pursue policies aimed at a high degree of sustainable convergence; whereas it is necessary that these Member States submit medium-term programmes, hereafter referred to as 'convergence programmes'; whereas

it is necessary to define the principal contents of such convergence programmes;

(10) Whereas in its Resolution of 16 June 1997 on the establishment of an exchange-rate mechanism in the third stage of Economic and Monetary Union, the European Council issued firm political guidelines in accordance with which an exchange-rate mechanism is established in the third stage of EMU, hereafter referred to as 'ERM2'; whereas the currencies of non-participating Member States joining ERM2 will have a central rate vis-à-vis the euro, thereby providing a reference point for judging the adequacy of their policies; whereas the ERM2 will also help to protect them and the Member States adopting the euro from unwarranted pressures in the foreign-exchange markets; whereas, so as to enable appropriate surveillance in the Council, non-participating Member States not joining ERM2 will nevertheless present policies in their convergence programmes oriented to stability thus avoiding real exchange rate misalignments and excessive nominal exchange rate fluctuations;

(11) Whereas lasting convergence of economic fundamentals is a prerequisite for sustainable exchange rate stability;

(12) Whereas it is necessary to lay down a timetable for the submission of stability programmes and convergence programmes and their updates;

(13) Whereas in the interest of transparency and informed public debate it is necessary that Member States make public their stability programmes and their convergence programmes;

(14) Whereas the Council, when examining and monitoring the stability programmes and the convergence programmes and in particular their medium-term budgetary objective or the targeted adjustment path towards this objective, should take into account the relevant cyclical and structural characteristics of the economy of each Member State;

(15) Whereas in this context particular attention should be given to significant divergences of budgetary positions from the budgetary objectives of being close to balance or in surplus; whereas it is appropriate for the Council to give an early warning in order to prevent a government deficit in a Member State becoming excessive; whereas in the event of persistent budgetary slippage it will be appropriate for the Council to reinforce its recommendation and make it public; whereas for non-participating Member States the Council may make recommendations on action to be taken to give effect to their convergence programmes;

(16) Whereas both convergence and stability programmes lead to the fulfilment of the conditions of economic convergence referred to in Article 104c,

Has Adopted this Regulation:Section 1 Purpose and Definitions

Article 1

This Regulation sets out the rules covering the content, the submission, the examination and the monitoring of stability programmes and convergence programmes as part of multilateral surveillance by the Council so as to prevent, at an early stage, the occurrence of excessive general government deficits and to promote the surveillance and coordination of economic policies.

Article 2

For the purpose of this Regulation 'participating Member States' shall mean those Member States which adopt the single currency in accordance with the Treaty and 'non-participating Member States' shall mean those which have not adopted the single currency.

Section 2 Stability Programmes

Article 3

1. Each participating Member State shall submit to the Council and Commission information necessary for the purpose of multilateral surveillance at regular intervals under Article 103 of the Treaty in the form of a stability programme, which provides an essential basis for price stability and for strong sustainable growth conducive to employment creation.
2. A stability programme shall present the following information:
   (a) the medium-term objective for the budgetary position of close to balance or in surplus and the adjustment path towards this objective for the general government surplus/deficit and the expected path of the general government debt ratio;
   (b) the main assumptions about expected economic developments and important economic variables which are relevant to the realization of the stability programme such as government investment expenditure, real gross domestic product (GDP) growth, employment and inflation;
   (c) a description of budgetary and other economic policy measures being taken and/or proposed to achieve the objectives of the programme, and, in the case of the main budgetary measures, an assessment of their quantitative effects on the budget;

(d) an analysis of how changes in the main economic assumptions would affect the budgetary and debt position.

3. The information about paths for the general government surplus/deficit ratio and debt ratio and the main economic assumptions referred to in paragraph 2 (a) and (b) shall be on an annual basis and shall cover, as well as the current and preceding year, at least the following three years.

Article 4

1. Stability programmes shall be submitted before 1 March 1999. Thereafter, updated programmes shall be submitted annually. A Member State adopting the single currency at a later stage shall submit a stability programme within six months of the Council Decision on its participation in the single currency.

2. Member States shall make public their stability programmes and updated programmes.

Article 5

1. Based on assessments by the Commission and the Committee set up by Article 109c of the Treaty, the Council shall, within the framework of multilateral surveillance under Article 103, examine whether the medium-term budget objective in the stability programme provides for a safety margin to ensure the avoidance of an excessive deficit, whether the economic assumptions on which the programme is based are realistic and whether the measures being taken and/or proposed are sufficient to achieve the targeted adjustment path towards the medium-term budgetary objective.

   The Council shall furthermore examine whether the contents of the stability programme facilitate the closer coordination of economic policies and whether the economic policies of the Member State concerned are consistent with the broad economic policy guidelines.

2. The Council shall carry out the examination of the stability programme referred to in paragraph 1 within at most two months of the submission of the programme. The Council, on a recommendation from the Commission and after consulting the Committee set up by Article 109c, shall deliver an opinion on the programme. Where the Council, in accordance with Article 103, considers that the objectives and contents of a programme should be strengthened, the Council shall, in its opinion, invite the Member State concerned to adjust its programme.

3. Updated stability programmes shall be examined by the Committee set up by Article 109c on the basis of assessments by the Commission; if necessary, updated programmes may also be examined by the Council in accordance with the procedure set out in paragraphs 1 and 2 of this Article.

Article 6

1. As part of multilateral surveillance in accordance with Article 103 (3), the Council shall monitor the implementation of stability programmes, on the basis of information provided by participating Member States and of assessments by the Commission and the Committee set up by Article 109c, in particular with a view to identifying actual or expected significant divergence of the budgetary position from the medium-term budgetary objective, or the adjustment path towards it, as set in the programme for the government surplus/deficit.

2. In the event that the Council identifies significant divergence of the budgetary position from the medium-term budgetary objective, or the adjustment path towards it, it shall, with a view to giving early warning in order to prevent the occurrence of an excessive deficit, address, in accordance with Article 103 (4), a recommendation to the Member State concerned to take the necessary adjustment measures.

3. In the event that the Council in its subsequent monitoring judges that the divergence of the budgetary position from the medium-term budgetary objective, or the adjustment path towards it, is persisting or worsening, the Council shall, in accordance with Article 103 (4), make a recommendation to the Member State concerned to take prompt corrective measures and may, as provides in that Article, make its recommendation public.

Section 3 Convergence Programmes

Article 7

1. Each non-participating Member State shall submit to the Council and the Commission information necessary for the purpose of multilateral surveillance of regular intervals under Article 103 in the form of a convergence programme, which provides an essential basis for price stability and for strong sustainable growth conducive to employment creation.

2. A convergence programme shall present the following information in particular on variables related to convergence:

(a) the medium-term objective for the budgetary position of close to balance or in surplus and the adjustment path towards this objective for the general government surplus/deficit; the expected path for the general government debt ratio; the medium-term monetary policy objectives; the relationship of those objectives to price and exchange rate stability;

(b) the main assumptions about expected economic developments and important economic variables which are relevant to the realization of the convergence programme, such as government investment expenditure, real GDP growth, employment and inflation;

(c) a description of budgetary and other economic policy measures being taken and/or proposed to achieve the objectives of the programme, and, in the case of the main budgetary measures, an assessment of their quantitative effects on the budget;

(d) an analysis of how changes in the main economic assumptions would affect the budgetary and debt position.

3. The information about paths for the general government surplus/deficit ratio, debt ratio and the main economic assumptions referred to in paragraph 2 (a) and (b) shall be on an annual basis and shall cover, as well as the current and preceding year, at least the following three years.

Article 8

1. Convergence programmes shall be submitted before 1 March 1999. Thereafter, updated programmes shall be submitted annually.

2. Member States shall make public their convergence programmes and updated programmes.

Article 9

1. Based on assessments by the Commission and the Committee set up by Article 109c of the Treaty, the Council shall, within the framework of multilateral surveillance under Article 103, examine whether the medium-term budget objective in the convergence programme provides for a safety margin to ensure the avoidance of an excessive deficit, whether the economic assumptions on which the programme is based are realistic and whether the measures being taken and/or proposed are sufficient to achieve the targeted adjustment path towards the medium-term objective and to achieve sustained convergence.

The Council shall furthermore examine whether the contents of the convergence programme facilitate the closer coordination of economic policies and whether the economic policies of the Member

State concerned are consistent with the broad economic policy guidelines.

2. The Council shall carry out the examination of the convergence programme referred to in paragraph 1 within at most two months of the submission of the programme. The Council, on a recommendation from the Commission and after consulting the Committee set up by Article 109c, shall deliver an opinion on the programme. Where the Council, in accordance with Article 103, considers that the objectives and contents of a programme should be strengthened, the Council shall, in its opinion, invite the Member State concerned to adjust its programme.

3. Updated convergence programmes shall be examined by the Committee set up by Article 109c on the basis of assessments by the Commission; if necessary, updated programmes may also be examined by the Council in accordance with the procedure set out in paragraphs 1 and 2 of this Article.

Article 10

1. As part of multilateral surveillance in accordance with Article 103 (3), the Council shall monitor the implementation of convergence programmes on the basis of information provided by non-participating Member States in accordance with Article 7 (2) (a) of this Regulation and of assessments by the Commission and the Committee set up by Article 109c of the Treaty, in particular with a view to identifying actual or expected significant divergence of the budgetary position from the medium-term budgetary objective, or the adjustment path towards it, as set in the programme for the government surplus/deficit.

    In addition, the Council shall monitor the economic policies of non-participating Member States in the light of convergence programme objectives with a view to ensure that their policies are geared to stability and thus to avoid real exchange rate misalignments and excessive nominal exchange rate fluctuations.

2. In the event that the Council identifies significant divergence of the budgetary position from the medium-term budgetary objective, or the adjustment path towards it, it shall, with a view to given early warning in order to prevent the occurrence of an excessive deficit, address in accordance with Article 103 (4), a recommendation to the Member State concerned to take the necessary adjustment measures.

3. In the event that the Council in its subsequent monitoring judges that the divergence of the budgetary position from the medium-term budgetary objective, or the adjustment path towards it, is persisting or

worsening, the Council shall, in accordance with Article 103 (4), make a recommendation to the Member State concerned to take prompt corrective measures and may, as provided in that Article, make its recommendation public.

Section 4 Common Provisions

Article 11

As part of the multilateral surveillance described in this Regulation, the Council shall carry out the overall assessment described in Article 103 (3).

Article 12

In accordance with the second subparagraph of Article 103 (4) the President of the Council and the Commission shall include in their report to the European Parliament the results of the multilateral surveillance carried out under this Regulation.

Article 13

This Regulation shall enter into force on 1 July 1998.

This Regulation shall be binding in its entirety and directly applicable in all Member States.

Done at Brussels, 7 July 1997.

For the Council

The President

J.-C. JUNCKER

Council Regulation (EC) No 1466/97 of 7 July 1997 on the strengthening of the surveillance of budgetary positions and the surveillance and coordination of economic policies[1]

Amended by:

-Council Regulation (EC) No 1055/2005 of 27 June 2005[2]

[No 1466/97 of 7 July 1997][3]

THE COUNCIL OF THE EUROPEAN UNION,

---

[1] OJ L 209, 2.8.1997, p. 1.   [2] OJ L 174, 7.7.2005, p. 1.

[3] NB: The preamble and the recitals of both the original and the amending Regulation are reproduced.

Having regard to the Treaty establishing the European Community, and in particular Article 103(5) thereof,

Having regard to the proposal from the Commission[4],

Acting in accordance with the procedure referred to in Article 189c of the Treaty[5],

(1) Whereas the Stability and Growth Pact is based on the objective of sound government finances as a means of strengthening the conditions for price stability and for strong sustainable growth conducive to employment creation;

(2) Whereas the Stability and Growth Pact consists of this Regulation which aims to strengthen the surveillance of budgetary positions and the surveillance and coordination of economic policies, of Council Regulation (EC) No 1467/97[6] which aims to speed up and to clarify the implementation of the excessive deficit procedure and of the Resolution of the European Council of 17 June 1997 on the Stability and Growth Pact[7], in which, in accordance with Article of the Treaty on European Union, firm political guidelines are issued in order to implement the Stability and Growth Pact in a strict and timely manner and in particular to adhere to the medium term objective of budgetary positions of close to balance or in surplus, to which all Member States are committed, and to take the corrective budgetary action they deem necessary to meet the objectives of their stability and convergence programmes, whenever they have information indicating actual or expected signi cant divergence from the medium-term budgetary objective;

(3) Whereas in stage three of Economic and Monetary Union (EMU) the Member States are, according to Article 104 of the Treaty, under a clear Treaty obligation to avoid excessive general government deficits; whereas under Article 5 of Protocol (No 11) on certain provisions relating to the United Kingdom of Great Britain and Northern Ireland to the Treaty, Article 104(1) does not apply to the United Kingdom unless it moves to the third stage; whereas the obligation under Article 116(4) to endeavour to avoid excessive deficits will continue to apply to the United Kingdom;

(4) Whereas adherence to the medium-term objective of budgetary positions close to balance or in surplus will allow Member States to deal

---

[4] OJ C 368, 6.12.1996, p. 9.
[5] Opinion of the European Parliament of 28 November 1996 (OJ C 380, 16.12.1996, p. 28), Council Common Position of 14 April 1997 (OJ C 146, 30.5.1997, p. 26) and Decision of the European Parliament of 29 May 1997 (OJ C 182, 16.6.1997).
[6] See p. 6 of this Official Journal.   [7] OJ C 236, 1.8.1997, p. 1.

with normal cyclical fluctuations while keeping the government deficit within the 3 % of GDP reference value;

(5) Whereas it is appropriate to complement the multilateral surveillance procedure of Article 99 (3) and (4) with an early warning system, under which the Council will alert a Member State at an early stage to the need to take the necessary budgetary corrective action in order to prevent a government deficit becoming excessive;

(6) Whereas the multilateral surveillance procedure of Article 99 (3) and (4) should furthermore continue to monitor the full range of economic developments in each of the Member States and in the Community as well as the consistency of economic policies with the broad economic guidelines referred to in Article 99 (2); whereas for the monitoring of these developments, the presentation of information in the form of stability and convergence programmes is appropriate;

(7) Whereas there is a need to build upon the useful experience gained during the first two stages of economic and monetary union with convergence programmes;

(8) Whereas the Member States adopting the single currency, hereafter referred to as 'participating Member States', will, in accordance with Article 121, have achieved a high degree of sustainable convergence and in particular a sustainable government nancial position; whereas the maintenance of sound budgetary positions in these Member States will be necessary to support price stability and to strengthen the conditions for the sustained growth of output and employment; whereas it is necessary that participating Member States submit medium-term programmes, hereafter referred to as 'stability programmes'; whereas it is necessary to de ne the principal contents of such programmes;

(9) Whereas the Member States not adopting the single currency, hereafter referred to as 'non-participating Member States', will need to pursue policies aimed at a high degree of sustainable convergence; whereas it is necessary that these Member States submit medium-term programmes, hereafter referred to as 'convergence programmes'; whereas it is necessary to de ne the principal contents of such convergence programmes;

(10) Whereas in its Resolution of 16 June 1997 on the establishment of an exchange rate mechanism in the third stage of economic and monetary union, the European Council issued rm political guidelines in accordance with which an exchange rate mechanism is established in the third stage of EMU, hereafter referred to as 'ERM2'; whereas the currencies of non-participating Member States joining ERM2 will

have a central rate vis-à-vis the euro, thereby providing a reference point for judging the adequacy of their policies; whereas the ERM2 will also help to protect them and the Member States adopting the euro from unwarranted pressures in the foreign-exchange markets; whereas, so as to enable appropriate surveillance in the Council, non-participating Member States not joining ERM2 will nevertheless present policies in their convergence programmes oriented to stability thus avoiding real exchange rate misalignments and excessive nominal exchange rate fluctuations;

(11) Whereas lasting convergence of economic fundamentals is a prerequisite for sustainable exchange rate stability;

(12) Whereas it is necessary to lay down a timetable for the submission of stability programmes and convergence programmes and their updates;

(13) Whereas in the interest of transparency and informed public debate it is necessary that Member States make public their stability programmes and their convergence programmes;

(14) Whereas the Council, when examining and monitoring the stability programmes and the convergence programmes and in particular their medium-term budgetary objective or the targeted adjustment path towards this objective, should take into account the relevant cyclical and structural characteristics of the economy of each Member State;

(15) Whereas in this context particular attention should be given to significant divergences of budgetary positions from the budgetary objectives of being close to balance or in surplus; whereas it is appropriate for the Council to give an early warning in order to prevent a government deficit in a Member State becoming excessive; whereas in the event of persistent budgetary slippage it will be appropriate for the Council to reinforce its recommendation and make it public; whereas for non-participating Member States the Council may make recommendations on action to be taken to give effect to their convergence programmes;

(16) Whereas both convergence and stability programmes lead to the fulfilment of the conditions of economic convergence referred to in Article 104(c),

Has Adopted this Regulation

[No 1055/2005 of 27 June 2005]
THE COUNCIL OF THE EUROPEAN UNION,
Having regard to the Treaty establishing the European Community, and in particular Article 99(5) thereof,

Having regard to the proposal from the Commission,

Having regard to the opinion of the European Central Bank[8],

Acting in accordance with the procedure laid down in Article 252 of the Treaty[9],

Whereas:

(1) The Stability and Growth Pact initially consisted of Council Regulation (EC) No 1466/97 of 7 July 1997 on the strengthening of the surveillance of budgetary positions and the surveillance and coordination of economic policies[10], Council Regulation (EC) No 1467/97 of 7 July 1997 on speeding up and clarifying the implementation of the excessive deficit procedure[11] and the Resolution of the European Council of 17 June 1997 on the Stability and Growth Pact[12]. The Stability and Growth Pact has proven its usefulness in anchoring scal discipline, thereby contributing to a high degree of macroeconomic stability with low inflation and low interest rates, which is necessary to induce sustainable growth and employment creation;

(2) On 20 March 2005 the Council adopted a report entitled 'Improving the implementation of the Stability and Growth Pact' which aims to enhance the governance and the national ownership of the fiscal framework by strengthening the economic underpinnings and the effectiveness of the Pact, both in its preventive and corrective arms, to safeguard the sustainability of public finances in the long run, to promote growth and to avoid imposing excessive burdens on future generations. The report was endorsed by the European Council in its conclusions of 23 March 2005[13], which stated that the report updates and complements the Stability and Growth Pact, of which it is now an integral part;

(3) According to the 20 March 2005 ECOFIN report endorsed by the spring 2005 European Council, the Member States, the Council and the Commission reaffirm their commitment to implement the Treaty and the Stability and Growth Pact in an effective and timely manner, through peer support and peer pressure, and to act in close and constructive cooperation in the process of economic and scal surveillance, in order to guarantee certainty and effectiveness in the rules of the Pact;

---

[8] OJ C 144, 14.6.2005, p. 17.

[9] Opinion of the European Parliament of 9 June 2005 (OJ C 124 E, 25.5.2006, pp. 517–520), Council Common Position of 21 June 2005 (OJ C 188 E, 2.8.2005, pp. 1–10), and Decision of the European Parliament of 23 June 2005.

[10] OJ L 209, 2.8.1997, p. 1.   [11] OJ L 209, 2.8.1997, p. 6.

[12] OJ C 236, 2.8.1997, p. 1.

[13] Annex 2 to conclusions of the European Councilof 22 and 23 March 2005.

(4) Regulation (EC) No 1466/97 needs to be amended in order to allow the full application of the agreed improvement of the implementation of the Stability and Growth Pact;

(5) The Stability and Growth Pact lays down the obligation for Member States to adhere to the medium-term objective for their budgetary positions of 'close to balance or in surplus' (CTBOIS). In the light of the economic and budgetary heterogeneity in the Union, the medium-term budgetary objective should be differentiated for individual Member States, to take into account the diversity of economic and budgetary positions and developments as well as of fiscal risk to the sustainability of public finances, also in the face of prospective demographic changes. The medium-term budgetary objective may diverge from CTBOIS for individual Member States. For euro area and ERM2 Member States, there would thus be a de ned range for the country-specific medium-term budgetary objectives, in cyclically adjusted terms, net of one-off and temporary measures;

(6) A more symmetrical approach to fiscal policy over the cycle through enhanced budgetary discipline in economic good times should be achieved, with the objective to avoid pro-cyclical policies and to gradually reach the medium-term budgetary objective. Adherence to the medium-term budgetary objective should allow Member States to deal with normal cyclical fluctuations while keeping the government deficit below the 3% of GDP reference value and ensure rapid progress towards fiscal sustainability. Taking this into account, it should allow room for budgetary manoeuvre, in particular for public investment;

(7) Member States that have not yet reached their medium-term budgetary objective should take steps to achieve it over the cycle. In order to reach their medium-term budgetary objective, Member States of the euro zone or of ERM2 should pursue a minimum annual adjustment in cyclically adjusted terms, net of one-offs and other temporary measures;

(8) In order to enhance the growth-oriented nature of the Pact, major structural reforms which have direct long-term cost-saving effects, including by raising potential growth, and therefore a verifiable impact on the long-term sustainability of public finances, should be taken into account when defining the adjustment path to the medium-term budgetary objective for countries that have not yet reached this objective and in allowing a temporary deviation from this objective for countries that have already reached it. In order not to hamper structural reforms that unequivocally improve the long-term sustainability of public finances, special attention should be paid to pension reforms

introducing a multi-pillar system that includes a mandatory, fully funded pillar, because these reforms entail a short-term deterioration of public finances during the implementation period;

(9) Deadlines set for the examination of stability and convergence programmes by the Council should be extended in order to allow for a thorough assessment of stability and convergence programmes,

Has Adopted this Regulation:

Section 1

Purpose and Definitions

Article 1

This Regulation sets out the rules covering the content, the submission, the examination and the monitoring of stability programmes and convergence programmes as part of multilateral surveillance by the Council so as to prevent, at an early stage, the occurrence of excessive general government deficits and to promote the surveillance and coordination of economic policies.

Article 2

For the purpose of this Regulation 'participating Member States' shall mean those Member States which adopt the single currency in accordance with the Treaty and 'non-participating Member States' shall mean those which have not adopted the single currency.

Section 1A

Medium-Term Budgetary Objectives

Article 2a

Each Member State shall have a differentiated medium-term objective for its budgetary position. These country-specific medium-term budgetary objectives may diverge from the requirement of a close to balance or in surplus position. They shall provide a safety margin with respect to the 3% of GDP government deficit ratio; they shall ensure rapid progress towards sustainability and, taking this into account, they shall allow room for budgetary manoeuvre, considering in particular the needs for public investment.

Taking these factors into account, for Member States that have adopted the euro and for ERM2 Member States the country-specific medium-term budgetary objectives shall be specified within a defined range between -1% of GDP and balance or surplus, in cyclically adjusted terms, net of one-off and temporary measures.

A Member State's medium-term budgetary objective can be revised when a major structural reform is implemented and in any case every four years.

Section 2

Stability Programmes

Article 3

1. Each participating Member State shall submit to the Council and Commission information necessary for the purpose of multilateral surveillance at regular intervals under Article 99 of the Treaty in the form of a stability programme, which provides an essential basis for price stability and for strong sustainable growth conducive to employment creation.

2. A stability programme shall present the following information:
   (a) the medium-term budgetary objective and the adjustment path towards this objective for the general government surplus/deficit and the expected path of the general government debt ratio;
   (b) the main assumptions about expected economic developments and important economic variables which are relevant to the real-isation of the stability programme such as government investment expenditure, real gross domestic product (GDP) growth, employment and inflation;
   (c) a detailed and quantitative assessment of the budgetary and other economic policy measures being taken and/or proposed to achieve the objectives of the programme, comprising a detailed cost-benefit analysis of major structural reforms which have direct long-term cost-saving effects, including by raising potential growth;
   (d) an analysis of how changes in the main economic assumptions would affect the budgetary and debt position;
   (e) if applicable, the reasons for a deviation from the required adjust-ment path towards the medium term budgetary objective.

3. The information about paths for the general government surplus/deficit ratio and debt ratio and the main economic assumptions referred to in paragraph 2(a) and (b) shall be on an annual basis and

shall cover, as well as the current and preceding year, at least the following three years.

Article 4

1. Stability programmes shall be submitted before 1 March 1999. Thereafter, updated programmes shall be submitted annually. A Member State adopting the single currency at a later stage shall submit a stability programme within six months of the Council Decision on its participation in the single currency.
2. Member States shall make public their stability programmes and updated programmes.

Article 5

1. Based on assessments by the Commission and the Committee set up by Article 114 of the Treaty, the Council shall, within the framework of multilateral surveillance under Article 99 of the Treaty, examine the medium-term budgetary objective presented by the Member State concerned, assess whether the economic assumptions on which the programme is based are plausible, whether the adjustment path towards the medium-term budgetary objective is appropriate and whether the measures being taken and/or proposed to respect that adjustment path are sufficient to achieve the medium-term objective over the cycle.

   The Council, when assessing the adjustment path toward the medium-term budgetary objective, shall examine if the Member State concerned pursues the annual improvement of its cyclically-adjusted balance, net of one-off and other temporary measures, required to meet its medium-term budgetary objective, with 0.5% of GDP as a benchmark. The Council shall take into account whether a higher adjustment effort is made in economic good times, whereas the effort may be more limited in economic bad times.

   When defining the adjustment path to the medium-term budgetary objective for Member States that have not yet reached this objective and in allowing a temporary deviation from this objective for Member States that have already reached it, under the condition that an appropriate safety margin with respect to the deficit reference value is preserved and that the budgetary position is expected to return to the medium-term budgetary objective within the programme period, the Council shall take into account the implementation of major structural reforms which have direct long-term cost-saving effects, including by raising potential growth, and therefore a verifiable impact on the long-term sustainability of public finances.

Special attention shall be paid to pension reforms introducing a multi-pillar system that includes a mandatory, fully funded pillar. Member States implementing such reforms shall be allowed to deviate from the adjustment path to their medium-term budgetary objective or from the objective itself, with the deviation reflecting the net cost of the reform to the publicly managed pillar, under the condition that the deviation remains temporary and that an appropriate safety margin with respect to the deficit reference value is preserved.

The Council shall furthermore examine whether the contents of the stability programme facilitate the closer coordination of economic policies and whether the economic policies of the Member State concerned are consistent with the broad economic policy guidelines.

2. The Council shall carry out the examination of the stability programme referred to in paragraph 1 within at most three months of the submission of the programme. The Council, on a recommendation from the Commission and after consulting the Committee set up by Article 114, shall deliver an opinion on the programme. Where the Council, in accordance with Article 99, considers that the objectives and contents of a programme should be strengthened, the Council shall, in its opinion, invite the Member State concerned to adjust its programme.

3. Updated stability programmes shall be examined by the Committee set up by Article 114 on the basis of assessments by the Commission; if necessary, updated programmes may also be examined by the Council in accordance with the procedure set out in paragraphs 1 and 2 of this Article.

Article 6

1. As part of multilateral surveillance in accordance with Article 99(3), the Council shall monitor the implementation of stability programmes, on the basis of information provided by participating Member States and of assessments by the Commission and the Committee set up by Article 114, in particular with a view to identifying actual or expected signi cant divergence of the budgetary position from the medium-term budgetary objective, or the adjustment path towards it, as set in the programme for the government surplus/deficit.

2. In the event that the Council identi es signi cant divergence of the budgetary position from the medium-term budgetary objective, or the adjustment path towards it, it shall, with a view to giving early warning in order to prevent the occurrence of an excessive deficit, address, in

accordance with Article 99(4), a recommendation to the Member State concerned to take the necessary adjustment measures.

3. In the event that the Council in its subsequent monitoring judges that the divergence of the budgetary position from the medium-term budgetary objective, or the adjustment path towards it, is persisting or worsening, the Council shall, in accordance with Article 99(4), make a recommendation to the Member State concerned to take prompt corrective measures and may, as provides in that Article, make its recommendation public.

Section 3

Convergence Programmes

Article 7

1. Each non-participating Member State shall submit to the Council and the Commission information necessary for the purpose of multilateral surveillance of regular intervals under Article 99 in the form of a convergence programme, which provides an essential basis for price stability and for strong sustainable growth conducive to employment creation.

2. A convergence programme shall present the following information in particular on variables related to convergence:

   (a) the medium-term budgetary objective and the adjustment path towards this objective for the general government surplus/deficit and the expected path of the general government debt ratio; the medium-term monetary policy objectives; the relationship of those objectives to price and exchange rate stability;

   (b) the main assumptions about expected economic developments and important economic variables which are relevant to the realisation of the convergence programme, such as government investment expenditure, real GDP growth, employment and inflation;

   (c) a detailed and quantitative assessment of the budgetary and other economic policy measures being taken and/or proposed to achieve the objectives of the programme, comprising a detailed cost-benefit analysis of major structural reforms which have direct long-term cost-saving effects, including by raising potential growth;

   (d) an analysis of how changes in the main economic assumptions would affect the budgetary and debt position;

   (e) if applicable, the reasons for a deviation from the required adjustment path towards the medium term budgetary objective.

3. The information about paths for the general government surplus/ deficit ratio, debt ratio and the main economic assumptions referred to in paragraph 2(a) and (b) shall be on an annual basis and shall cover, as well as the current and preceding year, at least the following three years.

Article 8

1. Convergence programmes shall be submitted before 1 March 1999. Thereafter, updated programmes shall be submitted annually.
2. Member States shall make public their convergence programmes and updated programmes.

Article 9

1. Based on assessments by the Commission and the Committee set up by Article 114 of the Treaty, the Council shall, within the framework of multilateral surveillance under Article 99 of the Treaty, examine the medium-term budgetary objective presented by the Member State concerned, assess whether the economic assumptions on which the programme is based are plausible, whether the adjustment path towards the medium-term budgetary objective is appropriate and whether the measures being taken and/or proposed to respect that adjustment path are sufficient to achieve the medium-term objective over the cycle.

   The Council, when assessing the adjustment path toward the medium-term budgetary objective, shall take into account whether a higher adjustment effort is made in economic good times, whereas the effort may be more limited in economic bad times. For ERM2 Member States, the Council shall examine if the Member State concerned pursues the annual improvement of its cyclically adjusted balance, net of one-off and other temporary measures, required to meet its medium-term budgetary objective, with 0.5% of GDP as a benchmark.

   When defining the adjustment path to the medium-term budgetary objective for Member States that have not yet reached this objective and in allowing a temporary deviation from this objective for Member States that have already reached it, under the condition that an appropriate safety margin with respect to the deficit reference value is preserved and that the budgetary position is expected to return to the medium-term budgetary objective within the programme period, the Council shall take into account the implementation of major structural reforms which have direct long-term cost-saving effects, including by raising potential growth, and therefore a verifiable impact on the long-term sustainability of public finances.

Special attention shall be paid to pension reforms introducing a multi-pillar system that includes a mandatory, fully funded pillar. Member States implementing such reforms shall be allowed to deviate from the adjustment path to their medium-term budgetary objective or from the objective itself, with the deviation reflecting the net cost of the reform to the publicly managed pillar, under the condition that the deviation remains temporary and that an appropriate safety margin with respect to the deficit reference value is preserved.

The Council shall furthermore examine whether the contents of the convergence programme facilitate the closer coordination of economic policies and whether the economic policies of the Member State concerned are consistent with the broad economic policy guidelines.

2. The Council shall carry out the examination of the convergence programme referred to in paragraph 1 within at most three months of the submission of the programme. The Council, on a recommendation from the Commission and after consulting the Committee set up by Article 114, shall deliver an opinion on the programme. Where the Council, in accordance with Article 99, considers that the objectives and contents of a programme should be strengthened, the Council shall, in its opinion, invite the Member State concerned to adjust its programme.

3. Updated convergence programmes shall be examined by the Committee set up by Article 114 on the basis of assessments by the Commission; if necessary, updated programmes may also be examined by the Council in accordance with the procedure set out in paragraphs 1 and 2 of this Article.

Article 10

1. As part of multilateral surveillance in accordance with Article 99(3), the Council shall monitor the implementation of convergence programmes on the basis of information provided by non-participating Member States in accordance with Article 7(2) (a) of this Regulation and of assessments by the Commission and the Committee set up by Article 114 of the Treaty, in particular with a view to identifying actual or expected signi cant divergence of the budgetary position from the medium-term budgetary objective, or the adjustment path towards it, as set in the programme for the government surplus/deficit.

In addition, the Council shall monitor the economic policies of non-participating Member States in the light of convergence programme objectives with a view to ensure that their policies are geared to stability and thus to avoid real exchange rate misalignments and excessive nominal exchange rate fluctuations.

2. In the event that the Council identifies significant divergence of the budgetary position from the medium-term budgetary objective, or the adjustment path towards it, it shall, with a view to given early warning in order to prevent the occurrence of an excessive deficit, address in accordance with Article 99(4), a recommendation to the Member State concerned to take the necessary adjustment measures.

3. In the event that the Council in its subsequent monitoring judges that the divergence of the budgetary position from the medium-term budgetary objective, or the adjustment path towards it, is persisting or worsening, the Council shall, in accordance with Article 99(4), make a recommendation to the Member State concerned to take prompt corrective measures and may, as provided in that Article, make its recommendation public.

Section 4

Common Provisions

Article 11

As part of the multilateral surveillance described in this Regulation, the Council shall carry out the overall assessment described in Article 99(3).

Article 12

In accordance with the second subparagraph of Article 99(4) the President of the Council and the Commission shall include in their report to the European Parliament the results of the multilateral surveillance carried out under this Regulation.

Article 13

This Regulation shall enter into force on 1 July 1998.

This Regulation shall be binding in its entirety and directly applicable in all Member States.

Council Regulation (EC) No 1467/97 of 7 July 1997 on speeding up and clarifying the implementation of the excessive deficit procedure

THE COUNCIL OF THE EUROPEAN UNION,

Having regard to the Treaty establishing the European Community, and in particular the second subparagraph of Article 104c (14) thereof,

Having regard to the proposal from the Commission[1],

Having regard to the opinion of the European Parliament[2],

Having regard to the opinion of the European Monetary Institute,

(1) Whereas it is necessary to speed up and to clarify the excessive deficit procedure set out in Article 104c of the Treaty in order to deter excessive general government deficits and, if they occur, to further their prompt correction; whereas the provisions of this Regulation, which are to the above effect and adopted under Article 104c (14) second subparagraph, constitute, together with those of Protocol (No 5) to the Treaty, a new integrated set of rules for the application of Article 104c;

(2) Whereas the Stability and Growth Pact is based on the objective of sound government finances as a means of strengthening the conditions for price stability and for strong sustainable growth conducive to employment creation;

(3) Whereas the Stability and Growth Pact consists of this Regulation, of Council Regulation (EC) No 1466/97[3] which aims to strengthen the surveillance of budgetary positions and the surveillance and coordination of economic policies and of the Resolution of the European Council of 17 June 1997 on the Stability and Growth Pact[4], in which, in accordance with Article D of the Treaty on European Union, firm political guidelines are issued in order to implement the Stability and Growth Pact in a strict and timely manner and in particular to adhere to the medium term objective for budgetary positions of close to balance or in surplus, to which all Member States are committed, and to take the corrective budgetary action they deem necessary to meet the objectives of their stability and convergence programmes, whenever they have information indicating actual or expected significant divergence from the medium-term budgetary objective;

(4) Whereas in stage three of Economic and Monetary Union (EMU) the Member States are, according to Article 104c of the Treaty, under a clear Treaty obligation to avoid excessive government deficits;

---

[1] OJ No C 368, 6. 12. 1996, p. 12.   [2] OJ No C 380, 16. 12. 1996, p. 29.
[3] See p. 1 of this Official Journal.   [4] OJ No C 236, 2. 8. 1997, p. 1.

whereas under Article 5 of Protocol (No 11) to the Treaty, paragraphs 1, 9 and 11 of Article 104c do not apply to the United Kingdom unless it moves to the third stage; whereas the obligation under Article 109e (4) to endeavour to avoid excessive deficits will continue to apply to the United Kingdom;

(5) Whereas Denmark, referring to paragraph 1 of Protocol (No 12) to the Treaty has notified, in the context of the Edinburgh decision of 12 December 1992, that it will not participate in the third stage; whereas, therefore, in accordance with paragraph 2 of the said Protocol, paragraphs 9 and 11 of Article 104c shall not apply to Denmark;

(6) Whereas in stage three of EMU Member States remain responsible for their national budgetary policies, subject to the provisions of the Treaty; whereas the Member States will take the necessary measures in order to meet their responsibilities in accordance with the provisions of the Treaty;

(7) Whereas adherence to the medium-term objective of budgetary positions close to balance or in surplus to which all Member States are committed, contributes to the creation of the appropriate conditions for price stability and for sustained growth conducive to employment creation in all Member States and will allow them to deal with normal cyclical fluctuations while keeping the government deficit within the 3 % of GDP reference value;

(8) Whereas for EMU to function properly, it is necessary that convergence of economic and budgetary performances of Member States which have adopted the single currency, hereafter referred to as 'participating Member States', proves stable and durable; whereas budgetary discipline is necessary in stage three of EMU to safeguard price stability;

(9) Whereas according to Article 109k (3) Articles 104c (9) and (11) only apply to participating Member States;

(10) Whereas it is necessary to define the concept of an exceptional and temporary excess over the reference value as referred to in Article 104c (2) (a); whereas the Council should in this context, inter alia, take account of the pluriannual budgetary forecasts provided by the Commission;

(11) Whereas a Commission report in accordance with Article 104c (3) is also to take into account whether the government deficit exceeds government investment expenditure and take into account all other relevant factors, including the medium-term economic and budgetary position of the Member State;

(12) Whereas there is a need to establish deadlines for the implementation of the excessive deficit procedure in order to ensure its

expeditious and effective implementation; whereas it is necessary in this context to take account of the fact that the budgetary year of the United Kingdom does not coincide with the calendar year;

(13) Whereas there is a need to specify how the sanctions provided for in Article 104c could be imposed in order to ensure the effective implementation of the excessive deficit procedure;

(14) Whereas reinforced surveillance under the Council Regulation (EC) No 1466/97 together with the Commission's monitoring of budgetary positions in accordance with paragraph 2 of Article 104c should facilitate the effective and rapid implementation of the excessive deficit procedure;

(15) Whereas in the light of the above, in the event that a participating Member State fails to take effective action to correct an excessive deficit, an overall maximum period of ten months from the reporting date of the figures indicating the existence of an excessive deficit until the decision to impose sanctions, if necessary, seems both feasible and appropriate in order to exert pressure on the participating Member State concerned to take such action; in this event, and if the procedure starts in March, this would lead to sanctions being imposed within the calendar year in which the procedure had been started;

(16) Whereas the Council recommendation for the correction of an excessive deficit or the later steps of the excessive deficit procedure, should have been anticipated by the Member State concerned, which would have had an early warning; whereas the seriousness of an excessive deficit in stage three should call for urgent action from all those involved;

(17) Whereas it is appropriate to hold the excessive deficit procedure in abeyance if the Member State concerned takes appropriate action in response to a recommendation under Article 104c (7) or a notice issued under Article 104c (9) in order to provide an incentive to Member States to act accordingly; whereas the time period during which the procedure would be held in abeyance should not be included in the maximum period of ten months between the reporting date indicating the existence of an excessive deficit and the imposition of sanctions; whereas it is appropriate to resume the procedure immediately if the envisaged action is not being implemented or if the implemented action is proving to be inadequate;

(18) Whereas, in order to ensure that the excessive deficit procedure has a sufficient deterrent effect, a non-interest-bearing deposit of an appropriate size should be required from the participating Member State concerned, whenever the Council decides to impose a sanction;

(19) Whereas the definition of sanctions on a prescribed scale is conducive to legal certainty; whereas it is appropriate to relate the amount of the deposit to the GDP of the participating Member State concerned;

(20) Whereas, whenever the imposition of a non-interest-bearing deposit does not induce the participating Member State concerned to correct its excessive deficit in due time, it is appropriate to intensify the sanctions; whereas it is then appropriate to transform the deposit into a fine;

(21) Whereas appropriate action by the participating Member State concerned in order to correct its excessive deficit is the first step towards abrogation of sanctions; whereas significant progress in correcting the excessive deficit should allow for the lifting of sanctions in accordance with paragraph 12 of Article 104c; whereas the abrogation of all outstanding sanctions should only occur once the excessive deficit has been totally corrected;

(22) Whereas Council Regulation (EC) No 3605/93 of 22 November 1993 on the application of the Protocol on the excessive deficit procedure annexed to the Treaty establishing the European Community[5] contains detailed rules for the reporting of budgetary data by Member States;

(23) Whereas, according to Article 109f (8), where the Treaty provides for a consultative role for the European Central Bank (ECB), references to the ECB shall be read as referring to the European Monetary Institute before the establishment of the ECB,

Has Adopted this Regulation: Section 1 Definitions and Assessments

Article 1

1. This Regulation sets out the provisions to speed up and clarify the excessive deficit procedure, having as its objective to deter excessive general government deficits and, if they occur, to further their prompt correction.

2. For the purpose of this Regulation 'participating Member States' shall mean those Member States which adopt the single currency in accordance with the Treaty and 'non-participating Member States' shall mean those which have not adopted the single currency.

---

[5] OJ L 332, 31. 12. 1993, p. 7.

Article 2

1. The excess of a government deficit over the reference value shall be considered exceptional and temporary, in accordance with Article 104c(2) (a), second indent, when resulting from an unusual event outside the control of the Member State concerned and which has a major impact on the financial position of the general government, or when resulting from a severe economic downturn.

   In addition, the excess over the reference value shall be considered temporary if budgetary forecasts as providedby the Commission indicate that the deficit will fall below the reference value following the end of the unusual event or the severe economic downturn.

2. The Commission when preparing a report under Article 104c (3) shall, as a rule, consider an excess over the reference value resulting from a severe economic downturn to be exceptional only if there is an annual fall of real GDP of at least 2 %.

3. The Council when deciding, according to Article 104c (6), whether an excessive deficit exists, shall in its overall assessment take into account any observations made by the Member State showing that an annual fall of real GDP of less than 2 % is nevertheless exceptional in the light of further supporting evidence, in particular on the abruptness of the downturn or on the accumulated loss of output relative to past trends.

Section 2 Speeding up the Excessive Deficit Procedure

Article 3

1. Within two weeks of the adoption by the Commission of a report issued in accordance with Article 104c (3), the Economic and Financial Committee shall formulate an opinion in accordance with Article 104c (4).

2. Taking fully into account the opinion referred to in paragraph 1, the Commission, if it considers that an excessive deficit exists, shall address an opinion and a recommendation to the Council in accordance with Article 104c (5) and (6).

3. The Council shall decide on the existence of an excessive deficit in accordance with Article 104c (6), within three months of the reporting dates established in Article 4 (2) and (3) of Regulation (EC) No 3605/93. When it decides, in accordance with Article 104c (6), that an excessive deficit exists, the Council shall at the same time make recommendations to the Member State concerned in accordance with Article 104c (7).

4. The Council recommendation made in accordance with Article 104c (7) shall establish a deadline of four months at the most for effective action to be taken by the Member State concerned. The Council recommendation shall also establish a deadline for the correction of the excessive deficit, which should be completed in the year following its identification unless there are special circumstances.

Article 4

1. Any Council decision to make public its recommendations, where it is established that no effective action has been taken in accordance with Article 104c (8), shall be taken immediately after the expiry of the deadline set in accordance with Article 3 (4) of this Regulation.
2. The Council, when considering whether effective action has been taken in response to its recommendations made in accordance with Article 104c (7), shall base its decision on publicly announced decisions by the Government of the Member State concerned.

Article 5

Any Council decision to give notice to the participating Member State concerned to take measures for the deficit reduction in accordance with Article 104c (9) shall be taken within one month of the Council decision establishing that no effective action has been taken in accordance with Article 104c (8).

Article 6

Where the conditions to apply Article 104c (11) are met, the Council shall impose sanctions in accordance with Article 104c (11). Any such decision shall be taken no later than two months after the Council decision giving notice to the participating Member State concerned to take measures in accordance with Article 104c (9).

Article 7

If a participating Member State fails to act in compliance with the successive decisions of the Council in accordance with Article 104c (7) and (9), the decision of the Council to impose sanctions, in accordance with paragraph 11 of Article 104c, shall be taken within ten months of the reporting dates pursuant to Regulation (EC) No 3605/93 as referred to in Article 3 (3) of this Regulation. An expedited procedure shall be used in the case of a deliberately planned deficit which the Council decides is excessive.

Article 8

Any Council decision to intensify sanctions, in accordance with Article 104c (11), other than the conversion of deposits into fines under Article 14 of this Regulation, shall be taken no later than two months after the reporting dates pursuant to Regulation (EC) No 3605/93. Any Council decision to abrogate some or all of its decisions in accordance with Article 104c (12) shall be taken as soon as possible and in any case no later than two months after the reporting dates pursuant to Regulation (EC) No 3605/93.

Section 3 Abeyance and Monitoring

Article 9

The excessive deficit procedure shall be held in abeyance:
- if the Member State concerned acts in compliance with recommendations made in accordance with Article 104c (7),
- if the participating Member State concerned acts in compliance with notices given in accordance with Article 104c (9).

2. The period during which the procedure is held in abeyance shall be included neither in the ten month period referred to in Article 7 nor in the two month period referred to in Article 6 of this Regulation.

Article 10

1. The Commission and the Council shall monitor the implementation of action taken:
   - by the Member State concerned in response to recommendations made under Article 104c (7),
   - by the participating Member State concerned in response to notices given under Article 104c (9).

2. If action by a participating Member State is not being implemented or, in the Council's view, is proving to be inadequate, the Council shall immediately take a decision under Article 104c (9) or Article 104c (11) respectively.

3. If actual data pursuant to Regulation (EC) No 3605/93 indicate that an excessive deficit has not been corrected by a participating Member State within the time limits specified either in recommendations issued

under Article 104c (7) or notices issued under Article 104c (9), the Council shall immediately take a decision under Article 104c (9) or Article 104c (11) respectively.

Section 4 Sanctions

Article 11

Whenever the Council decides to apply sanctions to a participating Member State in accordance with Article 104c (11), a non-interest-bearing deposit shall, as a rule, be required. The Council may decide to supplement this deposit by the measures provided for in the first and second indents of Article 104c (11).

Article 12

1. When the excessive deficit results from non-compliance with the crite-rion relating to the government deficit ration in Article 104c (2) (a), the amount of the first deposit shall comprise a fixed component equal to 0,2 % of GDP, and a variable component equal to one tenth of the difference between the deficit as a percentage of GDP in the preceding year and the reference value of 3 % of GDP.
2. Each following year, until the decision on the existence of an excessive deficit is abrogated, the Council shall assess whether the participating Member State concerned has taken effective action in response to the Council notice in accordance with Article 104c (9). In this annual assessment the Council shall decide, in accordance with Article 104c (11), and without prejudice to Article 13 of this Regulation, to intensify the sanctions, unless the participating Member State concerned has complied with the Council notice. If an additional deposit is decided, it shall be equal to one tenth of the difference between the deficit as a percentage of GDP in the preceding year and the reference value of 3 % of GDP.
3. Any single deposit referred to in paragraphs 1 and 2 shall not exceed the upper limit of 0,5 % of GDP.

Article 13

A deposit shall, as a rule, be converted by the Council, in accordance with Article 104c (11), into a fine if two years after the decision to require the participating Member State concerned to make a deposit, the excessive deficit has in the view of the Council not been corrected.

Article 14

1. In accordance with Article 104c (12), the Council shall abrogate the sanctions referred to in the first and second indents of Article 104c (11) depending on the significance of the progress made by the participating Member State concerned in correcting the excessive deficit.

Article 15

In accordance with Article 104c (12), the Council shall abrogate all outstanding sanctions if the decision on the existence of an excessive deficit is abrogated. Fines imposed in accordance with Article 13 of this Regulation will not be reimbursed to the participating Member State concerned.

Article 16

Deposits referred to in Articles 11 and 12 of this Regulation shall be lodged with the Commission. Interest on the deposits, and the fines referred to in Article 13 of this Regulation constitute other revenue referred to in Article 20l of the Treaty and shall be distributed among participating Member States without a deficit that is excessive as determined in accordance with Article 104c (6) in proportion to their share in the total GNP of the eligible Member States.

Section 5 Transitional and Final Provisions

Article 17

For the purpose of this Regulation and for as long as the United Kingdom has a budgetary year which is not a calendar year, the provisions of sections 2, 3 and 4 of this Regulation shall be applied to the United Kingdom in accordance with the Annex.

Article 18

This Regulation shall enter into force on 1 January 1999.

This Regulation shall be binding in its entirety and directly applicable in all Member States.

Done at Brussels, 7 July 1997.

For the Council
The President
J.-C. JUNCKER

Annex

Time Limits Applicable to The United Kingdom

1. In order to ensure equal treatment of all Member States, the Council, when taking decisions in Sections 2, 3 and 4 of this Regulation, shall have regard to the different budgetary year of the United Kingdom, with a view to taking decisions with regard to the United Kingdom at a point in its budgetary year similar to that at which decisions have been or will be taken in the case of other Member States.
2. The provisions specified in Column I shall be substituted by the provisions specified in Column II.

Column I	Column II
"as a rule, within four months of the reporting dates established in Article 4 (2) and (3) of Council Regulation (EC) No 3605/93" (Article 3(3))	"as a rule, within six months after the end of the budgetary year in which the deficit occurred"
"the year following its identification" (Article 3(4))	"the budgetary year following its identification"
"as a rule, within sixteen months of reporting dates established in Article 4 (2) and (3) of Regulation (EC) No 3605/93" (Article 7)	"as a rule, within eighteen months from the end of the budgetary year in which the deficit occurred"
"the preceding year" (Article 12(1))	"the preceding budgetary year" '

Council Regulation (EC) No 1467/97 of 7 July 1997 on speeding up and clarifying the implementation of the excessive deficit procedure[1]

Amended by:
- Council Regulation (EC) No 1056/2005 of 27 June 2005[2]
  [No 1467/97 of 7 July 1997][3]
  THE COUNCIL OF THE EUROPEAN UNION,
  Having regard to the Treaty establishing the European Community, and in particular the second subparagraph of Article 104c (14) thereof,
  Having regard to the proposal from the Commission[4],
  Having regard to the opinion of the European Parliament[5],
  Having regard to the opinion of the European Monetary Institute,

---

[1] OJ L 209, 2.8.1997, p. 6.   [2] OJ L 174, 7.7.2005, p. 5.
[3] NB: The preamble and the recitals of both the original and the amending Regulation are reproduced.
[4] OJ C 368, 6.12.1996, p. 12.   [5] OJ C 380, 16.12.1996, p. 29.

(1) Whereas it is necessary to speed up and to clarify the excessive deficit procedure set out in Article 104c of the Treaty in order to deter excessive general government deficits and, if they occur, to further their prompt correction; whereas the provisions of this Regulation, which are to the above effect and adopted under Article 104c(14) second subparagraph, constitute, together with those of Protocol (No 5) to the Treaty, a new integrated set of rules for the application of Article 104c;

(2) Whereas the Stability and Growth Pact is based on the objective of sound government finances as a means of strengthening the conditions for price stability and for strong sustainable growth conducive to employment creation;

(3) Whereas the Stability and Growth Pact consists of this Regulation, of Council Regulation (EC) No 1466/97[6] which aims to strengthen the surveillance of budgetary positions and the surveillance and coordination of economic policies and of the Resolution of the European Council of 17 June 1997 on the Stability and Growth Pact[7], in which, in accordance with Article D of the Treaty on European Union, firm political guidelines are issued in order to implement the Stability and Growth Pact in a strict and timely manner and in particular to adhere to the medium term objective for budgetary positions of close to balance or in surplus, to which all Member States are committed, and to takethe corrective budgetary action they deem necessary to meet the objectives of their stability and convergence programmes, whenever they have information indicating actual or expected signi cant divergence from the medium-term budgetary objective;

(4) Whereas in Stage III of economic and monetary union (EMU) the Member States are, according to Article 104c of the Treaty, under a clear Treaty obligation to avoid excessive government deficits; whereas under Article 5 of Protocol (No 11) to the Treaty, paragraphs 1, 9 and 11 of Article 104c do not apply to the United Kingdom unless it moves to the third stage; whereas the obligation under Article 109e (4) to endeavour to avoid excessive deficits will continue to apply to the United Kingdom;

(5) Whereas Denmark, referring to paragraph 1 of Protocol (No 12) to the Treaty has notified, in the context of the Edinburgh decision of 12 December 1992, that it will not participate in the third stage; whereas, therefore, in accordance with paragraph 2 of the said

[6] See p. 1 of this Official Journal.   [7] OJ C 236, 2.8.1997, p. 1.

Protocol, paragraphs 9 and 11 of Article 104c shall not apply to Denmark;

(6) Whereas in Stage III of EMU Member States remain responsible for their national budgetary policies, subject to the provisions of the Treaty; whereas the Member States will take the necessary measures in order to meet their responsibilities in accordance with the provisions of the Treaty;

(7) Whereas adherence to the medium-term objective of budgetary positions close to balance or in surplus to which all Member States are committed, contributes to the creation of the appropriate conditions for price stability and for sustained growth conducive to employment creation in all Member States and will allow them to deal with normal cyclical fluctuations while keeping the government deficit within the 3% of GDP reference value;

(8) Whereas for EMU to function properly, it is necessary that convergence of economic and budgetary performances of Member States which have adopted the single currency, hereafter referred to as 'participating Member States', proves stable and durable; whereas budgetary discipline is necessary in stage three of EMU to safeguard price stability;

(9) Whereas according to Article 109k(3) Articles 104c(9) and (11) only apply to participating Member States;

(10) Whereas it is necessary to de ne the concept of an exceptional and temporary excess over the reference value as referred to in Article 104c(2)(a); whereas the Council should in this context, *inter alia*, take account of the pluri-annual budgetary forecasts provided by the Commission;

(11) Whereas a Commission report in accordance with Article 104c(3) is also to take into account whether the government deficit exceeds government investment expenditure and take into account all other relevant factors, including the medium-term economic and budgetary position of the Member State;

(12) Whereas there is a need to establish deadlines for the implementation of the excessive deficit procedure in order to ensure its expeditious and effective implementation; whereas it is necessary in this context to take account of the fact that the budgetary year of the United Kingdom does not coincide with the calendar year;

(13) Whereas there is a need to specify how the sanctions provided for in Article 104c could be imposed in order to ensure the effective implementation of the excessive deficit procedure;

(14) Whereas reinforced surveillance under the Council Regulation (EC) No 1466/97 together with the Commission's monitoring of

budgetary positions in accordance with paragraph 2 of Article 104c should facilitate the effective and rapid implementation of the excessive deficit procedure;

(15) Whereas in the light of the above, in the event that a participating Member State fails to take effective action to correct an excessive deficit, an overall maximum period of ten months from the reporting date of the figures indicating the existence of an excessive deficit until the decision to impose sanctions, if necessary, seems both feasible and appropriate in order to exert pressure on the participating Member State concerned to take such action; in this event, and if the procedure starts in March, this would lead to sanctions being imposed within the calendar year in which the procedure had been started;

(16) Whereas the Council recommendation for the correction of an excessive deficit or the later steps of the excessive deficit procedure, should have been anticipated by the Member State concerned, which would have had an early warning; whereas the seriousness of an excessive deficit in stage three should call for urgent action from all those involved;

(17) Whereas it is appropriate to hold the excessive deficit procedure in abeyance if the Member State concerned takes appropriate action in response to a recommendation under Article 104c(7) or a notice issued under Article 104c(9) in order to provide an incentive to Member States to act accordingly; whereas the time period during which the procedure would be held in abeyance should not be included in the maximum period of ten months between the reporting date indicating the existence of an excessive deficit and the imposition of sanctions; whereas it is appropriate to resume the procedure immediately if the envisaged action is not being implemented or if the implemented action is proving to be inadequate;

(18) Whereas, in order to ensure that the excessive deficit procedure has a sufficient deterrent effect, a non-interest-bearing deposit of an appropriate size should be required from the participating Member State concerned, whenever the Council decides to impose a sanction;

(19) Whereas the definition of sanctions on a prescribed scale is conducive to legal certainty; whereas it is appropriate to relate the amount of the deposit to the GDP of the participating Member State concerned;

(20) Whereas, whenever the imposition of a non-interest-bearing deposit does not induce the participating Member State concerned to correct its excessive deficit in due time, it is appropriate to intensify the

sanctions; whereas it is then appropriate to transform the deposit into a fine;

(21) Whereas appropriate action by the participating Member State concerned in order to correct its excessive deficit is the first step towards abrogation of sanctions; whereas significant progress in correcting the excessive deficit should allow for the lifting of sanctions in accordance with paragraph 12 of Article 104c; whereas the abrogation of all outstanding sanctions should only occur once the excessive deficit has been totally corrected;

(22) Whereas Council Regulation (EC) No 3605/93 of 22 November 1993 on the application of the Protocol on the excessive deficit procedure annexed to the Treaty establishing the European Community[8] contains detailed rules for the reporting of budgetary data by Member States;

(23) Whereas, according to Article 109f(8), where the Treaty provides for a consultative role for the European Central Bank (ECB), references to the ECB shall be read as referring to the European Monetary Institute before the establishment of the ECB,

Has Adopted This Regulation

[No 1056 /2005 of 27 June 2005]

THE COUNCIL OF THE EUROPEAN UNION,

Having regard to the Treaty establishing the European Community, and in particular the second subparagraph of Article 104(14) thereof,

Having regard to the proposal from the Commission,

Having regard to the opinion of the European Central Bank[9],

Having regard to the opinion of the European Parliament[10],

Whereas:

(1) The Stability and Growth Pact initially consisted of Council Regulation (EC) No 1466/97 of 7 July 1997 on the strengthening of the surveillance of budgetary positions and the surveillance and coordination of economic policies[11], Council Regulation (EC) No 1467/97 of 7 July 1997 on speeding up and clarifying the implementation of the excessive deficit procedure[12] and the Resolution of the European Council of 17 June 1997 on the Stability and Growth Pact[13]. The Stability and Growth Pact has proven its usefulness in anchoring

---

[8] OJ L 332, 31.12.1993, p. 7.   [9] OJ C 144, 14.6.2005, p. 16.
[10] Opinion of 9 June 2005 (OJ C 124 E, 25.2. 2006, pp. 524–526).
[11] OJ L 209, 2.8.1997, p. 1.   [12] OJ L 209, 2.8.1997, p. 6.
[13] OJ C 236, 2.8.1997, p. 1.

fiscal discipline, thereby contributing to a high degree of macroeconomic stability with low inflation and low interest rates, which is necessary to induce sustainable growth and employment creation.

(2) On 20 March 2005 the Council adopted a report entitled 'Improving the implementation of the Stability and Growth Pact' which aims to enhance the governance and the national ownership of the fiscal framework by strengthening the economic underpinnings and the effectiveness of the Pact, both in its preventive and corrective arms, to safeguard the sustainability of public finances in the long run, to promote growth and to avoid imposing excessive burdens on future generations. The report was endorsed by the European Council in its conclusions of 23 March 2005[14], which stated that the report updates and complements the Stability and Growth Pact, of which it is now an integral part.

(3) According to the 20 March 2005 ECOFIN report endorsed by the spring 2005 European Council, the Member States, the Council and the Commission reaffirm their commitment to implement the Treaty and the Stability and Growth Pact in an effective and timely manner, through peer support and peer pressure, and to act in close and constructive cooperation in the process of economic and fiscal surveillance, in order to guarantee certainty and effectiveness in the rules of the Pact.

(4) Regulation (EC) No 1467/97 needs to be amended in order to allow the full application of the agreed improvement of the implementation of the Stability and Growth Pact.

(5) The guiding principle for the application of the excessive deficit procedure is the prompt correction of an excessive deficit. The procedure should remain simple, transparent and equitable.

(6) The concept of exceptional excess over the reference value resulting from a severe economic downturn should be revised. In doing so, due account should be taken of the economic heterogeneity in the European Union.

(7) The Commission should always prepare a report on the basis of Article 104(3) of the Treaty. In its report, it should examine whether the exceptions provided for in Article 104 (2) apply. The Commission report under Article 104(3) should appropriately reflect developments in 3the medium-term economic position and in the medium-term budgetary position. Furthermore, due consideration should be given to any other factors which, in the opinion of the Member State

---

[14] Annex 2 to conclusions of the European Council of 22 and 23 March 2005.

concerned, are relevant in order to comprehensively assess in qualitative terms the excess over the reference value.

(8) Careful consideration should be given in all budgetary assessments in the framework of the excessive deficit procedure to an excess close to the reference value which reflects the implementation of pension reforms introducing a multi-pillar system that includes a mandatory, fully funded pillar, because the implementation of those reforms leads to a short-term deterioration of the budgetary position, while the long-term sustainability of public finances clearly improves. In particular, when assessing under Article 104(12) of the Treaty whether the excessive deficit has been corrected, the Commission and the Council should assess developments in EDP deficit figures while also considering the net cost of the reform to the publicly managed pillar.

(9) The procedural deadlines for Council decisions in the excessive deficit procedure should be extended in order to allow the Member State concerned to better frame its action within the national budgetary procedure and to develop a more coherent package of measures. In particular, the deadline for the Council to decide on the existence of an excessive deficit in accordance with Article 104(6) of the Treaty should be set, as a rule, to four months after the reporting dates established in Article 4(2) and (3) of Council Regulation (EC) No 3605/93 of 22 November 1993 on the application of the Protocol on the excessive deficit procedure annexed to the Treaty establishing the European Community[15]. This would address the cases in which the budgetary statistical data has not been validated by the Commission (Eurostat) shortly after the reporting dates established in Regulation (EC) No 3605/93.

(10) In order to ensure a prompt correction of excessive deficits, it is necessary for Member States that are in a situation of excessive deficit to take effective action and to achieve an annual minimum fiscal improvement in their cyclically adjusted balance, net of one-off and temporary measures. As a benchmark, countries in excessive deficit will be required to achieve an annual minimum fiscal effort in cyclically adjusted terms, net of one-off and temporary measures.

(11) Maximum time periods within which Member States are to take effective action and measures should be extended to allow better framing of the action in the national budgetary procedures and the development of more articulated packages of measures.

---

[15] OJ L 332, 31.12.1993, p. 7. Regulation as last amended by Regulation (EC) No 351/2002 (OJ L 55, 26.2.2002, p. 23).

(12) If the Member State concerned has taken effective action in response to a recommendation under Article 104(7) of the Treaty or a notice issued under Article 104(9) and unexpected adverse economic events with major negative consequences for government finances prevent the correction of the excessive deficit within the time limit set by the Council, it should be possible for the Council to issue a revised recommendation under Article 104(7) or a revised notice under Article 104(9).

(13) The current overall maximum period of 10 months from the reporting dates established in Article 4(2) and (3) of Regulation (EC) No 3605/93 until the decision to impose sanctions would be inconsistent with the amended deadlines in each step of the procedure and the possibility to issue revised recommendations under Article 104(7) of the Treaty or revised notices under Article 104(9). The overall maximum period should therefore be adjusted in accordance with these amendments.

(14) The provisions applicable to the implementation of the excessive deficit procedure in the case of the United Kingdom, which are set out in the Annex to Regulation (EC) No 1467//97, also need to be modified to reflect those changes,

Has Adopted This Regulation:

Section 1

Definitions and Assessments

Article 1

1. This Regulation sets out the provisions to speed up and clarify the excessive deficit procedure, having as its objective to deter excessive general government deficits and, if they occur, to further their prompt correction.

2. For the purpose of this Regulation 'participating Member States' shall mean those Member States which adopt the single currency in accordance with the Treaty and 'non-participating Member States' shall mean those which have not adopted the single currency.

Article 2

1. The excess of a government deficit over the reference value shall be considered exceptional and temporary, in accordance with

Article 104(2) (a), second indent, when resulting from an unusual event outside the control of the Member State concerned and which has a major impact on the financial position of the general government, or when resulting from a severe economic downturn.

In addition, the excess over the reference value shall be considered temporary if budgetary forecasts as provided by the Commission indicate that the deficit will fall below the reference value following the end of the unusual event or the severe economic downturn.

2. The Commission and the Council, when assessing and deciding upon the existence of an excessive deficit in accordance with Article 104(3) to (6) of the Treaty, may consider an excess over the reference value resulting from a severe economic downturn as exceptional in the sense of the second indent of Article 104(2)(a) if the excess over the reference value results from a negative annual GDP volume growth rate or from an accumulated loss of output during a protracted period of very low annual GDP volume growth relative to its potential.

3. The Commission, when preparing a report under Article 104(3) of the Treaty shall take into account all relevant factors as indicated in that Article. The report shall appropriately reflect developments in the medium-term economic position (in particular potential growth, prevailing cyclical conditions, the implementation of policies in the context of the Lisbon agenda and policies to foster research and development and innovation) and developments in the medium-term budgetary position (in particular, fiscal consolidation efforts in 'good times', debt sustainability, public investment and the overall quality of public finances). Furthermore, the Commission shall give due consideration to any other factors which, in the opinion of the Member State concerned, are relevant in order to comprehensively assess in qualitative terms the excess over the reference value and which the Member State has put forward to the Commission and to the Council. In that context, special consideration shall be given to budgetary efforts towards increasing or maintaining at a high level financial contributions to fostering international solidarity and to achieving European policy goals, notably the unification of Europe if it has a detrimental effect on the growth and fiscal burden of a Member State. A balanced overall assessment shall encompass all these factors.

4. If the double condition of the overarching principle – that, before the relevant factors mentioned in paragraph 3 are taken into account, the general government deficit remains close to the reference value and its excess over the reference value is temporary – is fully met, these factors shall also be taken into account in the steps leading to the decision on the existence of an excessive deficit, foreseen in paragraphs 4, 5 and 6

of Article 104 of the Treaty. The balanced overall assessment to be made by the Council shall encompass all these factors.

5. The Commission and the Council, in all budgetary assessments in the framework of the excessive deficit procedure, shall give due consideration to the implementation of pension reforms introducing a multi-pillar system that includes a mandatory, fully funded pillar.

6. If the Council has decided, on the basis of Article 104(6) of the Treaty, that an excessive deficit exists in a Member State, the Commission and the Council shall take into account the relevant factors mentioned in paragraph 3 also in the subsequent procedural steps of Article 104, including as specified in Articles 3(5) and 5(2) of this Regulation. However those relevant factors shall not be taken into account for the decision of the Council under Article 104(12) of the Treaty on the abrogation of some or all of its decisions under paragraphs 6 to 9 and 11 of Article 104.

7. In the case of Member States where the deficit exceeds the reference value, while remaining close to it, and where this excess reflects the implementation of a pension reform introducing a multi-pillar system that includes a mandatory, fully funded pillar, the Commission and the Council shall also consider the cost of the reform to the publicly managed pillar when assessing developments in EDP deficit figures. For that purpose, consideration shall be given to the net cost of the reform on a linear degressive basis for a transitory period of five years. This net cost shall be taken into account also for the decision of the Council under Article 104(12) of the Treaty on the abrogation of some or all of its decisions under paragraphs 6 to 9 and 11 of Article 104, if the deficit has declined substantially and continuously and has reached a level that comes close to the reference value.

Section 2

Speeding Up The Excessive Deficit Procedure

Article 3

1. Within two weeks of the adoption by the Commission of a report issued in accordance with Article 104(3), the Economic and Financial Committee shall formulate an opinion in accordance with Article 104(4).

2. Taking fully into account the opinion referred to in paragraph 1, the Commission, if it considers that an excessive deficit exists, shall

address an opinion and a recommendation to the Council in accordance with Article 104(5) and (6).

3. The Council shall decide on the existence of an excessive deficit in accordance with Article 104(6) of the Treaty, as a rule within four months of the reporting dates established in Article 4(2) and (3) of Regulation (EC) No 3605/93. When it decides that an excessive deficit exists, the Council shall at the same time make recommendations to the Member State concerned in accordance with Article 104(7) of the Treaty.

4. The Council recommendation made in accordance with Article 104(7) of the Treaty shall establish a deadline of six months at most for effective action to be taken by the Member State concerned. The Council recommendation shall also establish a deadline for the correction of the excessive deficit, which should be completed in the year following its identification unless there are special circumstances. In the recommendation, the Council shall request that the Member State achieves a minimum annual improvement of at least 0.5% of GDP as a benchmark, in its cyclically adjusted balance net of one-off and temporary measures, in order to ensure the correction of the excessive deficit within the deadline set in the recommendation.

5. If effective action has been taken in compliance with a recommendation under Article 104 (7) and unexpected adverse economic events with major unfavourable consequences for government finances occur after the adoption of that recommendation, the Council may decide, on a recommendation fromthe Commission, to adopt a revised recommendation under Article 104(c). The revised recommendation, taking into account the relevant factors mentioned in Article 2(3) of this Regulation, may notably extend the deadline for the correction of the excessive deficit by one year. The Council shall assess the existence of unexpected adverse economic events with major unfavourable consequences for government finances against the economic forecasts in its recommendation.

Article 4

1. Any Council decision to make public its recommendations, where it is established that no effective action has been taken in accordance with Article 104(8), shall be taken immediately after the expiry of the deadline set in accordance with Article 3(4) of this Regulation.

2. The Council, when considering whether effective action has been taken in response to its recommendations made in accordance with Article 104(7), shall base its decision on publicly announced decisions by the Government of the Member State concerned.

Article 5

1. Any Council decision to give notice to the participating Member State concerned to take measures for the deficit reduction in accordance with Article 104(9) of the Treaty shall be taken within two months of the Council decision establishing that no effective action has been taken in accordance with Article 104(8). In the notice, the Council shall request that the Member State achieves a minimum annual improvement of at least 0.5% of GDP as a benchmark, in its cyclically adjusted balance net of one-off and temporary measures, in order to ensure the correction of the excessive deficit within the deadline set in the notice.

2. If effective action has been taken in compliance with a notice under Article 104(9) of the Treaty and unexpected adverse economic events with major unfavourable consequences for government finances occur after the adoption of that notice, the Council may decide, on a recommendation from the Commission, to adopt a revised notice under Article 104(9) of the Treaty. The revised notice, taking into account the relevant factors mentioned in Article 2(3) of this Regulation, may notably extend the deadline for the correction of the excessive deficit by one year. The Council shall assess the existence of unexpected adverse economic events with major unfavourable consequences for government finances against the economic forecasts in its notice.

Article 6

Where the conditions to apply Article 104(11) are met, the Council shall impose sanctions in accordance with Article 104(11). Any such decision shall be taken no later than four months after the Council decision giving notice to the participating Member State concerned to take measures in accordance with Article 104(9).

Article 7

If a participating Member State fails to act in compliance with the successive decisions of the Council in accordance with Article 104(7) and (9) of the Treaty, the decision of the Council to impose sanctions, in accordance with Article 104(11), shall be taken as a rule within 16 months of the reporting dates established in Article 4(2) and (3) of Regulation (EC) No 3605/93. In case Article 3(5) or 5(2) of this Regulation is applied, the 16-month deadline is amended accordingly. An expedited procedure shall be used in the case of a deliberately planned deficit which the Council decides is excessive.

Article 8

Any Council decision to intensify sanctions, in accordance with Article 104 (11), other than the conversion of deposits into fines under Article 14 of this Regulation, shall be taken no later than two months after the reporting dates pursuant to Regulation (EC) No 3605/93. Any Council decision to abrogate some or all of its decisions in accordance with Article 104(12) shall be taken as soon as possible and in any case no later than two months after the reporting dates pursuant to Regulation (EC) No 3605/93.

Section 3

Abeyance and Monitoring

Article 9

1. The excessive deficit procedure shall be held in abeyance:
   - if the Member State concerned acts in compliance with recommendations made in accordance with Article 104(7),
   - if the participating Member State concerned acts in compliance with notices given in accordance with Article 104(9).
2. The period during which the procedure is held in abeyance shall be included neither in the period referred to in Article 6 nor in the period referred to in Article 7 of this Regulation.
3. Following the expiry of the period referred to in the first sentence of Article 3(4) and following the expiry of the period referred to in the second sentence of Article 6 of this Regulation, the Commission shall inform the Council if it considers that the measures taken seem sufficient to ensure adequate progress towards the correction of the excessive deficit within the time limits set by the Council, provided that they are fully implemented and that economic developments are in line with forecasts. The Commission statement shall be made public.

Article 10

1. The Commission and the Council shall monitor the implementation of action taken:
   - by the Member State concerned in response to recommendations made under Article 104(7),
   - by the participating Member State concerned in response to notices given under Article 104(9).
2. If action by a participating Member State is not being implemented or, in the Council's view, is proving to be inadequate, the Council shall

immediately take a decision under Article 104(9) or Article 104(11) respectively.

3. If actual data pursuant to Regulation (EC) No 3605/93 indicate that an excessive deficit has not been corrected by a participating Member State within the time limits specified either in recommendations issued under Article 104(7) or notices issued under Article 104(9), the Council shall immediately take a decision under Article 104(9) or Article 104(11) respectively.

Section 4

Sanctions

Article 11

Whenever the Council decides to apply sanctions to a participating Member State in accordance with Article 104(11), a non-interest-bearing deposit shall, as a rule, be required. The Council may decide to supplement this deposit by the measures provided for in the first and second indents of Article 104(11).

Article 12

1. When the excessive deficit results from non-compliance with the criterion relating to the government deficit ration in Article 104(2)(a), the amount of the first deposit shall comprise a fixed component equal to 0.2% of GDP, and a variable component equal to one tenth of the difference between the deficit as a percentage of GDP in the preceding year and the reference value of 3% of GDP.

2. Each following year, until the decision on the existence of an excessive deficit is abrogated, the Council shall assess whether the participating Member State concerned has taken effective action in response to the Council notice in accordance with Article 104(9). In this annual assessment the Council shall decide, in accordance with Article 104 (11), and without prejudice to Article 13 of this Regulation, to intensify the sanctions, unless the participating Member State concerned has complied with the Council notice. If an additional deposit is decided, it shall be equal to one tenth of the difference between the deficit as a percentage of GDP in the preceding year and the reference value of 3% of GDP.

3. Any single deposit referred to in paragraphs 1 and 2 shall not exceed the upper limit of 0.5% of GDP.

Article 13

A deposit shall, as a rule, be converted by the Council, in accordance with Article 104(11), into a fine if two years after the decision to require the participating Member State concerned to make a deposit, the excessive ficit has in the view of the Council not been corrected.

Article 14

1. In accordance with Article 104(12), the Council shall abrogate the sanctions referred to in the first and second indents of Article 104(11) depending on the significance of the progress made by the participating Member State concerned in correcting the excessive deficit.

Article 15

In accordance with Article 104(12), the Council shall abrogate all out-standing sanctions if the decision on the existence of an excessive deficit is abrogated. Fines imposed in accordance with Article 13 of this Regulation will not be reimbursed to the participating Member State concerned.

Article 16

Deposits referred to in Articles 11 and 12 of this Regulation shall be lodged with the Commission. Interest on the deposits, and the fines referred to in Article 13 of this Regulation constitute other revenue referred to in Article 269 of the Treaty and shall be distributed among participating Member States without a deficit that is excessive as deter-mined in accordance with Article 104(6) in proportion to their share in the total GNP of the eligible Member States.

Section 5

Transitional and Final Provisions

Article 17

For the purpose of this Regulation and for as long as the United Kingdom has a budgetary year which is not a calendar year, the provisions of sections 2, 3 and 4 of this Regulation shall be applied to the United Kingdom in accordance with the Annex.

Article 18

This Regulation shall enter into force on 1 January 1999.

This Regulation shall be binding in its entirety and directly applicable in all Member States.

Annex

Time Limits Applicable to the United Kingdom

In order to ensure equal treatment of all Member States, the Council, when taking decisions in Sections 2, 3 and 4 of this Regulation, shall have regard to the different budgetary year of the United Kingdom, with a view to taking decisions with regard to the United Kingdom at a point in its budgetary year similar to that at which decisions have been or will be taken in the case of other Member States.

The provisions specified in Column I shall be substituted by the provisions specified in Column II.

COLUMN 1	COLUMN 2
'as a rule, within four months of the reporting dates established in Article 4(2) and (3) of Council Regulation (EC) No 3605/93' *(Article 3(3))*	'as a rule, within six months after the end of the budgetary year in which the deficit occurred'
'the year following its identification' *(Article 3(4))*	'the budgetary year following its identification'
'as a rule, within 16 months of reporting dates established in Article 4(2) and (3) of Regulation (EC) No 3605/93' *(Article 7)*	'as a rule, within 18 months from the end of the budgetary year in which the deficit occurred'
'the preceding year' *(Article 12(1))*	'the preceding budgetary year'

Political Communication (Council Resolution 1997 and ECOFIN Communication 2005)

Resolution of The European Council on the Stability and Growth Pact Amsterdam, 17 June 1997 (97/C 236/01)[1]

Official Journal C 236, 02/08/1997 P. 0001 – 0002

I. Meeting in Madrid in December 1995, the European Council confirmed the crucial importance of securing budgetary discipline

---

[1] http://eur-lex.europa.eu/LexUriServ/LexUriServ.do?uri=CELEX:31997Y0802(01):EN: HTML.

in stage three of Economic and Monetary Union (EMU). In Florence, six months later, the European Council reiterated this view and in Dublin, in December 1996, it reached an agreement on the main elements of the Stability and Growth Pact. In stage three of EMU, Member States shall avoid excessive general government deficits: this is a clear Treaty obligation (1). The European Council underlines the importance of safeguarding sound government finances as a means to strengthening the conditions for price stability and for strong sustainable growth conducive to employment creation. It is also necessary to ensure that national budgetary policies support stability oriented monetary policies. Adherence to the objective of sound budgetary positions close to balance or in surplus will allow all Member States to deal with normal cyclical fluctuations while keeping the government deficit within the reference value of 3 % of GDP.

II. Meeting in Dublin in December 1996, the European Council requested the preparation of a Stability and Growth Pact to be achieved in accordance with the principles and procedures of the Treaty. This Stability and Growth Pact in no way changes the requirements for participation in stage three of EMU, either in the first group or at a later date. Member States remain responsible for their national budgetary policies, subject to the provisions of the Treaty; they will take the necessary measures in order to meet their responsibilities in accordance with those provisions.

III. The Stability and Growth Pact, which provides both for prevention and deterrence, consists of this Resolution and two Council Regulations, one on the strengthening of the surveillance of budgetary positions and the surveillance and coordination of economic policies and another on speeding up and clarifying the implementation of the excessive deficit procedure.

IV. The European Council solemnly invites all parties, namely the Member States, the Council of the European Union and the Commission of the European Communities, to implement the Treaty and the Stability and Growth Pact in a strict and timely manner. This Resolution provides firm political guidance to the parties who will implement the Stability and Growth Pact. To this end, the European Council has agreed upon the following guidelines:

The Member States

1. commit themselves to respect the medium-term budgetary objective of positions close to balance or in surplus set out in their stability

or convergence programmes and to take the corrective budgetary action they deem necessary to meet the objectives of their stability or convergence programmes, whenever they have information indicating actual or expected significant divergence from those objectives;

2. are invited to make public, on their own initiative, the Council recommendations made to them in accordance with Article 103 (4);

3. commit themselves to take the corrective budgetary action they deem necessary to meet the objectives of their stability or convergence programmes once they receive an early warning in the form of a Council recommendation issued under Article 103 (4);

4. will launch the corrective budgetary adjustments they deem necessary without delay on receiving information indicating the risk of an excessive deficit;

5. will correct excessive deficits as quickly as possible after their emergence; this correction should be completed no later than the year following the identification of the excessive deficit, unless there are special circumstances;

6. are invited to make public, on their own initiative, recommendations made in accordance with Article 104c (7);

7. commit themselves not to invoke the benefit of Article 2 (3) of the Council Regulation on speeding up and clarifying the excessive deficit procedure unless they are in severe recession; in evaluating whether the economic downturn is severe, the Member States will, as a rule, take as a reference point an annual fall in real GDP of at least 0,75 %.

The Commission

1. will exercise its right of initiative under the Treaty in a manner that facilitates the strict, timely and effective functioning of the Stability and Growth Pact;

2. will present, without delay, the necessary reports, opinions and recommendations to enable the Council to adopt decisions under Article 103 and Article 104c; this will facilitate the effective functioning of the early warning system and the rapid launch and strict application of the excessive deficit procedure;

3. commits itself to prepare a report under Article 104c (3) whenever there is the risk of an excessive deficit or whenever the planned or actual government deficit exceeds the reference value of 3 % of GDP, thereby triggering the procedure under Article 104c (3);

4. commits itself, in the event that the Commission considers that a deficit exceeding 3 % of GDP is not excessive and this opinion differs from that of the Economic and Financial Committee, to present in writing to the Council the reasons for its position;
5. commits itself, following a request from the Council under Article 109d, to make, as a rule, a recommendation for a Council decision on whether an excessive deficit exists under Article 104c (6).

The Council

1. is committed to a rigorous and timely implementation of all elements of the Stability and Growth Pact in its competence; it will take the necessary decisions under Article 103 and Article 104c as is practicable;
2. is urged to regard the deadlines for the application of the excessive deficit procedure as upper limits; in particular, the Council, acting under Article 104c (7), shall recommend that excessive deficits be corrected as quickly as possible after their emergence, no later than the year following their identification, unless there are special circumstances;
3. is invited always to impose sanctions if a participating Member State fails to take the necessary steps to bring the excessive deficit situation to an end as recommended by the Council;
4. is urged always to require a non-interest bearing deposit, whenever the Council decides to impose sanctions on a participating Member State in accordance with Article 104c (11);
5. is urged always to convert a deposit into a fine after two years of the decision to impose sanctions in accordance with Article 104c (11), unless the excessive deficit has in the view of the Council been corrected;
6. is invited always to state in writing the reasons which justify a decision not to act if at any stage of the excessive deficit or surveillance of budgetary positions procedures the Council did not act on a Commission recommendation and, in such a case, to make public the votes cast by each Member State.
   (1) Under Article 5 of Protocol 11, this obligation does not apply to the United Kingdom unless it moves to the third stage; the obligation under Article 109e (4) of the Treaty establishing the European Community to endeavour to avoid excessive deficits shall continue to apply to the United Kingdom.

Ecofin Communication (2005)

Improving the implementation of the Stability and Growth Pact – Council Report to the European Council –

This report presents proposals for strengthening and clarifying the implementation of the Stability and Growth Pact, with the aim of improving the coordination and monitoring of economic policies according to Article 99 of the Treaty and of avoiding excessive deficits as required by Article 104(1) of the Treaty.

The Council confirms that the Stability and Growth Pact, built on Treaty Articles 99 and 104, is an essential part of the macroeconomic framework of the Economic and Monetary Union. By requesting Member States to coordinate their budgetary policies and to avoid excessive deficits, it contributes to achieving macroeconomic stability in the EU and plays a key role in securing low inflation and low interest rates, which are essential contributions for delivering sustainable economic growth and job creation.

The Council recalls the Declaration on Article III-184 (annexed to the Final Act of the Constitution), which reaffirmed the European Council's commitment to the goals of the Lisbon Strategy – job creation, structural reforms, and social cohesion – and which stated on budgetary policy : "The Union aims at achieving balanced economic growth and price stability. Economic and budgetary policies thus need to set the right priorities towards economic reforms, innovation, competitiveness and strengthening of private investment and consumption in phases of weak economic growth. This should be reflected in the orientations of budgetary decisions at the national and Union level in particular through restructuring of public revenue and expenditure while respecting budgetary discipline in accordance with the Constitution and the Stability and Growth Pact."

The two nominal anchors of the Pact – the 3% of GDP reference value for the deficit ratio and the 60% of GDP reference value for the debt ratio – have proven their value and continue to be the centrepiece of multilateral surveillance. However, the European Council noted in June 2004 the need to strengthen and to clarify the implementation of the Stability and Growth Pact, in order to foster transparency and national ownership of the EU fiscal framework and to improve enforcement of its rules and provisions.

The Pact has to be applied across countries in a fair and consistent way and be understood by public opinion. The Council reaffirms that a rules-based system is the best guarantee for commitments to be enforced and for all Member States to be treated equally. In strengthening and clarifying the Pact it is essential to secure a proper balance between the higher degree of economic judgement and policy discretion in the surveillance and co-ordination of budgetary policies and the need for keeping the rules-based framework simple, transparent and enforceable.

However, in a European Union of 25 countries, characterised by considerable heterogeneity and diversity and given the experience of 5 years in EMU, an enriched common framework with a stronger emphasis on the economic rationale of its rules would allow to better cater for differences in economic situations across the EU. The objective is therefore to enhance the economic underpinnings of the existing framework and thus strengthen credibility and enforcement. The aim is not to increase the rigidity or flexibility of current rules but rather to make them more effective.

On this basis, the reform aims at better responding to the shortcomings experienced so far through greater emphasis to economic developments and an increased focus on safeguarding the sustainability of public finances. Also, the instruments for EU economic governance need to be better interlinked in order to enhance the contribution of fiscal policy to economic growth and support progress towards realising the Lisbon strategy.

Following the Commission Communication of 3 September 2004 on "Strengthening economic governance and clarifying the implementation of the Stability and Growth Pact", the Council has worked in order to make concrete proposals for a reform of the Stability and Growth Pact.

The Council, in reviewing the Stability- and Growth-Pact provisions, detected mainly five areas where improvements could be made:

(i) enhance the economic rationale of the budgetary rules to improve their credibility and ownership;
(ii) improve "ownership" by national policy makers;
(iii) use more effectively periods when economies are growing above trend for budgetary consolidation in order to avoid pro-cyclical policies;
(iv) take better account in Council recommendations of periods when economies are growing below trend;
(v) give sufficient attention in the surveillance of budgetary positions to debt and sustainability.

In making the proposals for a reform of the Stability and Growth Pact, the Council gave due consideration to enhance the governance and the national ownership of the fiscal framework, to strengthen the economic underpinnings and the effectiveness of the Pact, both in its preventive and corrective arms, to safeguard the sustainability of public finances in the long run, to promote growth and to avoid imposing excessive burdens on future generations.

In accordance with the Luxembourg Resolution on economic policy coordination, the Council confirms that enhanced coordination of fiscal policies must adhere to the Treaty principle of subsidiarity, respecting the prerogatives of national Governments in determining their structural and budgetary policies, while complying with the provisions of the Treaty and the Stability and Growth Pact.

Ministers indicate in the present report the necessary legislative changes in order to make operational their views on the reform of the Stability and Growth Pact. They intend to keep changes to a minimum and look forward to proposals of the Commission to put their views into effect.

1.   Improving governance

In order to increase the legitimacy of the EU fiscal framework and to strengthen support for its goals and institutional arrangements, the Council considers that Member States, the Commission and the Council, while avoiding any institutional shift, must deliver on their respective responsibilities, in particular:

(1) The Commission and the Council respect the Member States' responsibility to implement the policies of their choice within the limits set by the Treaty, in particular by Articles 99 and 104, while the Member States have to comply with the recommendations of the Council;

(2) The Commission has to exercise its right of initiative in a timely manner and apply the rules effectively, while the Council and the Member States respect the Commission's responsibility as guardian of the Treaty and its procedures;

(3) The Council has to exercise responsibly its margin of discretion, while the Member States and the Commission respect the Council's responsibility for the coordination of economic policies within the European Union and its role for the proper functioning of economic and monetary union;

(4) The Member States, the Council and the Commission should reaffirm their commitment to implement the Treaty and the Stability and Growth Pact in an effective and timely manner, through peer support and peer pressure, and to act in close and constructive cooperation in the process of economic and fiscal surveillance, in order to guarantee certainty and effectiveness to the rules of the Pact.

The Council emphasises the importance of improving governance and strengthening national ownership of the fiscal framework through the proposals outlined hereafter.

1.1. *Cooperation and communication*

The Council, the Commission and the Member States should apply the Treaty and the Stability and Growth Pact in an effective and timely manner. Parties should act in close and constructive cooperation in the process of economic and fiscal surveillance in order to guarantee certainty and effectiveness to the rules of the Pact.

In the spirit of transparency and accountability, due consideration should be given to full and timely communication among institutions as well as with the general public. In particular, in order to foster a frank and confidential exchange of views, the Council, the Commission and the Member States should commit to exchange advance information on their intentions at all stages of the budgetary monitoring and excessive deficit procedure, without prejudice to their respective prerogatives.

1.2. *Improving peer support and applying peer pressure*

The Council agrees that increasing the effectiveness of peer support and peer pressure is an integral part of a reformed Stability and Growth Pact. The Council and the Commission should commit to motivate and to make public their positions and decisions at all appropriate stages of the procedure of the Pact.

Peer support and peer pressure at euro area level should be given in the framework of the coordination carried out in the Eurogroup and be based on a horizontal assessment of national budgetary developments and their implications for the euro area as a whole. Such an assessment should be done at least once a year before the summer.

1.3. *Complementary national budgetary rules and institutions*

The Council agrees that national budgetary rules should be complementary to the Member States' commitments under the Stability and Growth Pact. Conversely, at EU level, incentives should be given and disincentives removed for national rules to support the objectives of the Stability and Growth Pact. In this context, the Council points out disincentives stemming from the impact in the fiscal framework of certain ESA95 accounting and statistical rules.

The implementation of existing national rules (expenditure rules, etc.) could be discussed in stability and convergence programmes, with due caution and as far as they are relevant for the respect of EU budgetary rules, as Member States are committed at European level to respect the latter, and compliance with EU budgetary rules constitutes the focus of the assessment of the stability and convergence programmes.

The Council considers that domestic governance arrangements should complement the EU framework. National institutions could play a more prominent role in budgetary surveillance to strengthen national ownership, enhance enforcement through national public opinion and complement the economic and policy analysis at EU level.

1.4.   *A stability programme for the legislature*

The Council invites Member States, when preparing the first update of their stability/convergence programme after a new government has taken office, to show continuity with respect to the budgetary targets endorsed by the Council on the basis of the previous update of the stability/convergence programme and – with an outlook for the whole legislature – to provide information on the means and instruments which it intends to employ to reach these targets by setting out its budgetary strategy.

1.5.   *Involvement of national Parliaments*

The Council invites Member States' governments to present stability/ convergence programmes and the Council opinions thereon to their national Parliaments. National Parliaments may wish to discuss the follow-up to recommendations in the context of the early warning and the excessive deficit procedures.

1.6.   *Reliable macroeconomic forecasts*

The Council recognises that it is important to base budgetary projections on realistic and cautious macroeconomic forecasts. It also recognises the important contribution that Commission forecasts can provide for the coordination of economic and fiscal policies.

In their macroeconomic and budgetary projections, Member States, in particular euro area Member States and Members States participating in ERM II, should use the "common external assumptions" if provided by the Commission in due time. Member States are free to base their stability/convergence programmes on their own projections. However, divergences between the national and the Commission forecasts should be explained in some detail. This explanation will serve as a reference when assessing *a posteriori* forecast errors.

Given the inevitability of forecast errors, greater emphasis should be placed in the stability/convergence programmes on conducting comprehensive sensitivity analyses and/or developing alternative scenarios, in order to enable the Commission and the Council to consider the complete range of possible fiscal outcomes.

1.7.   *Statistical governance*

The Council agrees that the implementation of the fiscal framework and its credibility rely crucially on the quality, reliability and timeliness of fiscal statistics. Reliable and timely statistics are not only essential for the assessment of government budgetary positions; full transparency of such statistics will also allow the financial markets to better assess the creditworthiness of the different Member States, providing an important signalling function for policy errors.

The core issue remains to ensure adequate practices, resources and capabilities to produce high quality statistics at the national and European level with a view to ensuring the independence, integrity and account-ability of both national statistical offices and Eurostat. Furthermore, the focus must be on developing the operational capacity, monitoring power, independence and accountability of Eurostat. The Commission and the Council in the course of 2005 are dealing with the issue of improving the governance of the European statistical system.

Member States and EU institutions should affirm their commitment to produce high quality and reliable budgetary statistics and to ensure mutual cooperation to achieve this goal. Imposing sanctions on a Member State should be considered when there is infringement of the obligations to duly report government data.

2.   Strengthening the preventive arm

There is broad consensus that periods of growth above trend should be used for budgetary consolidation in order to avoid pro-cyclical policies. The past failure to reach the medium-term budgetary objective of 'close to balance or in surplus' calls for a strengthening of the preventive arm of the Stability and Growth Pact, through a renewed commitment by Member States to take the budgetary action necessary to converge towards this objective and respect it.

2.1.   *Definition of the medium-term budgetary objective*

The Stability and Growth Pact lays down the obligation for Member States to adhere to the medium term objective (MTO) for their budgetary positions of "close to balance or in surplus" (CTBOIS).

In light of the increased economic and budgetary heterogeneity in the EU of 25 Member States, the Council agrees that the MTO should be differentiated for individual Member States to take into account the diversity of economic and budgetary positions and developments as well as of fiscal risk to the sustainability of public finances, also in the face of prospective demographic changes.

The Council therefore proposes developing medium-term objectives that, by taking account of the characteristics of the economy of each Member State, pursue a triple aim. They should firstly provide a safety margin with respect to the 3% deficit limit. They should also ensure rapid progress towards sustainability. Taking this into account, they should allow room for budgetary manoeuvre, in particular taking into account the needs for public investment.

MTOs should be differentiated and may diverge from CTBOIS for individual Member States on the basis of their current debt ratio and potential growth, while preserving sufficient margin below the reference value of -3% of GDP. The range for the country-specific MTOs for euro area and ERM II Member States would thus be, in cyclically adjusted terms, net of one-off and temporary measures, between -1% of GDP for low debt/high potential growth countries and balance or surplus for high debt/low potential growth countries.

The long-term sustainability of public finances would be supported by the convergence of debt ratios towards prudent levels.

Implicit liabilities (related to increasing expenditures in the light of ageing populations) should be taken into account, as soon as criteria and modalities for doing so are appropriately established and agreed by the Council. By the end of 2006, the Commission should report on progress achieved towards the methodology for completing the analysis by incorporating such implicit liabilities.

The Council stresses however that fiscal policy cannot be expected in the short term to cope with the full structural effects of demographic ageing and it invites Member States to pursue their efforts in implementing structural reforms in the areas related to the ageing of their populations as well as towards increasing employment and participation ratios.

Medium-term budgetary objectives could be revised when a major reform is implemented and in any case every four years, in order to reflect developments in government debt, potential growth and fiscal sustainability.

2.2.   *Adjustment path to the medium-term objective*

The Council considers that a more symmetrical approach to fiscal policy over the cycle through enhanced budgetary discipline in periods of economic recovery should be achieved, with the objective to avoid pro-cyclical policies and to gradually reach the medium term objective, thus creating the necessary room to accommodate economic downturns and reduce government debt at a satisfactory pace, thereby contributing to the long-term sustainability of public finances.

Member States should commit at a European level to actively consolidate public finances in good times. The presumption is to use unexpected extra revenues for deficit and debt reduction.

Member States that have not yet reached their MTO should take steps to achieve it over the cycle. Their adjustment effort should be higher in good times; it could be more limited in bad times. In order to reach their MTO, Member States of the euro zone or of ERM-II should pursue an annual adjustment in cyclically adjusted terms, net of one-offs and other temporary measures, of 0.5% of GDP as a benchmark. "Good times" should be identified as periods where output exceeds its potential level, taking into account tax elasticities.

Member States that do not follow the required adjustment path will explain the reasons for the deviation in the annual update of the stability/convergence programmes. The Commission will issue policy advice to encourage Member States to stick to their adjustment path. Such policy advice will be replaced by early warnings in accordance with the Constitution as soon as it becomes applicable.

2.3. *Taking structural reforms into account*

The Council agrees that, in order to enhance the growth oriented nature of the Pact, structural reforms will be taken into account when defining the adjustment path to the medium-term objective for countries that have not yet reached this objective and in allowing a temporary deviation from this objective for countries that have already reached it, with the clear understanding that a safety margin to ensure the respect of the 3% of GDP reference value for the deficit has to be guaranteed and that the budgetary position would be expected to return to the MTO within the programme period.

Only major reforms which have direct long-term cost-saving effects, including by raising potential growth, and therefore a verifiable positive impact on the long-term sustainability of public finances, will be taken into account. A detailed cost-benefit analysis of those reforms from the budgetary point of view would need to be provided in the framework of the annual update of stability/convergence programmes.

These proposals should be introduced into Regulation 1466/97.

Moreover, the Council is mindful that the respect of the budgetary targets of the Stability and Growth Pact should not hamper structural reforms that unequivocally improve the long-term sustainability of public finances. The Council acknowledges that special attention must be paid to pension reforms introducing a multi-pillar system that includes a mandatory, fully funded pillar. Although these reforms entail a short-term deterioration of public finances during the implementation period, the long-term sustainability of public finances is clearly improved. The Council therefore agrees that Member States implementing such reforms should be allowed to deviate from the adjustment path towards the MTO, or from the MTO itself. The deviation from the MTO should reflect the net cost of the reform to the publicly managed pillar, provided the deviation remains temporary and an appropriate safety margin to the reference value is preserved.

3.   Improving the implementation of the excessive deficit procedure

The excessive deficit procedure should remain simple, transparent and equitable. Nevertheless, the experience of recent years shows possible scope for improvement in its implementation.

The guiding principle for the application of the procedure is the prompt correction of an excessive deficit.

The Council underlines that the purpose of the excessive deficit procedure is to assist rather than to punish, and therefore to provide incentives for Member States to pursue budgetary discipline, through enhanced surveillance, peer support and peer pressure. Moreover, policy errors should be clearly distinguished from forecast errors in the implementation of the excessive deficit procedure. If nevertheless a Member State fails to comply with the recommendations addressed to it under the excessive deficit procedure, the Council has the power to apply the available sanctions.

3.1.   *Preparing a Commission report under Article 104(3)*

In order to avoid excessive government deficits, as called for by Article 104(1) of the Treaty, the reports, prepared by the Commission according to Article 104(3) of the Treaty as a result of its monitoring, form the basis of the EFC opinion, the ensuing Commission assessment and ultimately the Council decision on the existence of an excessive deficit as well as on its recommendations, including on the deadlines for the correction of the deficit.

The Council and the Commission are resolved to clearly preserve and uphold the reference values of 3% and 60% of GDP as the anchors of the monitoring of the development of the budgetary situation and of the ratio of government debt to GDP in the Member States. The Commission will always prepare a report on the basis of Article 104(3) of the Treaty. The Commission shall examine in its report if one or more of the exceptions foreseen respectively in Article 104(2)(a) and (b) apply. The Council hereafter proposes revisions or clarifications to the scope of those exceptions.

As foreseen by the Treaty, the Commission shall moreover take into account in its report whether the Member State's government deficit exceeds government investment expenditure and take into account all other relevant factors, including the medium-term economic and budgetary position of the Member State. The Council hereafter proposes clarifications to the concept of "all other relevant factors".

3.2. An "exceptional and temporary" excess of the deficit over the reference value

The Treaty provides, in Article 104(2)(a) second indent, for an exception if an excess over the reference value is only exceptional and temporary and if the ratio remains close to the reference value.

Whereas, in order to benefit from that exception, the ratio has always to remain close to the reference value, Regulation 1467/97 gives definitions as to when an excess over the reference value, but still close to it, shall be considered exceptional and temporary: in order to be considered as exceptional, the excess has to result from an unusual event outside the control of the Member State and with a major impact on the financial position of the general government, or it has to result from a severe economic downturn. In order for the excess to be temporary, the Commission's budgetary forecast must indicate that the deficit will fall below the reference value following the end of the unusual event or the severe economic downturn.

A severe economic downturn is presently defined – as a rule – as an annual fall of real GDP of at least 2%. Moreover, in the case of an annual fall of real GDP of less than 2%, Regulation 1467/97 still allows the Council to decide that no excessive deficit exists, in the light of further evidence, in particular on the abruptness of the downturn or on the accumulated loss of output relative to past trends.

The Council considers that the current definition of "a severe economic downturn" given in Article 2(2) of Regulation 1467/97 is too restrictive. The Council considers that paragraphs (2) and (3) of Article 2 in Regulation 1467/97 need to be adapted in order to allow both the Commission and the Council, when assessing and deciding upon the existence of an excessive deficit, according to paragraphs (3) to (6) of Article 104 of the Treaty, to consider as exceptional an excess over the reference value which results from a negative growth rate or from the accumulated loss of output during a protracted period of very low growth relative to potential growth.

3.3.   *"All other relevant factors"*

Article 104(3) of the Treaty requests that, in preparing the report on the non-fulfilment of the criteria for compliance with budgetary discipline, the Commission "shall also take into account whether the government deficit exceeds government investment expenditure and take into account all other relevant factors, including the medium-term economic and budgetary position of the Member State". A balanced overall assessment has to encompass all these factors.

The Council underlines that taking into account "other relevant factors" in the steps leading to the decision on the existence of an excessive deficit (Article 104, paragraphs (4), (5) and (6)) must be fully conditional on the overarching principle that – before other relevant factors are taken into account – the excess over the reference value is temporary and the deficit remains close to the reference value.

The Council considers that the framework to take into account "all other relevant factors" should be clarified. The Commission's report under Article 104(3) should appropriately reflect developments in the medium-term economic position (in particular potential growth, prevailing cyclical conditions, the implementation of policies in the context of the Lisbon agenda and policies to foster R&D and innovation) and developments in the medium-term budgetary position (in particular, fiscal consolidation efforts in "good times", debt sustainability, public investment and the overall quality of public finances). Furthermore, due consideration will be given to any other factors, which in the opinion of the Member State concerned, are relevant in order to comprehensively assess in qualitative terms the excess over the reference value. In that context, special consideration will be given to budgetary efforts towards increasing or maintaining at a high level financial contributions to fostering international solidarity and to achieving European policy goals, notably the unification of Europe if it has a detrimental effect on the growth and fiscal burden of a Member State.

Clearly no redefinition of the Maastricht reference value for the deficit via the exclusion of particular budgetary items should be pursued.

If the Council has decided, on the basis of Article 104(6), that an excessive deficit exists in a Member State, the "other relevant factors" will also be considered in the subsequent procedural steps of Article 104. However, they should not be taken into account under Article 104(12), i.e. in the decision of the Council as to whether a Member State has corrected its excessive deficit.

These proposals should be introduced into Regulation 1467/97.

3.4.   *Taking into account systemic pension reforms*

The Council agrees that an excess close to the reference value which reflects the implementation of pension reforms introducing a multi-pillar system that includes a mandatory, fully funded pillar should be considered carefully. Although the implementation of these reforms leads to a short-term deterioration of the budgetary position, the long-term sustainability of public finances clearly improves.

The Commission and the Council, in all budgetary assessments in the framework of the EDP, will give due consideration to the implementation of these reforms.

In particular, when assessing under Article 104(12) whether the excessive deficit has been corrected, the Commission and the Council will assess developments in EDP deficit figures while also considering the net cost of the reform to the publicly managed pillar. Consideration to the net cost of the reform will be given for the initial five years after a Member State has introduced a mandatory fully-funded system, or five years after 2004 for Member States that have already introduced such a system. Furthermore, it will also be regressive, i.e. during a period of five years, consideration will be given to 100, 80, 60, 40 and 20 percent of the net cost of the reform to the publicly managed pillar.

3.5.   *Increasing the focus on debt and sustainability*

In line with the provisions of the Treaty, the Commission has to examine compliance with budgetary discipline on the basis of both the deficit and the debt criterion. The Council agrees that there should be increased focus on debt and sustainability, and reaffirms the need to reduce government debt to below 60% of GDP at a satisfactory pace, taking into account macroeconomic conditions. The higher the debt to GDP ratios of Member States, the greater must be their efforts to reduce them rapidly.

The Council considers that the debt surveillance framework should be strengthened by applying the concept of "sufficiently diminishing and approaching the reference value at a satisfactory pace" for the debt ratio in qualitative terms, by taking into account macroeconomic conditions and debt dynamics, including the pursuit of appropriate levels of primary

surpluses as well as other measures to reduce gross debt and debt management strategies. For countries above the reference value, the Council will
formulate recommendations on the debt dynamics in its opinions on the
stability and convergence programmes.

No change to the existing Regulations is required to that effect.

3.6.   Extending deadlines for taking effective action and measures

The Council considers that the deadline for adoption of a decision under
Article 104(6) establishing the existence of an excessive deficit should be
extended from three to four months after the fiscal notification deadline.
Moreover, the Council considers that the timing for taking effective
action following a recommendation to correct the excessive deficit
under Article 104(7) could be extended from 4 to 6 months, in order to
allow the Member State to better frame the action within the national
budgetary procedure and to develop a more articulated package of measures. This could facilitate the adoption of corrective packages of structural
(as opposed to largely temporary) measures. Furthermore, with longer
deadlines it would be possible to take an updated Commission forecast
into account, so that measures taken and significant changes in growth
conditions that could justify an extension of the deadlines would be
assessed together. For the same reasons, the one-month deadline for the
Council to take a decision to move from Article 104(8) to Article 104(9)
should be extended to two months, and the two-month deadline under
Article 104(9) should be extended to 4 months.

These proposals would require changes to the relevant Articles of
Regulation 1467/97.

3.7.   Initial deadline for correcting the excessive deficit

The Council considers that, as a rule, the deadline for correcting an
excessive deficit should be the year after its identification and thus, normally, the second year after its occurrence. The Council agrees however
that the elements to be taken into account in setting the initial deadline for
the correction of an excessive deficit should be better specified and should
include, in particular, an overall assessment of all the factors mentioned in
the report under Art. 104(3).

As a benchmark, countries in excessive deficit will be required to
achieve an annual minimum fiscal effort of at least 0.5 percent of GDP
in cyclically adjusted terms, net of one-off measures, and the initial deadline for the correction of the excessive deficit should be set taking into
account this minimum fiscal effort. If this effort seems sufficient to correct

the excessive deficit in the year following its identification, the initial deadline need not be set beyond that year.

However the Council agrees that in case of special circumstances, the initial deadline for correcting an excessive deficit could be set one year later, i.e. the second year after its identification and thus normally the third year after its occurrence. The determination of the existence of special circumstances will take into account a balanced overall assessment of the factors mentioned in the report under Article 104(3).

The initial deadline will be set without prejudice to the taking into account of systemic pension reforms and without prejudice to deadlines applying to new and future Member States.

3.8.   *Revising the deadlines for correcting the deficit*

The Council agrees that deadlines for correcting the excessive deficit could be revised and extended if unexpected adverse economic events with major unfavourable budgetary effects occur during the excessive deficit procedure. Repetition of a recommendation under Article 104(7) or a notice under Article 104(9) of the Treaty is possible and should be used if effective action has been taken by the Member State concerned in compliance with the initial recommendation or notice. This should be specified in Regulation 1467/97.

Member States would be required to give evidence of having taken effective action following recommendations. If effective action was taken in response to previous recommendations and unforeseeable growth developments justify a revision of the deadlines for correcting the excessive deficit, the procedure would not move to the next step. The growth forecast contained in the Council recommendation would be the reference against which unforeseeable growth developments would be assessed.

ECJ Judgment 13 July 2004

Case C-27/04

Commission of the European Communities

v

Council of the European Union

(Action for annulment – Article 104 EC – Regulation (EC) No 1467/97 – Stability and Growth Pact – Excessive government deficits – Council decisions under Article 104(8) and (9) EC – Required majority not achieved – Decisions not adopted – Action challenging 'decisions not to adopt the formal instruments contained in the Commission's recommendations' – Inadmissible – Action challenging 'Council conclusions')

In Case C-27/04,

Commission of the European Communities, represented by M. Petite, A. van Solinge and P. Aalto, acting as Agents, with an address for service in Luxembourg, applicant,

v

Council of the European Union, represented by J.-C. Piris, T. Middleton and J. Monteiro, acting as Agents, defendant,

APPLICATION for annulment of Council measures of 25 November 2003, namely:

- decisions not to adopt, in respect of the French Republic and the Federal Republic of Germany, the formal instruments contained in Commission recommendations pursuant to Article 104(8) and (9) EC;

- conclusions adopted in respect of each of those two Member States, entitled 'Council conclusions on assessing the actions taken by [the French Republic and the Federal Republic of Germany respectively] in response to recommendations of the Council according to Article 104(7) of the Treaty establishing the European Community and considering further measures for deficit reduction in order to remedy the situation of excessive deficit', in so far as those conclusions involve holding the excessive deficit procedure in abeyance, recourse to an instrument not envisaged by the Treaty and modification of the recommendations decided on by the Council under Article 104(7) EC,

The Court (Full Court),

composed of: V. Skouris, President, P. Jann, C. W. A. Timmermans, A. Rosas, C. Gulmann (Rapporteur), J.-P. Puissochet and J. N. Cunha Rodrigues, Presidents of Chambers, R. Schintgen, F. Macken, N. Colneric, S. von Bahr, R. Silva de Lapuerta and K. Lenaerts, Judges,

Advocate General: A. Tizzano,

Registrar: M.-F. Contet, Principal Administrator,

having regard to the decision of the President of the Court of 13 February 2004 that the case was to be determined in accordance with an expedited procedure pursuant to Article 62a of the Rules of Procedure, after hearing oral argument from the parties at the hearing on 28 April 2004,

after hearing the Advocate General,

gives the following

Judgment

1. By application lodged at the Court Registry on 27 January 2004, the Commission of the European Communities brought an action under Article 230 EC for annulment of measures of the Council of the European Union of 25 November 2003, namely:
   - decisions not to adopt, in respect of the French Republic and the Federal Republic of Germany, the formal instruments contained in Commission recommendations pursuant to Article 104(8) and (9) EC, and
   - conclusions adopted in respect of each of those two Member States, entitled 'Council conclusions on assessing the actions taken by [the French Republic and the Federal Republic of Germany respectively] in response to recommendations of the Council according to Article 104(7) of the Treaty establishing the European Community and considering further measures for deficit reduction in order to remedy the situation of excessive deficit' ('the Council's conclusions'), in so far as those conclusions involve holding the excessive deficit procedure in abeyance, recourse to an instrument not envisaged by the Treaty and modification of the recommendations decided on by the Council under Article 104(7) EC.

Legal context

2 Article 104 EC provides:

'1. Member States shall avoid excessive government deficits.

2. The Commission shall monitor the development of the budgetary situation and of the stock of government debt in the Member States with a view to identifying gross errors. In particular it shall examine compliance with budgetary discipline …

…

5. If the Commission considers that an excessive deficit in a Member State exists or may occur, the Commission shall address an opinion to the Council.

6. The Council shall, acting by a qualified majority on a recommendation from the Commission, and having considered any observations

which the Member State concerned may wish to make, decide after an overall assessment whether an excessive deficit exists.

7. Where the existence of an excessive deficit is decided according to paragraph 6, the Council shall make recommendations to the Member State concerned with a view to bringing that situation to an end within a given period. Subject to the provisions of paragraph 8, these recommendations shall not be made public.

8. Where it establishes that there has been no effective action in response to its recommendations within the period laid down, the Council may make its recommendations public.

9. If a Member State persists in failing to put into practice the recommendations of the Council, the Council may decide to give notice to the Member State to take, within a specified time-limit, measures for the deficit reduction which is judged necessary by the Council in order to remedy the situation.

   In such a case, the Council may request the Member State concerned to submit reports in accordance with a specific timetable in order to examine the adjustment efforts of that Member State.

10. The rights to bring actions provided for in Articles 226 and 227 may not be exercised within the framework of paragraphs 1 to 9 of this Article.

11. As long as a Member State fails to comply with a decision taken in accordance with paragraph 9, the Council may decide to apply or, as the case may be, intensify one or more of the following measures:

   - to require the Member State concerned to publish additional information, to be specified by the Council, before issuing bonds and securities,
   - to invite the European Investment Bank to reconsider its lending policy towards the Member State concerned,
   - to require the Member State concerned to make a non-interest-bearing deposit of an appropriate size with the Community until the excessive deficit has, in the view of the Council, been corrected,
   - to impose fines of an appropriate size.
   - The President of the Council shall inform the European Parliament of the decisions taken.

12. The Council shall abrogate some or all of its decisions referred to in paragraphs 6 to 9 and 11 to the extent that the excessive deficit in the Member State concerned has, in the view of the Council, been corrected. If the Council has previously made public recommendations, it shall, as soon as the decision under paragraph 8 has been

abrogated, make a public statement that an excessive deficit in the Member State concerned no longer exists.

13. When taking the decisions referred to in paragraphs 7 to 9, 11 and 12, the Council shall act on a recommendation from the Commission by a majority of two thirds of the votes of its members weighted in accordance with Article 205(2), excluding the votes of the representative of the Member State concerned.

14. Further provisions relating to the implementation of the procedure described in this article are set out in the Protocol on the excessive deficit procedure annexed to this Treaty.

The Council shall, acting unanimously on a proposal from the Commission and after consulting the European Parliament and the ECB, adopt the appropriate provisions which shall then replace the said Protocol.

...'

3 Under Article 104(9) and (13) EC, read in conjunction with Article 122 (3) and (5) EC, when the Council takes decisions envisaged by Article 104(9) the voting rights of Member States which have not adopted the single currency are suspended.

4 The European Council, in its Resolution on the Stability and Growth Pact adopted in Amsterdam on 17 June 1997 (OJ 1997 C 236, p. 1; 'the Resolution of the European Council of 17 June 1997'), recalled the crucial importance of securing budgetary discipline in stage three of Economic and Monetary Union ('EMU') and then adopted guidelines addressed to the Member States, the Commission and the Council.

5 The resolution states in the guidelines concerning the Council that the latter:

'1. is committed to a rigorous and timely implementation of all elements of the Stability and Growth Pact in its competence; it will take the necessary decisions under Article [99] and Article [104] as is practicable;

...

3. is invited always to impose sanctions if a participating Member State fails to take the necessary steps to bring the excessive deficit situation to an end as recommended by the Council;

...

6. is invited always to state in writing the reasons which justify a decision not to act if at any stage of the excessive deficit or surveillance of budgetary positions procedures the Council did not act on a Commission recommendation and, in such a case, to make public the votes cast by each Member State.'

6 Sections 2 and 3 of Council Regulation (EC) No 1467/97 of 7 July 1997 on speeding up and clarifying the implementation of the excessive deficit procedure (OJ 1997 L 209, p. 6) provide as follows:

'Section 2

Speeding up the excessive deficit procedure

Article 3

...

3. The Council shall decide on the existence of an excessive deficit in accordance with Article [104(6)], within three months of the reporting dates established in Article 4(2) and (3) of Regulation (EC) No 3605/93. When it decides, in accordance with Article [104(6)], that an excessive deficit exists, the Council shall at the same time make recommendations to the Member State concerned in accordance with Article [104(7)].
4. The Council recommendation made in accordance with Article [104(7)] shall establish a deadline of four months at the most for effective action to be taken by the Member State concerned. The Council recommendation shall also establish a deadline for the correction of the excessive deficit, which should be completed in the year following its identification unless there are special circumstances.

Article 4

1. Any Council decision to make public its recommendations, where it is established that no effective action has been taken in accordance with Article [104(8)], shall be taken immediately after the expiry of the deadline set in accordance with Article 3(4) of this Regulation.

...

Article 5

Any Council decision to give notice to the participating Member State concerned to take measures for the deficit reduction in accordance with Article [104(9)] shall be taken within one month of the Council decision establishing that no effective action has been taken in accordance with Article [104(8)].

Article 6

Where the conditions to apply Article [104(11)] are met, the Council shall impose sanctions in accordance with Article [104(11)]. Any such decision shall be taken no later than two months after the Council decision giving notice to the participating Member State concerned to take measures in accordance with Article [104(9)].

Article 7

If a participating Member State fails to act in compliance with the successive decisions of the Council in accordance with Article [104(7) and (9)], the decision of the Council to impose sanctions, in accordance with paragraph 11 of Article [104], shall be taken within ten months of the reporting dates pursuant to Regulation (EC) No 3605/93 as referred to in Article 3(3) of this Regulation. An expedited procedure shall be used in the case of a deliberately planned deficit which the Council decides is excessive.

...

Section 3

Abeyance and monitoring

Article 9

1. The excessive deficit procedure shall be held in abeyance:
   - if the Member State concerned acts in compliance with recommendations made in accordance with Article [104(7)],
   - if the participating Member State concerned acts in compliance with notices given in accordance with Article [104(9)].
2. The period during which the procedure is held in abeyance shall be included neither in the ten month period referred to in Article 7 nor in the two month period referred to in Article 6 of this Regulation.

...'

Facts

The Council's decisions pursuant to Article 104(6) and (7) EC

7 An excessive deficit procedure was initiated in relation to the Federal Republic of Germany in November 2002. By Decision 2003/89/EC of 21 January 2003 on the existence of an excessive deficit in Germany –

Application of Article 104(6) of the Treaty establishing the European Community (OJ 2003 L 34, p. 16), the Council decided, on a recommendation from the Commission, that an excessive deficit existed in that Member State. In accordance with Article 104(7) EC and Article 3(4) of Regulation No 1467/97, it recommended the German Government to bring that deficit to an end as rapidly as possible, by implementing various measures. It set 21 May 2003 as the deadline for taking the measures recommended. Since the measures taken by the Federal Republic of Germany were considered to be effective at that date, the excessive deficit procedure was implicitly held in abeyance.

8 An excessive deficit procedure was initiated in relation to the French Republic in April 2003. By Decision 2003/487/EC of 3 June 2003 on the existence of an excessive deficit in France – Application of Article 104(6) of the Treaty establishing the European Community (OJ 2003 L 165, p. 29), the Council decided, on a recommendation from the Commission, that an excessive deficit existed in that Member State. In accordance with Article 104(7) EC and Article 3(4) of Regulation No 1467/97, it recommended the French Government to bring that deficit to an end as rapidly as possible and by 2004 at the latest, by means of various measures. It set 3 October 2003 as the deadline for taking the necessary measures.

The Commission's recommendations pursuant to
Article 104(8) and (9) EC

9 On 8 October 2003 the Commission sent to the Council a recommendation for a decision founded on Article 104(8) EC, in order for the Council to establish that the French Republic had undertaken no effective action in response to the Council's recommendation under Article 104(7) EC.

10 On 21 October 2003 the Commission recommended that the Council decide, under Article 104(9) EC, to give notice to the French Republic to take measures to reduce its deficit. It recommended the Council to give that Member State notice, in particular, to put an end to its excessive deficit situation by 2005 at the latest and to achieve in 2004 an annual reduction in the cyclically-adjusted budget deficit equal to 1% of its gross domestic product ('GDP').

11 As regards the Federal Republic of Germany, the Commission ultimately considered that the measures taken in response to the Council's recommendation under Article 104(7) EC were inappropriate. On 18 November 2003 the Commission therefore sent to the

Council a recommendation for a decision founded on Article 104(8) EC, in order for it to establish that the action taken by the Federal Republic of Germany to correct the excessive deficit situation was proving to be inadequate.

12 On the same day, the Commission recommended that the Council decide, under Article 104(9) EC, to give notice to the Federal Republic of Germany to take measures to reduce its deficit. It recommended the Council to give that Member State notice, in particular, to put an end to its excessive deficit situation by 2005 at the latest and to achieve in 2004 an annual reduction in the cyclically-adjusted balance of 0.8% of GDP.

The Council meeting (economic and financial affairs) of 25 November 2003

13 At its meeting of 25 November 2003, the Council took votes on the Commission recommendations for Council decisions under Article 104(8) EC in respect of the French Republic and the Federal Republic of Germany. In accordance with Article 104(13) EC, all the Member States other than the Member State concerned took part in the two votes. Since the required majority was not achieved, the decisions were not adopted.

14 The Council also took votes on the Commission recommendations for Council decisions under Article 104(9) EC in respect of the same Member States. In accordance with Article 104(13) EC and 122(3) and (5) EC, only the Member States which have adopted the single currency, other than the Member State concerned, took part in those two votes. Since the required majority was not achieved, the decisions were not adopted.

15 On the same day, applying the voting rules which relate to decisions envisaged by Article 104(9) EC, the Council adopted essentially similar conclusions with regard to each of the two Member States concerned.

16 In paragraph 1 of the conclusions, the Council indicates the considerations which it has taken into account in assessing the budgetary situation of the Member State concerned.

17 In paragraph 2 of the conclusions, it notes that the Member State concerned adopted several measures following the recommendation made to it under Article 104(7) EC.

18 In paragraph 3 it 'welcomes the public commitment by [the Member State concerned] to implement all the necessary measures to ensure that the deficit will be below 3% of GDP in 2005 at the latest'.

19 In paragraph 4 the Council makes recommendations for the Member State concerned 'in the light of the Commission Recommendation and the commitments made by [that Member State]'. The recommendations concern, in particular, the annual deficit reduction for 2004 and 2005 and continuing to seek to achieve budgetary consolidation after 2005. The Council also recommends that the Member State concerned 'put an end to the present excessive deficit situation as rapidly as possible and at the latest by 2005'.

20 Paragraphs 5 and 6 are worded as follows:

'5. In the light of the recommendations and the commitments by [the Member State concerned] set out above, the Council decided not to act, at this point in time, on the basis of the Commission Recommendation for a Council decision under Article 104(9).

6. The Council agrees to hold the Excessive Deficit Procedure for [the Member State concerned] in abeyance for the time being. The Council stands ready to take a decision under Article 104(9), on the basis of the Commission Recommendation, should [the Member State concerned] fail to act in accordance with the commitments set out in these conclusions as it would emerge from the assessment based on paragraph 7 below.'

21 In paragraph 7 the Council invites the Member State concerned to submit reports, without setting a specific timetable, and recommends assessment by the Council and the Commission of the progress achieved by that State.

Forms of order sought

22. The Commission claims that the Court should:
   - annul, first, the decisions of the Council not to adopt the formal instruments contained in the Commission's recommendations pursuant to Article 104(8) and (9) EC and, second, the Council's conclusions in so far as they involve holding the excessive deficit procedure in abeyance, recourse to an instrument not envisaged by the Treaty and modification of the recommendations decided on by the Council under Article 104(7) EC;
   - order the Council to pay the costs.

23. The Council contends that the Court should:
   - declare the action inadmissible;
   - in the alternative, dismiss it;
   - order the Commission to pay the costs.

Admissibility of the action

24 The Council pleads that the action is inadmissible in seeking annulment both of the Council's failure to adopt the formal instruments contained in the Commission's recommendations pursuant to Article 104(8) and (9) EC and of the Council's conclusions concerning, respectively, the French Republic and the Federal Republic of Germany.

The claim for annulment of the Council's failure to adopt the formal instruments contained in the Commission's recommendations pursuant to Article 104(8) and (9) EC

Arguments of the parties

25 The Council submits that, in not adopting the Commission's recommendations, it did not take, even implicitly, any actionable decision. It points out that, under the Treaty, the procedure for requiring an institution to act is constituted by the action for failure to act provided for in Article 232 EC. Pursuant to that provision, the Commission may bring an action before the Court for a declaration that the Council has infringed the Treaty by failing to act. However, the conditions for recourse to this legal remedy are not met in the present case: the Council has not first been called upon to act by the Commission, nor was it legally required to adopt the decisions referred to in Article 104(8) and (9) EC. In any event, it cannot be alleged to have failed to act since it took a vote on the Commission's recommendations.

26 The Council contends that the judgment in Case C-76/01 P *Eurocoton and Others* v *Council* [2003] ECR I-0000, in which the Court held that the Council's failure to adopt a proposal submitted to it by the Commission for a regulation imposing a definitive anti-dumping duty produced legal effects for individuals and constituted an act open to challenge, is not relevant here. Anti-dumping proceedings, unlike the excessive deficit procedure, directly affect certain businesses and it must be ensured that the procedural guarantees granted to them by Community legislation are effective. Furthermore, in anti-dumping proceedings the Council may no longer adopt the Commission's proposal after expiry of the period laid down for that purpose. That is not so in the case of Commission recommendations to the Council pursuant to Article 104(8) and (9) EC. Since no mandatory and definitive period has expired, the Council remains entitled to adopt those recommendations and the Commission remains entitled to seek the adoption of its recommendations or to draw up fresh ones.

27 The Commission states in response that, under the system established by Article 104 EC, the vote by which the Council adopts a position on the Commission's recommendation seeking the determination provided for in Article 104(8) or the giving of notice provided for in Article 104(9) constitutes in every case a decision, be it positive or negative, depending on the result of the vote, and therefore an act open to challenge, in accordance with the case-law resulting from *Eurocoton*, cited above.

28 In short, by refusing to determine that the French Republic and the Federal Republic of Germany had taken no effective measures, the Council decided, albeit implicitly, that, contrary to the Commission's view, those two countries had in actual fact taken effective measures.

Findings of the Court

29 As provided in Article 104(13) EC, and without prejudice to Article 122(3) and (5) EC, when the Council takes the decisions referred to in Article 104(7), (8) and (9) EC it acts on a recommendation from the Commission by a majority of two thirds of the votes of its members weighted in accordance with Article 205(2) EC, excluding the votes of the representative of the Member State concerned.

30 Accordingly, the Council decision, referred to in Article 104(8) EC, to make its recommendations public where it establishes that there has been no effective action in response to them can exist only if it is adopted by the majority stated in the preceding paragraph of this judgment. The same is true of the Council decision, referred to in Article 104(9) EC, to give notice to the Member State concerned to take, within a specified time-limit, measures for the deficit reduction which is judged necessary by the Council in order to remedy the excessive deficit situation.

31 Thus, where the Commission recommends to the Council that it adopt decisions under Article 104(8) and (9) EC and the required majority is not achieved within the Council, no decision is taken for the purpose of those provisions.

32 Nor is there any provision of Community law prescribing a period on the expiry of which an implied decision under Article 104(8) or (9) EC is deemed to arise and establishing the content of that decision.

33 While it is true that, as stated in the 16th recital in the preamble to Regulation No 1467/97, the seriousness of an excessive deficit in stage three calls for urgent action from all those involved and that regulation lays down deadlines which must be observed, the fact remains that expiry of those deadlines does not preclude the Council from adopting

the acts recommended by the Commission. As is apparent from the 12th recital in the preamble to Regulation No 1467/97, the deadlines established in that regulation are intended to ensure expeditious and effective implementation of the excessive deficit procedure. It would therefore contradict this objective for expiry of the deadlines to result in the lapse of the Council's power to adopt the acts recommended by the Commission in the course of that procedure. Such lapse would require the procedure to be recommenced where appropriate.

34 In light of the foregoing, failure by the Council to adopt acts provided for in Article 104(8) and (9) EC that are recommended by the Commission cannot be regarded as giving rise to acts open to challenge for the purposes of Article 230 EC.

35 It should be remembered that, if the Council does not adopt formal instruments recommended by the Commission pursuant to Article 104(8) and (9) EC, the latter can have recourse to the legal remedy provided for by Article 232 EC, in compliance with the conditions prescribed therein.

36 Accordingly, the action is inadmissible in so far as it seeks annulment of the Council's failure to adopt the formal instruments contained in the Commission's recommendations pursuant to Article 104(8) and (9) EC.

The claim for annulment of the Council's conclusions concerning, respectively, the French Republic and the Federal Republic of Germany

Arguments of the parties

37 The Council submits that its conclusions are texts of a political nature and not acts entailing legal effects. The conclusions do not in any way prejudice the Commission's rights and powers. Their sole aim and effect is to record the situation reached in the ongoing excessive deficit procedures after the Council had considered the matter and not adopted the Commission's recommendations.

38 The holding in abeyance of the excessive deficit procedures initiated against the Federal Republic of Germany and the French Republic does not result in the slightest from the conclusions themselves. It results automatically from the fact that the Commission's recommendations were not adopted by the Council, without its having to adopt an express and legally binding decision in that regard.

39 The Council points out in this connection that only Article 9(1) of Regulation No 1467/97 provides for holding the excessive deficit procedure in abeyance. This provision merely envisages its being held in abeyance in two particular situations, without indicating in

what other circumstances it is possible or prohibited to do so and without establishing any mechanism for determining or declaring that it is being held in abeyance. Holding an ongoing procedure in abeyance is implicit. It flows from expiry of the period laid down by a measure adopted on the basis of Article 104(7) or (9) EC.

40 In any event, the fact that the procedure was expressly stated by the Council in its political conclusions to be held in abeyance does not in any way alter the fact that the conclusions do not have legal effects. It follows that their annulment would not alter in fact or in law the state of the ongoing excessive deficit procedures.

41 The Commission contends that if the holding in abeyance of those ongoing procedures against the French Republic and the Federal Republic of Germany had been the automatic consequence of the failure to adopt the decisions recommended by the Commission, the Council could have simply recorded that they were held in abeyance, without so deciding in a formal determination accompanied by new recommendations.

42 It is in actual fact possible to hold the excessive deficit procedure in abeyance only in the two situations set out in Article 9(1) of Regulation No 1467/97. Accordingly, inasmuch as the Council refused to determine that the Member States concerned had not taken effective action, thereby deciding that they had complied with the recommendations adopted under Article 104(7) EC, it could have held the ongoing excessive deficit procedures in abeyance only by decisions taken in accordance with the procedural and voting rules applicable under the latter provision. However, the Council's conclusions were adopted in accordance with the procedural and voting rules applicable under Article 104(9) EC.

43 The Council's conclusions are sui generis measures whose main legal effect is to free the Council and the Member States concerned from the binding legal framework formed by Article 104 EC and Regulation No 1467/97, replacing it with new guidelines governing assessment of the conditions for applying Article 104(9) EC and a new framework for monitoring the excessive deficits of the Member States concerned.

Findings of the Court

44 It is settled case-law that an action for annulment must be available in the case of all measures adopted by the institutions, whatever their nature or form, which are intended to have legal effects (see Case 22/70 *Commission* v *Council* (the '*ERTA*' case) [1971] ECR

263, paragraph 42, and Case C-316/91 *Parliament* v *Council* [1994] ECR I-625, paragraph 8).

45 In the present case, it must be established whether the Council's conclusions are intended to have such effects.

46 In paragraph 6 of those conclusions, the Council stated that it agreed to hold the excessive deficit procedure in abeyance for the time being and it declared itself ready to take a decision under Article 104(9) EC if it were to appear that the Member State concerned was not complying with the commitments which it had entered into, set out in the conclusions.

47 First, inasmuch as the decisions to hold the ongoing excessive deficit procedures in abeyance are conditional on compliance with the commitments made by the Member States concerned, they do not, contrary to the Council's submissions, merely confirm that the procedures are de facto held in abeyance, as a result of the failure to adopt the acts recommended by the Commission within the framework of Article 104(8) and (9) EC.

48 Also, the commitments in question are unilateral commitments, made by the two Member States concerned outside the framework of the recommendations previously decided upon under Article 104(7) EC. The Council thus renders any decision to be taken under Article 104 (9) EC conditional on an assessment which will no longer have the content of the recommendations adopted under Article 104(7) EC as its frame of reference, but the unilateral commitments of the Member State concerned.

49 Finally, in acting in that way the Council also in reality modifies the recommendations previously adopted under Article 104(7) EC, particularly inasmuch as in the conclusions it puts back the deadline for bringing the government deficit below the ceiling of 3% of GDP and consequently alters the extent of the consolidation measures sought.

50 It follows from the foregoing that the Council's conclusions are intended to have legal effects, at the very least inasmuch as they hold the ongoing excessive deficit procedures in abeyance and in reality modify the recommendations previously adopted by the Council under Article 104(7) EC.

51 Accordingly, the action is admissible in so far as it is directed against those conclusions.

Substance

52 The Commission seeks the annulment of the Council's conclusions adopted in respect of each of the Member States concerned in so far as

they involve holding the excessive deficit procedure in abeyance, recourse to an instrument not envisaged by the Treaty and modification of the recommendations decided on by the Council under Article 104(7) EC.

Arguments of the parties

53 The Commission submits that the Council, having recommendations for decisions under Article 104(8) and (9) EC before it, adopted 'conclusions', a measure not provided for by the Treaty and, in particular, Article 104 EC. The Council could not adopt instruments other than those provided for by Article 104 EC, namely decisions, which are binding measures. It was all the less able to do so because the conclusions include decisional elements such as the holding of the procedures in abeyance and recommendations to the Member States concerned.

54 In holding the excessive deficit procedure in abeyance, the Council's conclusions infringe the first indent of Article 9(1) of Regulation No 1467/97, under which that procedure is to be held in abeyance if the Member State concerned acts in compliance with recommendations adopted in accordance with Article 104(7) EC. The decisions to hold the procedure in abeyance do not show that this condition was met. Quite to the contrary, it is clear from the conclusions that the Council agreed with the Commission's analysis that led necessarily to the conclusion that this condition was not satisfied. Nor were the decisions to hold the procedure in abeyance adopted in compliance with the voting rules laid down in Article 104(13) EC, since they were adopted by the Member States in the euro area with the exception of the Member State concerned, and not by all the Member States other than the Member State concerned. Since it could only have been possible for the procedure to be legally held in abeyance at the stage of Article 104(7) EC, the voting rules should, by reason of parallelism of procedural requirements, have been those applicable at that stage.

55 The Commission does not contest the economic justification for the decisions to modify the recommendations decided upon by the Council under Article 104(7) EC, in particular so far as concerns the extension of the period within which the excessive deficits should be eliminated. However, it submits that the Council could not, without observing the procedures prescribed by the Treaty, adopt recommendations contrary to those adopted previously.

56 The Council recalls the observations made by it, in connection with its plea of inadmissibility, regarding the political, and not legal, nature of

its conclusions and, in particular, its observation that the ongoing procedures were automatically held in abeyance when it did not adopt the measures recommended by the Commission.

57 In the Council's submission, annulment of its conclusions would not alter in fact or in law the state of the ongoing excessive deficit procedures. That is confirmed by the fact, acknowledged by the Commission, that those procedures have not been brought to a close and that the Commission remains free at any time, in the exercise of its right of initiative, to submit to the Council recommendations pursuant to Article 104(7), (8) or (9) EC, depending on its analysis of the situation at the time.

58 The Council further submits that the recommendations previously adopted by it under Article 104(7) EC had become at least partially obsolete. They had been overtaken by changes in the economic situation. Various factors, in particular the less favourable development of the economic situation compared with the forecasts available when the recommendations were adopted, had made it impossible for the Member States concerned to correct their deficits in the periods laid down.

59 An alternative approach would have been for the Council to adopt fresh recommendations under Article 104(7) EC. However, such a solution was not possible since the Commission decided not to place before the Council fresh recommendations founded on that provision.

60 Accordingly, the Council considered it expedient to adopt the contested conclusions which, while recording the change in the economic situation and the measures taken and commitments made by each of the two Member States concerned, indicated to the latter what, in the Council's view, they had to do in order to remedy their excessive deficit situation.

61. This approach presented a number of advantages:
- making clear that the excessive deficit procedures had not been brought to a close, but were simply held in abeyance following the failure to adopt the decisions recommended by the Commission;
- noting the measures which the French Republic and the Federal Republic of Germany undertook to take and the objectives which they undertook to attain;
- reaffirming the preparedness of the Council to act, in the future, under Article 104(9) EC should the Member States concerned not comply with their commitments;
- making clear the Council's attachment to the principles and rules of the Stability and Growth Pact.

62 The approach adopted meant that, after the decisions recommended by the Commission pursuant to Article 104(8) and (9) EC had not been adopted, silence on the part of the Council did not undermine the credibility of the Stability and Growth Pact, and leave businesses and the foreign exchange markets in a state of uncertainty with disastrous consequences.

63 The Council submits that the Treaty contains no provision that precludes proceeding in such a way.

64 It adds that the recommendations under Article 104(7) EC, adopted on 21 January 2003 in respect of the Federal Republic of Germany and on 3 June 2003 in respect of the French Republic, remain in force.

Findings of the Court

65 In essence, notwithstanding the terms in which its application is couched, the Commission seeks annulment of the Council's conclusions only in so far as they contain a decision to hold the excessive deficit procedure in abeyance and a decision modifying the recommendations previously made to the Member State concerned.

66 Its formal claim that those conclusions be annulled in so far as they also involve recourse to an instrument not envisaged by the Treaty does not constitute, in reality, a self-standing claim, but rather an argument made in support of the claim for annulment noted in the preceding paragraph of this judgment.

67 The latter claim is to be examined after first identifying the broad logic of the excessive deficit procedure.

Broad logic of the excessive deficit procedure

68 According to Article 4(1) and (2) EC, the activities of the Member States and the Community are to include the adoption of an economic policy which is based on the close coordination of Member States' economic policies and, concurrently, the adoption of EMU. In accordance with Article 4(3) EC, these activities entail compliance with the following guiding principles: stable prices, sound public finances and monetary conditions and a sustainable balance of payments.

69 Article 104(1) EC lays down that Member States are to avoid excessive government deficits.

70 The objective of the excessive deficit procedure laid down in Article 104 (2) to (13) EC is to encourage and, if necessary, compel the Member State concerned to reduce a deficit which might be identified.

71 The rules laid down in Article 104 EC are defined more precisely and strengthened by the Stability and Growth Pact, constituted, in particular, by the Resolution of the European Council of 17 June 1997 and Regulation No 1467/97.

72 The Resolution of the European Council of 17 June 1997 draws attention to the crucial importance of securing budgetary discipline in stage three of EMU. In the light of that observation, it solemnly invites the Council to be committed to a rigorous and timely implementation of all elements of the Stability and Growth Pact in its competence and to regard the deadlines for the application of the excessive deficit procedure as upper limits.

73 The eighth recital in the preamble to Regulation No 1467/97 states that budgetary discipline is necessary in stage three of EMU to safeguard price stability. It is observed in the 16th recital that the seriousness of an excessive deficit in stage three should call for urgent action from all those involved.

74 In this context, marked by the importance that the framers of the Treaty attach to observance of budgetary discipline and by the aim of the rules laid down for applying budgetary discipline, those rules are to be given an interpretation which ensures that they are fully effective.

75 It should be noted that, in accordance with Article 104(10) EC, the right of the Commission and the Member States to bring infringement proceedings against a Member State under Articles 226 EC and 227 EC may not be exercised within the framework of Article 104(1) to (9) EC.

76 As the Commission has pointed out, responsibility for making the Member States observe budgetary discipline lies essentially with the Council.

77 The excessive deficit procedure is a procedure in stages, which can result in the imposition of sanctions pursuant to Article 104(11) EC.

78 Article 104 EC specifies the manner in which each stage is carried out and the respective roles and powers of the institutions in question. Regulation No 1467/97, which was adopted unanimously on the basis of the second subparagraph of Article 104(14) EC, lays down a strict framework of deadlines to be met in the course of the excessive deficit procedure, in order, according to the 12th recital in its preamble, to ensure expeditious and effective implementation of the procedure. Article 9 of Regulation No 1467/97 provides that the excessive deficit procedure is to be held in abeyance where the Member State concerned acts in compliance with recommendations made or notice given pursuant to Article 104(7) and (9) EC respectively. Article 10 of the regulation provides for monitoring of the implementation of action taken by the Member State concerned.

79 For each of the stages of the procedure where the matter is placed before the Council there is a corresponding measure which the Commission recommends that the Council adopt. Each stage involves consideration by the Council as to whether the Member State has complied with its obligations under Article 104 EC and, in particular, those resulting from the recommendations and decisions previously adopted by the Council.

80 As the Commission acknowledges, the Council has a discretion. Commission recommendations, and not proposals within the meaning of Article 250 EC, are placed before it, and it may, in particular on the basis of a different assessment of the relevant economic data, of the measures to be taken and of the timetable to be met by the Member State concerned, modify the measure recommended by the Commission, by the majority required for adoption of that measure.

81 Nevertheless, it follows from the wording and the broad logic of the system established by the Treaty that the Council cannot break free from the rules laid down by Article 104 EC and those which it set for itself in Regulation No 1467/97. Thus, it cannot have recourse to an alternative procedure, for example in order to adopt a measure which would not be the very decision envisaged at a given stage or which would be adopted in conditions different from those required by the applicable provisions.

82 It is in the light of this finding that the issue of whether the Council's conclusions must be annulled in so far as they contain a decision to hold the excessive deficit procedure in abeyance and a decision modifying the recommendations previously adopted by the Council under Article 104(7) EC should be examined.

Holding the excessive deficit procedure in abeyance

83 The 17th recital in the preamble to Regulation No 1467/97 states that it is appropriate to hold the excessive deficit procedure in abeyance if the Member State concerned takes appropriate action in response to a recommendation under Article 104(7) EC or a notice issued under Article 104(9) EC in order to provide an incentive to Member States to act accordingly.

84 Article 9(1) of Regulation No 1467/97 provides that the excessive deficit procedure is to be held in abeyance where the Member State acts in compliance with a recommendation or notice of the Council.

85 Neither Article 104 EC nor Regulation No 1467/97 provides for the possibility of deciding to hold the procedure in abeyance in other situations.

86 As the Council maintains, the procedure may de facto be held in abeyance if a Commission recommendation is placed before the Council and the latter does not succeed in adopting a decision because the required majority is not achieved.

87 However, in the present case, the contested conclusions expressly state that the Council 'agrees to hold the Excessive Deficit Procedure for [the Member State concerned] in abeyance ...' and that it 'stands ready to take a decision under Article 104(9), on the basis of the Commission Recommendation, should [that Member State] fail to act in accordance with the commitments set out in these conclusions ...'.

88 By those statements, the Council does not simply record that the excessive deficit procedure is de facto held in abeyance because it has not been possible to adopt a decision recommended by the Commission, an inability which could be remedied at any time. In so far as the Council's conclusions make holding the procedure in abeyance conditional upon compliance by the Member State concerned with its commitments, they restrict the Council's power to give notice under Article 104(9) EC on the basis of the Commission's earlier recommendation, so long as the commitments are considered to be complied with. In so doing, the conclusions provide, in addition, that the Council's assessment for the purposes of a decision to give notice, that is to say for the purposes of pursuing the excessive deficit procedure, will no longer have as its frame of reference the content of the recommendations already made under Article 104(7) EC to the Member State concerned, but unilateral commitments of that Member State.

89 Such a decision to hold the procedure in abeyance infringes Article 104 EC and Article 9 of Regulation No 1467/97.

90 It should be added that, in accepting that the procedure may de facto be held in abeyance simply because the Council does not succeed in adopting a decision recommended by the Commission, the Court does not express a view as to whether, pursuant to Article 104(9) EC, the Council could be required to adopt a decision where the Member State persists in failing to put into practice its recommendations under Article 104(7) EC, a question which the Court is not called upon to answer in the present proceedings.

Modification of the recommendations adopted by the Council under Article 104(7) EC

91 In accordance with Article 104(13) EC, recommendations under Article 104(7) EC may be adopted only on a recommendation from

the Commission. As has been pointed out, the Council has the power to adopt a decision different from that recommended by the Commission.

92 However, where the Council has adopted recommendations under Article 104(7) EC, it cannot subsequently modify them without a fresh recommendation from the Commission since the latter has a right of initiative in the excessive deficit procedure, as the Council acknowledges.

93 In the present case, the Council adopted such recommendations for the Federal Republic of Germany on 21 January 2003 and for the French Republic on 3 June 2003.

94 The Council's conclusions were not preceded by Commission recommendations seeking the adoption, on the basis of Article 104(7) EC, of Council recommendations different from those adopted previously.

95 Furthermore, the recommendations contained in the Council's conclusions were adopted not in accordance with the voting rules prescribed for Council recommendations under Article 104(7) EC but in accordance with those prescribed for a decision under Article 104(9) EC, that is to say with only Member States in the euro area taking part in the vote.

96 The decision to adopt those Council recommendations, being contrary to Article 104(7) and (13) EC, is therefore unlawful.

97 The Council's conclusions adopted in respect of the French Republic and the Federal Republic of Germany respectively must consequently be annulled in so far as they contain a decision to hold the excessive deficit procedure in abeyance and a decision modifying the recommendations previously adopted by the Council under Article 104(7) EC.

Costs

98 In accordance with Article 69(3) of the Rules of Procedure, where each party succeeds on some and fails on other heads, or where the circumstances are exceptional, the Court may order that the costs be shared or that the parties bear their own costs. Since each of the parties has failed in part, it is appropriate to order each of them to bear their own costs.

On those grounds,

The Court

hereby:

1. **Declares the action of the Commission of the European Communities inadmissible in so far as it seeks annulment of**

the failure of the Council of the European Union to adopt the formal instruments contained in the Commission's recommendations pursuant to Article 104(8) and (9) EC;

2. **Annuls the Council's conclusions of 25 November 2003 adopted in respect of the French Republic and the Federal Republic of Germany respectively, in so far as they contain a decision to hold the excessive deficit procedure in abeyance and a decision modifying the recommendations previously adopted by the Council under Article 104(7) EC;**

3. **Orders the parties to bear their own costs**.

Skouris	Jann	Timmermans
Rosas	Gulmann	Puissochet
Cunha Rodrigues	Schintgen	Macken
Colneric		von Bahr
Silva de Lapuerta		Lenaerts

Delivered in open court in Luxembourg on 13 July 2004.

R. Grass	V. Skouris
Registrar	President

Bibliography

AFP (2008) 'Ruling out US-style bailout plan, EU looks to tougher regulation', retrieved on 3 February at http://afp.google.com/article/ALeqM5g9jbnEyG5T_3fj1eHwmqosgJ8mAQ.

Alesina, Alberto and Allan Drazen (1991) 'Why are stabilizations delayed', *American Economic Review*, **81**, 1170–88.

Allensbacher Archiv (1995) 'IfD-Umfragen 6013', Institut für Demoskopie, Allensbach.

Alt, James E. and Robert C. Lowry (1994) 'Divided government, fiscal institutions, and budget deficits – evidence from the States', *American Political Science Review*, **88**, 811–28.

Artis, Michael J. and Marco Buti (2000) '"Close to balance or in surplus" – a policy maker's guide to the implementation of the Stability and Growth Pact', *Journal of Common Market Studies*, **38**(4): 563–91.

— (2001) 'Setting medium-term fiscal targets in EMU', in Anne Brunila, Marco Buti and Daniele Franco (eds.) *The Stability and Growth Pact: The Architecture of Fiscal Policy in EMU*, New York: Palgrave, pp. 185–203.

Artis, Michael J. and Bernhard Winkler (1999) 'The Stability Pact: Trading off flexibility for credibility?' Andrew Hughes Hallett, Michael M. Hutchison and Svend E. Hougaard Jensen (eds.) *Fiscal Aspects of European Monetary Integration*, New York: Cambridge University Press, pp. 157–88.

Balassone, Fabrizio and Daniele Franco (2001) 'The SGP and the 'Golden Rule'', in Anne Brunila, Marco Buti, and Daniele Franco (eds.) *The Stability and Growth Pact: The Architecture of Fiscal Policy in EMU*, New York: Palgrave, pp. 371–93.

Balassone, Fabrizio and Raffaela Giordano (2001) 'Budget deficits and coalition governments', *Public Choice*, **106**, 327–49.

Beetsma, Roel M. W. J. (1999) 'The Stability and Growth Pact in a model with politically induced deficit biases', in Andrew Hughes Hallett, Michael M. Hutchison, and Svend E. Hougaard Jensen (eds.) *Fiscal Aspects of European Monetary Integration*, New York: Cambridge University Press, pp. 189–215.

— (2001) 'Does EMU need a stability pact?', in Anne Brunila, Marco Buti and Daniele Franco (eds.) *The Stability and Growth Pact: The Architecture of Fiscal Policy in EMU*, New York: Palgrave, pp. 23–52.

Beetsma, Roel and Heikki Oksanen (2007) 'Pension systems, ageing and the Stability and Growth Pact', *European Economy. Economic Papers*. 289. October 2007. European Commission. Brussels. 66 p. KC-AI-07-289-EN-N ISBN: 978–92–79–04642–1 ISSN: 1016–8060.

(2008) 'Pensions under ageing populations and the EU Stability and Growth Pact', *CESifo Economic Studies* **54**(4): 563–92.

Begg, Iain (ed.) (2002) *Europe: Government and Money; Running EMU: The Challenges of Policy Coordination*, London: The Federal Trust.

Begg, Iain and Waltraud Schelke (2004) 'Can fiscal policy co-ordination be made to work?', *Journal of Common Market Studies* **42**(5): 1047–55.

Blanchard, Olivier J. and Francesco Giavazzi (2004) 'Improving the SGP through a proper accounting of public investment', CPER Discussion Paper, 4220.

Börzel, Tanja (2005) 'Mind the gap: European integration between level and scope', *Journal of European Public Policy*, **12**(2): 217–36.

Bouwen, Pieter (2002) 'Corporate lobbying in the European Union: the logic of access', *Journal of European Public Policy*, **9**(3): 356–90.

Brunila, Anne, Marco Buti and Daniele Franco (2001) 'Introduction', in Anne Brunila, Marco Buti and Daniele Franco (eds.) *The Stability and Growth Pact: The Architecture of Fiscal Policy in EMU*, New York: Palgrave, pp. 1–22.

Buiter, Willem and Clemens Grafe (2002) 'Patching up the Pact: some suggestions for enhancing fiscal sustainability and macroeconomic stability in an enlarged European Union', CEPR Discussion Paper No. 3496.

Bulmer, Simon (1983) 'Domestic politics and European Community policy-making', *Journal of Common Market Studies*, **21**(4): 349–63.

Bundesministerium der Finanzen (1995) 'Stabilitätspakt für Europa – Finanzpolitik in der dritten Stufe der WWU', *Auszüge aus Presseartikeln 75*, 7 November 1995.

Burley, Anne-Marie and Walter Mattli (1993) 'Europe before the court: a political theory of legal integration', *International Organization*, **47**(1): 41–76.

Busch, Andreas (1994) 'The crisis in the EMS', *Government and Opposition*, **29**, 80–97.

Buti, Marco and Lucio R. Pench (2004) 'Why do large countries flout the Stability Pact? And what can be done about it?', *Journal of Common Market Studies* **42**(5): 1025–32.

Buti, Marco, Sylvester Eijffinger and Daniele Franco (2003) 'Revisiting the Stability and Growth Pact: grand design or internal adjustment', CEPR Working Paper No. 3692.

Caporaso, James (1996) 'The European Union and forms of State: Westphalian, regulatory or post-modern', *Journal of Common Market Studies*, **34**(1): 29–52.

CEC (1996a) 'Ensuring Budgetary Discipline in Stage Three of EMU', (II/409/ 96-EN of 19 July 1996).

(1996b) 'A Stability Pact to Ensure Budgetary Discipline in EMU', (II/163/96-EN of 18 March 1996).

(1996c) 'Towards a Stability Pact', (II/11/96-EN of 10 January 1996).

Centraal Plan Bureau (2003) 'Europe's future, Dutch mortgage market, institutions breaking the law', *CPB Report Quarterly Review of CPB Netherlands' Bureau for Economic Policy Analysis* SDU Publishers, The Hague, NL, p. 68.

Chang, Michele (2006) 'Reforming the Stability and Growth Pact: size and influence in EMU policymaking', *Journal of European Integration* **28**(1): 107–20.

Checkel, Jeffrey T. (1998) 'The constructivist turn in international relations theory', *World Politics* **50**(2): 324–48.

(2001) 'Why comply? Social learning and European identity change', *International Organization* **55**(3): 553–88.

Christiansen, Thomas, Knud-Erik Joergensen and Antje Wiener (1999) 'The social construction of Europe', *Journal of European Public Policy*, **6**(4): 528–44.

Cichowski, Rachel A. (2007) *The European Court and Civil Society*, Cambridge University Press.

Clift, Ben (2006) 'The new political economy of dirigisme: French macroeconomic policy, unrepentant sinning and the Stability and Growth Pact', *The British Journal of Politics and International Relations*, **8**(3): 388–409.

Collignon, Stefan (2004) 'Is Europe going far enough? Reflections on the EU's economic governance', *Journal of European Public Policy*, **11**(5): 909–25.

COM(96)496 (1996) 'Stability Pact for ensuring budgetary discipline in stage three of EMU', *Agence Europe*, Vol. Europe Documents 2010.

Commission of the European Communities (1990) 'One market, one money', *European Economy*, **44**.

(1991) 'The economics of EMU. Background studies for European Economy, 44 "One market, One money"', *European Economy*, Special Edition, No.1.

(1995) 'Europinion No. 5'.

(2007) 'Public finances in EMU – 2007', *European Economy*, **3**.

(2008a) 'Communication from the Commission to the Council and the European Parliament – Public finances in EMU – 2008 – The role of quality of public finances in the EU governance framework {SEC(2008) 2092}'.

(2008b) 'Communication of 29 October', COM(2008) 706.

(2008c) 'Communication from the Commission: A European Economic Recovery Plan for Growths and Jobs', Brussels, 26 November.

(2009) 'Interim Forecast January 2009'.

Committee for the Study of Economic and Monetary Union (1989) 'Report on Economic and Monetary Union in the European Community', Office for Official Publications of the EC, Luxembourg.

Corbey, Dorette (1993) *Stilstand is Vooruitgang: De Dialectiek van het Europese Integratieprocess*, Assen & Maastricht: Van Gorcum.

(1995) 'Dialectical functionalism: stagnation as a booster of European integration', *International Organization*, **49**(2): 253–84.

Costello, Declan (2001) 'The SGP: how did we get there?', in Anne Brunila, Marco Buti and Daniele Franco (eds.) *The Stability and Growth Pact: The Architecture of Fiscal Policy in EMU*, New York: Palgrave, pp. 106–36.

Council of the EU (2005) 'Meetings of the Eurogroup and the "Economic and Financial Affairs" Council: No agreement on the reform of the Stability and Growth Pact', press release 8 March. Consulted at www.eu2005.lu/en/actualites/communiques/2005/03/08ecofin/index.html.

Council Report to the European Council (2007) 'Improving the implementation of the Stability and Growth Pact', 7619/1/05 REV1 Annex II pp. 1–18.

Crowley, Patrick M. (2002) 'The Stability and Growth Pact: review, alternatives and legal aspects', *Current Politics and Economics of Europe*, **11**(3): 225–44.

de Búrca, Gráinne (2005) 'Rethinking law in neofunctionalist theory', *Journal of European Public Policy*, **12**(2): 310–26.

de Grauwe, Paul (2007) *Economics of Monetary Union*, Oxford University Press, 7th edition.

Deutsch, Karl W., L. J. Edinger, R. C. Macridis and R. L. Merritt (1967) *France, Germany and the Western Alliance. A Study of Elite Attitudes on European Integration and World Politics*, New York: Charles Scribner's Sons.

Deutsch, Karl, S. A. Burrell, R. A. Kann, M. Lee, M. Lichterman, R. E. Lindgren, F. L. Loewenheim and R. W. Van Wagenen (eds.) (1957) *Political Community and the North Atlantic State: International Organization in the Light of Historical Experience*, Princeton University Press.

Donnelly, Shawn (2005) 'Explaining EMU reform', *Journal of Common Market Studies*, **43**(5): 947–68.

Doukas, Dimitrios (2005) 'The frailty of the Stability and Growth Pact and the European Court of Justice: much ado about nothing?', *Legal Issues of Economic Integration*, **32**(3): 293–312.

(2006) 'Fiscal discipline versus political discretion in the EMU: can the European Court of Justice close the Pandora's Box?', Paper presented at the 6th Biennial Conference of the European Community Studies Association-Canada, Victoria BC, 19–20 May.

Drake, Helen (1995) 'Political leadership and European integration: the case of Jacques Delors', *West European Politics*, **18**(1): 140–60.

(2000) *Jacques Delors: Perspectives on a European Leader*, London: Routledge.

Dudek, Caroline M. and Pieter Omtzigt (2001) 'The role of Brussels in national pension reform', *EUI Working Papers – Robert Schuman Centre*, RSC 2001/47.

Dutzler, Barbara and Angelika Hable (2005) 'The European Court of Justice and the Stability and Growth Pact – just the beginning?', *European Integration online Papers (EIoP)*, Vol 9, No 5 available at http://eiop.or.at/eiop/texte/2005–005a.htm.

Dyson, Kenneth (1994) *Elusive Union: The Process of Economic and Monetary Union in Europe*, London; New York: Longman.

(2000) *The Politics of the Euro-zone: Stability or Breakdown?*, Oxford; New York: Oxford University Press.

(2002) 'Germany and the Euro: redefining EMU, handling paradox, and managing uncertainty and contingency', in K. Dyson (ed.) *European States and the Euro: Europeanization, Variation, and Convergence*, Oxford University Press, pp. 173–211.

Dyson, Kenneth and Kevin Featherstone (1996a) 'EMU and economic governance in Germany', *German Politics*, **5**(3): 325–56.

(1996b) 'Italy and EMU as Vincolo Esterno', *Journal of South European Society and Politics*, **2**(3): 272–99.

(1999) *The Road to Maastricht: Negotiating Economic and Monetary Union*, Oxford; New York: Oxford University Press.

Dyson, K., K. Featherstone and G. Michalpoulos (1995) 'Strapped to the mast: EC central bankers between global financial markets and regional integration', *Journal of European Public Policy*, **2**(3): 465–87.

ECB (2000) *Monthly Bulletin*, March.

(2003) 'Statement of the Governing Council on the ECOFIN Council conclusions regarding the correction of excessive deficits in France and Germany', press release 25 November.

(2005a) 'Statement of the Governing Council on the ECOFIN Council's report on improving the implementation of the Stability and Growth Pact', press release, 21 March.

(2005b) 'The reform of the Stability and Growth Pact: an assessment', speech by José Manuel González-Páramo, Member of the Executive Board of the ECB conference on "New Perspectives on Fiscal Sustainability" Frankfurt, 13 October.

Eichengreen, Barry J. (1996) 'Saving Europe's automatic stabilisers', *National Institute Economic Review*, **159**(1): 92–8.

Eichengreen, Barry J. and Charles Wyplosz (1998) 'The Stability Pact: more than a minor nuisance?', *Economic Policy*, **26**, 65–114.

Enderlein, Henrik (2001) 'Wirtschaftspolitik in der Währungsunion: Die Auswirkungen der Europäischen Wirtschafts- und Währungsunion auf die finanz- und lohnpolitischen Institutionen in den Mitgliedsländern', Bremen, Cologne.

(2004) 'Break it, don't fix it!', *Journal of Common Market Studies*, **42**(5): 1039–46.

EUObserver (2008a) 'US bank crisis smashes hole in European markets', 16 September.

(2008b) 'Europe throws cash at nervous markets', 17 September.

(2008c) 'Germany and UK want global financial regulator', 22 September.

(2008d) 'Capitalism must be regulated, says Sarkozy', 24 September.

(2008e) '"Laissez-faire"capitalism is finished, says France', 26 September.

(2008f) 'Banking crisis claims Belgo-Dutch giant', 29 September.

(2008g) 'Europe scrambles to save banking system', 30 September.

Euractiv (2008a) 'France urged to respect stability pact rule', 10 February.

(2008b) 'US-style "financial socialism" not an option for Europe', 19 September.

(2008c) 'EU leaders remain split on bail-out', 6 October.

European Commission (2009) Interim forecast, European Economy, January (press conference of 19 January), p. 47.

European Council (1995) 'Presidency conclusions Madrid European Council of 15 and 16 December 1995', www.consilium.europa.eu/ueDocs/cms_Data/docs/pressData/en/ec/00400-C.EN5.htm.

Falkner, Gerda, O. Treib, M. Hartlapp and S. Leiber (2005) *Complying with Europe: EU Harmonisation and Soft Law in the Member States*, Cambridge University Press.

Fatas, Antonio and Ilian Mihov (2003) 'On constraining fiscal policy discretion in EMU', *Oxford Review of Economic Policy*, **19**, 112–31.

Fatas, Antonio, J. von Hagen, A. Hughes Hallett, A. Sibert and R. R. Strauch (2003) *Stability and Growth in Europe: Towards a Better Pact*, London: Center for Economic Policy Research.

Finnemore, Martha (1996) *National Interests in International Society*, Ithaca, NY: Cornell University Press.

Fischer, Jonas and Gabriele Giudice (2001) 'The stability and convergence programmes', in Anne Brunila, Marco Buti and Daniele Franco (eds.) *The Stability and Growth Pact: The Architecture of Fiscal Policy in EMU*, New York: Palgrave, pp. 158–84.

Fischer, Jonas, L. Jonung and M. Larch (2006) '101 proposals to reform the Stability and Growth Pact', European Economy, Economic Papers, No. 267 (available on http://ec.europa.eu/economy_finance/index_en.htm), December.

Garrett, Geoffrey (1994) 'The politics of Maastricht', in J. A Frieden (ed.) *The Political Economy of European Monetary Unification*, Boulder, Colorado: Westview Press, pp. 47–66.

Genberg, Hans (1990) 'In the shadow of the Mark: exchange rate and monetary policy in Austria and Switzerland', in Paul de Grauwe (ed.) *Choosing an Exchange Rate Regime: The Challenge for Smaller Industrial Countries*, International Monetary Fund, Washington DC.

Giavazzi, Francesco and Alberto Giovannini (eds.) (1989) *Limiting Exchange Rate Flexibility: The European Monetary System*, Cambridge MA: MIT Press.

Gill, Stephen (2001) 'Constitutionalising capital: EMU and disciplinary neo-liberalism', in A. D. Morton (ed.) *Social Forces in the Making of the New Europe: The Restructuring of European Social Relations in the Global Political Economy*, Houndmills: Palgrave, pp. 47–69.

Goldstein, Judith and Keohane, Robert O. (eds.) (1993) *Ideas and Foreign Policy: Beliefs, Institutions, and Political Change*, Ithaca: Cornell University Press.

Grieco, Joseph M. (1995) 'The Maastricht Treaty, Economic and Monetary Union and the neorealist research programme', *Review of International Studies*, **21**, 21–40.

Gros, Daniel and A. Hobza (2001) 'Fiscal policy spillovers in the euro area: where are they?', *CEPS Working Documents*, 176.

Gros, Daniel and Niels Thygesen (1998) *European Monetary Integration*, Harlow: Longman.

Haas, Ernst B. (1958) *The Uniting of Europe: Political, Social, and Economical Forces, 1950–1957*, London: Stevens.

(1964) *Beyond the Nation-State. Functionalism and International Organization*, Stanford University Press.

(1968) *The Uniting of Europe: Political, Social, and Economic Forces, 1950–1957*, 2nd edition, Stanford University Press.

(1975) 'The obsolescence of regional integration theory', *Research Studies*, Vol. 25, Institute of International Studies, Berkeley.

(1976) 'Turbulent fields and the theory of regional integration', *International Organization*, **30**(2): 173–212.

(2001) 'Does constructivism subsume neo-functionalism?', in A. Wienerx (ed.) *The Social Construction of Europe*, London: Sage Publications, pp. 22–31.

(2004) 'Introduction: institutionalism or constructivism?', in *The Uniting of Europe: Political, Social, and Economic Forces, 1950–1957*, 3rd edition, University of Notre Dame Press, pp. xiii–lvi.

Haas, Peter M. (1992) 'Introduction: epistemic communities and international policy coordination', *International Organization*, **46**(1): 1–35.

Hahn, Hugo J. (1998) 'The Stability Pact for European Monetary Union: compliance with deficit limits as a constant legal duty', *Common Market Law Review*, **35**, 77–100.

Hall, Peter A. (1992) 'The movement from Keynesianism to monetarism', in F. Longstreth (ed.) *Structuring Politics: Historical Institutionalism in Comparative Analysis*, Cambridge University Press, pp. 90–113.

(ed.) (1989) *The Political Power of Economic Ideas: Keynesianism across Nations*, Princeton University Press.

Hall, Peter A. and Rosemary C. R. Taylor (1996) 'Political science and the three new institutionalisms', *Political Studies*, **44**(5): 936–57.

Hallerberg, Mark (2004) *Domestic Budgets in a United Europe*, Ithaca: Cornell University Press.

Hallstein, Walter (1979) *Die Europäische Gemeinschaft*, Econ-Verlag, Düsseldorf; Wien.

Hanny, Birgit and Wolfgang Wessels (1998) 'The monetary committee: significant though not typical case', in M. P. C. M. v. Schendelen (ed.) *EU Committees as Influential Policymakers*, Aldershot: Ashgate, pp. 109–26.

Hauptmeier, Sebastian, M. Heipertz and L. Schuknecht (2007) 'Expenditure reform in industrialised countries – a case study approach', *Fiscal Studies*, **23**(3): 293–342.

Hellwig, Martin (2008) 'Systemic risk in the financial sector: an analysis of the sub-prime mortgage crisis', *Reprints of the Max Planck Institute for Research on Collective Goods*, **43**.

Heipertz, Martin (2001) 'How strong was the Bundesbank? A case study in the policy-making of German and European Monetary Union', *CEPS Working Documents*, **172**.

(2003) 'The Stability and Growth Pact – not the best but better than nothing. Reviewing the debate on fiscal policy in Europe's Monetary Union', *MPIfG Working Paper*, 03/10.

Heipertz, Martin and Amy Verdun (2004) 'The dog that would never bite? What we can learn from the origins of the Stability and Growth Pact, *Journal of European Public Policy*, **11**(5): 765–80.

(2005) 'The Stability and Growth Pact – theorizing a case in European integration', *Journal of Common Market Studies*, **43**(5): 985–1008.

Henning, R. (1994) 'Management of economic policy in the European Community', in G. J. Harrison (ed.) *Europe and the United States: Competition and Cooperation in the 1990s*, Armonk: Sharpe, pp. 15–29.

Hix, Simon (1994) 'Approaches to the study of the European Community: the challenge to comparative politics', *West European Politics*, **17**, 1–30.

Hodson, Dermot (2004) 'Macroeconomic co-ordination in the euro area: the scope and limits of the open method', *Journal of European Public Policy*, **11**(2): 231–248.

(2009) 'EMU and political union: what, if anything, have we learned from the euro's first decade?', *Journal of European Public Policy*, **16**(4): 508–26.

Hodson, Dermot and Imelda Maher (2001) 'The open method as a new mode of governance: the case of soft economic policy co-ordination', *Journal of Common Market Studies*, **39**(4): 719–46.

(2004), 'Soft law and sanctions: economic policy coordination and reform of the Stability and Growth Pact', *Journal of European Public Policy*, **11**(5): 798–813.

Hoekstra, Ruth, C. Horstmann, J. Knabl, D. Kruse, S. Wiedemann (2007) 'Germanizing Europe? The evolution of the European Stability and Growth Pact', *Working Papers on Economic Governance*, Hamburg University, No. 24

Hoffmann, Stanley (1966) 'Obstinate or obsolete: the fate of the nation-state and the case of Western Europe?', *Daedalus*, **95**, 862–916.

Hooghe, Liesbet (2002) *The European Commission and the Integration of Europe: Images of Governance*, Cambridge University Press.

Hooghe, Liesbet and Gary Marks (2001) *Multi-level Governance and European Integration*, Lanham: Rowman and Littlefield.

Hosli, Madeleine O. (2000) 'The creation of the European economic and monetary union (EMU): intergovernmental negotiations and two-level games', *Journal of European Public Policy*, 7(5): 744–66.

Howarth, David J. (2001) *The French Road to European Monetary Union*, Houndmills: Palgrave.

(2005) 'Making and breaking the rules: French policy on EU 'gouverment économique' and the Stability and Growth Pact' *European Integration Online Papers (EIoP)*, Vol. **9**, No. 15, http://eiop.or.at/eiop/texte/2005–015a.htm.

Huelshoff, Michael G. (1994) 'Domestic politics and dynamic issue linkages – a reformulation of integration theory', *International Studies Quarterly*, **38**(2): 255–79.

Hughes Hallett, Andrew and T. Warmedinger (1999) 'On the asymmetric effect of a common monetary policy', in C. Waller (ed.) *Common Money Uncommon Regions*, Bonn: Center for European Integration Studies.

Issing, Otmar (2002) 'On macroeconomic policy co-ordination in EMU', *Journal of Common Market Studies*, **40**(2): 345–58.

Italianer, Alexander (1993) 'Mastering Maastricht: EMU issues and how they were settled', in Klaus Gretschmann (ed.) *Economic and Monetary Union: Implications for National Policy-Makers*, Maastricht: European Institute for Public Administration, pp. 51–115.

Jachtenfuchs, Markus (2001) 'The governance approach to European integration', *Journal of Common Market Studies*, **39**(2): 245–64.

Jacobsen, John Kurt (1995) 'Review: much ado about ideas: the cognitive factor in economic policy', *World Politics*, **47**(2): 283–310.

Johnson, Peter A. (1998) *The Government of Money: Monetarism in Germany and the United States*, Ithaca: Cornell University Press.

Kaelberer, Matthias (2003) 'Knowledge, power and monetary bargaining: central bankers and the creation of monetary union in Europe', *Journal of European Public Policy*, **10**(3): 365–79.

Kassim, Hussein and Anand Menon (2003) 'The principal-agent approach and the study of the European Union: promise unfulfilled?', *Journal of European Public Policy*, **10**(1): 121–39.

Kenen, Peter B. (1969) 'The theory of Optimum Currency Areas: an eclectic view', in R. A. Mundell and A. K. Swoboda (eds.) *Monetary Problems of the International Economy*, University of Chicago Press, pp. 41–60.

(1995) *Economic and Monetary Union in Europe: Moving Beyond Maastricht*, Cambridge; New York: Cambridge University Press.

Kenen, Peter B. and Ellen E. Meade (2007) *Regional Monetary Integration*, Cambridge University Press.

Kennedy, Ellen (1991) *The Bundesbank: Germany's Central Bank in the International Monetary System*, London: Pinter.

Kohler-Koch, Beate and Rainer Eising (eds.) (1999) *The Transformation of Governance in the European Union*, London: Routledge.

Kotlikoff, Laurence J. and Bernd Raffelhüschen (1999) 'Generational accounting around the globe', *American Economic Review (Papers & Proceedings)*, **89**, 161–66.

Laffan, Brigid (1997) 'From policy entrepreneur to policy manager: the challenge facing the European Commission', *Journal of European Public Policy*, **4**(3): 422–38.

Leblond, Patrick (2006) 'The political Stability and Growth Pact is dead: long live the economic Stability and Growth Pact', *Journal of Common Market Studies*, **44**(5): 969–90.

Leeper, Eric M. (1991) 'Equilibria under active and passive monetary and fiscal policies', *Journal of Monetary Economics*, **27**, 129–47.

Lehment, Harmen and Joachim Scheide (1995) 'Der Fahrplan für die Europäische Währungsunion: Noch erheblicher Handlungs- und Klärungsbedarf', *Kiel Discussion Papers*, 259.

Lequesne, Christian and Philippe Rivaud (2003) 'The committees of independent experts: expertise in the service of democracy?', *Journal of European Public Policy*, **10**(5): 695–709.

Lindberg, Leon N. and Stuart A. Scheingold (1970) *Europe's Would-be Polity. Patterns of Change in the European Community*, Englewood Cliffs, New Jersey: Prentice Hall.

(eds.) (1971) *Regional Integration: Theory and Research*, Cambridge MA: Harvard University Press.

Lohmann, Susanne (1993) 'Electoral cycles and international policy-cooperation', *European Economic Review*, **37**, 1373–91.

Ludlow, Peter (1982) *The Making of the European Monetary System: A Case Study of Politics in the European Community*, London: Butterworth.

Luhmann, Niklas (1990) *Konstruktivistische Perspektiven, Soziologische Aufklärung*. Bd. 5. Köln: Westdeutscher Verlag.

Maes, Ivo and Amy Verdun (2005) 'Small states and the creation of EMU: Belgium and the Netherlands, pace-setters and gate-keepers', *Journal of Common Market Studies*, **43**(2): 327–48.

Magnusson, Lars (2002) 'The political transaction costs of the convergence criteria', in Lars Magnusson and Bo Strath (eds.) *From the Werner Plan to the EMU*, Brussels: Peter Lang, pp. 163–78.

March, James G. (1986) 'Bounded rationality, ambiguity, and the engineering of choice', in Jon Elster (ed.) *Rational Choice*, Oxford: Blackwell, pp. 142–70.

Marcussen, Martin (2000) *Ideas and Elites: The Social Construction of Economic and Monetary Union*, Vilborg: Aalborg University Press.

Martin, Lisa L. (1994) 'International and domestic institutions in the EMU process', in Jeffry A. Frieden (ed.) *The Political Economy of European Monetary Unification*, Boulder, Colorado: Westview Press, pp. 87–106.

(1995) 'The influence of national parliaments on European integration', in Jurgen von Hagen (ed.) *Politics and Institutions in an Integrated Europe*, Berlin: Springer, pp. 65–92.

Mayes David and Matti Virén (2004) 'Pressures on the Stability and Growth Pact from asymmetry in policy', *Journal of European Public Policy*, **11**(5): 781–97.

Mazey, Sonia and Jeremy Richardson (eds.) (1993) *Lobbying in the European Community*, Oxford University Press.

McKinnon, Ronald (1963) 'Optimum Currency Areas', *American Economic Review*, **53**, 717–25.

McNamara, Kathleen R. (1994) 'Economic and Monetary Union: do domestic politics really matter?', Paper presented at the American Political Science Association Annual Meeting.

(1998) *The Currency of Ideas: Monetary Politics in the European Union*, Ithaca, NY: Cornell University Press.

(1999) 'Consensus and constraint: ideas and capital mobility in European monetary integration', *Journal of Common Market Studies*, **37**(3): 455–76.

Milesi, Gabriel (1998) *Le Roman de l'euro*, Paris: Hachette littératures.

Moravcsik, Andrew (1991) 'Negotiating the Single European Act: national interests and conventional statecraft in the European Community', *International Organization*, **45**(1): 19–56.

(1993) 'Introduction: integrating international and domestic theories of international bargaining', in Robert D. Putnam (ed.) *Double-edged Diplomacy: International Bargaining and Domestic Politics*, Berkeley: University of California Press, pp. 3–42.

(1998) *The Choice for Europe: Social Purpose and State Power from Messina to Maastricht*, Ithaca, NY: Cornell University Press.

Morris, Richard, H. Ongena and L. Schuknecht (2006) 'The reform and implementation of the Stability and Growth Pact', *European Central Bank Occasional Paper Series*, No. 47, June.

Mundell, Robert A. (1961) 'A theory of optimum currency areas', *American Economic Review*, **51**, 657–75.

Mutimer, David (1989) '1992 and the political integration of Europe: neofunctionalism reconsidered', *Journal of European Integration*, **13**(1): 75–101.

New Europe (2008) 'EU sets out ambitious plans to tackle financial crisis', Issue 806, 3 November 2008, www.neurope.eu/articles/90387.php.

Niemann, Arne and Philippe C. Schmitter (2009) 'Neofunctionalism', in Antje Wiener and Thomas Diez (eds.) *European Integration Theory*, Oxford University Press.

OECD (1996) Quarterly Labour Market Statistics.

OJ 368 (1996) 'Proposal for a Council Regulation (EC) on speeding up and clarifying the implementation of the excessive deficit procedure', *Official Journal*, Vol. COM/96/0496 Final – CNS 96/0248, p. 12.

OJ 369 (1996) 'Proposal for a Council Regulation (EC) on the strengthening of the surveillance and coordination of budgetary policies', *Official Journal*, Vol. COM/96/0496 Final – Syn 96/0247, p. 9.

Padoan, Pier Carlo (1999) 'Is European monetary union endogenous?', *The International Spectator*, **34**(3): 29–44.

Parsons, Craig (2002) 'Showing ideas as causes: the origins of the European Union', *International Organization*, **56**(1): 47–84.

Peterson, John (2003) 'Policy networks', in Antje Wiener and Thomas Diez (eds.) *European Integration Theory*, Oxford; New York: Oxford University Press, pp. 117–33.

Pierson, Paul (1996) 'The path to European integration: a historical institutionalist analysis', *Comparative Political Studies*, **29**(2): 123–63.

Pisani-Ferry, Jean (2006) 'Only one bed for two dreams: a critical retrospective on the debate over the economic governance of the euro area', *Journal of Common Market Studies*, **44**(4): 823–44.

Presidency of the European Union (2008a) 'Summit of European G8 members – statement', Palais de l'Elysée, Saturday 4 October.

   (2008b) 'Presidency conclusions – Brussels, 15 and 16 October 2008', 14368/08.

Pollack, Mark A. (1997) 'Delegation, agency, and agenda setting in the European Community', *International Organization*, **51**(1): 99–134.

   (2001) 'International relations theory and European integration', *Journal of Common Market Studies*, **39**(2): 221–44.

Puetter, Uwe (2004) 'Governing informally: the role of the Eurogroup in EMU and the Stability and Growth Pact', *Journal of European Public Policy*, **11**(5): 854–70.

   (2006) *The Eurogroup: How a Secretive Circle of Finance Ministers Shape European Economic Governance*, Manchester University Press.

Putnam, Robert (1988) 'Diplomacy and domestic politics: the logic of two-level games', *International Organization*, **42**(3): 427–60.

Radaelli, Claudio M. (1995) 'The role of knowledge in the policy process', *Journal of European Public Policy*, **2**(2): 159–84.

   (1999) *Technocracy in the European Union*, London; New York: Longman.

   (2002) 'The Italian state and the euro: institutions, discourse, and policy regimes', in Kenneth Dyson (ed.) *European States and the Euro: Europeanization, Variation and Convergence*, Oxford University Press, pp. 212–37.

Richardson, Jeremy J. (2001) 'Policy-making in the EU: interests, ideas and garbage cans of primeval soup', in Jeremy Richardson (ed.) *European Union: Power and Policy-making*, London: Routledge, pp. 3–26.

Risse, Thomas (2000) '"Let's Argue!": Communicative action in world politics', *International Organization*, **54**(1): 1–40.

   (2004) 'Social constructivism', in Antje Wiener and Thomas Diez (eds.) *European Integration Theory*, Oxford University Press, pp. 159–76.

   (2005) 'Neofunctionalism, European identity, and the puzzles of European integration', *Journal of European Public Policy*, **12**(2): 291–309.

Risse-Kappen, Thomas (1996) 'Exploring the nature of the beast: international relations theory and comparative policy analysis meet the European Union', *Journal of Common Market Studies*, **34**(1): 53–80.

Rode, Reinhard (1991) *Germany, World Economic Power or Overburdened Eurohegemon?*, Peace Research Institute Frankfurt, Frankfurt am Main.

Rosamond, Ben (2005) 'The uniting of Europe, and the foundation of EU Studies: revisiting the neofunctionalism of Ernst B. Haas', *Journal of European Public Policy*, **12**(2): 237–54.

Sabatier, Paul and Hank Jenkins-Smith (eds.) (1993) *Policy Change and Learning: An Advocacy Coalition Approach*, Boulder: Westview Press.

Sachverständigenrat zur Begutachtung der gesamtwirtschaftlichen Entwicklung (1992) *Jahresgutachten 1992/93: Für Wachstumsorientierung – gegen lähmenden Verteilungsstreit*, Stuttgart: Metzler-Poeschel.

Sadeh, Tal and Amy Verdun (2009) 'Explaining Europe's Monetary Union: a survey of the literature', *International Studies Review*, **11**(2): 277–301.

Sandholtz, Wayne (1993) 'Choosing union: monetary politics and Maastricht', *International Organization*, **47**(1): 1–39.

Sarcinelli, Ulrich (1987) *Symbolische Politik: Zur Bedeutung Symbolischen Handelns in der Wahlkampfkommunikation der Bundesrepublik Deutschland*, Westdt. Verl., Opladen.

Sargent, Thomas J. and Neil Wallace (1981) 'Some unpleasant monetarist arithmetic', *Federal Reserve Bank of Minneapolis Quarterly Review*, **5**, 1–17.

Savage, James (2005) *Making the EMU: The Politics of Budgetary Surveillance and the Enforcement of Maastricht*, Oxford University Press.

Savage, James and Amy Verdun (2007) 'Reforming Europe's Stability and Growth Pact: lessons from the American experience in macrobudgeting', *Review of International Political Economy*, **14**(5): 842–67.

Schäfer, Armin (2002) 'Vier perspektiven zur Entstehung und Entwicklung der "Europäischen Beschäftigungspolitik"', *MPIfG Discussion Paper*, 02/9.

Scharpf, Fritz W. (1988) 'The joint decision trap – lessons from German Federalism and European-integration', *Public Administration*, **66**(3): 239–78.

(1997) *Games Real Actors Play: Actor-Centered Institutionalism in Policy Research*. Boulder, CO: Westview Press.

Scharpf, Fritz W. and Vivien A. Schmidt (eds.) (2000) *Welfare and Work in the Open Economy: Diverse Responses to Common Challenges*, Oxford University Press.

Schelkle, Waltraud (2004a) 'EMU's second chance: enlargement and the reform of fiscal policy co-ordination', *Journal of European Public Policy*, **11**(5): 890–908.

(2004b) 'Understanding new forms of European integration: a study in competing political economy explanations', in Erik Jones and Amy Verdun (eds.) *Political Economy Approaches to the Study of European Integration*, London: Routledge, pp. 149–69.

(2005) 'The political economy of fiscal policy co-ordination in EMU: from disciplinarian device to insurance arrangement', *Journal of Common Market Studies*, **43**(2): 371–91.

Schmitter, Philippe C. (2004) 'Neo-neo-functionalism', in Antje Wiener and Thomas Diez (eds.), *European Integration Theory*, Oxford University Press, pp. 45–74.

(2005) 'Ernst B. Haas and the legacy of neofunctionalism', *Journal of European Public Policy*, **12**(2): 255–72.

(2009) 'On the way to a post-functionalist theory of European integration', *British Journal of Political Science*, **39**(1): 211–15.

Schure, Paul and Amy Verdun (2007) 'States and the exercise of power in the new European Union', *Current Politics and Economics of Europe*, **18**(2): 181–202.

——— (2008) 'Legislative bargaining in the European Union: the divide between large and small Member States', *European Union Politics*, **9**(4): 459–86.

Schure, Paul, F. Passarelli and D. Scoones (2007) 'When the powerful drag their feet', mimeo, University of Victoria.

Siebert, Horst (2008) 'An international system to avoid financial instability', Kiel Working Papers, No. 1461.

Stark, Jürgen (2001) 'Genesis of a pact', in Anne Brunila, Marco Buti and Daniele Franco (eds.) *The Stability and Growth Pact: The Architecture of Fiscal Policy in EMU*, New York: Palgrave, pp. 77–105.

Steuer, Werner (1998) 'Der Europäische Stabilitäts- und Wachstumspakt', in Scharrer, H.-E. (ed.) *Die Europäische Wirtschafts- und Währungsunion: Regionale und globale Herausforderungen*, Bonn: Europa Union Verlag, pp. 101ff.

Stiglitz, Joseph (2003) 'The false promise of stability', *The Economic Times*, 15 May.

Stone Sweet, Alec and Wayne Sandholtz (eds.) (1998) *European Integration and Supranational Governance*, Oxford University Press.

Tanzi, Vito and Ludger Schuknecht (2000) *Public Spending in the 20th Century: A Global Perspective*, Cambridge University Press.

Tamborini, Roberto (2004) 'The "Brussels Consensus" on macroeconomic stabilization policies: a critical assessment', in Francisco Torres, Amy Verdun, Chiara Zilioli and Hubert Zimmermann (eds.) *Governing EMU: Economic, Political, Legal and Historical Perspectives*, Florence, Italy: European University Institute, pp. 157–76.

Tömmel, Ingeborg and Amy Verdun (eds.) (2009) *Innovative Governance in the European Union: The Politics of Multilevel Policy-Making*, Boulder, CO: Lynne Rienner.

Tranholm-Mikkelsen, Jeppe (1991) 'Neofunctionalism: obstinate or obsolete? A reappraisal in the light of the new dynamism of the European Community', *Millennium*, **20**(1): 1–22.

Tsoukalis, Loukas (1977) *The Politics and Economics of European Monetary Integration*, London: George Allen and Unwin.

Ubide, Angel (2004) 'Just reinforce the Pact', *Finance and Development*, **41**(2): 27–8.

UNDP (1998) 'World population ageing 1950–2050', UNDP Office of Development Studies, New York, NY.

van Esch, Femke A. W. J. (2002) 'Why states want EMU: developing a theory on national preferences', in Amy Verdun (ed.) *The Euro: European Integration Theory and Economic and Monetary Union*, Lanham: Rowman and Littlefield, pp. 51–65.

——— (2007) 'Mapping the road to Maastricht: a comparative study of German and French pivotal decision makers' preferences concerning the establishment of a European Monetary Union during the early 1970s and late 1980s', unpublished Phd thesis, Radboud University Nijmegen, Department of Management Sciences.

Verdun, Amy (1999) 'The role of the Delors Committee in the creation of EMU: an epistemic community?', *Journal of European Public Policy*, **6**(2): 308–28.

(2000a) *European Responses to Globalization and Financial Market Integration. Perceptions of Economic and Monetary Union in Britain, France and Germany*, Houndmills, Basingstoke; New York: Palgrave-Macmillan / St. Martin's Press.

(2000b) 'Governing by committee: the case of the Monetary Committee', in Thomas Christiansen and Emil Kirchner (eds.) *Committee Governance in the European Union*, Manchester University Press, pp. 132–44.

(2002a) 'Merging neofunctionalism and intergovernmentalism: lessons from EMU', in Amy Verdun (ed.) *The Euro: European Integration Theory and Economic and Monetary Union*, Lanham: Rowman and Littlefield, pp. 9–28.

(2002b) 'The Netherlands and EMU: a small open economy in search of prosperity', in Kenneth Dyson (ed.) *European States and the Euro: Playing the Semi-Sovereignty Game*, Oxford University Press, pp. 238–55.

(2003) 'La nécessité d'un "gouvernement économique" dans une UEM asymétrique. Les préoccupations françaises sont-elles justifiées?', *Politique Européenne*, No 10, spring, pp. 11–32.

(2009) 'Regulation and cooperation in Economic and Monetary Policy', in Ingeborg Tömmel and Amy Verdun (eds.), *Innovative Governance in the European Union: The Politics of Multilevel Policy-Making*, Boulder, CO: Lynne Rienner, pp. 75–86.

Waever, Ole (2004) 'Discursive approaches', in Antje Wiener and Thomas Diez (eds.) *European Integration Theory*, Oxford University Press, pp. 197–216.

Waigel, Theo (1995a) 'Dritte Lesung zum Haushaltsgesetz 1996 (10.11.1995)', Bonn, Bundestagsdrucksache 13/69.

(1995b) 'Zweite Lesung zum Haushaltsgesetz 1996 (07.11.1995)', Bonn, Bundestagsdrucksache 13/66.

Walt, Stephen M. (2000) 'Alliances: balancing and bandwagoning', in R. Jervis (ed.) *International Politics: Enduring Concepts and Contemporary Issues*, New York, NY: Longman, pp. 110–17.

Webb, Carole (1983) 'Theoretical perspectives and problems', in C. Webb (ed.) *Policy-making in the European Communities*, 2nd edition, Wiley, Chichester, pp. 1–41.

Wessels, Wolfgang (1997) 'An ever closer fusion? A dynamic macropolitical view on integration processes', *Journal of Common Market Studies*, **35**(2): 267–99.

Westlake, Martin (1995) *The Council of the European Union*, London: Cartermill.

Willett, Thomas D. (1999) 'A political economy analysis of the Maastricht and stability pact fiscal criteria', in Andrew Hughes Hallett, Michael M. Hutchison, and Svend E. Hougaard Jensen (eds.) *Fiscal Aspects of European Monetary Integration*, New York: Cambridge University Press, pp. 37–68.

Wolf, Dieter (2002) 'Neofunctionalism and intergovernmentalism amalgamated: the case of EMU', in Amy Verdun (ed.) *The Euro: European Integration Theory and Economic and Monetary Union*, Lanham: Rowman and Littlefield, pp. 29–49.

Woodford, Michael (1994) 'Monetary policy and price level determinacy in a cash-in-advance economy', *Economic Theory*, **4**(3): 345–80.

Wylie, Lloy (2002) 'EMU: A neoliberal construction', in Amy Verdun (ed.) *The Euro: European Integration Theory and Economic and Monetary Union*, Lanham: Rowman and Littlefield, pp. 69–89.

Youngs, Richard (1999) 'The politics of the single currency: learning the lessons of Maastricht', *Journal of Common Market Studies*, **37**(2): 295–316.

Index

Almunia, Joaquín, 181, 186, 189
Amato, Giuliano, 115, 116, 125
Amsterdam European Council, 2, 52, 63
Amsterdam resolution of the European
      Council, 168
Amsterdam summit, 31, 36, 39, 52, 59, 60
anti-EMU platform, 51
Arthuis, Jean, 31, 56, 61

Berlusconi, Silvio, 118, 119, 130, 157
Broad Economic Policy Guidelines, xvi, 69,
      77, 83, 98, 105, 165
Bundesbank
   criticism of EMU, 46
   monetarist institution, 92
   President, 47, 48
   role of the, 14, 41, 44, 48
Bundesverfassungsgericht, xvi, 46, 47

Chirac, Jacques, 31, 56, 58, 59, 133, 138,
      144, 149, 159
   Amsterdam summit, 60
   campaign, 55, 56
   defence spending, 159
   Dublin compromise, 59
   Dublin summit, 56, 57
   election campaign, 131
   fiscal policy, 55
   Kohl and, 31, 35, 38
   leader of RPR, 55
   and Lionel Jospin, 55
   parliamentary and presidential
         control, 129
   parliamentary elections, 58
   provisional formula and political
         interpretation of the SGP, 140
   remarks, 140
   and Schröder, 142
   tax cuts, 129
   violation of the SGP, 144
Clarke, Kenneth, 23, 35
Cologne Process, 114

Commission
   advancing the SGP dossier, 77
   close to balance or in surplus, 68
   de Silguy, 54
   Delors, 96
   draft legislative text, 5
   Hallstein, 83
   initiate sanctioning mechanism, 141
   Member States, 2, 99, 102, 126, 150, 262,
         263, 291
   objectives, 123
   perspective, 80
   President, 20, 65, 66, 135, 157
   Prodi, Romano, 118, 120, 132, 135,
         141, 157
   proposal, 5, 6, 36, 68, 69, 70, 71,
         91, 99, 100, 159, 210, 219, 222,
         241, 245
      against France and Germany, 147
      Council, 147, 206, 208, 283
      initiate all procedural steps under
            the EDP, 159
      qualified majority, 71
      reform, 152
   propose a solution, 5
   recommendation
      amended by, 159
      Council opinion, 190
      early warning, 78
      ECOFIN, 2
      EDP, 160, 161, 162
      existence of an excessive deficit in
            France, 138
      Germany and France, 160
      initiation of the EDP, 37
      on the basis of new, 161
      qualified majority, 1, 205, 206,
            207, 208
      stability programmes, 156
      to the ECOFIN Council, 136
      two-thirds of the votes, 208, 284
   reform plans on the SGP, 138

Commission (cont.)
  reform proposals, 138
  report, 33
  right of initiative, 2, 98
  role of the, 68
  as Secretary to the MC, 68
  services of the, 98
Commission and Council, 99, 102, 126,
    127, 154, 155, 160, 162, 197, 249,
    250, 262, 265, 269, 277
  amend the SGP regulations, 163
  assess developments in EDP, 247, 271
  budgetary assessments, 250, 271
  governance of the European statistical
    system, 265
  intentions of, 163
  monitor the implementation of action
    taken, 238, 253
  respective roles of, 162
Commission of the European Communities,
    xvi, 49, 72, 257, 273, 274, 275,
    294, 298
Common Foreign and Security
    Policy, 201
comparative political economy, xvi, 11
Constitution for Europe, 148
creation of the Pact, 87, 163
critical junctions, 80

de Silguy, Yves-Thibault, 54, 59, 67
deficit bias, 73, 74, 94, 170
Delors Committee, 25, 83, 97,
    105, 308
Delors Report, 25, 72
Delors, Jacques, 67, 96, 299
domestic politics approach, 42, 45, 61, 62,
    84, 106, 124, 127, 171, 173, 191,
    196, 199
Dublin European Council, 103
Dublin Marathon, 35
Duisenberg, Willem, 53, 97, 116,
    133, 145

early-warning system, 101
EC Treaty, 3
ECB
  General Council, 148
  independence, 71, 74, 77, 81
  monetary stance, 77
  President, 53, 116, 133, 145, 146
  statutes, 15, 46, 74, 80, 97
  supranational institution, 5, 8
ECB and the Bundesbank, 163
eclectic approach, 16, 175, 176, 193,
    201, 202

ECOFIN and the MC, vii, 22, 33
ECOFIN negotiations, 38
Economic and Financial Affairs Council,
    xvi, 1
Economic and Financial Committee, xvi, 4,
    5, 13, 15, 22, 28, 89, 97, 163, 203,
    236, 250, 259
economic and monetary integration,
    1, 67, 201
EDP
  dissuasive arm, 76, 78
  implementation of the EDP, 34, 170,
    178, 193
  politicised nature, 6
  strengthening through the pact, 94
EDP of the Maastricht Treaty, 2, 101
Eichel, Hans, 115, 117, 119, 120,
    121, 122, 123, 124, 125, 133,
    134, 135, 136, 140, 141, 146,
    147, 149, 150, 156, 157, 158,
    168, 175
  and Chancellor Schröder, 149
  and Mer, 136
  and Sarkozy, 168
electoral cycles, 45
Elysée Treaty, 39
EMU and the SGP, 13, 24, 104
epistemic communities, 10, 70, 88, 301
EU and the ECB, 75
EU Council of Economic and Financial
    Affairs, 2
EU Finance Ministers, 137, 181
euro and Economic and Monetary Union, 1
Eurogroup and peer group pressure, 118
Europe's economic slowdown, 121
Europe's single currency, 1
European Central Bank, i, xiii, xiv, xvi, 2, 4,
    51, 57, 181, 222, 235, 245, 305
European Commission see Commission
European Council
  importance of the European Council, 28
  Stage III of EMU, 47, 56
European Council and ECOFIN, 29
European Council conclusions, 77, 98, 188
European Council Summits, 19
European Council–ECOFIN Council–
    Monetary Committee, 29
European Councils of the heads of state and
    government, 21
European Court of Justice, i, vii, xvi, 2, 153,
    154, 162, 299
European Currency Unit (ECU), 53
European Economic Recovery Plan and
    European Recovery Programme,
    189, 190, 192, 195, 298

European integration theories, 4, 8, 11, 14, 19, 85, 113, 175, 193, 194, 197
European Monetary System (EMS), 5, 22
European Security and Defence Policy, 201
Excessive Deficit Procedure *see* EDP
Exchange Rate Mechanism (ERM), 5, 22
expertocracy *see* expertocratic approach
expertocratic approach, vii, 85, 87, 89, 96, 103, 104, 105, 106, 192, 200

financial and economic crisis, 3, 14, 35, 113, 174, 189, 193, 195, 196
fiscal Schengen, 26
Fischer, Joschka, 101, 157, 158, 159, 165, 166, 301
fixing the franc to the Deutschmark, 96
Florence European Council, 33
Franco-German meetings, 39, 120, 144
French Stability Programme, 139

German public opinion, 49, 106
global financial crisis, 179, 181, 186
golden rule, 136, 151
Gyurcsány, Ferenc, 176

Haas, Ernst B., 9, 64, 66, 301, 307
Haas, Peter M., 10, 88, 301
Hallstein, Walter, 83, 302
Hanover summit, 96
Harney, Mary, 119
heterogeneity of the currency zone, 82
Hoffmann, Stanley, 9, 19, 64, 303

ideational approaches, 11
IMF, xvi, 38, 90, 105, 188
implementation of the SGP, 12, 13, 89, 113, 149, 152, 159, 162, 166, 195, 199
improving the implementation of the SGP, 167, 300
integration theory *see* European integration theory
intergovernmentalism, 9, 11, 14, 19, 34, 37, 39, 41, 42, 124, 127, 171, 309
International Monetary Fund *see* IMF
Irish case, 118, 125, 126

Jospin, Lionel, 36, 55, 59, 60, 120, 129
    accepted the SGP, 31
    election campaign, 59
    and Kohl, 39
    led government, 58

Presidential and Parliamentary elections, 120
Prime Minister, 58
and Schröder, 120
Socialist opposition, 56
Juncker, Jean-Claude, ix, xv, 147, 152, 218, 240
    broker of the final deal between France and Germany, 35
    proposal, 34
    solution was brokered by, 37
Juppé government, 15, 34, 58
Juppé, Alain, 15, 34, 55, 56, 58

Kenen, Peter B., 57, 75, 303, 304
Keynesianism, 92, 93, 94, 302
knowledge-based approaches, 85
Kohl, Helmut
    Amsterdam European Council, 52
    and Chirac, 31, 35, 38
    government, 24, 25, 47, 48, 50, 51
    and Jospin, 39

Länderfinanzausgleich, 119
Lisbon Agenda, 158, 169
Lisbon Council, 78
Lisbon Treaty, 4, 160, 195
low budgetary deficit regime, 3
Luxembourg Presidency, 156

Maastricht deficit criterion, 24
Maastricht fatigue, 77, 115
Maastricht Treaty
    agreement based on the German Model, 24
    Articles and Protocols on the EDP, 8
    central bank independence, 57, 74
    Delors Committee and, 105
    economic policy cooperation, 8
    framework of the, 32, 106
    needs an amendment, 50
    negotiations, 72, 97
    ratification of the, 47
    restrictions imposed by, 27
McGreevy, Charlie, 119
McKinnon, Ronald I., 75, 305
medium-term deficit target, 99
medium-term objective, 114, 210, 219, 232, 242, 265, 267
Mer, Francis, 131–141, 145, 149, 150
    ECOFIN, 137
    text of the Council conclusions, 133
Merkel, Angela, 15, 175, 203
Mitterrand, 25, 26, 36, 55, 67, 97
monetarism, 92

Monetary Committee, xvi, 5, 13, 15, 88,
    203, 309
  actor experts, 105
  content of the SGP, 41, 84
  discussion on Waigel proposal, 36
  national representatives, 22, 62, 66
  negotiations on, 5
  representatives of the EU central banks, 47
  working of the, vii, 97
Monetary Committee and the
    Commission, 67
Monetary Committee creation of the SGP
    and EMU, 28
Monetary Committee official, 97, 98, 99
Monti, Mario, 114
Moravcsik, Andrew, 9, 19, 20, 305
Moscovici, Pierre, 59
multilevel governance and other governance
    approaches, 10
Mundell, Robert A., xv, 22, 75, 303, 305

National Stability Pact, 124
neofunctionalism, 19, 64, 65, 66, 79, 199,
    307, 309

OCA, xvii, 75, 76
OECD, xvii, 38, 56, 90, 94, 105, 305
open fiscal flank, 8, 54
Open Method of Coordination, 78
optimum currency area *see* OCA
Organisation for Economic Cooperation
    and Development *see* OECD

Plan Juppé, 56
policy learning, 85, 86, 88, 91, 97, 104,
    170, 171
political approach to the stability pact, 130
Presidency Conclusions, 4, 30, 167, 300
principal-agent, 11, 87, 303
Prodi, Romano, 135, 141
  Pacte de Stupidité, 135
  twin-track strategy, 136
Protocol on the EDP, 3, 30
Putnam, Robert D.
  two-level game, 43, 47, 305, 306

Raffarin, Jean-Pierre, 133, 138, 139, 141,
    144, 159
reform programme for the SGP, 136
reformed SGP, 2, 170, 174

Sachverständigenrat, 49, 50, 307
Sarkozy, Nicolas, 158, 186, 300
  Finance Minister, 159
  French President, 186, 187

Ministry of Finance, 159
Schröder, Gerhard, 115, 122, 123, 125,
    142, 144, 149, 158, 203
  accused the Commission, 123
  balanced budget, 139
  and Chirac, 142
  election campaign, 123
  employment pact, 114
  focusing on employment rather than
    inflation, 125
  government, 15, 164, 175
  and Jospin, 120
  narrowly won the general elections, 132
  Prime Minister of Lower Saxony, 50
  verbal pressure on the ECB, 140
severe economic downturn, 102, 121, 168,
    236, 246, 249, 269
severe recession, 29, 30, 33, 34, 35, 38, 258
socialisation, 20, 67, 84, 85, 86, 90, 91,
    104, 105
soft euro, 53
Solbes, Pedro, 118, 122–123, 129–147,
    154–156
Spanish Presidency, 29
Stability and Convergence Programmes, 4,
    115, 190
Stability Council, 5, 52, 80, 81
stability paradigm, 74, 87, 90, 92, 93, 95, 97,
    103, 105, 107, 108
Steinbrück, Peer, 175, 176
Stoiber, Edmund, 51, 123
Strasbourg summit, 25
Strauss-Kahn, Dominique, 59, 117
structure-agency, 11

Tietmeyer, Hans, xv, 48
Treaty Establishing the European
    Community, xvii, 5
Treaty on European Union, xvii, 210, 219,
    232, 242
Tremonti, Giulio, 130, 131
Trichet, Jean-Claude, 53, 55, 146

US Federal Reserve, 179

Verhofstadt, Guy, 120

Waigel, Theodor, xv
  and Arthuis, 31
  initiative, 23, 45, 71, 107
  proposal, 5, 23, 32, 36, 83, 91, 99, 107
  Stability Pact, 5, 24, 32, 52, 54, 95, 98, 107
Wicks Box, 35, 36, 38

Zalm, Gerrit, 73, 144, 164